From the Ballot to the Blackboard

From the Ballot to the Blackboard provides the first comprehensive account of the political economy of education spending across the developed and developing world. The book demonstrates how political forces such as democracy and political partisanship and economic factors such as globalization deeply impact the choices made by voters, parties, and leaders in financing education. The argument is developed through three stories that track the historical development of education: first, its original expansion from the elite to the masses; second, the partisan politics of education in industrialized states; and third, the politics of higher education. The book uses a variety of complementary methods to demonstrate the importance of redistributive political motivations in explaining education policy, including formal modeling, statistical analysis of survey data and both subnational and cross-national data, and historical case analyses of countries, including the Philippines, India, Malaysia, England, Sweden, and Germany.

Ben W. Ansell is Assistant Professor of Political Science at the University of Minnesota. He has published articles on education policy in *International Organization* and *World Politics*. He received his Ph.D. from Harvard University, where he was awarded the Senator Charles Sumner Dissertation Award. He has served as a member of the United Kingdom's Leitch Review of Skills, worked on education policy for Her Majesty's Treasury, and held visiting fellowships at the Centre for Economic Performance at the London School of Economics and the Max Weber Programme at the European University Institute.

Cambridge Studies in Comparative Politics

General Editor
Margaret Levi *University of Washington, Seattle*

Assistant General Editors
Kathleen Thelen *Northwestern University*
Erik Wibbels *Duke University*

Associate Editors
Robert H. Bates *Harvard University*
Stephen Hanson *University of Washington, Seattle*
Torben Iversen *Harvard University*
Stathis Kalyvas *Yale University*
Peter Lange *Duke University*
Helen Milner *Princeton University*
Frances Rosenbluth *Yale University*
Susan Stokes *Yale University*

Other Books in the Series

Continued after the Index

From the Ballot to the Blackboard

THE REDISTRIBUTIVE POLITICAL ECONOMY OF EDUCATION

BEN W. ANSELL

University of Minnesota

CAMBRIDGE
UNIVERSITY PRESS

CAMBRIDGE UNIVERSITY PRESS
Cambridge, New York, Melbourne, Madrid, Cape Town,
Singapore, São Paulo, Delhi, Mexico City

Cambridge University Press
32 Avenue of the Americas, New York NY 10013-2473, USA

Published in the United States of America by Cambridge University Press, New York

www.cambridge.org
Information on this title: www.cambridge.org/9781107616998

© Ben W. Ansell 2010

First published 2010
First paperback edition 2013

A catalogue record for this publication is available from the British Library

Library of Congress Cataloguing in Publication Data
Ansell, Ben W., 1977–
   From the ballot to the blackboard : the redistributive political economy
   of education / Ben W. Ansell.
      p.   cm. – (Cambridge studies in comparative politics)
   Includes bibliographical references and index.
   ISBN 978-0-521-19018-3 (hardback)
   1. Education – Finance – Case studies.   2. Education, Higher – Finance – Case studies.
   3. Education – Political aspects – Case studies.   4. Education and state – Case studies.
   I. Title.   II. Series.
   LB2824.A58   2009
   379.1′1–dc22   2009031385

ISBN 978-0-521-19018-3 Hardback
ISBN 978-1-107-61699-8 Paperback

To Jane

Contents

List of Tables

List of Figures

Preface

The prospect of an academic writing a book about the politics of education, indeed one with a chapter on higher education, might appear rather solipsistic. While the reader will be the best judge of the book's merits, I hope that I have avoided most of the perils of navel gazing. To the degree that I have achieved this ambition, thanks must go to the many people, both inside and outside academia, who have provided support and comfort along the way.

I would like to begin by thanking the most critical academic influences on this project: my dissertation committee. While this book has been subject to countless iterations and revisions since its genesis as my Ph.D. dissertation, many of the ideas and empirical analyses contained within date from that project and, consequently, owe a great deal to my advisors. Beth Simmons, an advisor at both Berkeley and Harvard, was a constant source of advice and support. Beth first sparked my interest in the connection between international and comparative political economy, and her extensive notes and comments were essential in honing and focusing my ideas. Torben Iversen has been the greatest intellectual influence on the content of this book. I'd like to thank him for his indefatigable energy and for his interest in this project – for seeing it from informal chats in his office through to the final copyedits of a finished manuscript. Finally, Michael Hiscox's input was invaluable in terms of thinking through the international implications of my argument and for his generous supply of data. A number of other Harvard faculty aided me greatly in this project. I would like, in particular, to thank Jim Alt, Jeff Frieden, Peter Hall, and Pepper Culpepper.

I began my graduate career at Berkeley, receiving the lion's share of my training there, and no set of acknowledgments would be complete without referencing the many scholars there who helped to shape me as a researcher. I would like, in particular, to thank John Zysman, who first piqued my interest in political economy and who supported me through the Berkeley Roundtable on the International Economy. I also appreciated greatly the input of Jonah Levy, Bob Powell, Jim Robinson, Gerard Roland, Steve Weber, and Nick Ziegler.

Since leaving graduate school, I have been very fortunate to be at such a supportive department at the University of Minnesota. For their input into this project, I would like to single out Liz Beaumont, Teri Caraway, Bud Duvall, Kathryn Pearson, David Samuels, and Shawn Treier. Two colleagues in particular, John Freeman and Phil Shively, made extensive notes on elements of the manuscript, for which I am especially grateful. Outside of my previous and current departments, a whole host of other scholars have provided aid and insight, in particular John Ahlquist, Pablo Beramendi, Mark Copelovitch, Mark Kayser, Lane Kenworthy, Mike Kellerman, Irfan Nooruddin, Will Phelan, Jonas Pontusson, Philipp Rehm, Frances Rosenbluth, Ken Scheve, Hillel Soifer, David Soskice, David Stasavage, John Stephens, Erik Wibbels, and Anne Wren.

I would also like to thank the many institutions that have provided me with funding from the genesis to the completion of this project. From Harvard University, I thank the Center for European Studies and the Weatherhead Center for International Affairs for funding research and time to write my dissertation. During the writing of my dissertation, I was based at the Centre for Economic Performance at the London School of Economics, thanks to John Van Reenen and Richard Layard. I was also based at Her Majesty's Treasury, where I had the great fortune to work on British education strategy. For support at the Treasury, I would like to thank Ed Miliband, Jitinder Kohli, Ella Joseph, Lord Sandy Leitch, and Chris Martin. During the completion of the final manuscript, I was a Visiting Fellow of the Max Weber Programme at the European University Institute (EUI). I would like to thank Susan Garvin, Lotte Holm, Peter Mair, Sven Steinmo, Karin Tilmans, and, particularly, Ramon Marimon for their support at the EUI.

Completing the final manuscript was also greatly aided by the efficiency and diligence of my editors at Cambridge University Press. My thanks go to Lew Bateman, Margaret Levi, Shelby Peak, Emily Spangler, and my copy editor, Andy Saff. Kathy Thelen, who shepherded my book through the final revisions for submission to the Studies in Comparative Politics series, deserves special thanks for her detailed comments.

Finally, and most importantly, I would like to thank my family, who have always been willing to listen, often at considerable transatlantic cost – to my incomprehensible accounts of how the book was progressing. It was their intellectual interest in the world, their ability to be at once opinionated and non-judgmental, and their constant love and support that molded me. I cannot repay them enough or do justice to them, so I just want to express pure thanks to my brother Ed Ansell, my father Tony Ansell, and my mother Penny Ansell. My son Theo I cannot really thank for his intellectual input just yet, but he has been a constant delight and I hope one day he enjoys looking over the book, even if just to note the absence of "scary monsters." And above all, I want to thank my wife, Jane Gingrich, to whom I dedicate this book. Jane has been both the inspiration behind my work and the core of my life outside. A more intelligent and caring friend and scholar I could never hope to meet. This book could not have happened without her.

1

The Redistributive Political Economy of Education

1.1 TWO PUZZLES, TWO INSIGHTS

In 1951, the Indian government, buoyed by the fresh hopes of newly won independence, declared its intent that India should universally educate its population. It announced a program of massive government spending that would culminate in a sustained 6 percent of national income being devoted to public education spending. This ambition, codified in India's first Five Year Plan, was reiterated several times over the ensuing decades: by the Kothari Commission in 1966, and in the National Policy on Education in 1986 (Ghosh, 2000). Yet, even by 1995 India was spending barely half of this amount and remained home to one-third of the world's illiterates. The heady goals of the early independence movement were patently unmet in the field of human development. By the early 1990s, the debate around education in India was imbued with depression and recriminations. Why was India, a country famed for its unique level of democratic success in the developing world, unable to provide for the human development of its population?

This puzzle looks all the more confusing when we consider India's near-neighbor across the Andaman Sea: Malaysia. Governed under a semi-autocratic regime by leaders from the United Malays National Organisation (UMNO) party since 1969, Malaysia's executive is little constrained by the legislature, civil liberties are restricted, and opposition parties have been unable to secure government. While Malaysia is hardly a tyranny, it is significantly less open to political opposition and popular debate than is India. Given the UMNO's unbroken rule and the lack of channels for popular discontent, one might expect that the Malaysian masses would remain as uneducated as their Indian counterparts. Yet Malaysia's spending on education, as a proportion of national income, has consistently doubled Indian spending, reaching nearly 8 percent of gross domestic product (GDP) by 2001, a figure that places Malaysia among the ranks of Denmark, Sweden, and Norway. Why then was autocratic Malaysia a more effective educator than democratic India?

When we turn to the developed world, the politics of education spending appear no less puzzling. At the other end of the educational spectrum from

1

extending education to the illiterate masses lie the contemporary politics of funding higher education. Here we also see paradoxical behavior. We often think of left-wing parties as the advocates of increased public spending on transfers and social services. Right-wing parties, conversely, are associated with policies that reduce transfers and introduce private fees into services. Yet when we examine higher education policy in advanced industrial states, we see precisely the reverse scenario. In the United Kingdom, it was the left-wing New Labour Party that introduced tuition fees into higher education against the vociferous opposition of the right-wing Conservatives. Conversely, in Sweden, where the Social Democratic Party has been the long-time advocate of expanding social services and welfare spending, it was the center-right coalition led by the Moderate Party that removed quotas on university enrollment and began a massive injection of public funds into the Swedish higher education system. Why do the politics of higher education look so dissimilar to our traditional understanding of partisanship social policy in advanced industrial states?

These two puzzles – the failure of democracies such as India to expand access to education to the masses, and the reversal of typical partisan patterns of government spending in the realm of higher education in the UK and Sweden – highlight the inadequacy of standard political economy theories in explaining education policy. Education is held by international development agencies, growth economists, and politicians of every stripe to be the catalyst of modern economic growth. Yet from the most basic task of providing primary education to the illiterate up to the modern university, the pinnacle of the education system, we see a range of surprising and often pessimism-inducing outcomes, as countries fail to meet their professed educational ambitions or channel money in apparently unsuitable and ineffective ways. If education really is the policy equivalent of a "free lunch," why do so many states fail to educate more than 50 percent of their population? And if, as common consensus would have it, higher education is the key to the West's sustained success in an era of globalization, why do political parties disagree so vehemently over what funding reforms are most appropriate?

This book presents a unified theory of education policy that can explain these puzzles. The theory is built around two key insights. The first is that education is essentially redistributive. This assertion alone does not distinguish this work from the standard analysis of public spending conducted by political economists. However, the redistributive politics of education is rather more nuanced than that of most other fiscal transfers. On the one hand, universal education is the sharpest edge of progressive redistribution. Not only does it transfer resources from the rich to pay for the education of the poor, but it also potentially undermines the position of the rich – and their children – in the distribution of income. That is, education promotes meritocracy over heredity. Furthermore, an increased supply of education to the masses weakens the returns that the skilled elite accrue from their education. Consequently, it appears to be in the best interests of the elite to block education spending where they can, as in, for example, autocracies. Symmetrically, we should expect to see increased education spending associated with political institutions and organizations that represent the interests of the poor – for example, democracies and left-wing parties.

So, at first glance, education might appear to be a particularly distasteful public good from the perspective of the rich. However, the progressivity of education depends entirely on *who* actually receives that education. Where the provision of education can be limited to a subgroup of the population, redistribution might actually flip from being progressive to regressive. For example, the wealthy are typically disproportionately represented in higher education. As such, public spending on universities is often fiscally regressive, amounting to a redistribution of resources from the school-educated poor and middle class to the college-educated rich. More generally, where public education is extended to the rich and middle class but excludes the poor, there is an opening for the rich, who might prefer to finance their children's education privately, to ally with the uneducated poor in an anti-education "ends against the middle" alliance. Thus, education spending is a powerful tool that political actors manipulate for their own redistributive ends and it can produce a broad array of sometimes rather unlikely political coalitions. Education is, at heart, a political decision.

The second insight is that one cannot examine education policy without connecting it to broader trends in the labor market, chief of which is a state's relative integration with the global economy. India's failure to educate its citizens was not the result of the caste system or hidden flaws in its democracy. Instead, the chief obstacle to Indian education has been India's sheltering from the global economy. This conclusion may appear surprising, given the apparently harsh impact of globalization on welfare spending in developing states (Rudra, 2003; Wibbels, 2006). However, once we analyze the impact of trade policy on the supply of and demand for education, this outcome seems rather less unlikely. Globalization allows citizens to "export their skills," meaning that the domestic supply of education can increase without undermining the return to education. Similarly, the demand for educated labor also conditions the parameters of education policy. As states absorb new technologies that are highly complementary with skilled labor – for example, the computer and new media – the potential returns to education rise. To the degree that globalization facilitates this kind of technology transfer, it increases the state's incentive to invest in education. Thus, public education policy is heavily affected by the nature of the global market for educated labor.

This book develops its theory of education spending by tracing three stories, which roughly track the historical expansion of the government's role in education. It begins by considering the original expansion of education to the masses. While this is the earliest involvement of the government in education policy in most states, its historical occurrence has varied widely across countries. Universal primary education was achieved in the mid-nineteenth century in the United States of America but still remains unmet in many states in Africa and

Asia. Nonetheless, the second half of the twentieth century marked a period of mass expansion in public spending on education, as most states began or completed the process of universal primary, and often secondary, education. Public spending on education as a percentage of national income increased from a global average of 2.5 percent in 1960 to 4.6 percent in 1999. Clearly, this epochal change in the state's role in education deserves explanation.

But perhaps more dramatically, it is not only average education spending that has increased but also the variation within and across countries in that spending. Between 1960 and 1995, not only did the global mean of education double but so also did its standard deviation. Clearly some states were being left behind as others surged ahead – producing divergence, "big time," in education spending (Pritchett, 1995). Furthermore the trend in education spending is not always upward. Many countries have experienced a striking volatility in their education spending. Chile, for example, spent 2.5 percent of GDP on public education in 1960 under the Conservative government of Jorge Alessandri, 4.5 percent under the socialist government of Salvador Allende in the early 1970s, 2.5 percent under the right-wing dictatorship of Augusto Pinochet that followed, and 4.3 percent in 2000 under the center-left government of Ricardo Lagos. Countries as varied as Portugal, the Philippines, and Zimbabwe have seen fluctuations of a similar magnitude over the past four decades. What explains both the global secular increase in education spending and this kind of within-country volatility? This book's first story traces the impact of political institutions such as democracy and monarchy on education spending – demonstrating the redistributive political nature of education policy – and the effect of integration with the global economy – demonstrating the impact on education policy of changes in the labor market.

The second story moves along the historical path of education policy to the political battles that are fought over education today in the advanced industrial states. While debates over education in Western Europe and North America have often centered around the merits of denominational schooling, I show that the key determinant of education spending in the postwar era has been partisan control of government. However, this is partisanship very much constrained. On the one hand, political parties make campaign promises about education spending to the electorate. To this extent, they face bottom-up pressure to commit to these promises. On the other hand, these parties are also constrained by the nature of electoral institutions, which dictate what coalitions are required to enact policies. Furthermore, electoral institutions shape the manner in which both parties and voters trade off their preferences over education against more general redistribution. Thus, redistributive politics are continually at play in the financing of public education, both academic and vocational, but their extent is greatly limited by politicians' interactions with voters and political institutions.

The third story takes us to the zenith of modern education policy: higher education. Fifty years ago, the politics of higher education was extremely limited in scope. Fewer than 5 percent of citizens in even the most advanced industrial states attended university. Today, however, in many European, North American, and East Asian countries, university enrollments are tipping over the 50 percent mark. Since most university systems were publicly funded in 1950, how have governments adapted to this enrollment challenge? Do they continue to absorb the increasing numbers of students by cranking up public financing of higher education? Or do they ask students to pay for some of the necessary increase in funding themselves? Or do they prevent the expansion from occurring in the first place by limiting entry to the university system? This story brings us to the difficult question of why countries decide to change educational institutions and why they choose different strategies of reform. As before, I offer a redistributive explanation. Political parties choose to structure higher education systems following their constituencies' particular preferences, but they are constrained by the nature of the preexisting system. Thus the politics of higher education are quite distinct in mass systems as opposed to those that remain elitist.

1.2 THE ARGUMENT OF THIS BOOK

In constructing my argument in this book, I develop three theoretical claims: (a) that education is a tool of *targeted redistribution*, (b) that seemingly domestic education policy cannot be viewed apart from the *global labor market for education*, and (c) that *political and educational institutions* strongly condition education policy. In this section, I address these claims in turn before situating my argument, in the following section, within the broader context of theories about education in the social sciences.

Targeted Redistribution

The first claim is that education is a tool of targeted redistribution. In particular, I argue that the redistributive effects of education depend entirely on *who receives* that education and *who pays* for it. Where education is universal, public education will be fiscally progressive. If only the wealthy receive some form of public education (for example, higher education), then public education spending will be fiscally regressive. Finally, if education is provided to a majority, but not all, of the population, there may be the possibility of a rich-poor alliance, at the expense of the middle class, to reduce education spending, if the rich can purchase substitute education in the private market. Thus the multidirectional nature of public education means that a broad array of coalitions are possible: The poor and middle class might advocate for universal education, the rich and middle class might advocate for increased spending on secondary education from which the poor are excluded, or the poor and rich might advocate for reduced overall education spending.

Given the complex coalitions and patterns of redistribution that might emerge, how can we effectively theorize about likely outcomes? To untie this Gordian knot, we need to examine the different impacts of various forms of education spending on the distribution of income. The simple act of providing, for example, universal primary education has several crosscutting redistributive impacts: It takes money from the rich to pay for the education of the poor; it increases the country's relative factor endowment of skilled labor; it increases the chance that the shape of the future distribution of income will be decided by merit rather than birthright; and it creates positive externalities for other individuals by increasing the efficiency of transactions in the economy. Examining other, more limited, forms of education spending such as university funding adds the further complication that education is targeted to some groups rather than others. To clarify the mechanisms at work, I discuss in turn the several redistributive forces tied to public education: fiscal effects, scarcity effects, lottery effects, externalities, and targeting.

Fiscal effects are determined by the cost per student educated, the number of students educated, and the progressivity of the tax rate. If taxation is progressive and education is provided in a uniform amount to all citizens, the tax system will redistribute resources among those who receive education from the wealthiest to the poorest. Accordingly, when states democratize and the poorer masses gain control of political decision making, we expect taxation to rise and public education spending to increase. A similar logic applies with the election of left-wing governments that favor higher taxation and hence more funding for public goods such as education. However, this simple assertion must be qualified: if the provision of education is limited but taxation is universal, those who fail to receive education but pay for it are clear losers. In many societies, the poor have to pay taxes that are used to educate solely the elite and middle class, setting up a potential "ends against the middle" coalition against education. Furthermore, even when education provision is universal, tax systems themselves vary in their progressivity – at the limit, a universal education system funded by a lump-sum tax may be hardly redistributive at all.

Scarcity effects refer to the relative scarcity of educated and non-educated labor in the workforce. As with other factors of production such as land and capital, the supply of education in the economy will determine its rate of return. Accordingly, if an educated elite can limit the further expansion of education, they will reap scarcity rents from their skills. However, as education expands to the middle class and the poor, these rents will be dissipated substantially. Thus, the elite have a vested interest in "protecting" the rents accruing to their education and, thus, in keeping education spending minimal. As with the pattern of fiscal redistribution, we would expect democratization to reflect the interest of the masses in expanding education, not the interest of the rich in protecting their rents. However, scarcity effects are not constant across states. The structure of the labor market, whether it is integrated with the global product market and the relative skill bias of technology, will condition the impact of scarcity effects.

Lottery effects are the third manner in which public education hurts the rich. If natural ability is uniformly distributed throughout society and education provides a way of "matching" ability to income, we should expect education to help the able poor and harm the less able rich. Education, then, acts as a "lottery" mechanism in relation to parental income, encouraging meritocracy rather than heredity and making the intergenerational transfer of wealth more random. As lottery effects become more important, education becomes yet more threatening to the rich and encouraging to the poor, so much so that the rich might actually prefer to "buy off" the poor with simple transfers of cash rather than allow even minimal education spending. This provides the implication, tested throughout the book, that regimes or parties that favor the rich will try to shift the balance of government spending away from education and toward other government consumption that proves less of a meritocratic risk.

So far, education appears to be a curse on the rich. Yet this anti-elitist effect is not the full story. Like many other public goods, education produces positive *externalities*. Since these externalities are not privately capturable, education might be undersupplied on aggregate in a purely private market, justifying government intervention. However, unlike most other public goods, education is not a collectively used good like a park or clean air. Instead, education must be provided to new individuals in order to increase the provision of the public good. Thus, the elite face an intriguing trade-off: They want to benefit from the externalities of an educated workforce, but in order to reap these returns, they have to suffer the negative fiscal, scarcity, and lottery effects of having *other* educated people. Externalities thus provide an *economic* justification for providing public education but they do not necessarily provide a *political* justification if the other negative redistributive forces dominate. Unlike most public goods, the simple logic of the collective action problem cannot explain outcomes in education policy.

If externalities alone do not encourage the elite to provide public education, there may be another mechanism through which we see the elite advocate increased spending. If the elite can *target education* toward only themselves, they may become more enthusiastic proponents of public education, albeit of a very limited kind. This creates the possibility not only of progressive redistribution but regressive redistribution. Higher education, for example, is typically biased in its enrollment toward the children of the wealthy. Thus, high-income groups may favor increased education funding if it can be targeted toward higher education and away from universal goods such as primary education. The possibility of targeting is not limited to groups with high income: In countries where the political ethnic elite does not coincide with the economic elite, we may see targeting of education toward the politically powerful ethnicity, as in Malaysia. Generally, though, political and economic hierarchies are closely aligned and thus autocracies are associated with a greater ratio of targeted spending (higher education) to universal spending (primary education).

The Labor Market and Education

The second key claim of this book is that education policy cannot be divorced from the labor market. The preceding analysis of targeted redistribution did not directly address the demand for education in the economy, nor the determinants of the returns to education. While the redistributive urge alone may in some cases be sufficient to explain education provision, in most cases this political motivation cannot be divorced from the economic forces that govern the use of education as a factor in production. Thus we must move from an analysis of the political market to the labor market.

Two key elements of the labor market are emphasized throughout this book: the effects of the *supply* of education and the *demand* for education on policy outcomes. In the first case, I extend the preceding analysis of scarcity effects by examining the response of skilled wages to the supply of education under different conditions. Under some circumstances, scarcity effects are highly pronounced. In these cases, an expansion of educated workers dramatically reduces the return to education because the change in the supply of education is enough to alter dramatically the relative scarcity of skills in the product market *at large*. In other cases, changes in the supply of education have little effect on the return to education. As an example, Cambridge, Massachusetts, produces enormous numbers of workers with graduate qualifications without, however, noticeably reducing the return to that education received by each worker. Why is this possible? Why don't the educated workers of Cambridge, Massachusetts, bid down each other's wages? The reason that the returns to education are sustained is because these workers do not only sell the fruit of their educated labor to one another and the remaining, presumably "unskilled," citizens of Cambridge. Rather, they sell their factor endowments to millions of other Americans and indeed citizens in other countries, who purchase goods that embody the skilled labor of these graduates.

Extending this analogy, when a country expands education, provided that this country sells its goods into the global market, any change in its domestic supply of educated labor will not affect the domestic returns to education. Put differently, most countries are too small to have changes in their factor endowments alter global factor endowments and prices. If, however, the country is autarkic and consumes all its own production, then necessarily a national shift in education will change the availability of skilled labor in the relevant (national) labor market and thus reduce the returns to education. Thus, in globalizing states, there is a less negative effect on the skill premium when education expands. Consequently, we should expect the already educated, typically the economic elite, to be less adamantly opposed to education in such states.

The structure of the labor market is also greatly affected by the shape of labor demand. Shocks to labor demand often result from technological change. The discovery of new production techniques or technologies can have a substantial impact on the relative demand for skilled and unskilled labor. Claudia Goldin and Lawrence Katz (1998) refer to this as the relative "skill-bias" of technology. Thus, all else equal, when a skill-biased technology, such as computing, emerges, we should expect producer demand to shift toward inputs of skilled rather than unskilled labor, causing a rise in the skill premium. As with skill supply, there is a further impact related to global product and labor markets. When countries open up to international markets, they face competition from foreign firms with more advanced technology. Furthermore, as Daron Acemoglu (2003) argues, the kinds of technology that are being transferred have become more skill-biased over the past half-century; for example, computers require moderate skills to operate. This provides a strong demand-side impetus to public education spending. Thus, through its effects on both labor supply and demand, globalization fundamentally alters the political dynamics surrounding education spending.

Education and Institutions

The third key claim of this book is that political and educational institutions constrain targeted redistribution and shape the effect of labor market structure on education policy. That is, institutions provide the framework in which the key causal forces of redistributive preferences and labor market dynamics operate. I have argued that the structure of the labor market can change the incentives of actors to acquire education, thereby altering the set of *economic constraints or opportunities* within which the redistributive politics of education take place. Examining political and educational institutions, we see instead a set of *political constraints and opportunities.* Throughout this book, we shall see that policy makers, be they constitutional monarchs or cabinet leaders, are constrained by the nature of the political institutions that govern their ability to acquire, execute, and maintain power. While actors may have intense preferences over education, the course of true preferences never did run smooth. The redistributive goals of actors and their consequent preferred education policies are subject to what is institutionally possible. The structure of institutions addresses three questions: Who gets to participate in decisions over education policy? What possible coalitions between groups can emerge? And are groups out of power able to constrain or block reforms?

The first question addresses regime type. Autocracies typically translate into rule by and for the elite in society. We have established that because of the fiscal, scarcity, and lottery effects of public education the elite will attempt to limit education spending to themselves. However, they can succeed in this goal only where they control political decision making, that is, where they are the "selectorate" (Bueno de Mesquita et al., 2003). Under such autocratic conditions, we would expect generally low levels of overall education spending and a focus on tertiary education for the elite rather than universal primary education. Following democratization, if the elite relinquish power to the masses – who benefit from the fiscal and lottery effects of education – public education will both transfer funds from the wealthy to the poor and increase potential intergenerational income mobility. As participation expands, so too will universal education provision.

The rise of democracy provides an answer to the question of which groups have their preferences represented, but it raises the further question of what kinds of coalitions will form between newly represented groups. In a one-dimensional world where politics aligns on a rich-poor redistributive axis, the middle class will dominate politically as they become the "median voter" of democracy. In that case, we expect education provision to expand up to the middle class, who benefit from both the fiscal transfer of resources from the rich and the lottery effect of increasing meritocracy in the distribution of income. However, the destiny of the poor remains less clear. If externalities to education are sufficiently high, or if the poor have sufficient representation, we might expect education to become universal. Thus, a democratic pro-education alliance between the middle class and the poor is likely.

But it is possible that the middle class will fail to provide for the poor, leaving them both uneducated and anti-education. As Michael Ross (2005) has noted, democracy does not always provide the kinds of public goods that the poor want – it is the middle class who typically pull the political strings in democracy. Thus, if we move beyond a simple one-dimensional model of politics to a multidimensional coalitional model, where groups must trade off education versus simple cash transfers, we might find the poor willing to ally with the rich in an anti-education, "ends against the middle" alliance. This outcome is apparent in situations as diverse as Latin American populism, coalitional patterns under proportional representation, and the introduction of university tuition fees in the contemporary Organization for Economic Cooperation and Development (OECD).

The final political question is whether groups out of government can block reform. Political actors may favor various forms of targeted redistribution, but their ability to achieve these goals is dependent on overriding opposing actors. Parliamentary and electoral institutions can curtail governing parties. Electoral systems such as majoritarianism work against coalition forming and split the middle class, leading to more sharply defined education outcomes. Conversely, in proportional electoral systems, the necessity of coalition building moderates swings in education spending and creates new trade-offs between "pure" redistribution and education. Finally, subnational entities might have veto power or control over spending outcomes – for example, subnational states have significant control over university financing in both Germany and the United States.

One more institutional factor is noteworthy: the institutional structure of the education system itself, which can affect the translation of redistributive preferences into educational outcomes. Previous decisions about education policy shape future ones; for example, the growth of education in South Korea followed a sequential path from primary to tertiary education. Moreover, education institutions themselves produce a particular labor market structure. The existence of streamed secondary schooling, where students must choose either academic or vocational schools, impacts both partisan preferences over vocational enrollment and, more generally, enrollment into universities. In the context of universities, mass higher education enrollment has quite different repercussions for the college premium and hence political redistributive preferences than does a restricted higher education system. In the former case, it will be representatives of the masses who prefer to fund higher education, whereas in the latter case it will be the representatives of the elite and the upper middle class. The structure of educational institutions strongly channels education policy.

1.3 THE THEORETICAL DEBATE OVER EDUCATION

If "education is, at heart, a political decision," this begs a series of questions. What type of education? Funded by whom? For what end? What do we mean by politics: distributional politics, identity politics, *realpolitik*? How are preferences over education developed and channeled politically? Questions along these lines have inspired an extensive amount of research across the social sciences. Economists have undertaken analyses examining the extent to which externalities produced by educational investment justify state intervention in education. Sociologists have examined how Western forms of education provision are mimicked by developing nations as they establish public services. Political scientists have produced a variety of studies examining the impact of partisan preferences on broad educational aggregates. This is not an empty field of study by any means.

However, despite the fecundity of this field of research, there has not been an overarching study of how a broad range of political and economic factors affect education spending. Generally, studies have been limited to examining the effect of single variables on one particular facet of education spending. Missing is a generalized model of the political economy of education, which might generate hypotheses about how a broad variety of factors might affect spending on a variety of aspects of education. This book integrates the analysis of targeted redistribution, labor market structure, and institutional constraints to build such a unified theory. To make this theory distinct, it is useful to examine other approaches to explaining the extent of education provision from the social sciences: economics, sociology, and political science.

The vast modern literature on the economics of education began with the foundational work of Gary Becker (1964) and Theodore Schultz (1961). This literature uses the standard economic assumptions of rational individual utility maximization and examines how individuals treat education as an investment, balancing their discounted future returns from education against the present cost of acquiring it. In as much as there is any reason for public involvement in the provision of education, market failures provide the key justification. Credit constraints, imperfect information, time-inconsistent preferences, and externalities are examined as potential market failures justifying state intervention (Poterba, 1995). This literature thus takes an efficiency-focused approach in analyzing education. There is relatively little analysis of the political economy of education provision – that is, of the distributive impact of education and how this might affect policy choices over the optimal level of spending.

To the degree that economists have modeled the determinants of education provision, as in Perotti (1993) or Saint Paul and Verdier (1993), the typical underlying assumption is that all investment is privately made. Accordingly, most economists view education provision as a private optimization problem, with the extent of education provision determined by the aggregation of individual investments. Yet, this model bears almost no resemblance to the actual provision of education worldwide, which is for the most part publicly provided. In contrast, this book develops a full political economy model where education is publicly funded through the tax system and policy decisions are made *politically*. This places this work in the company of those economists who have examined the political economy of public education spending – for example, Besley and Coate (1991), Fernandez and Rogerson (1995), Gradstein, Justman, and Meier (2005), and Roemer (2006). This emerging literature has begun to integrate the standard economic analysis of education with the political economy literature explaining the size of government – for example, Meltzer and Richard (1981) and Persson and Tabellini (2002). The models in this book are consequently developed in this spirit.

I turn toward two different strands of economic literature in terms of defining precisely how labor market structure impacts education policy. First, I argue that the impact of the *supply* of education on the returns to education is a function of a state's integration with the global market. Autarkic states face a collapse in the returns to education following an expansion in provision; thus, educated elites will attempt to block further spending. Highly open states, conversely, can support much higher levels of education supply without necessarily reducing the return to education. This argument builds off Samuelson's (1948) Factor Price Equalization theory, which asserts that all factor returns will converge to a globally uniform level when trade is completely free, provided that countries are sufficiently diversified in their production. This implies that skilled wages are unaffected by domestic skill supply in any one state, though they are impacted by total global supply of education. Rybzynski (1955) demonstrates that under Samuelson's conditions, changes in factor supply will affect only the composition of industrial output, not factor returns. Thus, as states globalize, the impact of increasing education spending will be increasingly found in industrial structure rather than relative wages, an assertion confirmed by recent work by Hanson and Slaughter (2002).

I also make use of a recent literature in labor economics on "skill-biased technological change." This work focuses on the importance of technological change in altering the *demand* for education. Goldin and Katz (1998) develop a theory of how technological change can become biased towards skilled or unskilled labor, and the impact of such changes on the relative economic well-being and preferences of each group. In particular, they trace the development of industrialization from the skill-biased artisanal process, through unskilled labor–biased factory line production, to the increasing use of skill-biased technology such as computers in post-industrial and high-technology production. This shift to automated and digitally enhanced production massively increases the demand for skilled labor in order to operate this expensive new capital. Acemoglu (2003) argues that globalization, through technology transfer, is actually spreading this skill bias internationally, as states shift from labor-biased heavy industrial production to skill-biased production, thereby increasing demand for education. Hence, in combining insights from both international and labor economics, I am able to examine how education provision is impacted by global integration.

In contrast to the individual investment models of economists, the cross-national sociological literature on education provision takes a systemic view of education. Three particular theories of education provision have traditionally dominated the sociological debate. The first theory – mainstream social differentiation theory – was a by-product of the dominant social functionalist approach of the 1950s and 1960s. Most closely associated with Parsons (1957), this approach argued that education was used in order to create "horizontal differentiation" between individuals serving different societal roles. The rise of modernity leads to an increasing functional complexity of society, leading to greater and greater horizontal specialization, and hence a greater demand for education that can provide individuals with the cognitive skills needed to fit into this framework. The second theory – critical social differentiation theory – argued instead that education socialized individuals into *vertically* differentiated roles; that is, education was a tool of social control by the elite (Bourdieu and Passeron, 1977; Bowles and Gintis, 1976). In this framework, growth in education spending might reflect growing control of the social elite over the lower classes. Finally, the third approach, pioneered by Boli, Ramirez and Meyer (1985), saw the international expansion of mass education as the adaptation of Western governance structures by developing nations, through a form of "isomorphism." Developing states adopted the Western mass education system not as a form of social differentiation but as a form of "universalistic integration" into the world system. Thus, in the formulation of Boli and his colleagues, education spending increased as the modern West's social and economic systems were absorbed by developing nations, regardless of whether their level of "functional complexity" actually required this level of education.

This study differs significantly in its argument from the sociological literature, not only because it is built from an individualist model of political preferences rather than a systemic worldview, but also because it sees interest groups as attempting to *deny* one another education rather than use it as a functional tool to socialize or control individuals. Although education clearly can be used for "nation-building" purposes (Weber, 1976), the correlation between education and income is so profound (Mincer, 1974) that it is difficult to imagine that an autocratic elite would choose education as the most effective manner to keep their subjects down. If anything, the suggestion is the reverse: that an educated mass is dangerous for the elite (Acemoglu and Robinson, 2006; Verdier and Bourguignon, 2000). Furthermore, education is costly to provide and threatening to the established social order not constitutive of it. Nineteenth century elites were much more concerned with keeping education spending minimal and avoiding meritocracy than they were with using education as a direct tool of social control (Lindert, 2003a). The isomorphism argument, for its part, may explain the transmission of Western *styles* of education but it certainly did not lead to Western *levels* of education spending. For example, India has long had a British-inspired education system, yet its levels of education spending have been pitifully low. Finally, these systemic arguments are typically very difficult to test since they specify broad levels of "modernity" and "social control" as independent variables – concepts that are almost impossible to operationalize and difficult to distinguish in some cases from education itself.

The focus on redistributive politics thus distinguishes this work from the economics literature and structural functionalism, while the focus on the impact of the labor market and political institutions on education distinguishes this book from vertical differentiation and Marxist analyses. Thus, this is fundamentally a *political and institutional* explanation of education policy. However, it also differs substantially from the traditional depiction of education in the political science literature. The classic view of education in the political science literature typically focused on the social content of education – that is, education as used to socialize individuals into the religious, nationalist, or economic goals of the state. For Gellner (1983), education was used as a tool of "social genetics," which the state could use to reproduce effectively a loyal, nationalistic citizenry. Education fulfilled the function of control by the state. Weber (1976) reached a similar conclusion in his analysis of the development of the French state. Education was used by the Third Republic to spread the French language and French national identity to the parochial peasantry and thereby to strengthen the state vis-à-vis society. In more recent work, Kalyvas (1996) has stressed the importance of education for the religious political parties of late nineteenth century Europe. In particular, for the Catholic states, secular education was a threat to the Church's dominance of social relations. Thus, battles over education between secular and religious parties were essentially conflicts over whether the state's socialization of the citizenry would be tinged by sword or cross. In these accounts, the citizenry remain a passive vessel into which the state would pour its socializing education.

This project essentially reverses this statist view of education by building a theory of education preferences from the individual level up. While I argue that education policy is strongly constrained by political institutions, it is at heart determined by the preferences not of a reified "state" but by the preferences of individuals whose political interests are represented in government. And citizens have every reason to demand education themselves, given that it is the chief predictor of economic success. Individuals of different incomes and economic class will consequently have sharply different preferences over education spending, and policy reflects these political battles rather than the assumed preferences of the state itself.

The classic political science analysis of "statist education" has been replaced by a more recent comparative political economy literature in political science. A number of authors have examined the basic effects of political institutions such as democracy and partisanship on public spending on education. Busemeyer (2007) and Boix (1998), for example, have shown a positive relationship between socialist control of government and the level of education spending in the

OECD. Lake and Baum (2001) have examined the impact of democracy on secondary school enrollment ratios. Other authors have analyzed the impact of democratization on aggregate education spending in Latin America (Brown and Hunter, 2004) and Africa (Stasavage, 2005). However, these studies are for the most part somewhat fragmentary in that their range of cases and time periods is limited and their analysis of education is generally limited to a single facet of education policy. Conversely, this study examines, among other issues, aggregate education spending, education spending relative to other public goods, higher education spending, private education spending, voters' preferences over education, and partisan educational rhetoric. Moreover, many of these studies do not present a general model of the political economy of education spending; rather, they draw on broad trends and correlations. As such, it is difficult to extend these arguments, given that they are couched in simple bivariate, associative terms. Finally, these works give short shrift to the impact of the global economy on education; in particular, they fail to draw out the implications of globalization for labor supply and demand.

The Varieties of Capitalism (VoC) literature developed in Hall and Soskice (2001) does more closely address the intersection of global economic forces and redistributive politics. The VoC framework argues that labor market institutions and patterns of redistribution form poles of comparative advantage for developed countries in the global economy; thus seemingly domestic policies such as innovation, corporate governance, social insurance, and wage bargaining have a global logic – they permit states to specialize in international commerce. This analysis of the links between the global economy and institutionally differentiated production is innovative and telling. However, it does not extend fully satisfactorily to the study of education. The analysis of education in this literature – for example, Estevez-Abe, Iversen, and Soskice (2001) and Thelen (2004) – focuses almost exclusively on the differences between vocational and general education systems, drawing on the links between these forms of education and labor market bargaining and risk insurance but not explicitly on their links to the global market nor to redistributive politics more broadly.

A particular absence in the VoC literature is the role of higher education in advanced industrial countries – a surprising omission given the emphasis placed on this educational sector by most commentators and politicians. Where higher education is examined, it is considered part of a general-skills approach that promotes innovation and is found in Liberal Market Economies (LMEs). This contrasts with the emphasis on specific vocational skills in Coordinated Market Economies (CMEs). The focus on vocational education may fit the binary model of LMEs and CMEs, but this glosses over the striking difference *among* CMEs between mass Nordic higher education systems and their elitist continental counterparts. A further concern with the VoC literature is that its emphasis on national institutional complementarities empties the argument of partisan politics. Vocational education in particular is examined through the lens of "efficiency" or "complementarity" rather than as also host to redistributive politics. As we shall see, there is evidence that even in vocational training,

TABLE 1.1. *Situating the Debate around Education*

	Global Labor Market	No Global Labor Market
Redistributive	This Book VoC	Comparative Political Economy Vertical Differentiation
Not Redistributive	New Growth Labor Economics Human Capital and Signaling	World Systems Theory Statist Education Theory

partisan politics can bite. More generally, while inequality and social insurance are important components of the VoC framework, there is a countervailing neglect of the redistributive politics of education. This book aims to fill that gap.

Table 1.1 summarizes the interdisciplinary literature on education policy, clarifying the axes of distinction between major approaches and noting that the theory developed in this book combines the emphasis on the redistributive dimension of education stressed in political science and in critical sociological work, with the labor market analysis more typical of economics and the Varieties of Capitalism literature in political economy.

1.4 THREE STORIES ABOUT EDUCATION

This book develops and tests its argument by telling three stories. These stories move roughly along the timeline of education policy experienced by most states, starting at the original decision to expand basic education to the masses, moving to the partisan politics of mass compulsory education, and concluding with the transition to mass higher education systems in advanced industrial states. This section lays out the plan of the book, which follows the logic of the developmental tale of the three stories. Each chapter explores both theoretical and empirical questions, building the basic theory off a simple formal model of education, before testing this theory on statistical evidence, and tracing the logic of the causal mechanism in a variety of case studies.

The Expansion of Education to the Masses: Chapters 2 and 3

Chapter 2 begins the story of the original extension of education to the mass public. I develop a baseline formal model of political preferences over public education spending. This model begins by setting out the determinants of individual preferences over education and shows how different political institutions permit varied forms of redistribution through education policy and how different political coalitions might form around these policies. The model is then extended to show how the redistributive politics of education are altered under different labor market conditions, focusing, in particular, on the impact of opening a state to the global economy. From the formal model, an array of hypotheses is developed, then tested using a variety of statistical methods, on a dataset of 115 countries stretching from 1960 to 2000. In particular, I show that democracies are likely to have higher public education spending than autocracies, and I test what components of democracy and autocracy make such a pattern particularly likely. I further find that democracies spend less on private education and tilt their education spending toward primary education rather than higher education. I also show, counterintuitively, that states that open their economies to the global market have greater education spending and that this effect is significantly stronger in autocracies and developing states.

Chapter 3 continues the story of expanding education to the masses through a series of case studies that more closely pry into the causal effects of regime type and global integration on education spending. The cases are chosen so as to test the causal mechanisms across the full range of counterfactuals and include countries that display particularly unusual configurations of regime type and openness. I begin by examining the Philippines, which has had significant volatility in both regime type and its level of integration with the global economy since the days of Spanish rule. I discuss the differing impacts of Spanish, American, and Japanese colonialism before moving to the variously democratic and autocratic regimes governing the Philippines in the postwar era. I also examine the impact on education policy of Philippine trade strategy, noting that its reliance on import substitution industrialization (ISI) weakened its demand for education. Secondly, I turn to a case comparison of India and Malaysia in terms of the impact of openness on their education policy since independence. India and Malaysia provide an interesting contrast, since both lie "off the diagonal" of open democracies and autarkic autocracies. I show that the paradox of democratic India's failure to educate its citizenry can be explained by its dalliance with ISI development. Similarly, the paradox that authoritarian Malaysia is a world leader in education spending can be resolved by reference to Malaysia's early turn to export-oriented development. Thirdly, I compare the development of East Asia and Latin America, revisiting the well-known debate on their relative success by suggesting it can be best explained by examining the *interdependence* between openness and education, which permitted the rise of East Asia up the value chain but condemned Latin America to a two-tier economy with a majority unskilled workforce. This contrast is developed through a case comparison of Brazil and South Korea in the postwar era. A final set of cases attempts to distinguish the effects of democracy and globalization by examining three states that experienced shocks to each variable in distinct periods: Portugal, Spain, and Greece, who all democratized in the 1970s and joined the European Community in the 1980s.

The Partisan Politics of Education: Chapter 4

The second story is that of the partisan politics of education as they play out in the advanced industrial states. These states had, for the most part, achieved universal primary and secondary education by 1950. However, even with mass enrollment achieved, there has remained considerable cross-country variation in overall education spending. Denmark, for example, continues to spend almost three times as much on education as a proportion of national income as compared to Greece. Furthermore, wealthy states often see major shifts in education spending over time. In 1975, the UK spent around 6.5 percent of GDP on public education, but this declined to 4.5 percent by the late 1990s, then jumped back to 5.6 percent of GDP by 2006. Since most politicians, whatever their partisan persuasion, publicly declare their interest in public education, particularly as a way of improving national productivity, this kind of variance within the subset of advanced industrial states is somewhat surprising. Chapter 4 argues that this cross-national variation, and cross-time variation within states, can best be explained by examining the interplay of partisan politics and electoral institutions.

Chapter 4 develops and tests a model of voters, parties, and elections. I show that income differences and party identification are the major determinants of individual preferences over both public and private education and I find that parties aggregate these preferences rather effectively. This implies that party promises to provide education policies that cut against basic partisan preferences are unlikely to be credible. Instead, parties have distinct and systematic preferences over education policy, expressed in their manifesto declarations and revealed in their policy enactments once in office. The chapter tests the impact of switches in party control on both overall education spending, and education spending relative to other government consumption, showing a powerful positive effect of left-wing control of government on education spending. Vocational education shows a different pattern, however, with right-wing parties associated with higher vocational enrollments, at least when school systems are streamed. The chapter goes on to show how electoral institutions constrain the ability of parties to make their preferred policies and open up the potential for new and unlikely coalitions.

High Politics in Higher Education: Chapter 5

The final story centers on the transition to a mass higher education system in advanced industrial countries. Universities have been the site of major institutional reform over the past few decades. In the immediate postwar era, almost all developed states had an elite, publicly subsidized higher education system. However, since the early 1990s a number of states have developed truly mass higher education systems, albeit using quite distinct funding mechanisms. Several states, including Australia and New Zealand, have introduced tuition fees to support expansion, whereas the Scandinavian countries have accompanied expansion with public funds. Still other states, including Germany and Italy, retain elite, publicly funded systems. Chapter 5 focuses on the determinants of changes in higher education provision, focusing on the redistributive dimension of funding what often amounts to a regressive public good.

I develop the concept of a "trilemma" among the extent of enrollment, the degree of subsidization, and the public cost of higher education, producing three models of higher education systems: the Partially Private, the Mass Public, and the Elite. I develop a formal analysis of the trade-offs within this trilemma by examining individual preferences, the aggregation of these preferences by political parties, and the preconditions for institutional change among these systems. I then conduct a series of empirical tests of the implications of the model. I firstly demonstrate the existence of the trilemma at a cross-sectional level in the OECD. I then turn to establishing voter preferences over higher education funding, noting how the national structure of higher education conditions them. I then turn to a panel data analysis of higher education spending and enrollment across the OECD during the 1980s and 1990s. To examine institutional change and partisan preferences in greater detail, I continue with a case comparison of higher education reforms since 1960 in England, Sweden, and Germany. I conclude the chapter with a statistical analysis of the determinants of appropriations and tuition fees across the U.S. states between 1982 and 2007. Throughout the chapter, I show a "conditional" partisan pattern, wherein at low levels of existing enrollment, right-wing parties are the chief advocates of spending and expansion, but at high levels of enrollment these partisan patterns reverse.

2

The Expansion of Education to the Masses

Theory and Data

The southern African kingdoms of Swaziland and Lesotho appear at first glance to be twins. Both states have populations of just over one million, low per capita incomes, near-identical demographic structures, and mountainous terrains, and are enveloped (entirely in the case of Lesotho) by the country of South Africa. Hence, one might expect both countries to face similar challenges in providing public infrastructure and investment. However, in terms of education spending, the countries stand in sharp contrast, with Lesotho spending twice as much of its national income on education as Swaziland. This distinction is a new one. In the mid-1980s, the two countries both spent around 6 percent of national income on education. But in the early 1990s, Lesotho began to diverge from Swaziland, at points spending over 10 percent of its national income, whereas Swaziland's investment actually declined.

What explains this divergence? In Lesotho in 1993, Major General Elias Phisoana Ramaema handed over power to a democratically elected government headed by the previously banned Basutoland Congress Party. Although that government faced a variety of challenges to its control over the following five years, including two attempted coups, democracy has slowly become institutionalized and Lesotho has experienced peaceful and fair elections over the past decade. While far from an exemplar of democracy, Lesotho compares well to Swaziland, which has been controlled since 1986 by King Mswati III, who retains the ability to hire and dismiss the prime minister and other government figures at will. The Polity index of democracy rates Lesotho as a +8 (where +10 is the highest score) but Swaziland as a −9 (where −10 is the lowest score). Figure 2.1 suggests that the transition to democracy in Lesotho in 1993, while Swaziland remained resolutely autocratic, was closely related to the ensuing divergence in education spending across the two countries. Is democracy, then, the path to education?

The case of South Korea provides a striking counterpoint to the tiny kingdoms of southern Africa. South Korea had, until the 1990s, a highly authoritarian military government. Yet it was also the developing world's leader

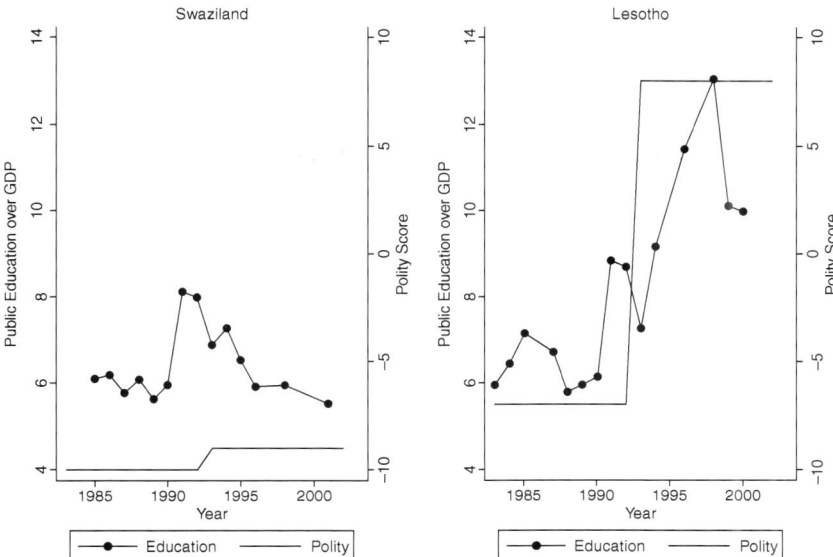

FIGURE 2.1. Education and Democracy in Swaziland and Lesotho

in the provision of education. During two decades of military rule, South Korea actually expanded secondary enrollment from 35 percent of the age cohort in 1965 to 88 percent in 1987 and achieved universal primary enrollment, at a time when many democratic developing countries, such as India, were struggling to educate over half of their population. Why did South Korea succeed in educational investment where other autocracies, from Swaziland to Brazil, failed? South Korea's distinction was its outward orientation in economic development. By moving toward a strategy of export-oriented industrialization, the South Koreans boosted demand for a mass skilled workforce and prevented the collapse in returns to education that occurred in inward-looking autocracies such as Egypt. Thus openness proved a substitute for democracy in South Korea, providing a second path to education.

Do these two paths to education hold more generally? In this chapter, I demonstrate that both a country's political regime and its level of integration with the global economy matter enormously for its level of education spending and the manner in which that spending is distributed. Put simply, political openness and economic openness appear to be the key drivers of the expansion of education. Burrowing deeper into the data, we can view these forces as substitute choices for states – globalizing autocracies and autarkic democracies can both become educational leaders. However, the consistent major educational spenders are precisely those countries with long histories of democracy and openness, such as Denmark and New Zealand.

This is a somewhat surprising finding. The standard assumption of a "race to the bottom" in public spending among states exposed to globalization suggests we might expect lower education spending in highly open states. Furthermore, those theories that do suggest increased public spending in globalizing states tend to emphasize the *compensational* role of this spending – for example, insurance against unemployment (Katzenstein, 1985; Garrett, 1998; and Rodrik; 2000) – rather than its effects on the *composition* of the state's endowments. While the positive relationship between the expansion of the franchise to the masses and the expansion of education is more intuitive, even here the finding cuts against the grain of much existing research. For example, historical and sociological accounts of education often emphasize the role of education in solidifying authoritarian control of the state and expanding the military, so even the positive role of democracy is not obvious (Weber, 1976; Krebs, 2006). Consequently, the empirical findings of this chapter, and their theoretical underpinnings, have important repercussions for how we should think about the role of education in development policy. While many international institutions have shifted toward a focus on improving human capital and "capabilities" (Sen, 2000), this development strategy is unlikely to be effective in countries that are "predisposed" to lower levels of education spending because of redistributive conflict: autocracies and autarkies.

Beyond these twin findings about the relationship between democracy and globalization and overall education spending, this chapter digs further into the determinants of a variety of aspects of education spending. We will see that private education spending is highly *negatively* correlated with democracy and that as states democratize they also tilt their public spending away from higher education toward mass primary education. Thus the impact of democracy is felt not only in *how much* education is made available but the particular *types* of education that emerge. Moreover, this chapter shows that the effects of democracy on education appear driven neither by the greater stability of regimes nor by the reduction of factionalism under democracy but fundamentally by the degree to which the public at large is represented by, and can control, policy making.

Globalization also impacts the types of education produced in states. In particular, I show in this chapter that while highly open developed states are increasingly focusing on higher education vis-à-vis primary education, the reverse is true in the developing world. Consequently, while many commentators in the developed world view education as the "solution" to globalization and increasing low-wage competition from the developing world, the very type of education spending provoked by globalization in developed countries is likely to exacerbate economic inequality.

I begin this chapter in Section 2.2 by focusing on the enormous cross-national and historical variation in education spending. In doing so, I show that this variation cannot be easily explained by appealing to broad differences in economic development or regional culture. Having outlined the variation to be explained in this chapter, I discuss the existing debate over democracy and globalization in Section 2.3. Then, in Section 2.4, I develop a theory of education spending. Here I integrate insights from the expansive literatures on democracy and globalization before developing a simple formal framework producing a broad variety of hypotheses about the determinants of education spending. In Section 2.5,

I test these hypotheses on a dataset of over one hundred states from 1960 to 2000, examining a variety of aggregate measures of education including both public and private spending. Section 2.6 extends the earlier analysis, disaggregating both regime type – differentiating among democracies and autocracies rather than between them – and education spending itself, focusing on tertiary education versus primary education. Section 2.7 concludes the chapter.

2.2 VARIATION IN EDUCATION SPENDING

The analysis of public education investment would be less than stimulating if most countries spent similar levels of national resources on education. Yet, existing theories provide relatively little guidance as to what cross-national variance might look like, or even whether it ought to be anticipated at all. The standard economic view of public education as a solution to market failures suggests that the level of spending adopted by states should be fairly constant, at least within groups of similarly developed nations. Similarly, sociological theories of education provision presume similar levels of state effort across states that are similarly "modern," or where the nation-state is most fully established. Overall, most existing accounts of comparative education policy suggest that economic development and social modernization are the key drivers of change. Furthermore, other than a general upward trend in education spending, existing theories provide little indication that education spending should show much temporal variation. Unlike much social spending that is driven by the business cycle, we might expect education spending to be relatively constant across time within countries.

However, education spending is both highly variant internationally and highly volatile within nations. I begin by considering cross-national variation. Figure 2.2 is a "box and whisker" plot of the proportion of national income spent on public education within each main geographical region in the world. The edges of the box show the countries that lie between the 25th and 75th percentile in terms of education spending within that particular region, with the line within the box representing the median country for that region. The branches (or "whiskers") extending from the box mark the 10th and 90th percentiles for the region and the dots mark countries beyond these two extremes. A number of implications stand out.

First, there is substantial variation among countries within *every* region in the world. It is not the case that the wealthy countries of Europe have similarly high levels of education spending, nor that the mostly poor countries of Sub-Saharan Africa have uniformly low levels of spending. The "development" story told by the standard economic and sociological theories of education provision becomes problematic when one examines the cross-national record. Second, the median across regions also varies dramatically – for example, *on average* African countries spend less than do European ones. Here we have some evidence that development might indeed matter, but so too might other attributes, such as democracy or openness, that are shared by countries with similar levels

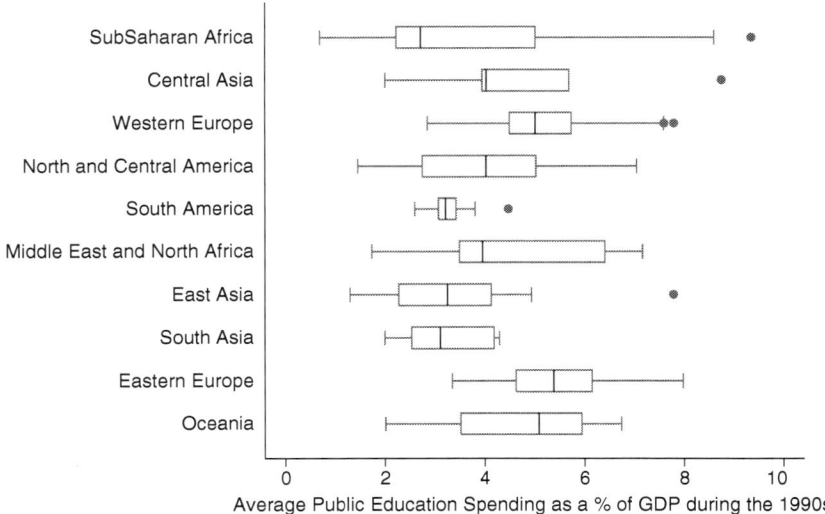

FIGURE 2.2. Cross-national and Regional Variation in Education Spending

of development. Third, the variation that exists is *substantively* important. The highest-spending state in Africa, Lesotho, spends ten times what the lowest-spending state, Equatorial Guinea, does. Given the similar demographic profiles of these states, such substantial variation has very real implications for the sustainable development and level of welfare of these states.

Thus, the global educational story is one marked by a massive diversity of experience. But is this just a function of some states being more "education-friendly" than others? The standard cultural or nation-building view of education expects little variation *within* countries in terms of their education provision. If education is a process of socializing one's citizenry from above, or is a "grassroots" phenomenon with some cultures simply more attuned to study, we should expect little cross-time variation in education provision other than a gradual upward trend as socialization reaches toward the periphery of the state. Cross-national analyses of education are thus typically static – some countries just have more education-directed cultures – or monotonic – education expands slowly and surely until the last illiterate is transformed into an acculturated student. Yet, as with cross-national variation, this consensus on temporal stability is unmatched by the data.

Figure 2.3 provides a salutary example of just how variable education spending can be in as little as a decade. The figure depicts public education spending as a percentage of national income in the Philippines from 1960 to 2000. The volatility of education policy is striking. In 1960, the Philippines spent around 2 percent of national income on public education, and this level was more or less maintained until the mid-1970s. However, from the late 1970s until the mid-1980s, education spending plummeted to just over 1 percent. Following this dip, spending then rose to 3 percent of national income by 1990 and then

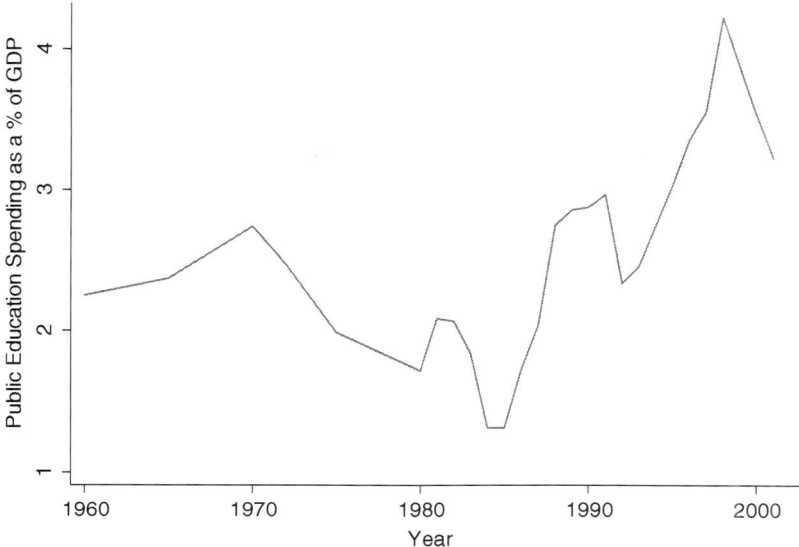

FIGURE 2.3. Education Spending in the Philippines, 1960 to 2000

to over 4 percent by 2000, before sharply dropping once more. In Chapter 3, we will explore the Philippine case in much greater detail, but suffice it to say, it is clear that constant cultural explanations – for example, a Filipino "love of education" – are unable to explain the reality of sharp fluctuation.

2.3 A REDISTRIBUTIVE THEORY OF EDUCATION EXPANSION

In this section, I set about exploring the causes of the vast cross-sectional and temporal variation in education spending described in the preceding section. I develop a redistributive theory of education expansion, building off two extensive literatures familiar to political scientists and economists: scholarship that focuses on (a) the impact of democracy on redistributive politics, and (b) the effect of globalization on public spending. Drawing insights from this literature, in the following section I develop a simple formal model of education spending, constructing a causal mechanism that connects political institutions and the structure of the global labor market to outcomes in education spending.

Democracy and Redistributive Politics

Since John Stuart Mill, political economists have puzzled over the precise relationship between democracy and education. For Mill (1856) democracy was in itself educational – by participating in political action, individuals would learn how to become citizens. Many other authors have viewed education as a prerequisite for democracy. Lipset (1959), for example, saw education as a precondition for the development of a pro-democratic middle class that would hasten modernization. In more contemporary work, Boix (2003) views education as hastening democracy but not because of any inherent "democratizing" nature of education itself but through education's effect of compressing income distribution. Still other authors actually elide the distinction between democracy and education: Ross's (2001) analysis of whether oil inhibits democracy also asks whether oil inhibits public education, assuming a near-equivalency between the two. Education and democracy thus have a long-standing relationship in political economy. But the direction of the relationship is unclear.

While there is an extended literature on whether education promotes democracy, few works address the reverse issue of how aggregate education funding is affected by this most basic of political institutions. There is a small developing literature that has examined the effects of democracy on educational outcome variables such as secondary school enrollments and literacy rates (Lake and Baum, 2001). There is less work that directly addresses actual public spending, that is, inputs into education driven by the political process. Those studies that have examined this effect on spending tend to be limited to particular groups of states: developing nations (Rudra and Haggard, 2005), Africa (Stasavage, 2005), Latin America (Brown and Hunter, 2004), and developed states in the nineteenth century (Lindert, 2004).

In Chapter 1, I argued that preferences over public education spending are negatively related to income because education redistributes income, both present and future, from the rich to the poor. Thus, any political system that tilts representation toward the wealthier members of society should have lower public spending on education. Countries with property franchises for voting (the United Kingdom before 1918), those that systematically exclude poorer ethnic groups from political participation (South Africa under apartheid), or those that reflect the preferences only of the ruling elite or family (e.g., the Swazi or Saudi monarchies) will consequently have lower public education spending. Thus, the chief determinant of education spending will be the extent to which the polity's decision makers are "representative agents" of the population affected by their decisions. Where the franchise is limited or the executive unconstrained, policies will reflect the redistributive interests of the elite. This view of democracy resembles the "selectorate" concept developed by Bueno de Mesquita and his colleagues (2004), which differentiates among regimes by the size of the group that can "select" the ruling executive. It is useful to compare the conceptualization of democracy employed in this project to those used in other well-known studies of the effects of democracy on public policies. These alternate theories can be divided into three main categories: the monopolistic theory of democracy; the stability of succession theory of democracy; and the contestation model.

The monopolistic theory of democracy analyzes the state through the economic model of the firm. According to this theory, autocracies are able to carve out large monopoly rents in their provision of public services because barriers to political entry are high. This implies that autocracies are systematically restricting the supply of public goods such as education with a view to bidding up taxes and favors by citizens who want access to these scarce commodities (Shleifer and Vishny, 1992; Lake and Baum, 2001). The difficulty with ascertaining the validity of this theory is that it requires data on the autocracy's gains from monopolization, and such data – for example, corruption indices – are notoriously unreliable. Moreover, it is rarely the case that nominal tax rates are particularly high in autocracies.[1] Finally, those people able to bid up taxes or bribes for scarce resources tend to be those who could already access education – not the poorest members of society. Rather than accepting a rent-seeking model of autocracy where education is scarce in order to blackmail citizens for resources, why not assume that the elite in control of autocracies simply prefer not to fund education publicly because of the negative redistributive effects of provision? The monopolistic theory elides this distinction because it focuses on a disembodied state rather than on a government that reflects the redistributive preferences of a particular subset of society more generally.

The stability theory argues that the stability of succession explains public good provision, particularly the supply of investment goods such as education. In regimes with highly unstable succession, the ruler is likely to prefer short-term predation. Conversely, where succession is stable, rulers will undertake (and skim rents from) long-term investment (Olson 1993). Despotic rulers are thus likely to under-invest in public goods such as education. Democracies conversely allow both stability of succession and the potential return to office through reelection – thus leading to higher provision of public goods (Quinn and Wooley, 2001). This theory differs in implications from the monopolistic model in that it implies that monarchies, because they permit stable succession, should have higher investment in public goods vis-à-vis other autocracies. As we shall see, however, the stability of succession has no apparent impact on education spending. Even if monarchs are long-sighted, they behave myopically with regard to education.

The contestation model is proposed by Stasavage (2005) in his analysis of African education spending. Stasavage essentially reverses Bates' (1981) argument that autocratic states, facing greater threat of removal by urban workers than by rural peasants, will distort the agricultural market to benefit the former at the expense of the latter. Stasavage notes that this favoritism should be reversed as states democratize and rulers become more reliant on the voting mass in rural areas. Since education spending – particularly at the primary level – benefits these rural citizens disproportionately, democracies will expand education spending and target it toward universal provision. Stasavage's model is the closest to that developed in this study in that it focuses on responses to an increased selectorate. Yet it is not obvious that the logic of rural–urban politics is appropriate outside of the African context. Moreover, the example of states such as India, which are democratic and yet have failed to extend education effectively to rural areas, rather belies Stasavage's purported

---

[1] Exceptions include communist states, which, in any case, had particularly high education spending for autocracies.

mechanism.[2] Furthermore, as I show in Section 2.7, empirical analysis of the degree of factionalism within democracies, a potential analog to Stasavage's mechanism, shows no strong effect on education spending.

Most of the preceding theories assume a binary structure of politics: the state versus society, urban versus rural. The model developed in this chapter takes a more continuous approach, allowing for gradations in democracy to expand political representation step by step.[3] Rather than viewing the state as necessarily predatory, the model depicts it as the embodiment of the redistributive preferences of its own selectorate. Where the selectorate's preferences vary from the masses' preferred policies, political institutions will fail to represent the democratic consensus on education spending. This implies that dictatorships will have much lower public education spending than will democracies, with the elite preferring spending to remain private. Furthermore, public spending in dictatorships will be targeted toward the children of the elite, typically toward the university sector rather than primary education. Finally, such public spending as there is in autocracies will be tilted away from education, which has particularly negative redistributive consequences for the rich, and toward other forms of simple government consumption. Dictatorships might prefer to "buy off" the poor rather than educate them. This implies that not only *absolute* but also *relative* education spending will be lower in autocracies. These arguments are developed formally in the following section. However, before doing so, I turn from the political to the economic marketplace.

Globalization and the Labor Market

Education policy and globalization might not appear to be obvious theoretical bedfellows. Education looks like the paradigmatic "domestic" policy. Not only is education policy focused on domestic students and schools, but typically states cannot directly export and import the service of education. However, education is not as immobile as it might superficially appear. Through the trade of goods and services that *embody* skilled labor, and through the transfer of technology, individuals can sell their education abroad and buy the education of foreigners. Global trade thus alters the returns to education in a manner as profound as its effects on the return to capital or on unskilled labor (Rogowski, 1989). This force works through two channels. The first channel is through the effects of openness on whether the returns to skill are affected by the *supply* of skills. The second channel is through the effects of openness on the *demand* for skills, through the mechanism of technology transfer.

The supply argument is a basic corollary of the Factor Equalization Theory developed by Samuelson (1948). The argument claims that if countries trade

---

[2] On the Indian paradox, see Chapter 3 and Weiner (1990).

[3] An approach also followed in Lindert (2003a), which concerns itself with the incremental expansion of democracy in nineteenth century Europe and the consequent effect on public education.

goods with one another that are both in each country's "zone of diversification,"[4] then domestic prices for these goods will converge with global prices. With global prices and global production of all goods, all factors will be paid the *same rate of return* for their role in production. What is particularly important to note is that this rate is *not* determined by the domestic supply of factors. At the extreme, countries could have highly "unbalanced" factor supplies (for example, a workforce where almost every member has a university degree) without any change in the rate of return to that factor. Changes in factor supply would affect only the composition of output (that is, the mix of goods produced) rather than factor returns – an outcome known as the Rybczynski theorem (Rybczynski, 1955).

While such extreme price and wage convergence is rarely achieved when states trade, the fact that trade necessarily leads to some convergence in factor returns means a reduction in the *factor supply elasticity of factor returns*, that is, the rate at which relative returns respond to changes in relative supply. As states become increasingly open, this elasticity converges to zero. In fact, near-zero elasticities have been measured in some of the most open trading systems in the world – for example, between the states of the United States. Hanson and Slaughter (2002) found that changes in the supply of skilled and unskilled workers within U.S. states had no effect on the relative wages of skilled and unskilled workers. If California absorbed scores of unskilled workers, instead of reducing the return to unskilled labor, industrial composition would simply shift toward low-cost production such as agriculture. Similarly, the relative skilled wage premium in Massachusetts was found to be unaffected by the internal migration of college graduates to that state during the 1990s. While the U.S. case is extreme, a similar pattern emerged in the negligible response of skilled wages to the mass expansion of higher education in Western Europe (Machin, 1998).

The stability of skilled wages with respect to skill supply implies that when states expand education in an open economy, the negative effects that are experienced by the holders of skill in autarkies do not occur. At the margin, then, education provision would be preferable in open economies vis-à-vis closed ones. Closed economies are unable to absorb the extra production of education-intensive goods, which bids down skilled wages or produces educated unemployment, harming the already educated, who thus prefer lower education spending. Any autarkic state that finds expanding education merely produces educated unemployment or collapsing wages is likely to limit further expansion. The negative impact of education provision is greatly reduced in open economies where the skilled can essentially sell their factor endowments to foreign bidders – here education can be expanded without such negative consequences. This supply-side impact of openness will be most pronounced in states where the educated elite control political decision making – that is, in autocracies. Section 2.5 shows

---

[4] The "zone of diversification" is the set of goods that states will continue to produce under free trade. If this set just includes one good per state, we have complete specialization.

that there does appear to be a stronger positive effect of openness on education spending in such states.

The demand-side story differs somewhat from the supply elasticity effect and is derived from the recent combination of new growth theory and trade economics, best represented in the work of Daron Acemoglu. Acemoglu (2003) argues, building off earlier work by Pissarides (1997), that globalization impacts wages through the mechanism of technology transfer. As states globalize, they are exposed to new technologies, which compete against indigenously developed technologies. On the assumption that the global technology is superior, businesses must adapt to these new technologies or become replaced. Adaptation to new technologies *necessarily* requires a small trained workforce who can implement changes in production. So far, then, globalization is likely to be associated with increases in the demand for education at the margin – but largely confined to the very high-skill engineering sectors. However, Acemoglu argues that the process of technological transfer is much more extensive than just the requirement for such technicians. Most new technologies tend to be those that are complementary with highly skilled labor (Goldin and Katz, 1998). For example, computers cannot be used in a production process merely by being turned on by unskilled workers – they require trained operators to use them effectively (Autor, Levy, and Murnane, 2001). Modern manufacturing requires workers who can manipulate and innovate processes on the go – a switch from labor-biased Fordist production to flexible specialization (Piore and Sabel, 1984). Such technologies, then, require a more educated labor force, thus increasing the demand for public education. Note that we might expect this effect of globalization to be stronger in states that were not previously exposed to such technologies, indicating that the effect of openness on education should be stronger in developing countries.

Increased openness also affects education spending *relative* to other government spending. The likely impact is mixed. On the one hand, globalization potentially reduces the antipathy of the elite toward education vis-à-vis other forms of spending, potentially increasing education's share of the budget.[5] On the other hand, globalization might reduce relative education spending, if it provokes increased activity in other forms of spending. Many political economists – from Cameron (1978) to Garrett (1998) to Rodrik (2000) – have argued that overall government consumption increases following the opening of the economy. Such arguments tend to assume that the volatility caused by openness will lead to a Keynesian compensatory response through public employment or social insurance. This raises the question of whether governments will respond to globalization with a *compensatory* strategy or a strategy that involves changing the *composition* of the workforce through education. The compensational

---

[5] Openness also lessens the chance of an anti-education, pro-redistribution alliance between the rich and poor, with the rich no longer willing to trade off a small amount of increased education for a large amount of other public goods for the poor.

pattern, however, is only likely to occur in countries where unskilled workers are particularly threatened by globalization, that is, in developed states. Combining these implications, I expect relative education spending to rise generally under openness but to be pronounced more strongly in developing states and autocracies.

The final impact of globalization to note is its effect on the composition of education spending between primary and tertiary education. The neoclassical theory of international trade assumes that trading states will export factors in which they are relatively well endowed and develop their industrial structures accordingly. This implies that open developing states should export goods embodying lower skills – those produced by primary education – whereas open developed states should export goods embodying higher education. Open developing states should thus invest in primary education, and open developed states should invest in higher education. Conversely, autarkic developing states will under-invest in primary education and over-invest in higher education, with the reverse pattern occurring for autarkic developed states.

2.4 A SIMPLE MODEL OF EDUCATION EXPANSION

In this section, I develop a simple formal model that integrates the roles of regime type and globalization in determining education spending. In doing so, I focus on the effect of political institutions and labor market structure on the ability of groups to target redistribution to themselves. The model focuses on distributional conflict between the rich, the middle class, and the poor, examining the preferences held by each group over different levels and types of education spending, and how the structure of the labor market impacts these preferences. Consequently, the model is a conflictual one, where groups' preferred education policies come at the expense of the preferences of others. However, how much the winners win and the losers lose depends on how a set of crosscutting redistributive factors adds up.

I begin by imagining a country with three groups of individuals: a high-income group (the "elite"), a middle-income group (the "middle class"), and a poor group (the "poor"). Individuals earn income from two sources. Firstly, they receive group "wealth" q_i, where $i \in \{H, M, P\}$, where $q_H > q_M > q_P$. For the purposes of the model, it is not important where this element of income comes from – but it is important to note that it is not derived from the labor market. We can think of it as some form of unequally distributed wealth. It is taxation of this wealth that will make any fiscally progressive tax policy "bite" for the rich and benefit the poor, regardless of the returns to education. It also allows us to distinguish between the middle class and the poor when both are unskilled and between the middle class and the rich when both are skilled. Individuals also receive income in the form of returns to their factor endowments of skilled and unskilled labor, which I assume derive from whether they received education or not. Individuals are either fully skilled or unskilled.

The returns to skilled and unskilled labor, w_s and w_u, are defined by their relative productivity and their relative abundance. In particular, I assume that skilled productivity, σ_s, is always higher than unskilled productivity, σ_u. However, the skill premium is reduced by the relative abundance of skilled labor vis-à-vis unskilled labor. Skilled individuals will benefit financially when there are relatively few other skilled individuals and will suffer as the proportion of the population with skills expands. The proportion of the population who are skilled is $S \in [0,1]$, and the degree to which skilled wages are reduced by an expansion in S, through education spending, is defined by the skilled labor supply elasticity parameter, b. A relative abundance of skilled labor implies a relative scarcity of unskilled labor, which is reflected by the unskilled labor supply elasticity parameter, a. These two labor supply elasticity parameters a and b reflect the degree to which the scarcity effect impacts wages. If they equal zero, then the relative supply of skilled and unskilled labor has *no* effect on the returns to education. Conversely, if they are positive, then an increase in the abundance of one of the factors reduces its return.

To define w_j, we need to examine labor market equilibria for skilled and unskilled wages, determined by their relative productivity and abundance.

$$w_s = \sigma_s - bS \tag{1}$$

$$w_u = \sigma_u + aS \tag{2}$$

Skilled wages are decreasing in the relative abundance of skills and increasing in the productivity of skilled labor, whereas unskilled wages are increasing in the relative abundance of skills and in the productivity of unskilled labor. I make one further important assumption about earnings, which links the wealth and wage functions. I assume that all individuals who receive the skilled wage (that is, who receive education) have higher individual wealth than those who do not. This implies that skill provision begins with the richest member of society and gradually extends to the poorest.[6] I define an individual's "inverse skill index" as $s_i \in [0,1]$, where the person with $s_i = 0$ will be the first to receive education under public education expansion, and the person with $s_i = 1$ will be the last. This inverse skill index is inversely related to the individual wealth parameter q_i, as laid out in the following relationships:

$$s_i = f(q_i), \quad f'(q_i) < 0; \quad f(\min q_i) = 1; \quad f(\max q_i) = 0 \tag{3}$$

---

[6] If I did not make this assumption and assumed that education was distributed uniformly throughout society but in a probabilistic manner, the basic results would still hold. In the case where the poor receive education first, the results would hold provided that the elite were also receiving private education and that expanded public education had a negative scarcity effect on the returns to private education. I explore this alternative at length in Chapter 5.

Individuals with s_i below the level of education provision S receive education; those with higher levels of s_i do not receive education. The following equation summarizes this:

$$s_i \leq S \Leftrightarrow w_j = w_s$$
$$s_i > S \Leftrightarrow w_j = w_u \tag{4}$$

As S increases, the number of individuals earning skilled wages also increases from the richest to the poorest member of society. Combining the income equations produces the following:

$$y_i = q_i + w_j \left(s_i \left(q_i\right), S\right)$$
$$y_i = q_i + \sigma_s - bS \quad for \ s_i \leq S$$
$$y_i = q_i + \sigma_u + aS \quad for \ s_i > S \tag{5}$$

We can see from these basic income equations how the relative scarcity effects, a and b, influence the preferences of different individuals. For those who already possess education, any expansion is a net negative for them since their wages will be reduced by a factor b. Conversely, those who receive education for the first time receive a jump in their income equal to the skill premium $w_s - w_u$. Finally, as long as a is greater than zero, the unskilled actually benefit indirectly through skill provision as unskilled labor becomes relatively scarcer. Figure 2.4 demonstrates the effects of education provision on skilled and unskilled wages.

To examine the political impact of expanding education expansion, I assume that the high-income group already has education, the middle-income group is its likely recipients, and the poor group remains unskilled. To pay for public education, individuals must have their income taxed. I assume education is provided with constant marginal cost c.[7] Thus the total cost of education will simply be cS. I also assume a flat tax on income t, which is used solely to fund education spending. This assumption about taxation being flat – or "linear" – is clearly an abstraction from the kinds of taxation we see both today and historically. On the one hand, most developed nations have progressive tax schedules where the rich pay a higher portion of their income in taxes than the poor.[8] On the other hand, in many developing countries, immature tax bureaucracies force a reliance on taxes that are easy to collect – excise and sales taxes – which are fairly regressive (Gordon and Li, 2005). I split the difference between these forces and assume a flat tax and a uniform education "subsidy," which is granted to everyone whose wealth income is high enough to warrant receiving education, according to Equation (4). Note that if *everyone* received education, this

---

[7] Assuming increasing marginal costs does not alter the qualitative results, although education expands less far than in the case of uniform costs, meaning that the poor are less likely to receive education.

[8] In Chapter 5, I explore how altering the relative "progressivity" of taxes changes spending preferences.

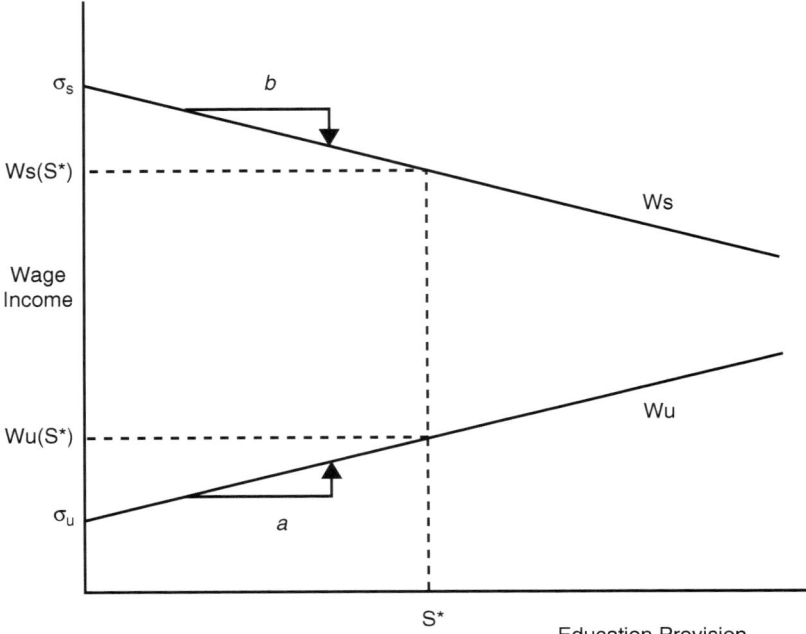

FIGURE 2.4. The Baseline Labor Market Model

form of fiscal tax and transfer scheme would be progressive, since although taxation is linear, all individuals would receive the same "amount" of education. However, if education is *limited*, then the poorer members of society are paying a flat proportion of their incomes in taxes but receiving nothing in return. Hence the relative expansion of education determines whether the tax system as a whole is progressive or highly regressive and who consequently benefits from existing and future education spending.

Normalizing the population of the country to one, we can denote total tax take as the tax rate t multiplied by average income $\bar{y}$. I examine a two-generational model, where parents, who live for one period, must decide how much to tax themselves to provide education for their children, who live in the following period.[9] These two periods are denoted period zero and period one. For the moment, I limit education provision to the public sector so even the rich must pay some positive level of taxation if they wish to see their children educated. This leads to the budget constraint, where total period zero tax take equals the cost of period one education:

$$t\bar{y}_0 = cS_1 \Leftrightarrow t = \frac{cS_1}{\bar{y}_0} \tag{6}$$

---

[9] There is no time-inconsistency problem, in that tax rates decided in round zero systematically lead to spending levels in round one. The discounting parameter does, however, absorb some of the uncertainty about whether investments will come to fruition.

Each family's utility is comprised of period zero income, net of taxes, and period one income – discounted by δ – which is determined by whether children receive skilled or unskilled wages $w_{j1}(S_1)$ and by the level of "externalities" produced by education: $g(S_1) = gS_1$. I assume that education produces positive externalities – where the receipt of education by one citizen benefits all other citizens. Family utility can thus be defined fully as:

$$U_i = \left(1 - \frac{cS_1}{\overline{y}_0}\right) y_{i0} + \delta\left[q_{i1} + w_{j1}(S_1) + gS_1\right] \tag{7}$$

I take the derivative of this utility function with respect to the level of public education provision, S_1, to produce the following result, which makes clear the general effect of education expansion on each group:

$$\frac{dU_i}{dS_1} = -c\frac{y_{i0}}{\overline{y}_0} + \delta\left[\frac{\partial w_{j1}(S_1)}{\partial S_1} + g\right] \tag{8}$$

The basic effects on utility of expanding education are as follows. Firstly, there is a strictly negative impact on parental income because of the tax cost of providing education, weighted by relative income. This impact is very similar to the famous Meltzer-Richard result (Meltzer and Richard, 1981), wherein the richer an individual is, the more he or she is hurt by a flat tax and uniform subsidy scheme. However, there are two further impacts of education spending: firstly, the impact of education provision on period one wage income received by the family's children; and secondly, the impact of education provision on externalities, also in period one. The latter effect is strictly positive – every citizen benefits to some degree from other educated citizens. However, the former effect depends on whether the individual in question belongs to the high-income, medium-income, or poor group, as follows:

$$\frac{dU_H}{dS_1} = -c\frac{q_H + w_{s0}}{\overline{y}_0} + \delta[-b + g] \tag{9}$$

$$\frac{dU_M}{dS_1} = -c\frac{q_M + w_{u0}}{\overline{y}_0} + \delta\left[(\sigma_s - bS_1) - (\sigma_u + aS_1) + g\right] \tag{10}$$

$$\frac{dU_P}{dS_1} = -c\frac{q_P + w_{u0}}{\overline{y}_0} + \delta[a + g] \tag{11}$$

Equations (9) through (11) demonstrate a multidirectional impact of expanding education provision. For the high-income group, expanding education spending is doubly distasteful. Not only do they pay the highest absolute amount in taxes, and hence suffer most from the basic logic of a fiscally progressive tax system, but they are also negatively impacted by the increased abundance of educated people, which chips away at their scarcity rent from being educated. The magnitude of this negative effect is dependent on the skill scarcity parameter b. The middle class, conversely, is the chief beneficiary of increased education provision, with their income jumping up by the skill premium. If their income is below the mean – and standard models of the income distribution assume that median income is significantly below the mean – then they are clear fiscal beneficiaries of the distributive impact of education spending. Finally, the poor may actually benefit from education spending, even if they do not receive education, provided the unskilled scarcity parameter a and externalities are large enough and that their loss of taxed income is relatively minor. Thus the combination of the fiscal effects of redistribution, the scarcity effects of increased abundance in education, the existence of positive externalities, and the fact that education expansion is typically made to a *targeted* group (in this case, the middle class) all combine to produce a slightly unusual "ends against the middle" pattern, where the middle class are the chief winners of educational expansion, with the elite the clear losers and the poor in a somewhat ambiguous position.

Regime Change and Education Spending

I now turn to a set of important questions about how changes in political institutions and the structure of the labor market impact the preferences of these different groups over public education. I begin by asking how a regime change from autocracy to democracy would affect education spending, assuming that following democratization, the locus of political power switches from the elite to the middle class. Given the group preferences previously detailed, we should consequently expect education spending to expand, at a minimum to include members of the middle class since they would benefit from the jump in the skill premium as they receive skilled rather than unskilled wages. To be more precise, when the middle class controls political power, their optimal level of education is defined as follows (by rewriting Equation (10)):

$$S_{1M}^{*} = \frac{1}{b+a}\left[g + (\sigma_s - \sigma_u) - c\left(\frac{y_{M0}}{\delta \overline{y}_0} \right) \right] \tag{12}$$

A few conclusions can be drawn from this optimality condition. First, as the skill premium or the externalities produced by education rise, education spending should jump up. Second, if returns to skilled or unskilled labor are strongly affected by the domestic supply of skills – that is, if a or b are high – the increase in education spending following democracy will be moderated. This is the *scarcity effect* previously mentioned. Finally, if the cost of extending education is high, or if the middle class is relatively wealthy compared to the poor, education spending could also be limited as the tax costs of provision for the middle class become higher. This is the *fiscal redistribution* effect. Thus, even following democratization, it is not obvious that the newly empowered middle class would provide education to the poor. As Ross (2005) notes, democracy is not always "good for the poor" if it leads to public spending targeted toward the middle class.

So, under what conditions will education be extended to the poor? First, if the poor explicitly control political decision making, we would expect education provision to expand fully throughout the economy, even against middle-class and elite preferences. Second, externalities from further education spending may be high enough, or costs low enough, to encourage the middle class to extend education to the poor. Finally, if b is small enough, the negative effects of expanding education will attenuate, facilitating provision to the poor. Generally, then, I expect democratization, which replaces elite with mass control of political decision making, to be associated with increased education spending. Similarly, when democracies fail to consolidate and suffer a reversion to authoritarianism, I expect a retraction of state involvement in education, coming in the form of reduced spending on poorer students or perhaps the removal of education entirely from that group. This produces Hypothesis One:

> *Hypothesis One: The expansion of democracy will increase education spending. Reversion to autocracy will reduce education spending.*

The Role of Globalization on Education Spending

I now move to examining the impact of globalization on each group's preferred level of education spending. As I have argued, when countries integrate with the global market, there are two main channels through which education is affected: first, the degree to which the supply of education affects the returns to skill, and second, an increase in the demand for education by domestic businesses.

I begin by considering the effects of the supply channel, which within the model operates through the scarcity parameters a and b. The discussion in Section 2.3 highlighted the "law of one wage" developed by Samuelson (1948), which presumes that as countries become fully integrated with the global economy, the returns to factors become determined by global rather than domestic supply. Applying this logic to the supply of skills, this implies that the parameters a and b will asymptote toward zero. This alters Equations (9) through (11), as can be seen in Equations (13) through (15):

$$\frac{dU_H}{dS_1} = -c\frac{q_H + w_{s0}}{\overline{y}_0} + \delta g \tag{13}$$

$$\frac{dU_M}{dS_1} = -c\frac{q_M + w_{u0}}{\overline{y}_0} + \delta\left[(\sigma_s - \sigma_u) + g\right] \tag{14}$$

$$\frac{dU_P}{dS_1} = -c\frac{q_P + w_{u0}}{\overline{y}_0} + \delta g \tag{15}$$

What is the impact of removing the scarcity effects (that is, setting them to zero)? For both the elite and for the middle class, global integration affects the impact of expanding education. Since the expansion of education no longer reduces skilled wages, the elite have one less reason to dislike further education provision, and if externalities outweigh tax costs, they might even favor a limited expansion. For the middle class, the impact is less direct, working through the change in the skill premium. Nonetheless, the effect is still positive. However, for the poor, globalization actually weakens the positive effects of education expansion on utility. Since we are assuming that the poor's children will not receive education, the only benefit they now receive from expansion is through externalities: No longer will they obtain scarcity rents for their unskilled labor.

The equations imply two propositions. Firstly, if either the elite or the middle-class control government, education spending should expand when states globalize. Given that we would typically expect one of these two groups to be politically strongest in most states (that is, in elite-controlled autocracies or median voter–driven democracies), on average education spending should rise when countries integrate with the global economy. Secondly, since the impact of globalization on preferences over education spending is most positive for the elite and least positive – and potentially negative – for the poor, the positive impact of globalization on education should be stronger in autocracies – rule by the elite – than in democracies, where the poor have greater political power. These provide Hypotheses Two (a) and Two (b):

> *Hypothesis Two (a): Increased integration with the global economy will lead to increased education spending in both democracies and autocracies.*
> *Hypothesis Two (b): Increased integration with the global economy has a larger positive supply-side effect on education spending in autocracies than in democracies.*

As noted in Section 2.3, globalization also has impacts on the demand side, with global integration leading to technology transfer to developing states. Domestic firms require a skilled workforce in order to implement this technology or they risk being driven out of business. Hence, globalization raises the demand for education, essentially by raising the productivity of educated workers. Skilled wages are now determined by $w_s = \gamma(\bar{\sigma} - \sigma_s) + \sigma_s - bS_1$, where $\bar{\sigma}$ is the level of technological productivity in the most developed state, and $\gamma \in [0, 1]$ is the degree to which globalization leads a country to close the gap between domestic productivity and that of the most developed state. The utility function is now changed to:

$$U_i = \left(1 - \frac{cS_1}{\bar{y}_o}\right) y_{i0} + \delta\left[q_{i1} + w_{j1}\left(S_1, \gamma, \bar{\sigma}\right) + g\left(S_1, \gamma, \bar{\sigma}\right)\right] \tag{16}$$

In this formulation, round one wages (following globalization) depend on the degree to which skilled wages approach the productivity of the most developed state. Externalities also depend on these parameters, since reaping the rewards of technological adaptation requires a larger skilled workforce, given that production will change throughout the entire economy. We can look at how the effect of education expansion S on utility is itself affected by the technology transfer parameter γ by examining their cross derivative:

$$\frac{\partial^2 U_H}{\partial S_1 \partial \gamma} = \delta \frac{\partial^2 g(S_1)}{\partial S_1 \partial \gamma} \geq 0 \tag{17}$$

$$\frac{\partial^2 U_M}{\partial S_1 \partial \gamma} = \delta \frac{\partial^2 g(S_1)}{\partial S_1 \partial \gamma} + \delta\left[\gamma\left(\bar{\sigma} - \sigma_s\right)\right] > 0 \tag{18}$$

$$\frac{\partial^2 U_P}{\partial S_1 \partial \gamma} = \delta \frac{\partial^2 g(S_1)}{\partial S_1 \partial \gamma} \geq 0 \tag{19}$$

If there is a complementarity between the extent of education provision and the technology transfer parameter in terms of externalities (produced by skill-biased technological change), the right-hand sides of Equations (17) through (19) will be positive, and all groups will desire higher levels of education spending following globalization. Furthermore, the middle group always prefers higher levels of education provision following globalization because of the boost in the skill premium. Thus, the demand-side impact of globalization should be generally positive, complementing Hypothesis Two (a). Moreover, as the gap between developed and developing nations decreases, the right-hand side of Equation (18) is reduced. This implies that the demand-side impact of globalization on education spending decreases as countries get wealthier, providing Hypothesis Two (c):

Hypothesis Two (c): Increased integration with the global economy has a greater demand-side effect on education spending in developing states than in developed states.

Education Spending Relative to Other Redistribution

A number of the preceding claims about the redistributive effects of public education could in fact be made with regard to *any* form of governmental redistribution. It is thus important to distinguish more clearly spending on education from a simple tax and transfer scheme. In this section, I alter the model by introducing an alternative form of "lump-sum" redistribution that governments can provide in addition to education. Doing so highlights the fact that education has specific redistributive effects that move beyond simple fiscal transfers – in particular, the scarcity effects discussed previously. The concept of "relative education spending" – that is, education spending as a proportion of all government spending – gets to the heart of this distinction between education and more basic redistribution. I extend the model by assuming that tax revenues can be split between education, as defined previously, and a simple transfer payment m, received by parents in round zero. I alter the budget constraint and the utility function accordingly:

$$t = \frac{m + cS_1}{\bar{y}_0} \tag{20}$$

$$U_i = \left(1 - \frac{m + cS_1}{\overline{y}_0}\right) y_{i0} + m + \delta\left[q_{i1} + w_{j1}(S_1) + gS_1\right] \tag{21}$$

To analyze how a change in political control from the elite to the middle class affects relative education spending, I compare the derivative of family utility with respect to the money transfer, m, versus the derivative of family utility with respect to education provision S for a fixed tax level t^*. Note that the total effects of m are felt through its indirect effects on S – since spending on S must be reduced if m is increased for a fixed tax rate. This highlights the potential *trade-off* between education and other government spending as felt by each income group. From the budget constraint, we can calculate the effect of increasing the lump-sum transfer m on the provision of education supply S as -1/c. Equations (22) through (24) show the effects of expanding the lump-sum transfer at a constant tax rate t^* on each of the three groups:

$$\left.\frac{dU_H}{dm}\right|_{t=t^*} = 1 - \frac{\delta}{c}[g - b] \tag{22}$$

$$\left.\frac{dU_M}{dm}\right|_{t=t^*} = 1 - \frac{\delta}{c}\left[(\sigma_s - bS_1) - (\sigma_u + aS_1) + g\right] \tag{23}$$

$$\left.\frac{dU_P}{dm}\right|_{t=t^*} = 1 - \frac{\delta}{c}[a + g] \tag{24}$$

Starting from a position where the high-income group is fully skilled and where their children alone will receive skills in round one, we can see that the elite would prefer taxes to be spent on the cash transfer (assuming externalities are not enormous). The elite prefer to slant government spending away from education expansion for two reasons: firstly because their children are already guaranteed education under the current system, and secondly, because expansion diminishes the scarcity rents they receive from education. The middle class, conversely, thinks differently. In their case, it is likely that the combined effect of the wage increase and externalities outweighs the simple cash transfer. They would, hence, prefer that government spending be slanted toward education. Thus, we should expect that a transition of political control from the high-income group to the middle-income group would lead to an increase in *relative education spending*.

There is, however, one caveat to this assertion. The preferences of the poor are less equivocally for education over cash transfers than are those of the middle class. If scarcity effects are fairly weak, or externalities low, the poor may prefer a simple cash transfer to education spending. The elite, then, might be able to form an alliance with the working class against the middle group by "bribing" the poor with cash transfers. Generally, we should expect that democratic electoral politics will lead to convergence to the median voter, and hence bequeath power to the middle class. However, if "ends against the middle" coalitions are possible, we might see a reduction in relative education spending.

The conditions under which such a coalition might emerge are quite interesting. The elite are most favorable to lump-sum redistribution when scarcity effects on skilled labor are strong – b is high – but the poor are most favorable to lump-sum redistribution when scarcity effects on unskilled labor are low – a is low. Thus an "ends against the middle" coalition is most likely in those states where skill supply effects are strong on skilled labor but nonexistent on unskilled labor – for example, an autarkic state with a lower class whose wages are suppressed either by autocratic fiat or because of a large reserve army of labor (Rudra, 2003). In such an autarky, the elite prefer to pay off the poor, and the poor are unaffected by relative skill supply; thus both prefer low levels of spending on education and high levels of transfers. Conversely, in highly globalized states, both the elite and middle class will become relatively more favorable toward education spending as opposed to transfers, preventing the "ends against the middle" alliance.

The effects of globalization may differ in advanced industrial states, where education is already near-universal, democracy is sustained, and unskilled wages are not suppressed. Here, openness is likely to promote government spending outside the realm of education. As Garrett (1998) and Rodrik (2000) argue, globalization in advanced industrial states leads to calls by the poor for protection from economic volatility. The government may use either lump-sum redistribution or public employment as ways of buffering against this threat. Whereas the poor in the developed world benefit from globalization in terms of increased wages, the reverse is likely to occur in developed states, pushing up "compensatory" spending. Furthermore, since education is almost universal in these states and they are already at the technological frontier, neither the supply- or demand-side effects of globalization will be important drivers of education spending. Thus, overall, we should expect globalization to be associated with reduced relative education spending in developed states. Hypotheses Three (a) through (c) emerge from this analysis:

> *Hypothesis Three (a): Transitions to democracy will lead to higher levels of spending on education relative to other government consumption.*
> *Hypothesis Three (b): In developing states and autocracies, relative education spending should increase under globalization and decrease under autarky.*
> *Hypothesis Three (c): In advanced industrial states, relative education spending is likely to decrease under globalization.*

Private Education Spending

To this point, I have focused solely on aggregate education provision funded by public revenues. Historically, however, much provision of education was done privately; indeed, before the nineteenth century, no country had education financed by the central government. Indeed, many countries still retain large private education sectors, which typically attract wealthier students. In this section, I tease out how the existence of a private educational sector might alter the previous results.

In a world without public education, individuals would choose to educate their children privately if $\beta(q_i + w_j) \geq c$, where β is the proportion of income that individuals are willing to devote to the purchase of education (as discussed previously, this could be derived from the expected wage premium accruing to education). Parents will buy private education only when the amount of income they are willing to devote to private education exceeds the cost of skilling their child. Since only richer individuals can meet this condition, we obtain the unsurprising result that the wealthy purchase private education and those who cannot afford to do so do not. It is worth noting that if this inequality holds for the median political decision maker, as in an autocracy, the entire educational sector will be private. Thus, in the absence of a public education sector, we expect autocracies to refrain from developing public education, whereas democracies, where the median voter cannot afford unsubsidized private education, will develop public education.

In a situation where a public education sector already exists, the trade-off changes somewhat. Now purchasers of private education are also paying for a public education. Thus, individuals will choose to purchase private education only if $\beta(w_j + q_i) \geq c + t^* \bar{y}_0 / S_1$. Parents' incomes will have to be substantially larger than in the previous scenario because parents will also be paying for an unused public education for their child. Moreover, as the tax rate set by the median voter rises, fewer and fewer parents can afford this double expenditure. Thus, the private educational sector will become smaller as public education becomes more broadly available: an education "substitution" effect. In situations where the median voter is relatively poor, as in a democracy, private education provision thus tends to be smaller. Furthermore, factors that increase the level of public provision, such as globalization, will reduce the level of private education provision because of substitution. This provides Hypotheses Four (a) and (b):

> *Hypothesis Four (a): Democracies will spend less on private education spending than autocracies.*
>
> *Hypothesis Four (b): A substitution effect will exist between public and private education spending. Factors such as globalization that increase the former should decrease the latter.*

The Composition of Education Spending

I conclude the formal model by examining the impact of permitting "targeted spending," in which increased education spending goes toward greater "depth" (more per student funding) rather than greater "breadth" (increasing student enrollment). Since the baseline model assumed that education enrollment moves from rich to poor, increased depth implies targeting resources toward the well-off, typically through higher education. The parameter π represents per-student funding (or depth). Governments can choose to expand depth, breadth, or both. The budget constraint is now as follows:

$$t = \frac{(c + \pi) S_1}{\bar{y}_0} \tag{25}$$

The effect of increasing the level of depth on wages is as follows:

$$w_s(\pi) = \pi \sigma_s - bS$$
$$w_u(\pi) = \sigma_u + aS \tag{26}$$

Only skilled wages are directly affected by the depth parameter, which pushes the return to skills upward. I now rephrase the generic utility function as follows:

$$U_i = \left(1 - \frac{[\pi + c]S_1}{\overline{y}_0}\right) y_{i0} + \delta\left[q_{i1} + w_{j1}[\pi, S_1] + gS_1\right] \tag{27}$$

To examine the effects of targeting, I fix the breadth of education, $S(\pi) = S$, and look at the autocratic case, where only the high-income group currently receives education. The derivatives of group utility with respect to the depth parameter are as follows:

$$\frac{dU_H}{d\pi} = -S_1 \frac{y_{H0}}{\overline{y}_0} + \delta\sigma_s \tag{28}$$

$$\frac{dU_M}{d\pi} = -S_1 \frac{y_{M0}}{\overline{y}_0} \tag{29}$$

$$\frac{dU_P}{d\pi} = -S_1 \frac{y_{P0}}{\overline{y}_0} \tag{30}$$

Equation (28) shows that increased depth of education spending is beneficial to the high-income group if the increase in the skill premium outweighs the tax costs of provision. In this autocratic situation, where only the elite are provided with public education, we see that only they stand to benefit from increased depth of funding. Both the middle classes and the poor, when shut out from education provision, unsurprisingly prefer not to increase the depth of funding. However, if education does cover the middle class, as in a democracy, the middle class might prefer increasing the depth of funding over expanding coverage. The key implication is that if education can be targeted to groups with higher levels of income, as with tertiary education as opposed to primary education, its provision will be fiscally regressive and thus favored in more autocratic regimes. This produces Hypothesis Five (a).

> *Hypothesis Five (a): Autocracies will favor a higher tertiary to primary education spending ratio than democracies.*

The impact of globalization on targeted spending differs from that on the expansion of education, since scarcity effects are less important because increased depth of spending does not affect relative skill supply. We can, however, derive a proposition from the Stolper-Samuelson theorem about the likely impact of globalization on the composition of education spending in developed versus developing countries. Developing states have an abundance of labor with fairly low education and a scarcity of university-educated individuals – hence when the economy opens, production will shift to sectors with high demand for workers with primary education, not university education. Conversely, developed states have a relative abundance of university-trained workers, thus global integration should lead to production shifts toward high-skill production demanding college education. If shifts in industrial demand provoke changes in government policy, this produces Hypothesis Five (b).

> *Hypothesis Five (b): Following globalization, the tertiary to primary education spending ratio should decrease in developing states and increase in developed states.*

Summarizing the Model

The simple model developed in the preceding subsection produces a large number of conclusions about the likely impact of political and economic forces on education spending. Beginning with the effects of changing political institutions on education spending, I argued that broadly we should expect democracies to have higher levels of public spending on education than autocracies. I noted that a country's international economic policy should also be a key determinant of education spending through its effect both on the supply-side effects of education on wages and on the demand of businesses for skilled labor. This produced three hypotheses: that economic integration with the global economy should lead to higher public spending on education; that this effect should be stronger in autocracies than democracies; and that this effect should be stronger in developing countries than developed states.

The next set of hypotheses related to "relative education spending," that is, education spending as compared to spending on broader redistribution. I argued that because simple redistribution does not alter relative wages, unlike education spending, it may be in the interest of the elite to lobby for lump-sum redistribution *as opposed* to education spending. Hence, democracy should be associated with higher education spending relative to other government spending. The effect of globalization will differ across states, with developing states and autocracies likely to have higher relative education spending when opening their economies, and developed states having lower relative education spending.

The fourth set of hypotheses dealt with private education spending. Here I argued that since private education spending must come from citizens' own pockets, it will be biased toward the wealthier members of society. Consequently, if these individuals control the government, as in an autocracy, we should expect higher private education spending. Furthermore, the size of the group that can afford private education decreases when there is a public alternative. Consequently, we should also expect private and public education spending to be substitutes. The final set of hypotheses pertained to the composition of education spending among primary, secondary, and tertiary education. Here I argued that the ability to target education to particular groups alters the simple rich/poor divide previously used. If the elite can target public education to themselves, they may in fact support increases in public education, provided it is to their own children. Consequently, I expect that in autocracies the share of public funding that goes to tertiary education, highly restricted in its enrollment, as opposed to primary education will be higher, with the reverse pattern in democracies. I also expect integration with the global economy to affect the composition of education spending. As states become more globally integrated, I expect them to shift their education spending toward their "comparative advantage," with developing states increasing their relative supply of primary education vis-à-vis tertiary spending and the reverse occurring in developed states.

2.5 THE EMPIRICAL ANALYSIS OF EXPANSION

Do the simple hypotheses developed in the preceding formal model actually hold up when exposed to data drawn from states across the world over the past half century? In this section, I test the propositions using a broad array of statistical techniques on a dataset of over one hundred countries, from every continent, from 1960 to 2000. In doing so, I show that there are robust and substantive forces connecting political institutions and globalization to education spending of a variety of types. I begin this section by briefly discussing the sample that I analyze in this section and the types of empirical measures I adopt to operationalize the concepts of education provision, regime type, and globalization. The remainder of the chapter is devoted to a series of tests of the hypotheses developed earlier.

Choosing a Sample

The preceding hypotheses were developed from a very general theory of education spending. Empirically, what is the most appropriate set of observations on which to test them? Answering this question is not especially simple. We must trade off the ease of data collection against the dilemma of selecting on the dependent variable – for example, by examining only states with flawless education data, we may be including only those states who spend high amounts of public money on education. This could cause serious inferential problems since we would be excluding low spenders systematically, biasing against our ability to make reliable claims (Herrara and Kapur, 2007). However, widening the sample is not without problems. Poorer and more autocratic countries have fewer sources of data, limiting the different aspects of education we can reliably analyze.

Thus, the tests in this chapter necessarily strike a bargain between the twin demands of inference and reliability. Where possible, I examine a sample of over one hundred states since 1960, as for example in the analyses of aggregate public education spending. Since this is a fairly basic measure, regularly collected by international agencies, the broad sample allows us to test the effects of regime type and globalization across the full range of autocracies and democracies, autarkies and globalizers. However, elsewhere – for example, in the examination of private education spending – data availability constricts us to a reduced sample, thus these estimates tend to have greater uncertainty. Nonetheless, throughout this section, I adopt a broad array of statistical techniques to test the robustness of my findings. In some cases, however, there is simply not enough data available from developing countries to conduct reliable analysis of, for example, manifesto data about partisan preferences on education spending. Consequently, Chapter 4 delves into much greater detail about the politics of education spending than is possible in this chapter, albeit at the expense of restricting the sample to developed states.

A couple of potential restrictions on the dataset should, however, be noted. Firstly, the countries included are all sized over one million in population. It is not obvious that the kind of logic that makes sense for a country of median size in the dataset (7.14 million) will be true when one examines microstates, which often tend to be dependent on the resources of outside states. For example, most children from microstates such as Liechtenstein and Luxembourg will seek higher education outside of these small states. Secondly, this is an unbalanced dataset. While some countries have over twenty-five data-points for the variables under analysis, others have just one observation – with an average number of observations per state of 13.4. Again, here we trade off coverage and inferential traction with data reliability and availability.[10]

Developing Measures

Before beginning the empirical analysis on this sample of countries, it is important to lay out exactly what I am testing against what. That is, what are the empirical proxies that I am using to operationalize the concepts and parameters employed in the formal model? In particular, how am I measuring education, regime type, and globalization? Beginning with the dependent variable, I employ a variety of measures of different aspects of education provision. The analysis starts by examining what I refer to as absolute education spending, which corresponds to the parameter S in the formal model and is the percentage of national income devoted to public education. This variable comes from the World Bank's World Development Indicators and covers all state expenditure on primary, secondary, and tertiary education. Across the sample, this variable has a mean of 4.2 and a standard deviation of 1.9. The variable has a number of advantages recommending its use in this study. Firstly, it has been widely used in the economic literature examining the causes of cross-national variation in growth (Barro and Lee, 1994; Hall and Jones, 1999). Secondly, because it is a ratio, it is comparable across states of different sizes and incomes in a way that absolute expenditure figures are not. Finally, it allows easy comparison with the percentage of income devoted to overall government expenditure, which

---

[10] I replicated the baseline regressions using a dataset with only five yearly observations, finding similarly robust results for the variables of interest.

demonstrates the *relative* significance of human capital expenditure vis-à-vis other options open to governments, which we will examine in the next section.

To test the hypotheses developed in this chapter, it does not suffice merely to show a correlation between aggregate measures of democracy and education and then assume that the mechanisms specified in the formal model have passed the empirical test. Democracy is a multifaceted and much-debated concept – as Orwell (1945) wrote, "not only is there no agreed definition, but the attempt to make one is resisted from all sides." Thus, solely using aggregate measures of democracy may elide important distinctions between democratic regimes and impose a false certainty over any estimated relationship. On the other hand, data availability problems combined with the debate about whether there truly are "degrees of democracy" mean that well-intentioned attempts to fully disaggregate democracy into the elements that we find most theoretically convincing may run up against real difficulties of operationalization.

How to operationalize democracy effectively has been a subject of extended debate in political science ever since the start of cross-national statistical analysis of the causes and effects of democracy (e.g., Lipset, 1959; Alvarez et al., 2000). The debate is centered around whether democracy can be viewed as a continuum or whether autocracies and democracies are qualitatively different and conceivable only as a dummy variable. The concept of democracy as a continuum finds its modern antecedent in Dahl's (1972) concept of polyarchy, which measures the degree to which individual citizens can fully participate in political decision making. If one can decide upon verifiable institutional or behavioral characteristics of regimes that relate to participation in political decision making, one can aggregate these characteristics in some manner to produce an ordinal, or indeed interval, level scale. The well-known Polity index takes this continuum approach, combining institutional characteristics of autocracy and democracy into an aggregated scale. In line with most studies of the effects of democracy on government behavior, this book mostly utilizes the Polity continuous measure of democratization, which provides extensive within-state and between-state variation.[11] In particular, the Polity index is appropriate for this study since its continuous nature better reflects the concept of an expanding "selectorate" than does a simple binary measure. However, the use of the Polity scale leaves one open to criticism that the scale is weakly defined – that it aggregates different concepts of democracy that may have more or less relevance to the theoretical links drawn between democracy and education in this book. As such, in Section 2.7, I estimate the effect of the components of the Polity index to better isolate which elements of democracy matter most.

Turning to globalization, how can this other diffuse concept be operationalized in a precise manner? The flurry of papers and books about globalization disguises a poverty of reliable measurements. In fact, most economists and

---

[11] The Polity variable is taken from the Polity IV dataset as developed by Marshall and Jaggers (2002). I also conducted all the estimations using a dummy measure of democracy taken from Alvarez et al. (2000), producing similarly robust results.

political scientists rely on a few trusty variables that operate at a highly aggregated level of analysis – for example, capital inflows as a proportion of national income, or total exports and imports.[12] In terms of testing theoretical mechanisms, such aggregates may not always be appropriate: They are fairly blunt instruments to test the myriad causal arguments suggested in the globalization literature, such as price volatility, regulatory competition, import penetration, technology transfer, and factor price response. Unfortunately, more nuanced data on the composition of trade and on technology transfer are scarce across the sample of this study. Because of this data availability dilemma, this chapter uses two macromeasures of globalization to examine the effects of openness on public spending, but it is important to be aware of the limitations of aggregate variables.

The first measure used in this chapter is called log openness and is calculated by taking the log of exports plus imports over GDP. This variable has been the standard measure for openness used throughout the political economy literature since Cameron (1978). It has the advantage of having a clear economic meaning since it deals directly with the national accounts. Logging the variable means a one-point shift implies a doubling of openness, allowing us to compare substantively important shifts in trade within states, regardless of their typical level of openness. However, this measure is less useful in terms of cross-sectional analysis since very large states tend to have low levels of log openness because of their high levels of internal trade, even if they have nominally open borders.[13]

A further problem with the openness variable is that it does not directly reflect how sheltered domestic companies are from international competition – the mechanism underlying the technology-transfer skill demand argument outlined in the previous section. While changes in openness may reflect the degree to which countries are relying on exports – and thus allowing wages to become set by international forces – they do not necessarily account for the imposition of implicit trade barriers that protect import-competing sectors from international competition. Given these problems with the baseline openness variable, this study also uses a measure of *trade orientation* developed by Hiscox and Kastner (2005). The Hiscox-Kastner measure essentially gauges the degree to which states deviate from the "optimal" level of imports that they would be undertaking in a protection-free environment. The measure is created by using a standard gravity model to predict a state's level of imports from each trading partner but with a dummy variable for each country-year. This dummy variable measures the country-year deviation from the sample mean level of protectionism, once the distance to and income of each trading partner have been controlled for. They then subtract from each country-year dummy a free-trade benchmark (that is, the lowest-valued dummy variable: Holland in 1964), and

---

[12] See, for example, Rodrik (2000), Boix (2003), and Nooruddin and Simmons (2006).

[13] In terms of fixed effects analysis, this problem matters somewhat less because in this case we are just examining deviations from country means.

thus increasing scores on the index represent greater degrees of implied protectionism. The version of the variable I use is built off a gravity model incorporating distance, the income of trading partners, and the labor and capital ratio between each trading partner.

The relative advantage of using the Hiscox-Kastner measure vis-à-vis the log openness measure is that it focuses on the degree of implied protectionism rather than on exposure to trade, picking up policy changes more effectively than the latter variable. It should also be less affected by the global business cycle than the log openness variable, since it measures deviations from the level of imports that would be predicted by the incomes of other states (plus distance and factor endowments). Finally, it is worth noting that there should be a direct relationship between the Hiscox-Kastner model and the demand-side formal model developed in the previous section. The demand-side story is one about import penetration leading to technological change, which links closely to the Hiscox-Kastner model since it directly measures the degree to which imports are permitted to penetrate the domestic economy.

A set of control variables is also included in the regressions in the following sections in order to counter the potential problem of omitted variables biasing the coefficient estimates obtained for the Polity variable. The first variable is a measure of demographic forces that might increase the demand for education spending: the proportion of the population under fifteen. Countries with very youthful populations will need to spend more of their national income on education than those with much older populations. The regressions also control for the log of population, the log of national income, and then the square of logged national income. Using the extra quadratic form allows us to control for the potentially nonlinear effect of growth on education spending – Wagner's Law implies growing countries will demand higher levels of public services but they may do so at a diminishing rate. Government spending other than on public education is also controlled for to ascertain whether public education spending is rising *separate* from other government consumption. Finally, all regressions control for a linear time trend in order to take account of any secular trends in education spending. A linear time trend is appropriate given that the insertion of time dummies into the analysis show a linear effect in their coefficient estimates.[14]

Empirical Analysis

I now turn to a series of statistical tests on a dataset of over 110 countries between 1960 and 2000. Throughout the analysis, I show the robust and substantively important effects of political and economic openness on education spending

---

[14] The models have all been tested using a variety of specifications for time, including quadratic terms, as well as with time dummies. Results remain largely unaffected – a result of the linear pattern produced when the dummies are used. The linear time trend is chosen in order to maximize degrees of freedom and to avoid the dilemma of overspecification (Achen, 2000; Braumoeller, 2004).

and how the magnitude of these effects depends on the context in which they occur. I begin by examining education spending as a percentage of national income (absolute education spending) before turning to the determinants of education spending relative to other government consumption (relative education spending); the interplay among openness, democracy, and development; and, finally, the determinants of private education spending.

Absolute Spending on Education

Table 2.1 presents the first set of tests, which analyze the effect of regime type and openness on aggregate education spending. I begin by examining the effects of the Polity score and log openness on public education spending as a percentage of GDP. Model A uses a pooled regression with corrections for serial autocorrelation and panel corrected standard errors (PCSE) to adjust for contemporaneous correlation (Beck and Katz, 1995). This setup analyzes variation both between and within countries. Model B, conversely, incorporates country fixed effects, which control for unobserved long-run differences between countries. Thus Model B examines only within-country changes. Both these techniques have varying advantages in statistical terms, with the fixed effects method assuaging concerns about omitted variable bias but reducing the variation under analysis.

Regardless of their relative strengths, both techniques produce extremely similar results for the estimated effects of democracy and openness on education spending. In both cases, the effect of democracy is highly robust and substantively significant. Table 2.1 displays long-run estimates for the effects of a two-standard deviation shift in the Polity score (15 points).[15] The predicted effect of such a change in regime type is to increase education spending somewhere between half a percent point and 1.5 percent points of GDP. The latter estimate includes both within- and between-country effects, the former includes only within effects, suggesting that over the very long run democratic countries gain advantages in education spending that cannot be made up over the medium term by democratizing states. Nonetheless, these are large effects, amounting to between a 10 and 30 percent increase in the education budget of the average state in the dataset. Openness too has sizable effects. A doubling of openness (around two standard deviations) increases education spending over the long run by between 0.6 and 1.4 percent points, a similar effect to that of democracy, raising the question of whether democracy and openness might be substitutes. I consider this question shortly.

Models C and D deal with a potential gremlin: It is conceivable that education may itself lead to democratization, a theme touched upon in many works of modernization theory.[16] If this effect is real, then the resulting endogeneity of the Polity score will seriously bias the coefficients since it will correlate with

---

[15] The long-run effect is calculated by dividing the coefficient on Polity by one minus the lagged dependent variable coefficient and multiplying by a shift of fifteen points.

[16] For example, see Lipset 1959.

TABLE 2.1. *Democracy, Log Openness, and Education Spending*

	Model A	Model B	Model C	Model D	Model E	Model F
	PCSE	Fixed	IV Lags	IV Region	PCSE	Fixed
	PUBED	PUBED	PUBED	PUBED	PUBED	PUBED
Lagged DV	0.792	0.608	0.627	0.607	0.770	0.648
	(0.034)***	(0.018)***	(0.019)***	(0.018)***	(0.037)***	(0.022)***
Polity Score	0.016	0.012	0.033	0.015	0.013	0.012
	(0.005)***	(0.005)**	(0.014)**	(0.009)*	(0.005)***	(0.006)**
Log Openness	0.282	0.232	0.824	0.224		
	(0.061)***	(0.089)***	(0.424)*	(0.091)**		
Hiscox-Kastner					−0.007	−0.015
					(0.003)***	(0.003)***
Population < 15	0.005	−0.015	−0.001	−0.015	0.007	0.017
	(0.006)	(0.011)	(0.012)	(0.011)	(0.009)	(0.013)
Log GDP	−0.390	2.180	2.581	2.120	0.148	1.565
	(0.251)	(0.833)***	(0.973)***	(0.843)**	(0.266)	(1.073)
(Log GDP)^2	0.010	−0.041	−0.052	−0.040	0.001	−0.031
	(0.005)*	(0.017)**	(0.022)**	(0.017)**	(0.005)	(0.021)
Log Population	−0.058	−0.012	0.028	−0.011	−0.161	−0.222
	(0.045)	(0.225)	(0.234)	(0.225)	(0.053)***	(0.258)
Govt. Exp.	0.003	0.003	0.003	0.003	0.021	0.006
	(0.006)	(0.006)	(0.007)	(0.006)	(0.008)**	(0.009)
Year	−0.019	−0.016	−0.022	−0.017	−0.014	0.000
	(0.004)***	(0.006)***	(0.007)***	(0.006)***	(0.004)***	(0.007)
Constant	41.430	5.829	9.882	8.405	27.129	−14.077
	(7.494)***	(14.297)	(19.586)	(15.332)	(7.568)***	(17.398)
Polity Δ	+1.538***	+0.460**	+1.327**	+0.573*	+0.848***	+0.511**
Openness Δ	+1.437***	+0.627***	+2.342*	+0.604**	−0.913***	−1.278***
Observations	1,501	1,501	1,484	1,501	1,022	1,022
Countries	113	113	113	113	65	65
R^2	0.83	0.50	0.49	0.50	0.85	0.54

Note: Models A and E include regional dummies. Standard errors are in parentheses.
***$p < 0.01$, **$p < 0.05$, *$p < 0.1$.

the error term. Consequently, I develop two instruments for democracy, used in Models C and D. The first instrument I employ is the five-year lag of the Polity score, used in Model C, which has a high correlation with the Polity score (0.86).[17] The second instrument, used in Model D, is the average Polity score in a country's region (correlation of 0.74). This variable is substantively exogenous: There is no reason to expect that the level of democracy in a region is caused by any one state's education policy. In both cases, we find significant effects of democracy and openness on public education, though they are somewhat less robust than in Model B. The substantive impact of democracy and openness is particularly striking in Model C, which uses lags as instruments, suggesting that if any endogeneity is occurring, it appears to be that increases in education spending under autocracy actually retard democratization.

Finally, Models E and F repeat the analysis from Models A and B but replace log openness with the Hiscox-Kastner measure, which reduces the dataset from 113 to 65 countries. Despite a much smaller sample size, the estimated effect of democracy is almost identical to Models A and B. Furthermore, I find highly significant effects of the Hiscox-Kastner variable in both models. The long-run effect of a two-standard deviation shift toward protectionism in this variable (a 30 percent increase in the gap between "ideal" and actual imports) produces a decrease of around 1 percent of GDP in public education spending. As with the earlier models, this provides strong confirmation of Hypotheses One and Two (a). Total government effort in the realm of education is closely and profoundly tied to the level of political and economic openness in the regime. But is education really special and distinct from general public spending? I now turn to this rather more nuanced tale.

Relative Spending

We have seen that public education is a beneficiary of both democratization and globalization. But is it particularly special? After all, we know from Cameron (1978), Garrett (1998), Rodrik (2000), and others that government consumption generally rises as openness expands. Table 2.2 tests whether education grows not only as a share of national income but also as a share of the government budget following regime change or economic integration. The six models tested here essentially mirror those used in Table 2.1, including pooled, fixed effects and instrumental variable analysis and examining the impact of both log openness and the Hiscox-Kastner measure. The only distinction is that I now remove the government spending variable, since this is the denominator of the dependent variable.

Models A through F show strong and robust positive effects of democracy on education spending relative to other government expenditure. Excluding Model D, which uses the lag instruments, the effect of a two-standard deviation increase in the Polity score is estimated to amount to 2 to 5 percent points

---

[17] For completeness, I also instrument log openness similarly, although there is little theoretical reason to be particularly concerned about endogeneity.

TABLE 2.2. *Democracy, Openness, and Relative Education Spending*

	Model A	Model B	Model C	Model D	Model E	Model F
	PCSE	Fixed Effects	IV. Region	IVS. 5 Yr Lags	HK Basic	HK Adjusted
Lag DV	0.595	0.383	0.382	0.370	0.336	0.336
	(0.013)***	(0.014)***	(0.015)***	(0.015)***	(0.014)***	(0.014)***
Polity	0.060	0.185	0.200	0.545	0.223	0.221
	(0.027)**	(0.038)***	(0.073)***	(0.103)***	(0.046)***	(0.046)***
Log (Open)	1.321	1.536	1.506	1.673		
	(0.394)***	(0.704)**	(0.715)**	(0.794)**		
HK					−0.084	−0.087
					(0.025)***	(0.025)***
Population < 15	−0.018	−0.119	−0.118	−0.076	0.061	0.065
	(0.026)	(0.088)	(0.088)	(0.092)	(0.101)	(0.101)
Log (GDP)	0.715	20.498	20.257	20.544	19.723	19.926
	(1.523)	(6.535)***	(6.610)***	(7.470)***	(8.503)**	(8.495)**
Log (GDP) Sq.	−0.018	−0.353	−0.347	−0.343	−0.396	−0.402
	(0.031)	(0.134)***	(0.136)**	(0.154)**	(0.168)**	(0.168)**
Log (Pop)	0.29	1.392	1.394	0.993	−0.967	−0.913
	(0.190)	(1.769)	(1.769)	(1.871)	(2.063)	(2.059)
Year	−0.017	−0.169	−0.174	−0.232	0.014	0.020
	(0.020)	(0.047)***	(0.050)***	(0.057)***	(0.055)	(0.055)
Constant	30.188	42.060	52.631	162.16	−139.392	−160.084
	(44.153)	(111.098)	(119.336)	(141.460)	(167.789)	(168.783)
Polity Δ	+2.222**	+4.498***	+4.853 ***	+12.976***	+5.038***	+4.992***
Openness Δ	+3.262***	+2.489**	+2.437 **	+2.656**	+2.353***	+2.398***
N	1,491	1,491	1,491	1,435	1,022	1,022
Countries	111	111	111	108	65	65

Note: Standard errors are in parentheses.
*** = p < 0.01, ** = p < 0.05, * = p < 0.1.

of government spending. The average percentage of government spending devoted to education in the dataset is 28 percent. Thus, this shift in regime type should push the ratio of education to government spending by between 8 and 18 percent. In the outlying case of Model D, the estimate would be an increase of over 40 percent. These results are very large and are comparable in terms of percentage changes with those obtained for absolute education spending. Consequently, they imply that increases in the size of government following democratization are largely driven by education spending. Or put differently, of all forms of spending, education best serves the redistributive and social policy goals of the newly empowered masses.

The effects for the openness variables are also sizable and robust and vary considerably less than those obtained for democracy. The impact of a two-standard deviation increase in log openness and a similar decrease in the Hiscox-Kastner variable is estimated to be between 2 and 3 percent points of government spending over the long run or between 8 and 12 percent of the average level of government spending. These results for the Hiscox-Kastner variable are nearly identical to those obtained with the log openness variable, suggesting that both variables are picking up similar effects over the aggregate sample. We turn in the next section to different subsamples, but before we do, it is worth considering the substantive implications of these results.

The predicted effects of a two-standard deviation shift in economic openness are a change of around 10 percent in the balance of government spending. While this is a sizable effect, it is not quite as large as the shift in absolute education spending, which shifts 15 to 30 percent. However, we might expect the effects of globalization on relative spending to be less dramatic than the effects of democratization, which are more comparable across absolute and relative spending. The reason for this is the well-known empirical finding, best represented in Rodrik (2000), that open states have larger governments. Since much of the increase in the size of the government is occurring for *compensatory* reasons as well as for *compositional* reasons, we should not be surprised that the ratio between these types of government spending is not altered as dramatically with democracy, where the redistributive potential of education dominates. Nonetheless, at the margin, it seems that globalization is forcing governments to bias spending toward public education at the expense of compensation. This logic of globalization suggests that the activist state attempting to create a competitive workforce is edging out the compensatory state. But is this full sample result actually consistent when we dig deeper into the data? In the next section, I explore the conditions under which the compositional hypothesis holds.

Interactive Effects between Democracy and Globalization

In Section 2.4, I argued that the mechanisms relating economic openness to increased education spending might be context-specific. The supply-side argument hinges on a powerful elite who accrue scarcity rents from education provision under autarky and hence prefer to block education expansion. Consequently, the beneficial supply-side effects of the globalization (detaching the returns to education from the supply of education) will be most strongly felt in autocratic states, where the elite control decision making. On the demand side, I argued that the importance of technology transfer in increasing demand for education will matter only in countries that are currently technology-poor, that is, in the developing world. In Tables 2.3 and 2.4, I test these propositions by splitting the full sample into two sets of subsamples – firstly autocracies and democracies, and secondly OECD and non-OECD states. I first examine the effects of globalization across these subsamples on absolute education spending before turning to relative education spending.

TABLE 2.3. *Absolute Education Spending: Comparing Subsamples*

	Model A	Model B	Model C	Model D	Model E	Model F	Model G	Model H
	ABS	ABS	ABS	ABS	ABS	ABS	ABS	ABS
	AUTOC	DEMOC	AUTOC	DEMOC	Non-OECD	OECD	Non-OECD	OECD
Lagged DV	0.545	0.617	0.585	0.681	0.585	0.706	0.614	.685
	(0.031)***	(0.024)***	(0.046)***	(0.027)***	(0.022)***	(0.034)***	(0.030)***	(0.035)***
Log Openness	0.307	0.078			0.310	-0.791		
	(0.141)**	(0.126)			(0.101)***	(0.216)***		
Hiscox-Kastner			-0.020	-0.019			-0.018	0.008
			(0.006)***	(0.004)***			(0.004)***	(0.007)
Polity Score					0.011	0.068	0.009	0.066
					(0.005)**	(0.013)***	(0.005)*	(0.014)***
Population <15	0-.040	0.016	0.002	0.018	-0.025	0.052	0.004	0.049
	(0.020)**	(0.016)	(0.024)	(0.017)	(0.013)*	(0.021)**	(0.016)	(0.022)**
Log GDP	2.912	2.731	2.033	1.959	1.973	3.058	0.462	3.637
	(1.484)*	(1.125)**	(2.206)	(1.269)	(1.061)*	(1.797)*	(1.507)	(1.924)*
(Log GDP)^2	-0.061	-0.053	-0.041	-0.043	-0.037	-0.068	-0.007	-0.081
	(0.031)**	(0.022)**	(0.044)	(0.024)*	(0.022)*	(0.034)*	(0.030)	(0.037)**

(continued)

TABLE 2.3. (continued)

	Model A ABS AUTOC	Model B ABS DEMOC	Model C ABS AUTOC	Model D ABS DEMOC	Model E ABS Non-OECD	Model F ABS OECD	Model G ABS Non-OECD	Model H ABS OECD
Log Population	0.498	−0.206	0.495	−0.406	0.483	−0.310	0.781	−0.413
	(0.529)	(0.348)	(0.767)	(0.370)	(0.324)	(0.806)	(0.493)	(0.872)
Govt. Exp.	−0.000	0.011	−0.000	−0.004	0.006	−0.026	0.009	−0.022
	(0.011)	(0.007)	(0.017)	(0.012)	(0.007)	(0.018)	(0.011)	(0.018)
Year	−0.023	−0.003	−0.016	0.009	−0.032	0.024	−0.029	0.018
	(0.017)	(0.008)	(0.025)	(0.009)	(0.010)***	(0.010)**	(0.015)*	(0.012)
Constant	4.556	−24.650	1.470	−31.982	30.951	−73.207	39.085	−68.512
	(29.565)	(19.887)	(41.711)	(21.076)	(17.852)*	(30.467)**	(26.393)	(31.131)**
Long Run Δ	+0.675**	+0.204	+0.839***	+0.750***	+0.747***	−2.690***	+0.844***	−0.279
Observations	680	822	377	639	1,122	379	647	375
Countries	73	77	39	48	92	21	45	20
R²	0.41	0.52	0.42	0.60	0.48	0.64	0.49	0.66

Note: All regressions include country fixed effects. Standard errors are in parentheses.
***$p < 0.01$, **$p < 0.05$, *$p < 0.1$.

TABLE 2.4. *Relative Education Spending: Comparing Subsamples*

	Model A AUTO	Model B DEMO	Model C AUTO	Model D DEMO	Model E Non-OECD	Model F OECD	Model G Non-OECD	Model H OECD
Lagged DV	0.626	0.296	0.653	0.286	0.371	0.666	0.321	0.662
	(0.035)***	(0.015)***	(0.044)***	(0.014)***	(0.016)***	(0.035)***	(0.018)***	(0.035)***
Log Openness	1.886	0.214			1.499	-2.333		
	(1.015)*	(1.047)			(0.841)*	(1.040)**		
Hiscox-Kastner			-0.074	-0.110			-0.085	0.056
			(0.039)*	(0.036)***			(0.032)***	(0.036)
Polity Score					0.191	0.296	0.220	0.311
					(0.045)***	(0.065)***	(0.058)***	(0.068)***
Population<15	-0.079	0.053	-0.027	0.265	-0.178	0.196	-0.003	0.179
	(0.136)	(0.132)	(0.165)	(0.144)*	(0.111)	(0.101)*	(0.139)	(0.102)*
Log GDP	8.097	37.740	4.836	28.192	14.523	26.349	8.118	30.171
	(10.324)	(9.363)***	(15.177)	(10.788)***	(8.770)*	(8.445)***	(13.150)	(8.883)***
(Log GDP)²	-0.136	-0.689	-0.137	-0.545	-0.218	-0.607	-0.153	-0.679
	(0.215)	(0.184)***	(0.300)	(0.206)***	(0.181)	(0.161)***	(0.260)	(0.168)***
Log Population	2.294	-3.739	-4.340	-3.942	3.611	2.984	2.917	4.008
	(3.795)	(2.901)	(5.142)	(3.151)	(2.751)	(3.857)	(4.233)	(4.100)
Year	-0.112	-0.053	0.210	0.079	-0.251	0.148	-0.092	0.102
	(0.119)	(0.062)	(0.172)	(0.072)	(0.084)***	(0.048)***	(0.133)	(0.056)*
Constant	77.830	-325.274	-369.188	-438.546	240.500	-603.392	50.692	-587.998
	(207.720)	(164.261)**	(286.524)	(176.976)**	(149.238)	(140.245)***	(229.001)	(140.94)***
Long Run Δ	+5.043*	+0.304	+6.398*	+4.622***	+2.383*	-6.985**	+3.756***	-4.950
Observations	672	820	376	640	1,113	378	648	375
Countries	72	76	39	48	90	21	45	20
R²	0.39	0.38	0.45	0.50	0.40	0.63	0.41	0.63

Note: All regressions include country fixed effects. Standard errors are in parentheses.
***$p < 0.01$, **$p < 0.05$, *$p < 0.1$.

All the models in the following two tables use fixed effects regression and are thus directly comparable to Models B and F in Tables 2.1 and 2.2. Table 2.3 begins by examining the differential impact of log openness on absolute education spending in autocracies and democracies (Models A and B). In both cases, the coefficient on openness is positive but it is only statistically significant in the autocracy subsample. As anticipated by Hypothesis Two (b), this result likely reflects the greater impact of supply-side forces on education in autocracies than in democracies. However, in Models C and D, which compare the effect of the Hiscox-Kastner variable in autocracies and democracies, I find coefficients of similar magnitude *and* statistical significance. Here we see that deviations from "free-trade" levels of imports have a similarly negative impact on education spending in both autocracies and democracies. Hypothesis Two (c) suggested that the demand-inducing effects of technology transfer would be stronger in developing states than in developed states but gave no reason to believe that they would differ across autocracies and democracies. Though the analogy is imperfect, if the Hiscox-Kastner variable better picks up demand-side forces such as technology transfer, with log openness picking up supply-side forces, this finding suggests that demand-side forces have equal impact on education across autocracies and democracies, whereas supply-side forces impact education differently.[18]

I directly test Hypothesis Two (c) in Models E through H, which break the sample into OECD and non-OECD subsamples.[19] Models E and F, using the log openness measure, show a striking pattern. In developing countries, the impact of openness is strongly positive, whereas in developed states it is strongly negative. For developing countries, this is likely a result of the demand-side impact of technology transfer combined with their greater likelihood of being autocratic. Why, however, is the impact of changes in log openness negative in developed states? First, these states are already democratic; hence the supply effects are minimal. Furthermore, they are the originators, not the recipients, of technology transfer, thus weakening the demand-side effects. Thus neither Hypothesis Two (b) nor Two (c) would expect a positive impact on education spending in advanced industrial states. Furthermore, most of these states have been open to trade since 1960 and did not experience the same kind of massive secular increase in openness that occurred in the developing world. Consequently, the main causes of changes in log openness are likely to be income or trade shocks, which cause generalized contractions in government spending, including education funding. Models G and H, using the Hiscox-Kastner measure, find a positive and significant effect of opening up in developing states and an insignificant effect in developed states. Since this variable controls for national income and the income of trading partners, international economic shocks are removed from the measure. Hence, the negative impact

---

[18] This result is *not* caused by the smaller size of the subsample. Using the same smaller subsample as Models C and D but with log openness, I find a similar pattern to Models A and B.

[19] The OECD subsample excludes Mexico, Korea, Turkey, and the Eastern European states.

of openness in advanced industrial countries from Model F is replaced by the insignificant impact predicted by Hypotheses Two (b) and Two (c). Importantly, developing countries do continue to see a positive effect on absolute education spending from increased openness, modeled in the case of Model G as reduced import protection.

In Table 2.4, I examine the impact of openness across different subsamples on relative education spending. The first two models compare the effects of log openness in autocracies and democracies. As in Table 2.3, only in autocracies do we see a sizable and robust effect, though it is statistically significant only at the 10 percent level. Despite this caveat, the predicted long-run effect is extremely large, double that obtained in the analysis of the full sample in Table 2.2. The implication is that autocracies are particularly likely to respond to increased openness with education spending rather than other forms of government spending.[20] Democracies, conversely, see no direct effect of log openness. Turning to the Hiscox Kastner score, again we find little difference between autocracies and democracies, as both show robust and substantive effects of a decrease in import protection, amounting to a long-run change of around 5 percent points of government spending.

When we turn to developed versus developing countries, a picture similar to that presented in Table 2.3 emerges. Models E and F compare the effects of log openness, finding it is related positively to relative education spending in developing states but sharply negatively in developed states. Models G and H demonstrate a similar picture, though the effect of the Hiscox-Kastner variable on relative education spending in developed states is not statistically significant. These results help us address the puzzle of the compensation versus composition hypotheses mentioned previously: Do advanced industrial countries react to trade shocks by reducing all government spending or do they tilt toward compensatory spending in such circumstances (as suggested by Garrett 1998)? The results in Model F indicate the latter choice is made. Large increases in trade in the OECD have led to absolute reductions in education spending, as we saw in Table 2.3, but not equivalent reductions in other forms of government consumption. Clearly, governments are making trade-offs between forms of spending but this is a surprising result, considering that education is often portrayed as a solution to the travails of globalization for advanced industrial countries. In fact, it is developing countries that seem to follow this advice more closely. This too is an unexpected result given the findings of Wibbels (2006), who suggests that developing states react to trade volatility by cutting health and education spending rather than pensions and unemployment, thereby creating "dependency revisited." Though neither log openness nor the Hiscox-Kastner measure is identical to the volatility measures used by Wibbels, these results suggest the spending patterns of developing states are more complicated than that negative picture.

---

[20] In fact, there is no estimated impact of openness on other government consumption in autocracies. In democracies, conversely, other government consumption increases under openness.

Private Spending

I now turn to examine the effects of democracy and openness on private education spending. Unfortunately, data availability is far worse for private than for public spending, since the former does not constitute part of the easily available national accounts. Consequently, the data I examine here range only between 1990 and 1998, across thirty-three countries, with a maximum of seven periods under analysis and a country average of just over three. These are not ideal data, but despite their obvious weaknesses, we nonetheless find powerful cross-sectional *and* dynamic effects of democracy and openness on private education spending. I examine, as a dependent variable, private spending as a percentage of national income, which has a mean of 0.89 and a standard deviation of 0.61. This variable, since it is measured relative to national income, is an exact analog to absolute public education spending, the previously used variable.

Table 2.5 employs two sets of models: a pooled regression adjusted for serial and contemporaneous correlation, and a fixed effects model. Models A and B use the first approach and differ in that Model B includes measures of both government spending and public education spending, which though reducing the dataset somewhat are likely to be important in determining private spending. Across both models, the Polity score is robustly negatively related to private spending. To get an idea of the magnitude of its effects, as in Table 2.1, I calculate the short- and long-run impact of a two-standard deviation increase in the Polity score (15 points) as, respectively, −0.510 and −1.598 percent points of GDP. These are strikingly large estimated effects and, intriguingly, they mirror the estimated changes we found for public spending following democratization, albeit with a negative sign. This suggests that democratization leads to the replacement of private by public education spending. The coefficient estimate for public education spending in Model B confirms this substitution effect – it is robust and negatively signed – and this is an effect independent of democracy (which as we have seen tends to produce greater public education spending). Finally, in Models A and B, openness appears, like democracy, to reduce private education spending. A doubling of openness reduces private education spending by 0.15 in the short run and 0.47 in the long run. The effect is notably less robust when controlling for public education spending and government spending, suggesting that the openness effect on private education spending is not independent of its stronger and more robust effect on public education spending shown earlier.

In fact, this negative effect of openness on private spending vanishes entirely when we examine solely within-country changes in Models C and D. Though we should be careful in attributing too much importance to fixed effects analysis on such a small timeframe, whereas the negative effects of democracy on private education spending appear robust even when we are just examining dynamics, the same cannot be said for openness, which suggests the latter's effects on private education spending are essentially cross-sectional.[21] The estimates

---

[21] The effects of openness on private education spending in Models A and B are robust to controls for both population and land area, suggesting that trade policy, rather than country size, is the driving force.

TABLE 2.5. *Private Education as a Proportion of National Income*

	Model A	Model B	Model C	Model D
	PCSE	PCSE	Fixed FX	Fixed FX
Lagged DV	0.681	0.623	0.087	0.072
	(0.127)***	(0.148)***	(0.110)	(0.101)
Polity	−0.034	−0.034	−0.410	−0.410
	(0.008)***	(0.012)***	(0.089)***	(0.205)*
Log Openness	−0.148	−0.171	−0.055	0.140
	(0.053)***	(0.102)*	(0.188)	(0.431)
GDP per Capita	−0.000	−0.000	−0.000	−0.000
	(0.000)	(0.000)	(0.000)***	(0.000)***
Log Pop	−0.021	−0.024	0.215	1.333
	(0.025)	(0.025)	(1.777)	(3.446)
Population < 15	0.009	0.001	0.017	−0.017
	(0.006)	(0.005)	(0.079)	(0.058)
Gov't Exp		0.007		0.010
		(0.014)		(0.041)
PUBED		−0.053		0.026
		(0.024)**		(0.069)
Year	−0.015	−0.015	0.094	0.071
	(0.034)	(0.038)	(0.011)***	(0.023)**
Constant	30.297	32.650	−183.886	−157.982
	(67.330)	(74.702)	(28.908)***	(38.773)***
N	109	90	109	90
Countries	33	30	33	30
R²	0.58	0.54	0.18	0.16

Note: Standard errors are in parentheses.
* significant at 10 percent; ** significant at 5 percent; *** significant at 1 percent.

for the effect of democracy are extremely large in the fixed effects analysis and should be viewed with some caution given the short timeframe and consequent limited democratic change in the dataset during that period. Nonetheless, even in unpromising data conditions, democracy appears to have a strong impact on private education spending, supporting Hypothesis Four (a). However, openness has a less clear effect on private education, as predicted by Hypothesis Four (b).

2.6 EXTENSIONS: DISAGGREGATING POLITICAL REGIMES AND EDUCATION

The preceding analysis has focused on democracy and education as aggregate concepts. I showed that increases in the Polity score, an aggregated index, appear to produce growth in aggregate public education spending. But precisely what element of democracy is doing the work? In Section 2.3, I distinguished between a variety of theories of regime type – the monopolistic, stability, and contestation theories – contrasting them to my more general theory of regimes as tools of redistributive control. This latter theory presumes that education policy will become more democratic the more that the government resembles a "representative agent" of the population at large. Is it the case that this depiction of democracy is actually the driving element in education policy? Furthermore, are there important distinctions among autocratic governments? For example, communist governments claim to be representatives of the proletariat, whereas political scientists typically view oil-rich autocracies to be particularly liable to lead to personalistic rule of a small elite. In this section, I disaggregate political regimes to investigate this question, firstly taking apart the Polity index, and secondly comparing autocracies. I then turn to disaggregating education spending itself into spending on primary versus tertiary education, showing that regime type and openness affect not only the level but also type of education.

I begin by disaggregating the Polity index, which divides the underlying institutional framework of democracy into several subvariables that measure particular institutional phenomena. These subvariables are divided into the regulation of executive recruitment, the competitiveness of executive recruitment, the openness of executive recruitment, constraints on the executive, the regulation of political participation, and the competitiveness of political participation. The subvariables are not ordered monotonically with respect to "greater" democracy and thus may reflect nonlinear effects or institutions that are not of themselves democratic or autocratic but interact with other measures. Examining these submeasures enables us to test the representative theory of democracy against alternatives such as the stability and contestation theories.

Table 2.6 shows the estimated effect of each subvariable on absolute education spending (using the same model as Table 2.1, Model B). The first subvariable examined is the regulation of executive recruitment, which varies from unregulated coups to regulated transfers of power. This variable provides a useful test of the stability hypothesis, since a more regulated transition presumably increases the incentives of both autocratic monarchs and democratic parties to invest in education for the long term. Yet the variable is statistically insignificant both as a three-point scale and as a dummy where the first two categories are combined. The stability theory is thus provided with no support in this analysis. The second subvariable is the competitiveness of executive recruitment, which does have a statistically significant positive effect on education spending. This variable moves from systems where leaders are selected, including both monarchies and military regimes, to those where leaders are elected. Presumably election implies that leaders will be more representative of the population at large than under selection, thereby mirroring the representativeness theory. It is noteworthy that the estimated first difference on this variable is similar in magnitude to that obtained for the Polity score as a whole. The final executive recruitment variable examines its openness. This four-point scale moves

TABLE 2.6. *Components of the Polity Measure*

	Coefficent Estimate	Short-Term First Diff.
Polity Index	0.012 (0.005)**	+0.240**
Regulation of Executive Recruitment (Three-Point)	0.041 (0.046)	+0.082
Regulation of Executive Recruitment (Dummy)	0.049 (0.066)	+0.049
Competitiveness of Executive Recruitment (Three-Point)	0.108 (0.044)**	+0.216**
Openness of Executive Recruitment (Four-Point)	0.078 (0.180)	+0.234
Openness of Executive Recruitment (Dummy)	0.194 (0.678)	+0.194
Regulation of Political Participation (Five-Point)	−0.011 (0.030)	−0.044
Regulation of Political Participation (Dummy)	−0.086 (0.123)	−0.086
Competitiveness of Political Participation (Five-Point)	0.028 (0.026)	+0.140
Competitiveness of Political Participation (Dummy)	0.123 (0.061)**	+0.123**
Constraints on the Executive (Seven-Point)	0.032 (0.014)**	+0.224**
N	1,463	
States	112	

Note: All regressions use the fixed effect specification employed in Model B of Table 2.1. Standard errors are in parentheses. ***$p < 0.01$, **$p < 0.05$, *$p < 0.1$.

from closed (hereditary succession) through two hybrid systems (selection and election of chief ministers) to fully nonhereditary. This last category includes a variety of autocratic governments with nonhereditary succession, including communist governments and military regimes as well as democracies. There is no statistically significant relationship obtained for this variable, either as a four-point scale or a dummy variable, where the first three categories are combined. Again we see that monarchies are not distinct categories of regime. Overall, analysis of executive recruitment strongly supports the selectorate view of democracy rather than the stability mechanism.

The next set of subvariables deal with political participation. The first is regulation of political participation, a five-point scale (unregulated, multiple identity, sectarian, restricted, and regulated). Essentially, this variable measures the

institutionalization of political parties and the degree to which they are faction-
alist/ethnic or mass/programmatic. Consequently, this measure provides a useful proxy for the contestation view of democracy and for theories that presume
heterogeneity will reduce public goods provision (Alesina, Baqir, and Easterly,
1999; Miguel, 2004). However, this variable has no apparent effect on education
spending, either as a continuous measure or as a dummy where the first four
categories are combined. Political competition built around primordial or identity differences does not appear determinative of education policy. The second
subvariable is the competitiveness of political participation, a five-point scale
moving from states where no competition is permitted, to those where at least
20 percent of the population are excluded from the vote, to factional, transitional, and competitive systems. While the variable as a whole is not statistically
significant, a dummy measure that breaks off the first two categories from the
others is significant at the 5 percent level. Put simply, what matters in terms
of political competition is not factionalism versus secular parties but limits on
the right to participate at all. The first two categories are distinct because they
deprive citizens of the right to participate (either as voters or parties). This corresponds closely to the selectorate theory and the formal model developed in
Section 2.3, since we are contrasting regimes where only the elite may participate, and hence policies reflect elite preferences, with those where the mass of
the population is granted participation and presumably representation.

The final subvariable relates to the existence of constraints on the executive,
moving from absolute control to shared parity with a legislature. Checking this
subvariable is important since it matters not only that the masses have a vote or
political parties but also that the execution of policy is responsive to their preferences. And indeed we find a strong substantive and robust effect of constraints
on the executive. Pulling these results together, we find that three elements of
democracy are important for education policy: whether the executive is elected
(or selected), the existence of constraints on that executive, and whether all citizens are permitted to participate in the political process. If all three components
are in place, policy making should be representative of citizens' aggregated preferences in the fashion suggested by the selectorate theory. However, I find no
support for the stability theory. Monarchies appear to differ from more despotic
regimes only in their degree of ceremony. Furthermore, factionalist politics are
not a barrier to high public good provision, at least with regard to education.
Instead, what matters is the degree to which final policy outcomes reflect the
political preferences of the masses for education spending.

Varieties of Autocracy

The previous section analyzed how different institutional components of democratic systems might affect public education spending. This section takes an
alternative tack: Is there an important distinction between qualitatively different forms of autocratic government? In particular, two idiosyncratic types of
autocracy are examined: communist states (or states with a communist legacy)

and states that are dependent on oil as their main export commodity. Since communist states were self-professedly established as "dictatorships of the proletariat," we might expect that such governments would spend more on public education than comparably autocratic noncommunist governments (Mulligan, Gil, and Sala-i-Martin, 2004). Conversely, many political scientists have characterized oil-exporter states as particularly rapacious and unresponsive to citizen demands (e.g., Boix, 2003; Morrison, 2005). Ross (2001) lists a number of potential reasons why oil states are likely to be antidemocratic. Firstly, income from oil exports may allow these states to buy off opposition. Secondly, oil states might use these resources to repress their citizenry. The third reason Ross terms the "modernization effect": Because oil dictators grow rich from primary good production, they fail to develop the capital or human capital stock that might lead to a market economy supportive of liberal democracy. This suggests an impact on education: Perhaps the presence of oil leads states to invest less in education as they substitute funding toward resource extraction.

Bringing this together, we should expect those states that have, or recently had, communist governments to spend significantly more on education than those states that never had a communist experience. Conversely, where states rely on oil as their main export good, we should expect them both to be more autocratic – and therefore spend less on education – and indeed to spend less on education more generally because of the "modernization effect." Furthermore, since the exports of these states are dominated by primary resources rather than production that requires a large skilled workforce, we should not expect the education-promoting effects of openness to be present in oil exporters – if anything, we should expect the opposite relationship in these states.

Table 2.7 displays a cross-sectional analysis of these hypotheses, using average levels of each independent variable from 1960 to 2000 and adding dummies for communist legacy and oil exporter status. The dependent variable is public spending on education. Since these are cross-sectional regressions, I control for regional effects by introducing regional dummies and clustered standard errors and also include the log of a country's land area in order to control for the fact that larger states will be less open than smaller states. Models A and C provide baselines against which to judge the effects of communism and oil exports. Model B excludes openness and land area but shows a very sizable positive impact of communism on education spending – over 2 percent points of GDP. This is an enormous gap – indeed, it is similar to the predicted effect of "full democratization" on the Polity variable. We might, consequently, infer that communist states were as representative of the median voter's education preferences as advanced democracies. Conversely, in oil exporters, education spending is 1.5 percent points lower. This is not merely a function of oil exporters tending to be from the North Africa and Mideast region or from Western Africa as in Nigeria and Gabon, since we are controlling for region in the regression. The coefficient on the Polity score remains significant and similar in magnitude, demonstrating that these particular forms of autocracy are not driving the results found elsewhere in this chapter. Model D introduces openness and land

TABLE 2.7. *Cross-sectional Analysis of Types of Autocracy*

	Model A	Model B	Model C	Model D
Polity	0.091	0.081	0.072	0.060
	(0.023)***	(0.031)**	(0.017)***	(0.027)**
Communist		2.088		1.436
		(0.903)**		(0.843)*
Oil		−1.491		−1.461
		(0.613)**		(0.496)**
Log Openness			1.473	1.495
			(0.698)**	(0.702)**
Log Area			0.335	0.313
			(0.176)*	(0.173)*
Population < 15	0.011	0.060	0.032	0.061
	(0.040)	(0.052)	(0.035)	(0.043)
Log GDP	−2.272	−2.117	−3.422	−3.015
	(1.619)	(1.540)	(1.681)**	(1.862)
Log GDP Sq	0.052	0.056	0.077	0.075
	(0.032)	(0.029)*	(0.034)**	(0.037)**
Log Pop	−0.365	−0.706	−0.316	−0.566
	(0.169)**	(0.194)***	(0.321)	(0.351)
GOVEX	0.117	0.125	0.068	0.071
	(0.038)***	(0.031)***	(0.064)	(0.055)
Constant	33.887	29.835	36.010	29.706
	(20.139)*	(18.654)	(21.702)	(23.012)
N	113	113	110	110
R^2	0.47	0.55	0.59	0.63

Note: All regressions include regional dummy variables. All regressions have Huber-White standard errors adjusted for regional clustering. Standard errors are in parentheses.
*** = $p < 0.01$, ** = $p < 0.05$, * = $p < 0.1$.

area. While the communist dummy becomes smaller and less significant, the oil exporter variable is near identical. Overall, these are fairly dramatic effects. But do these effects hold up under dynamic analysis?

Table 2.8 uses a fixed effects analysis to see whether the estimated effects of democracy and openness on education spending are different in communist and oil-exporter states than in the overall sample. Model A essentially replicates the baseline fixed effects model of Section 2.4 (Model B of Table 2.1). In Model B, however, I add two interactive terms: the Polity score multiplied by the communist dummy and by the oil exporter dummy. In both cases, we see evidence that the general positive effect of democracy on education spending found in the main sample is countered by a negative effect in these states. In fact, the estimated effect of democratization on education spending in the full

TABLE 2.8. *Dynamic Effects of Communism and Oil*

	Model A	Model B	Model C	Model D
Lagged DV	0.608	0.614	0.600	0.604
	(0.018)***	(0.018)***	(0.019)***	(0.018)***
Polity	0.012	0.019	0.010	0.018
	(0.005)**	(0.005)***	(0.005)**	(0.005)***
Polity*Comm		−0.021		−0.021
		(0.013)*		(0.013)*
Polity*Oil		−0.122		−0.147
		(0.026)***		(0.027)***
Log Openness	0.232	0.173	0.314	0.281
	(0.089)***	(0.089)*	(0.103)***	(0.102)***
Open*Comm			−0.113	−0.076
			(0.208)	(0.207)
Open*Oil			−0.661	−1.116
			(0.319)**	(0.328)***
Population < 15	−0.015	−0.020	−0.013	−0.017
	(0.011)	(0.011)*	(0.011)	(0.011)
Log GDP	2.180	2.261	2.257	2.438
	(0.833)***	(0.829)***	(0.839)***	(0.833)***
Log GDP Sq.	−0.041	−0.043	−0.043	−0.047
	(0.017)**	(0.017)**	(0.017)**	(0.017)***
Log Pop.	−0.012	−0.121	−0.038	−0.174
	(0.225)	(0.228)	(0.225)	(0.228)
Govt. Exp.	0.003	0.004	0.003	0.003
	(0.006)	(0.006)	(0.006)	(0.006)
Year	−0.016	−0.016	−0.016	−0.015
	(0.006)***	(0.006)***	(0.006)**	(0.006)**
Constant	5.829	6.816	3.456	2.872
	(14.297)	(14.404)	(14.476)	(14.538)
N	1,501	1,501	1,501	1,501
Countries	113	113	113	113
R^2	0.50	0.51	0.50	0.51

Note: All models have country fixed effects. Standard errors are in parentheses.
*** $p < 0.01$, ** $p < 0.05$, * $p < 0.1$.

sample actually increases once we control for its differential effects across types of autocracy.

In the communist states, the coefficient, though almost identical to that obtained for democracy in the full sample, is negatively signed; the implication is that changes in the level of democracy in communist (or ex-communist) states had *no* effect on education spending. These states already had high levels of education spending, controlling for demographic factors, and the transition to democracy merely maintained education spending at these unusually high levels. This is a not an unexpected finding. But when we turn to oil exporters, we see a more surprising result. Democratization in these countries is strongly associated with a *decrease* in education spending. The small number of these states and the absence of sustained democratization among them should give us pause in interpreting these results; nonetheless, it may be the case that following regime change, political life turns on competition for control of resources rather than on longer-run investment in education. Turning to Models C and D, which add interactive effects between openness and being communist or an oil exporter, we see that the estimated effects of democratization in these varying regimes remain robust. Furthermore, the effect of openness on education spending in communist states is not appreciably different from that in the sample as a whole. The same cannot be said for oil exporters. Increased openness in these states leads to *decreased* education spending. Presumably, the reliance on primary exports as opposed to export-oriented industrialization actually weakens the incentive to invest in education. As with democracy, this is an extremely strong negative effect, far larger in magnitude than the positive effect of openness found in the general sample. Thus the suggestion made by Ross (2001) that resource curses might retard industrial modernization, especially human-capital led industrialization, finds ample support in the data. Not all forms of openness are helpful to education, only those that increase the demand for education or that mitigate supply-side effects. Oil exports may produce an educational Dutch disease, wherein investment is channeled away from industries that might ensure long-run growth.

So far, I have focused largely on aggregate education spending, either as a proportion of national income or compared to government consumption more generally. This emphasis has largely been a function of data availability. Once we move beyond the national accounts, it becomes challenging to obtain comparable data for multiple countries across time. However, the formal model did explore the question of targeted spending and the conditions under which competing groups are able to channel funding toward forms of education spending that benefit themselves. In this concluding section, I examine the empirical record of the effects of democracy and openness on the composition of education spending. Although the data are much more fragmentary than in the earlier analyses, we again see powerful effects of political and economic openness on education. In particular, both autocratic and autarkic regimes appear to slant funding toward targeted higher education and away from universal primary education. For autocracies, this appears to be caused by their general desire to restrict spending to the elite. For autarkies, the reasoning is slightly more complex: Highly open states will trade their "comparative educational advantage" – thus developing states will trade in goods embodying mass basic education, such as light manufactures, whereas developed states will trade in goods embodying higher education, such as computers and financial services. According to the Hecksher-Ohlin theorem, this implies greater production in

TABLE 2.9. *Democracy, Openness, and Tertiary over Primary Per-Student Spending*

	Model A	Model B	Model C	Model D	Model E	Model F
	All	Non-OECD	OECD	All	Non-OECD	OECD
Polity Score	−1.092	−1.553	−0.681	−1.076	−1.517	−0.293
	(0.425)**	(0.550)***	(0.416)	(0.436)**	(0.570)**	(0.449)
Log Openness	−6.993	−14.025	1.187	−7.544	−15.307	0.830
	(3.623)*	(6.242)**	(0.468)**	(3.904)*	(7.090)**	(0.584)
Population<15	−0.169	−0.786	−0.061	−0.166	−0.768	0.008
	(0.401)	(0.599)	(0.089)	(0.422)	(0.623)	(0.093)
Log GDP	−23.354	−28.968	0.080	−23.666	−26.909	0.415
	(11.955)*	−26.141	(5.060)	(12.267)*	(27.740)	−(4.632)
(Log GDP)²	0.369	0.420	0.005	0.377	0.373	−0.002
	(0.239)	(0.561)	(0.094)	(0.245)	(0.592)	(0.086)
Log Population	3.122	4.227	−0.507	2.953	4.061	−0.486
	(2.049)	(3.163)	(0.353)	(2.151)	(3.540)	(0.342)
Govt. Exp.	0.024	0.262	0.054	0.024	0.279	0.086
	(0.269)	(0.382)	(0.035)	(0.273)	(0.393)	(0.035)**
Tertiary Enrol.				−0.035	−0.034	−0.025
				(0.121)	(0.263)	(0.015)
Primary Enrol.				0.027	0.061	−0.036
				(0.090)	(0.112)	(0.022)
Constant	349.056	482.578	7.115	355.909	462.897	3.923
	(141.356)**	(299.223)	(70.722)	(144.627)**	(312.594)	(64.724)
Observations	77	52	25	77	52	25
R²	0.67	0.71	0.82	0.67	0.71	0.88

Note: All regressions are adjusted for heteroskedasticity using weighted least squares. Regional dummies are included. Standard errors are in parentheses.
***$p < 0.01$, **$p < 0.05$, *$p < 0.1$.

services embodying the skills in which countries have a comparative advantage and this creates demand for basic skills in developing countries and higher education in developed states. Autarkies, however, are not exposed to these market pressures and may retain skill structures, and government spending patterns, quite opposite to their comparative advantage. Hence openness in developing countries should be associated with increased primary education spending but in developed countries with increased tertiary education spending.

Table 2.9 tests Hypotheses 5 (a) and 5 (b) on a dataset of country mean spending on primary and tertiary education during the 1990s. The dependent variable in this analysis is the ratio of tertiary to primary spending per student. Because time series evidence on the composition of education spending is fragmentary, it is necessary to conduct a cross-sectional analysis of the data rather than analyzing dynamic patterns. Models A through C use the standard set of

controls, whereas Models D through F also include measures of overall enrollment levels in tertiary and primary education, in order to isolate the impact of
increased per-student spending from changes in enrollment and to control for
economies of scale. Each set of tests examines three subsamples: firstly all the
cases, secondly non-OECD states, and thirdly OECD states.

Models A through C show the expected effect of democracy on the tertiary to
primary spending ratio as presented in Hypothesis Five (a). The ratio variable
has significant variability in the dataset, ranging from 0.4 to 85. A two-standard
deviation shift in democracy is predicted to lead to a reduction in the ratio variable of fifteen points in the full sample and twenty-three points in developing
states. For OECD states, the negative effect remains but is much smaller (the
highest level of the ratio is 4.6 in the OECD) and statistically insignificant.
These patterns are robust to inclusion of the enrollment variables in Models
D through F. These results suggest that autocratic governments do indeed tilt
funding of public education toward the kind of education that benefits the elite
because of unequal access. Investment in higher education might superficially
appear to be one of few virtuous investments in authoritarian states, yet it is
likely to actually reflect the rather baser motives of an autocratic elite attempting to retain education for itself.

Turning to the effect of openness, I find ample support for Hypothesis Five
(b). In the full sample, there is a statistically weak negative effect of openness
on the ratio variable. However, in developing states, there is a robust and sizable
negative effect of openness on the ratio variable, as states move resources to
sectors of comparative advantage, which demand lower-skilled labor. It is worth
highlighting that the size of the predicted effect is quite notable: A doubling
of openness is predicted to have a similar effect to a fifteen-point move on the
Polity scale. Conversely, Model C shows a robust positive effect of openness
on the ratio in OECD states, whose comparative advantage lies in university-
educated labor. Note that because this analysis is cross-sectional, we are comparing highly open OECD states with less open ones, and country size could
be a confounding variable. However, controlling for a state's area leaves the
coefficient on openness robust and similar in magnitude. This analysis is likely
picking up the very high levels of higher education investment found in the
highly open Scandinavian states. Models D through F replicate this pattern,
controlling for enrollment. The effects in Models D and E remain robust to
enrollment patterns, suggesting that economies of scale in provision are not
driving this result. However, Model F shows that the statistical significance of
openness on the ratio is weakened in the OECD once I control for enrollment
levels. The results on developing countries are robust throughout, though, and
suggest an important lesson for those seeking to promote educational investment to developing countries. It is not enough to increase education spending
en masse, since autarkic states are liable to channel investment in the kind of
targeted, elitist education that might be useful for creating a protected high-
technology import-substituting sector but is rather less effective in encouraging sustainable and universal development.

2.7 CONCLUSION

Although education might appear a political no-brainer for governments – a salve for economic growth and an effective manner to extend the control of the state over its citizenry – in fact, education spending varies dramatically worldwide. The results in this chapter suggest that, unlike many other public goods, the political logic of education extends far beyond the simple resolution of a collective action problem to a fierce redistributive battle between rich and poor. The outcome of this battle is largely determined by the political institutions and labor market structure that governments face. Autocracies block education spending, even when it might benefit economic growth, because it harms the elite. Democratization, conversely, permits the eventual rise of mass education. Although trade policy and education policy may seem almost tangential, this chapter has also shown that education spending is deeply affected by global integration and that this is a mostly positive relationship, despite the traditional view of globalization as threatening to public spending. While rich, advanced democracies might occasionally sacrifice education spending during trade-induced recessions, elsewhere the impact of the global economy on education is benign. Globalization forces up demand for skills because it facilitates technology transfer. Hence would-be students in developing nations have the most to gain from global integration. Furthermore, globalization can even encourage those erstwhile enemies of education, autocracies, to expand their education spending, as harmful scarcity effects are dissolved. Thus, as the global economy expands, the friends of education need not fear a "race to the bottom"; instead, an integrated world should mean an educated world.

3

The Expansion of Education

Historical Evidence

3.1 INTRODUCTION

Statistical analysis in the previous chapter has confirmed a substantively strong and statistically robust relationship between public education spending and our two chief causal candidates: democracy and openness. However, even after running this battery of tests, our candidates remain just that – correlations alone cannot directly test causation. To get a handle on the validity of the causal mechanisms developed in Chapter 2, we need to examine the historical experience of a variety of states in much greater detail. In this chapter, I provide an analysis of education policy across a broad array of states, both developed and developing, and from South Asia to Western Europe. The cases demonstrate a profound connection among political events, trade policies, and education provision and add both empirical richness and causal clarity to the quantitative analysis in Chapter 2.

The chapter begins by examining changes in both democracy and globalization and their effects on education spending in the Philippines. We see firstly that the tumultuous experience with different political regimes in the Philippines since the sixteenth century has had very powerful effects on education funding, particularly during and following the period of martial law declared under Ferdinand Marcos. The volatility of political representation in the Philippines demonstrates both the positive effect on education that follows independence and democratization and the negative effects on education of colonialism, empire, and autocracy. The Philippines has also experienced significant vacillation in its degree of integration with the international economy. Again, I show how closely this has tracked education spending.

The chapter then moves to a comparison of two critical cases that demonstrate the *separate* effects of democracy and openness. In particular, I examine the case of India, a democracy with surprisingly low education spending, and Malaysia, an autocracy with surprisingly high education spending. As we shall see, the key difference between the states has been their level of integration with the international economy over the past several decades. The failure of India to invest adequately in education is infamous, and while authors have blamed this on the caste system or opportunities to engage in child labor (Weiner, 1990), the recent opening of the international economy has spurred education spending while those other factors have remained constant.[1] Thus, it appears that it was India's experimentation with import substitution that led to a severe contraction in education spending. Conversely, the Malaysian case of autocratic but economically open government represents a familiar pattern in Asian development, where export orientation was accompanied by increased education spending, even under authoritarianism.

I turn in the next section to another focused comparison, this time between the regions of Latin America and East Asia, and in particular, contrasting Brazil and South Korea's experience with education and development since 1945. During the 1960s and 1970s, most states in both regions were under authoritarian rule. Yet, though the level of democracy was similar across the regions, East Asian states had far higher levels of investment in education and achieved enrollment levels unprecedented in the developing world, whereas Latin American countries essentially stagnated in both funding and enrollments. I argue that the distinguishing factor between these two regions was the effect of their contrasting trade policies, with Latin American countries deepening their import substitution industrialization (ISI) strategy, whereas East Asian states moved away from ISI to export-oriented policies. Consequently, the East Asian states experienced a much greater demand for education and were less exposed to a declining skill premium when they did expand education than were the Latin American states. Furthermore, whereas South Korea, for example, adopted a "sequential" investment strategy, moving from primary, through secondary, to tertiary funding from 1960 to 1995, Latin American states such as Brazil focused their investment at the highest echelons of the skill distribution. Holding the level of democracy constant, this section allows us to separate out the effects of openness on education, and contributes a new explanation to the long-running debate on what determined the regions' contrasting development experiences.

Finally, I examine a set of states that experienced sudden shocks to both democracy and openness. The three Southern European states of Portugal, Spain, and Greece all experienced sudden democratizations in the 1970s and then all joined the European Community during the 1980s. As we shall see, both of these shocks were followed in all three cases by increases in education spending. The suddenness and temporal separation of these events provide a useful way of distinguishing the effects of democracy and openness on education spending from other potentially important but gradual forces like economic growth – they allow us to imitate an interrupted time series methodology.

Before commencing with the specific case analyses, it is worthwhile discussing the logic behind this case selection. There is often a temptation to examine those cases that are most supportive to the argument. If case comparison is used as a misleading way of essentially narrowing the dataset to the point that

---

[1] In the case of child labor, openness has, if anything, increased returns to child labor, which in Weiner's thesis would imply reduced participation in education.

correlation between variables of interest is perfect, this rather negates the point of the exercise. Instead, cases should be used to explore the causal mechanism postulated by the author, rather than as a demonstration of correlation – the latter task being better suited to statistical analysis. Given this emphasis on causation, it is imperative to choose cases where there is significant change *within* states. Thus examining the Philippines, South Korea, and the Southern European states provides significant within-state variation in democracy and openness across a broad variety of countries.

A second aim of case analysis is to define clearly changes in the independent variables of interest in order to examine their consequent effects on education spending. Sharply defined phenomena should have sharp effects on the outcome of interest – this is the logic behind the method of interrupted time series. They also allow us better to distinguish between our independent variables when events happen separately. While democratic events and changes in openness are largely collinear in the case of the Philippines, this is not true in the case of the Southern European countries, which experienced their entry to the European trading community around a decade after democratization, or Brazil, where liberalization followed several years after democratization. South Korea, conversely, democratized several decades after adopting its outward-oriented development policy, providing the reverse example.

The final aim of case analysis should be the examination of critical case studies – that is, those cases that display unusual configurations on the set of independent variables. In this analysis, we examine both India – an unusually autarkic democracy – and Malaysia – an unusually open autocracy – and compare their experiences with education spending. It is important that theories not be tested on a limited range of states where all variables of interest are collinear. The cases of India and Malaysia are important because they show the causal mechanism at work in cases that are "off the diagonal" of closed autarkies and open democracies and thus allow us to picture the full counterfactual of *any* country choosing to open its economy.

One caveat is worth addressing before commencing the cases. As we shall see in the study of party manifestos in Chapter 4, rare is the politician who is vocally anti-education. Even dictators with little cause to fear popular disapproval rarely explicitly denounce public education, though even here, as the case of Antonio de Oliveira Salazar in Portugal shows, there are exceptions. Autarkic democracies often lay out grand claims about educating the masses before neglecting universal education and channeling money only to universities. Words and deeds do not always match in the politics of education. Thus, the cases in these chapters cannot always sharply demonstrate the intentionality of political actors, particularly in terms of cutting education or targeting it to preferred clients. Where I am able to, I draw on both politicians' expressed views and on evidence of citizen preferences; elsewhere, I must rely on policy outcomes to support my causal mechanism. Throughout, however, I endeavor to identify which actors were supportive or antagonistic toward education and how their preferences match up to the predictions of my theory.

3.2 THE PHILIPPINES: POLITICAL VOLATILITY, ECONOMIC INSTABILITY, AND EDUCATION

The history of education in the Philippines has been a volatile and troubled one, with brief interludes of success followed by long troughs of cutbacks and defunding of the education system. In this section, I trace the interlinked history of education, democracy, and openness in the Philippines since the Spanish invasion of the sixteenth century.

The Philippines experienced a variety of colonial regimes of varying degrees of repression – the Spanish, the Americans, and the Japanese – before independence, and then a variety of political regimes: from the emerging postwar democracy, to Ferdinand Marcos' declaration of martial law and the ensuing autocracy, to the Corazon Aquino transition to democracy, followed by the brief and corrupt interlude of Joseph Estrada's presidency. During the postwar period, the Philippines has also experimented with a variety of trade policies, also with significant repercussions for education spending. What is particularly dramatic about the experience of the Philippines is how closely changes in democracy and openness have been linked with education spending. Moreover, this pattern has held both in periods of liberalization and periods of political and economic repression. These cycles in education spending have predominated despite the widespread belief that the Philippines has an idiosyncratic pro-education culture: An official UNESCO report remarked that "a passion for education is one of the unique characteristics of the Filipino" (Synott, 2002). And yet this cultural affinity for education has proved a weak bulwark against the tides of politics. Education spending has varied widely since independence, regardless of cultural factors. Because of this substantial variation, the Philippines provides an excellent case for analyzing the causal mechanisms suggested in the preceding chapter.

I begin my historical analysis of education in the Philippines with the Spanish conquest of 1565. Spanish rule, which lasted nearly three and a half centuries, was essentially feudal, with the Philippines divided into three *encomiendas* (administrative districts): those of the King, those of the Church, and those granted to Spanish settlers.[2] Given that the government of the Philippines was essentially a colonialism of "direct rule" (as opposed to the British system of reliance on local elites, or "indirect rule"), public services, such as there were, were set up for the benefit of settlers and the Church. The selectorate governing the Philippines therefore represented a tiny fraction of the islands' population and the extent of the education system mirrored the repression of political rule. Schools were limited to the children of the settlers or were vessels for proselytization: as Synott (2002) remarks, "the Spanish established no true schooling system for the Filipinos, and teaching was restricted to the forced learning of the Catholic catechism." Anderson (1988) remarks that

---

[2] The *encomiendas* system was replaced by a typically Latin American *hacienda* system during the eighteenth century, which was, if anything, an even more feudal mechanism of governance.

"a serious education was not easy to acquire in the colony, where the Church was violently opposed to any inroads of liberalism from Madrid and controlled most local schools."

Demands for the spread of education were a key part of the independence movement in the Philippines, providing further evidence that democratization was the catalyst for education spending, rather than the reverse. During the nineteenth century, an incipient independence movement arose in both Madrid and Manila (the Spanish authorities accused it of *filibusterismo* or "subversion") with "education for Filipinos ... a key cause of the independence movement and a factor in the struggles that ensued" (Synott, 2002). The most famous leader of the movement, the Filipino author Jose Rizal, wrote *Noli Me Tangere*, a novel whose central character is attacked as he lays the cornerstone for his village's first schoolhouse, prompting the famous line: "In our country today, to know something is to be hanged" (Anderson, 1997). The aspiration for schooling, then, went hand in hand with the incipient democratic movement. Following the public execution of Rizal in 1896, Filipino revolt against Spain snowballed into full-scale civil war and the declaration of independence in 1898 (Franco, 2000).

Independence was a quickly frustrated dream for the Filipinos since, following the Spanish–American War of 1898, the dream of an independent Philippines was swiftly quashed by the imposition of American rule, which triggered a failed war of resistance leading to the deaths of two hundred thousand Filipinos. As part of their pacification program, the Americans established a centralized public school system for the first time in 1901, bringing over six hundred American teachers. Crucially for later Philippine development, the Americans removed religion from the school system (thereby removing the only aim of Spanish educators) and insisted that education be conducted in English (Anderson, 1988). Of course, the granting of a school system to the Philippines was not an entirely beneficent act – the Americans expressly hoped that the socialization and propaganda effects of schooling would mollify the Filipinos. Nonetheless, American imperialism was more benign than that of the Spanish, and the provision of education followed this political logic closely.

The Americans gradually extended political rights to the Filipinos, albeit with the heavy hand of imperial control of trade and foreign policy hanging overhead. Local elections were introduced in 1901, legislative elections in 1907, and finally presidential elections in 1935, the latter as the Americans began a gradual process of withdrawal from colonial control. Although these reforms marked the introduction of voting rights for the first time, the Filipino electorate was highly constrained: 1.15 percent of the total population were eligible to vote in 1907, and by 1935 this had only expanded to 11 percent of the population (Franco, 2000). Underlying this restriction of the franchise was a literacy requirement, highlighting how American rule had limited impact on education at the national level: Fewer than half of the adult population of the Christian islands of the Philippines could read or write by the outbreak of the Second World War. Most Filipino politicians of the era were tightly linked to their upper-class constituents – the land-holding *caciques* – and when Manuel Quezon was elected as the first Filipino president in 1935, his promises to introduce a "Social Justice" campaign were quickly discarded after meeting strong parliamentary opposition from the representatives of the *caciques*. Overall, American imperialism and the limited increase in representation had positive benefits on education spending and provision as compared to the era of Spanish rule, but by the end of the 1930s the demands of the unrepresented poor for education provision, among other social goods, were increasingly unmet, foundering on colonial or parliamentary disapproval.

The American imperial era in the Philippines was brought to an end by the Japanese invasion of the islands during the Second World War. Typical of Japanese colonialism, rule was repressive and education became solely devoted to propaganda (Synott, 2002). Given that warfare led to the near-total destruction of Manila and other Filipino cities, it is little surprise that the education system had basically collapsed by 1945 and it would take several years following the U.S. liberation before education spending recovered to prewar levels.

The Philippines gained independence after World War II, but this was independence very much under American influence. During the 1960s, the Philippines was a moderately democratic state, scoring +5 on the Polity index. U.S. influence meant that civil liberties were repressed, but a quasi-democratic electoral system was put in place and this political system began to respond to popular demands for increased education spending. From 1960 to 1965, under the Liberal government of Diosdado Macapagal, the Philippines expanded from 56 percent enrollment in primary education to around 97 percent (Kang, 2002). In 1966, Ferdinand Marcos was democratically elected president of the Philippines and one of his earliest acts of legislation was the 1966 Magna Carta for School Teachers. This act represented the culmination of popular demands for an increasingly professionalized education system in the Philippines and led to a rise of education spending of around one quarter between 1960 and 1970. Teachers were granted academic freedom, the ability to unionize, and, most critically in terms of education funding, a guarantee that teacher salaries would be indexed to the cost of living and accompanied by a set of extra allowances (Synott, 2002). This spending on both the quality and quantity of teaching was a necessary counterpart to the broader increases in enrollment bringing education to the masses.

In 1972, however, Marcos declared martial law, forcing a transition to personal rule.[3] Contemporaneously, educational expenditure, which had been rising from 2.2 percent to 2.8 percent of GDP before Marcos declared martial law, dropped sharply to below 2 percent for most of Marcos' remaining years of rule. Marcos' policies increasingly reflected the educational spending preferences of his elite client base. As Kang (2002) notes, "under martial law in the

---

[3] The Polity index for the islands plummeted from +5 to –9 following the declaration of martial law.

1970s the priorities of the government, as reflected in the budgetary allocations to defense and industry, shifted away from education," with education spending declining from 29.1 percent of government spending in 1965 to just 11.4 percent by 1975. The connection between decreasing education spending and political cronyism was rather tight: Crone (1993) argues that "the education system eroded seriously due to manipulation of funding for Marcos' pet projects." The decline worsened in the early 1980s, when the Philippine economy nose-dived into a prolonged recession, forcing major cutbacks in all areas of government investment. This budgetary collapse was largely the result of endemic corruption – money that had been channeled into the public sector was appropriated by the elites and the percentage of the population in poverty grew from 43.8 percent in 1971 to 58.9 percent in 1985 (Congressional Budget Office, 1997). Consequently, salaries for teachers dropped well below the poverty line. While resources exited the public education system, autocracy led to an increase in private spending. Enrollments in private primary schools increased 2.5 times faster than in public schools between 1965 and 1987 (Swinerton, 1991).

It was not until the late 1980s, after Marcos was forced to resign power, that educational expenditure recovered to its pre-1972 level, under the post-Marcos democracy of Corazon Aquino and her successors. One of Aquino's first acts as president was the convocation of a Congressional Commission study on education (EDCOM), which highlighted the collapse in funding relative to comparator nations, recommending massive reinvestment in public education, particularly teachers' salaries (Toh and Floresca-Cawagas, 1993). Consequently, by 1998, educational expenditure had tripled its late-Marcos level and climbed to over 4 percent of GDP, although it has dropped back subsequently to its late 1990s average of around 3.5 percent of GDP. Poorer Filipinos were the chief beneficiaries of expanded coverage thanks to a constitutional stipulation that education be made available free at the primary and secondary levels, stated in Article XIV of the Philippine Constitution of 1987. This dramatic post-Marcos increase was supported by a further stipulation in the new Philippine Constitution of 1987 that education should be the largest proportion of the state's budget. Indeed, the newly drafted constitution stipulated that expenditure on education should be at least 6 percent of GDP. Although this did not prove to be a manageable target given the actual achievement of 3.5 percent, it clearly demonstrates the determination of the new democratic government to specifically target education as a key policy device.[4] Together, these constitutional requirements amply demonstrate the close relationship between the transition to democracy and the preferences of the masses over education spending, given the new emphasis on increased spending and enrollment entitlements.

---

[4] It is also a useful confirmation that public education expenditure as a percentage of GDP is an appropriate dependent variable for the empirical analysis in this book, given that this measure was formally incorporated into the Philippine Constitution. Of course, constitutional stipulations alone may not necessarily amount to policy outcomes – India, too, had a 6 percent of GDP target from 1948 onward that it was unable to meet.

The rise of education spending in the post-1986 period accelerated under President Fidel Ramos, who proclaimed a liberalization agenda combined with substantial increases in education spending. However, the political volatility that has bedeviled the Philippines did not end with the overthrow of Marcos, nor did the responsiveness of education spending to regime change. Although the government of Joseph Estrada from 1998 to 2001 claimed to represent the uneducated poor and relied heavily on their electoral support, the reality of his rule was rather different. The Philippines entered a period of elite-driven corruption that rivaled the Marcos regime in its level of endemic bribery, if not its political repression. Little attention was paid to education spending. Teachers' salaries plummeted and their allowances for materials were cut (Synott, 2002). Many teachers were forced to take on second jobs or to work in the canteens at the school and split profits on food. The Estrada period saw a rapid reduction of education funding from 4.3 percent of national income to 3.3 percent, much of which has been attributed to Estrada's plunder of national income. The corruption spread from the top downward to the education ministry, which appropriated administrative funds to spend on luxury motor vehicles for bureaucrats' personal use.

By the end of Estrada's rule in 2001, teachers had become an important part of the resistance movement, producing a petition of nine demands for action – chief among them pay rises and funds for materials. Estrada's government resembles the "ends against the middle" coalition discussed in Chapter 2, wherein the elite and the poor align over a policy of increased simple redistribution and reduced education spending. Certainly, Estrada was highly unpopular among the Filipino middle class, whose parliamentary representatives seized on the revelations of endemic corruption in the Estrada government by instigating impeachment proceedings in 2001. This undermining of Estrada was countered by massive riots among the poor in support of Estrada (de Dios and Hutchcroft, 2003). However, although Estrada's base of support and the collapse in education funding superficially resemble an "ends against the middle" coalition, Estrada's "pro-poor" rhetoric and policy promises remained largely unfulfilled (Tordesillas, 2000). Once again, the volatility of political regimes in the Philippines had direct and powerful impacts on education funding, and again the pro-democracy movement was deeply invested in demands for increased education spending.

The interlinked pattern of regime type and education spending can be seen in Figure 3.1. The period of moderated democracy in the 1960s came to an abrupt end in the early 1970s, which led to a collapse in education spending thereafter. It is particularly striking that education spending reached its nadir in 1985, a year before the People Power revolution that overthrew Marcos. From 1986 onward, education spending increased dramatically, doubling between 1986 and 1989 and increasing to over 4 percent of national income by the late 1990s before the Estrada regime and the consequent slide in education funding, a collapse that has not been halted by the regime of Gloria Arroyo.

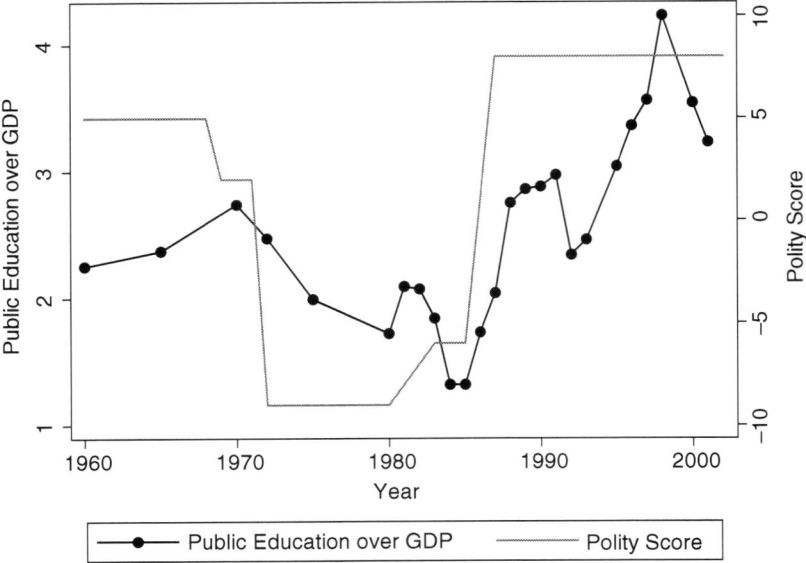

FIGURE 3.1. Democracy and Education Spending in the Philippines

The story of education funding in the Philippines has not solely been driven by political regime change, although this certainly appears to have had the most dramatic impact. The relationship of the Filipino economy to the global economy has varied considerably over the past fifty years, and this pattern of trade orientation also has a striking similarity to that seen in education spending. Figure 3.2 shows the change in the (inverted) adjusted Hiscox-Kastner variable over this time period, where positive values reflect greater trade orientation. Fluctuations of this variable appear to covary closely with those in education spending. Particularly noticeable is the stagnation in openness during the latter period of the Marcos dictatorship, with the Philippines essentially unchanged in its openness from 1974 to 1986. This period, as we saw earlier, also corresponds to the period of martial law and of massively reduced education spending. Following the 1986 return to democracy, we see openness shoot upward, essentially doubling by the mid-1990s, with a commensurate increase in education spending.

The relationship between openness and education spending appears to be tight in a bivariate analysis, but democracy and openness were also closely related during this period in the Philippines. To separate out the effects of openness from political change, I turn to an examination of Philippine trade policy in the era of independence. The legacy of colonial rule, as in many other Southeast Asian states, was a dependence on exports of agricultural and primary products to the metropole (Boyce, 1993). Under American rule, trade had expanded significantly but it was subject to significant limitations under the Payne-Aldrich and Philippine Tariff Acts of 1909, which allowed American goods free entry to

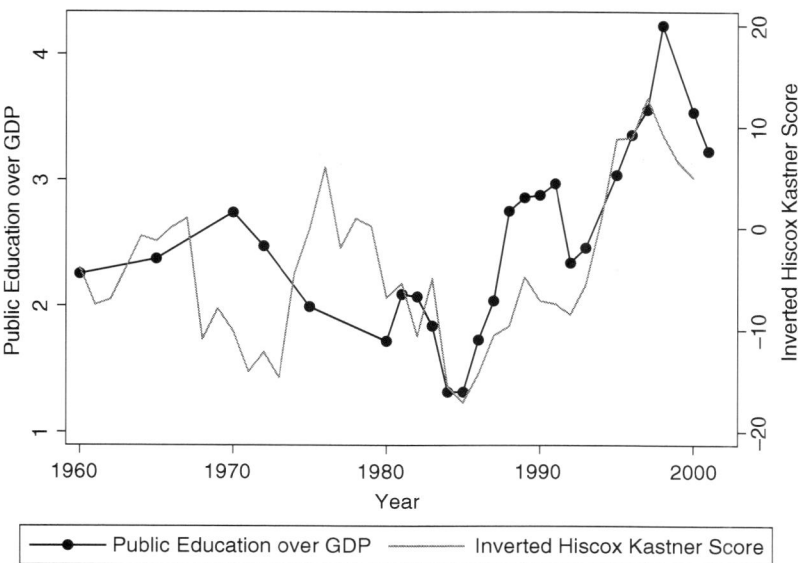

FIGURE 3.2. The Hiscox-Kastner Measure and Education Spending in the Philippines

Filipino ports but subjected Philippine agricultural exports to quotas and limited exports elsewhere. By 1930, 63 percent of Philippine imports came from the United States and 79 percent of Philippine exports went there (Hawes, 1987). These constraints on trade meant that industrial development was limited and educated labor was consequently in low demand. Trade with the United States certainly increased Philippine openness, but this failed to have a positive impact on education provision for two reasons. Firstly, agricultural production had few technological requirements and did not require an educated labor force, thereby limiting the demand side of education. Secondly, the Philippines was barely trading in manufactured goods with the United States and thus prices for these goods were not converging with the United States. Instead, U.S. companies used the Philippines as a dumping ground for cheap manufactures (de Dios and Hutchcroft, 2003), undermining the potential for increasing education supply without reducing the returns to education, since workers would find their wages undercut by American goods.

The post-political independence era was not an era of economic independence since the Philippines signed the Bell Trade Act with the United States in 1946. This act established a new series of quotas as well as "parity rights" to U.S. citizens for investment in the Philippines and a ban on the Philippines imposing export taxes; as Hawes (1987) notes, "it was a splendid example of neocolonialism." The restrictions on trade secured the continuation of agro-exports from the Philippines to the United States and limited the development of an industrial export orientation. Instead, Philippine industrialization turned inward, focusing on a heavily protected internal market (de Dios and Hutchcroft, 2003). As in the case of India – discussed in the next section – the bureaucratization of trade policy meant that control over the export sector was seized by relatively few well-connected families, who ran conglomerates combining agricultural and industrial businesses. Since industry was heavily protected, there was little technology transfer from abroad and hence demand for education failed to spike significantly upward. Instead, the Philippine economy began to mimic Latin American, rather than East Asian, development with little emphasis placed on educated labor (Haggard, 1986).

Ferdinand Marcos' declaration of martial law in 1972 was followed by a rhetorical shift toward export-oriented trade policy. Rhetoric was, however, largely unmatched by action, since Marcos, once keen to remove industrial firms from elite family control, set about protecting industry in the name of his own cronies. Export zones were established but remained niches. As McKay (2006) explains:

> ... despite these early moves to promote exports and foreign investments, the Marcos government did not make a fundamental shift away from the patrimonial policies of the past. This was largely because Marcos and other oligarchs, who through protection and monopolistic position could exploit a move into the export sector, were nevertheless in poor shape to compete internationally with vastly more efficient foreign multinationals.... Marcos pursed a contradictory but politically savvy, two-pronged strategy: he created a limited export platform or enclave economy to please foreign investors and development agencies while maintaining a highly protectionist domestic economy and coercive state to fend off political rivals and enrich himself and his closest allies.

Thus, Marcos' apparent trade orientation, proclaimed loudly for the benefit of international lenders, bore little resemblance to the structure of the Philippine economy outside the export zones (Bello, 2005). As Jayasuriya (1987) notes, "in 1980, Philippine industries had an average rate of effective protection of more than 70 per cent; this had not declined from the levels in the mid-1960s." With manufacturing protected and uncompetitive, the Philippines did not face the same demand for education felt in the East Asian "Tiger" economies. Contrary to Philippine comparative advantage, it was spending on higher education that grew most dramatically, with an annual growth rate of 5.2 percent during the early 1980s versus just 1.1 percent for primary education (Callanta, 1988). With local elites and Marcos cronies controlling these protected sectors, nor could the Philippine economy absorb such highly educated workers. Surveying Marcos' legacy in higher education, the education secretary, Lourdes Quisumbing, remarked in 1987 that "we have the supreme irony of [higher] education proceeding much faster than economic development, and creating difficult burdens for the country in terms of an educated unemployed" (Swinerton, 1991).

Political liberalization in 1986 was swiftly followed by economic liberalization under Aquino – who removed most import controls – and, in particular, under the Ramos administration. The 1991 recession also hurt education spending, but following this blip and the election of Ramos in 1992, education spending spiked upward to over 4 percent of national income. Ramos' "Philippines 2000" strategy connected trade liberalization and education spending, with his emphasis on following the East Asian model (Neher and Marlay, 1995). Under Ramos' administration, manufactured goods became the majority of Philippine exports for the first time, forcing up the demand for an educated labor force to aid in their production (de Dios and Hutchcoft, 2003). Despite the political turmoil of Joseph Estrada's corrupt government, the post-Ramos era has continued along the same economic lines, with manufactured exports supported by an increasingly educated Philippine workforce. In fact, between 1986 – the fall of Marcos – and 2005, the share of manufactures in exports from the Philippines increased from 25 percent to 88 percent, and the share of electronics increased from 13.3 percent in 1995 to 46.5 percent in 2005 (Ravenhill, 2008). As the Philippines has moved to a more diverse export profile, absorbed foreign technology, and extracted itself from restrictive trade policies – some imposed by the United States and some self-made – we should expect to see greater demand for and supply of education, as educated Filipinos are permitted to sell their skills on the global market. Overall, the dual transition to democracy and export orientation has strongly supported Philippine education spending, just as the combination of Marcos' autocracy and protectionism undermined it. I now turn to two states where democracy and openness have not coincided but rather the reverse.

3.3 INDIA AND MALAYSIA: COMPARING TWO EDUCATIONAL PUZZLES

India and Malaysia provide symmetric, contrasting puzzles. Why has India, perhaps the most successful democratic experiment in the developing world, failed so dramatically in terms of providing education to its citizenry? Why, conversely, has Malaysia had higher levels of investment than any other major state in Asia since the 1960s despite existing under a fairly oppressive authoritarian regime? Even controlling for their different sizes, populations, and levels of economic growth, India and Malaysia still appear to be significant outliers in terms of their relationship between democracy and education spending. In this section, I argue that the very different experiences of each country with regard to integration into the global economy have been the driving force behind their unusual education spending. Examining openness allows us to address these twin puzzles where regime type appears an insufficient explanation.

Before delving into the specific case analyses of India and Malaysia, it is worth examining their general trends in openness and spending across time and in comparison to their peer states. Figure 3.3 demonstrates how these patterns played out in four South Asian states – Bangladesh, India, Malaysia, and Thailand – from 1960 to 2000. Both between the states and within them, across time, openness has been strongly positively associated with education spending. While all four states have become increasingly open since 1960, they have done so from very different starting points. Over the period of the sample, there is a clear distinction between the relatively closed economies of Bangladesh and India and the more open economies of Malaysia and Thailand. For example, their mean levels of exports plus imports over GDP across the sample period

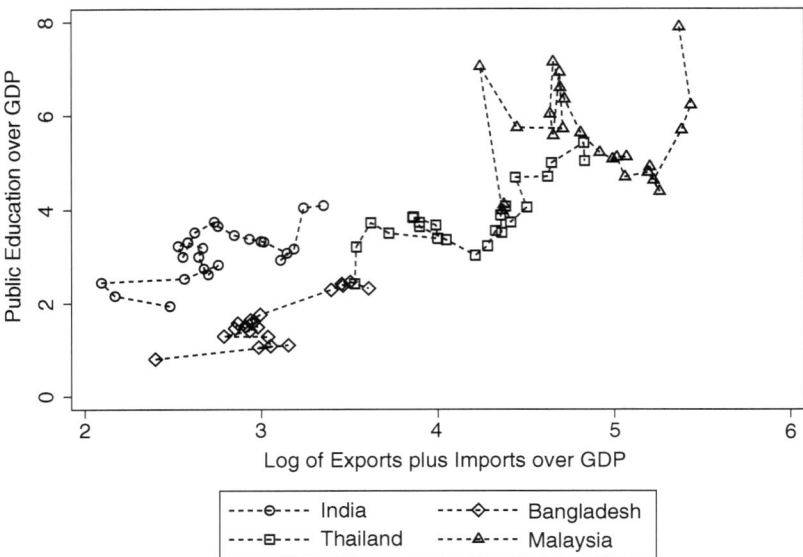

FIGURE 3.3. Education and Openness in Southern Asia

differ by an order of magnitude: Bangladesh's average is 22.2 percent and India scores 15.2 percent, whereas Thailand has an openness average of 59.3 percent and Malaysia the extreme of 121 percent of GDP.

This variation in education spending is perhaps somewhat surprising. The countries are all neighbors along the eastern coast of the Indian Ocean. Three out of four were British colonies in the early part of the twentieth century. None was particularly wealthy in 1960 – all had a GDP per capita below $1,000 (in 1995 $US). Although India obviously had a population and area dwarfing those of the other states, this hardly explains the enigma of Bangladeshi undereducation vis-à-vis Malaysia and Thailand. In fact, except for a couple of years at the end of the 1980s, India and Bangladesh have not had rates of public education higher than Thailand and Malaysia across the entire sample period. Perhaps most strangely, Malaysia and Thailand have been consistently less democratic than India (though not Bangladesh) across the period, yet their education spending has been consistently higher.

The key force behind these differences in education spending, then, appears not to be democracy but rather the degree of openness with the international economy. Indian import substitution has had the undesired (and perhaps unexpected) effect of both reducing demand for skills and creating an elite highly protective of their returns to education. Indian development was focused on developing domestic import-substituting industries, largely controlled by the political elites. The success of such industries depended rather more on easy access to import licenses and official corruption than on internationally competitive human capital. The Malaysians conversely have taken advantage of technological transfer from globalization and have been able to succeed with a policy of mass education without undermining the spoils of their elite. As such, the autocratic government of Mahatir Mohammed has been able to combine economic openness and high education spending with elite-driven rule.

India

India's failure to educate its workforce, particularly in rural areas, is infamous. Half of the Indian population remains illiterate (Lindert, 2004), which gives India 40 percent of the world's illiterates. This seems surprising on a number of levels. First, India has been a well-functioning democracy since 1947. Although politics are somewhat factional in India, Chapter 2 showed that the degree of factionalism within a political system does not appear to be a robust predictor of education spending. Rather, what matters is the degree to which citizens are enfranchised and the responsiveness of the executive to their demands, both of which have been high by developing state standards since Indian independence.[5] Second, Indian political rhetoric has consistently stressed the importance of education. Article 45 of the 1949 Indian Constitution declared that "the State shall endeavour to provide within a period of ten years from the commencement of this Constitution, for free and compulsory education for all children until they complete the age of 14 years" (Ghosh, 2000). Yet the aims of this article today remain unmet. In terms of spending, a target of 6 percent of national income for education spending has been uttered several times since the first Five Year Plan in 1951, including the Kothari Commission of 1968 and the National Policy on Education in 1986 (Tilak, 2003). However, this rhetoric has never been translated into effective action: Even today India spends just 4 percent of GDP on education.

There are three key reasons for this failure. The first is the decision to engage in an industrialization strategy of import substitution, which emerged in the mid-1950s as the consensus between the competing theories of economic nationalism (*swadeshi*), socialism, and Gandhian village production (Hardgrave and Kochanek, 2000). This strategy choked off foreign investment and hence foreign technology, reducing the demand for skilled labor. Second, the difficulty of obtaining export licenses in the "permit, license, quota Raj"[6] led to the absence of an external market for skilled labor. This meant that increases in education supply, such that there were, were swiftly followed by unemployment or lowered wages (Tilak, 2003). Thirdly, Indian education investment was

[5] It is worth noting that democracy has not been a complete failure in terms of education spending in India – in fact, India compares fairly favorably with autocratic and autarkic pre-1990s China, which consistently spent less than 2 percent of national income on education. Nonetheless, Indian autarky has kept education spending below what we would typically expect in a democracy, since most democracies are also fairly open in terms of trade orientation.

[6] This popular characterization of the bureaucratization of the economy under the Congress Party was coined by its 1960s opponent, the Swatranta Party (Erdman, 1963). The sheer difficulty of obtaining permits and licenses was a bone of contention for international aid organizations and economists for several decades; see, for example, Kreuger (1974).

focused almost exclusively on higher and upper secondary education that could provide the necessary skills for ISI production or to run the large Indian bureaucracy that managed, among other things, permits and licenses, as opposed to basic and primary education, which languished for decades. From independence through to the 1990s, this trade strategy had detrimental effects on both the size and composition of education spending.

The failure to meet government rhetoric about education began as the ink was drying on the Constitution. The new government of Jawaharlal Nehru established two education commissions: the Radhakrishnan Commission on higher education in 1948 and the Mudaliar Commission on secondary education in 1953. Ghosh (2000) notes that these commissions "dealt exclusively with two areas of education in which ruling elite groups were interested. Both these sections received large allocations of funds and underwent rapid expansion, resulting in ... severe problems of educated unemployment." Primary education, conversely, was neglected (Myrdal, 1972). These commissions and the Kothari Commission of 1968 were rather disdainful of "basic education" – village-based crafts and skills – instead emphasizing the importance of much higher-level skills that could be used to develop heavy industry for ISI development. The Kothari Commission, referring to rural education, announced "we recommend ... a particular emphasis on mathematics and the sciences .... [W]e have been unable to endorse the organization of formal courses in the schools for educating the primary producer" (Kothari Commission, 1968). Basic education in rural areas was not seen as aiding autarkic industrialization.

The relative emphasis placed on both education as a whole and on its different components can be seen by examining the composition of India's Five Year Plans. The plans reflected the rarely challenged Indian consensus that economic planning was a requisite of industrialization and were comprised of a mix of large-scale public works along with investment in social services. During the First Five Year Plan, education spending amounted to a fairly substantial 8 percent of all spending (around the same as the share devoted to power), half of which was devoted to elementary education (Ghosh, 2000). While this only amounted to around 15 percent of overall education spending, the share of education spending in the plans directly reflect government preferences over development, rather than non-policy variables such as demographic pressures. After the First Five Year Plan, education spending dropped to 5.8 percent of plan spending in the Second Five Year Plan and yet further to just 2.7 percent by the Sixth Five Year Plan in the early 1980s. Kumar (1998) notes that "basic education" had vanished from mention by the Fourth Plan.

During this period, the emphasis on elementary education was replaced by investment in higher education, with the former's share of spending reduced to 30 percent. Rudolph and Rudolph (1972) note that between 1951 and 1966, the share of higher education spending increased from a quarter to a third of the education budget: "India in 1961 may have spent a higher proportion of total educational expenditure on higher education than any other country." This pattern of decreased developmental funding for education vividly reflected the state's import substitution strategy. Tilak (2003) notes that:

1956 to 1969 marked the beginning of a drastic decline of resources allocated to elementary education and a doubling or trebling of resources allocated for higher education .... Relative emphasis shifted from the agricultural sector in favor of the industrial sector. Industrial development requires manpower, and higher education was looked upon for the supply of manpower. Phase III [1969–1986] showed a slight reversal of these trends. This may be partly attributable ... to the growth of educated unemployment, the mismatches in the labor market, and the resultant social unrest.

A number of points in Tilak's assessment are worth remarking upon. Firstly, the Indian developmental strategy was focused away from areas of comparative advantage (the agricultural sector, which following the Green Revolution became fairly competitive) toward import-substituting manufacture. The government began to limit investment in education and channel it toward the children of the elite, who were those most likely to attend higher education, in an ill-fated attempt to jump-start the Indian industrial sector. As Athreye (2005) argues, "India's achievements in tertiary education ... were the result of an overinvestment in education in preparation for general manufacturing import substitution, which did not happen." Because Indians were not exporting their manufactures abroad, the limited size of the market for such goods led to oversupply of high-end skills, a consequent increase in educated unemployment, and a collapse in the returns to advanced education. In 1974, 55 percent of high school graduates were unemployed, as were over a quarter of graduates (Ghosh, 2000). This undesirable pattern led to a further turn away from education funding in the 1970s and education essentially ceased to be a significant component of the Indian Five Year Plans until the mid-1990s. Non-plan education spending fared little better, hovering at around 2 percent of national income until the late 1980s.

What was the politics behind this neglect of education funding, especially in terms of universal elementary education? The answer lies in the peculiar political logic of the dominant Congress Party's support base, combined with their statist economic strategy. As Weiner (2001) notes, "in the early post-independence years Congress drew its electoral support from Muslims, scheduled castes and tribes, and from the higher castes." The former three groups were outsiders in the Indian polity, particularly the scheduled castes (or Dalits) and scheduled tribes with their inherited and immutable low social status. The latter groups, the higher castes such as the Brahmins and Baiyas were at the top of the social pyramid. In this sense, then, Congress's political base resembled an "ends against the middle" coalition. Universal education fell through the cracks, as the upper castes were supported through publicly financed higher education and secondary schooling (including subsidized private institutions) and the bottom castes were provided with "reservations" – quotas of jobs and places at universities for high-performing Dalits. The middle castes and classes were then doubly excluded: They were neither eligible for reservations nor were they able to access the limited secondary and higher education. In time, they would gravitate to the nationalist Bharitaya Janita Party, which railed against reservations (Basu, 2001). This political logic combined with the economic logic of ISI development focused on small high-technology sectors that employed the children of the upper castes, as too did the sizable bureaucracy needed to run a state-planned economy. Both sectors, but especially the bureaucracy, maintained sizable "reservations" for the lower castes. Widespread private sector development, especially in export sectors, was constricted, thereby weakening the demand for a broad-based medium-low skill workforce.

Examining the political motivations of these groups supports this claim. Indian elites were particularly antagonistic to mass education (Vanaik, 1990). J. P. Naik, the education planner, despaired that "education development, particularly at the secondary and higher stages is benefiting the 'haves' more than the 'have nots'" (Naik, 1965). Pranab Bardhan famously referred to the educated elite as a "proprietary class" who "enjoy a high scarcity value for the education and profession" such that "by managing to direct educational investment away from the masses, they have been able to protect their scarcity rent" (Bardhan, 1984). Bardhan's analysis of elite motivation is confirmed by survey evidence conducted in the 1980s in West Bengal, discussed by Acharya (1987). The upper strata in the survey community – the *jotedar* (landlords) and rich peasants – almost all of whose children attended school, were virulently anticompulsory education: Over 80 percent of them claimed it would cause them inconvenience and they were highly concerned it would lead to higher wages. From the other end of the social scale, the scheduled castes and tribes focused their energies on obtaining reservations rather than on universal enrollment; as Weiner (2001) argues, "reservations in education and employment proved to be a low cost strategy... because they permitted the government to pay little attention to primary and secondary school education." He also notes that those Indian states in which lower castes gained political prominence early often spent less on primary education, and where Dalits obtained the education ministry, as in Uttar Pradesh, they "invested state resources in constructing statues of Ambedkar, but did little to promote primary education."

Thus, we have seen that the Indian development strategy from the late 1950s to early 1990s, based as it was on autarkic industrialization, artificially deflated education spending and probably ended up causing more harm than good to long-run Indian wealth. Frustration with the 3.5 percent per annum "Hindu rate of growth" (fairly poor by developing country standards), combined with an economic crisis in the early 1990s, finally led to a breakthrough in economic policy and trade orientation under the administration of P. V. Narasimha Rao, who was elected in 1991. Rao's finance minister, Manmohan Singh, himself elected prime minister in 2004, was charged with developing and passing a broad range of liberalization policies in 1992. The Singh reforms permitted majority foreign ownership of Indian companies, reduced tariffs, and eliminated many quotas. In doing so, they catalyzed the development of India's rapidly growing high-technology and outsourcing industries, and following the reforms, the growth rate increased from around 5 to 7 percent.

Education policy changed along with trade and investment policies. From the Sixth Plan (1982–7) to the Eighth Plan (1992–7), the share of plans' education spending devoted to primary and secondary education rose from 14.4 precent to 61.1 percent (Moulin, 2004). Domestic demand from employers for educated workers, and from unskilled citizens for education, exploded. Sinha (2006) notes that "the 1990s saw an unprecedented demand for education even from the poorest households," as export-led growth led to the creation of new avenues of employment. In fact, India cannot educate workers fast enough at present for the skill demands of the newly globalized Indian companies and Western multinationals that have entered. Panagariya (2008) notes that "according to all available sources skilled wages in India have been rising faster than anywhere else in the world." Subramanian (2008) notes that these rises have been most prominent in the "export-oriented services." Thus, since the reforms of the early 1990s, the returns to skill have been rising, even as education is expanded, as we would expect following India's opening to the global economy.

Both business and government have responded to this increased demand for skill. Nambissan (2006) notes increased involvement from the corporate sector in developing independent initiatives and supporting government programs in elementary education. The government has been attempting to catch up with this demand and has been expanding education investment significantly; largely at the behest of these businesses' demands, between 1980 and 2000 education spending increased from 2.98 percent of GDP to 4.30 percent (Sinha, 2006). Where the government failed to catch up, an incipient private education sector developed, demonstrating that popular demand for education had been artificially suppressed by autarky. Tight labor markets in the high-tech industry led to increased private education training by major firms. Indeed, from 1998 to 1999, the government declared "a state of educational emergency" in response to skills gaps in the growing engineering sectors, setting up three new Indian Institutes of Technology (IIT) (Athreye, 2005). Despite this lag between demand and supply, an array of new education policies were unveiled during the 1990s and 2000s, often with the support of international agencies such as the World Bank.

Of particular importance to the transformation of Indian education was a set of policies introduced in the early 1990s, focusing on primary education. The District Primary Education Program (DPEP), begun in 1992, selected specific impoverished districts for targeted funding, with particular focus on areas with low female literacy. In 1995, the National Programme of Nutritional Support to Primary Education was launched, increasing its coverage of malnourished children from 33.4 million to 97.5 million by 1999 (Moulin, 2004). Finally the Education for All/Sarva Skiksha Abhiyan (SSA) program, begun in the mid-1990s and enacted in 2001, established a new series of target national enrollments for elementary education and sextupled elementary education funding, albeit relying on aid from the World Bank (Sadgopal, 2006; Bose and Vaugier-Chatterjee, 2004).

Two policy moves in the first years of the twenty-first century intensified this new governmental commitment to elementary education. Firstly, in 2002 a constitutional amendment passed to make elementary education a "fundamental right" – while Article 45 of the original Constitution expressed intent for the state to provide universal elementary education, it was nonbinding and hence not obeyed (Kumar, 2006). The 2002 change provided citizens the right to use the Indian court system to petition for access to education (Sinha, 2006). The second important development was the 2004 budget, which placed a 2 percent levy on all central government revenues to finance this commitment (Mehrotra, 2006). Thus, constitutional commitments have finally produced budgetary action in India.

A number of commentators and economists have suggested that as India globalizes, the demand for education could rise even further, with a consequent decline in illiteracy rates if these demands are met by public provision. Wood and Calandrino (2000) perform a series of econometric simulations in which they predict demand for skills if India were to become as open to trade as China.[7] They predict the following changes: a 23 percent decline in demand for illiterates, a 12 percent rise in the demand for primary education, a 31 percent increase in demand for secondary education, and a 64 percent rise in demand for college graduates. Do these increased demands for skill seem to be filtering through to policy? In fact, it does appear that supply is responding fairly successfully, though India is still overeducating at the secondary level vis-à-vis the primary level. Expansion is particularly focused on areas with large skills gaps, especially engineering. Revealingly, while no IIT had been established since the original five were established between 1950 and 1961, between 1994 and 2008 eight new IITs have been brought into being by the government, with another three in the pipeline.

The interplay between openness and education is also manifest at the subnational level in India.[8] Figure 3.4 shows that the trade orientation of subnational states appears to be positively related to literacy rates, at least when accounting for the unique case of Kerala (represented as "KE" in the figure). The figure shows the relationship in 2001 between openness and literacy rates in 2001 across fourteen Indian states.[9] The literacy data represent the proportion of literate adults in the state's population, coming from Kingdon et al. (2004) and ranging between under 50 percent (Bihar, represented in the figure as "BI") to over 90 percent (Kerala). The measure for openness is a ranking created by

---

[7] The comparison of India to China in terms of openness is hardly unimaginable. Indeed, in many ways it is surprising that India is actually less open than China given the generally positive correlation between democracy and openness.

[8] There are some caveats to this claim. While Indian states vary quite widely in their level of integration with the global economy, much trade *policy* (and indeed the "level of democracy") is nonetheless national, so we should examine subnational differences with some caution.

[9] India has twenty-eight states, but some were only created during the last several years (for example, Jharkhand was carved out of Bihar in 2000) and many others are extremely small. The fourteen states under analysis all have populations of over 20 million.

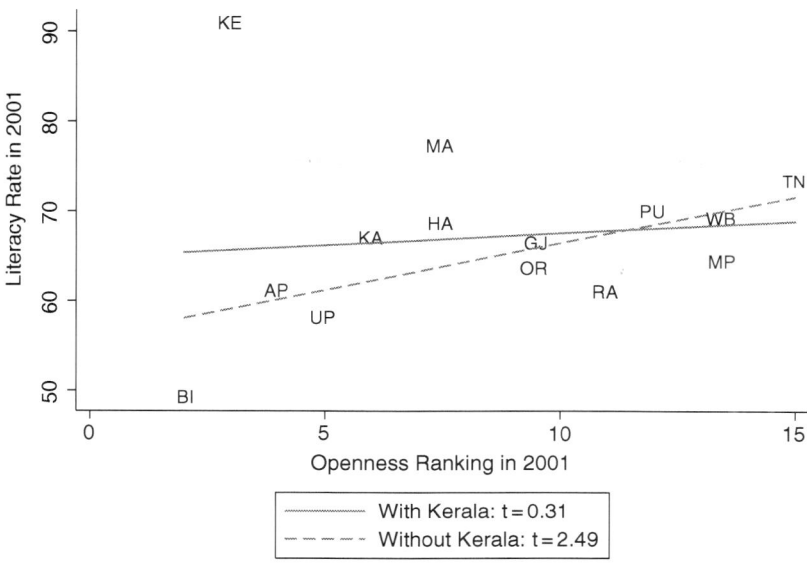

FIGURE 3.4. Literacy and Openness across the Indian States in 2001

Marjit, Kar, and Maiti (2006), where "openness" is defined as "consistency of [a state's] production structure with the trade pattern of the country"; in this sense, openness reflects the overall "export orientation" of the state's industrial structure. The ranking is ordered from least open (Bihar) to most open (Tamil Nadu, represented in the figure as "TN").

Overlaid on the plot are two regression lines, one with the case of Kerala included and the other without. Kerala, which has very high literacy rates but is relatively closed, is a highly influential outlier. Once Kerala is excluded, there is a statistically significant and positive relationship between openness and literacy among the other thirteen states. Bihar, Andhra Pradesh, and Uttar Pradesh all have low literacy rates and industrial structures specializing in import-competing industries, whereas Tamil Nadu, West Bengal and the Punjab have substantially higher literacy rates and are dominated by exporting sectors. As Arora, Gambardella, and Klepper (2005) note, education policies in these latter states were particularly important for the development of export markets in software and high-technology products. Across the Indian states, higher openness is associated with literacy rates around 15 percent points higher. There is also some evidence that states that have become more open over time have increased primary education spending as a proportion of state GDP (this latter variable is from Kingdon et al., 2004). Regressing the change in primary education spending on the change in openness rankings between 1991 and 1998 for all states, I find a positive effect, statistically significant at the 5 percent level, with a coefficient implying that a five-point improvement in a state's ranking would be associated with an increase in primary education spending of 0.3 percent of state GDP – a 10 percent increase in the average state's spending. Thus the relationship outlined in this section between openness and primary education spending in the developing world appears also to hold at the subnational level.

Two outliers stand out from the relationship between openness and education outcomes among the Indian states: Maharashtra and Kerala. The former can be partly explained by the dominance of a high-education, non-traded sector – finance – since Mumbai, Maharashtra's capital, is also India's financial capital. The story of Kerala – a closed state that is the country's educational leader – is more intriguing. Keralan politics have been dominated by the Left Democratic Front, a coalition headed by the Communist Party of India, which has regularly controlled local government since 1947 and "stood for a platform of equality and social development" (Kingdon et al., 2004). Communist dominance, as we saw earlier in the analysis of autocracies in Chapter 2, led to substantially greater investment in education than in other Indian states. However, it was also combined with heavy state regulation on the economy, especially external trade, and consequently Kerala remained, until the 1990s, relatively closed to trade. The combination of high education spending and a closed economy was not especially happy, in that returns to education were low and educated unemployment high, as the supply theory developed in the previous chapter would predict. Indeed, more than 1.6 million Keralans were forced to move abroad (Prakash, 1998) and millions more migrated to other Indian states. Thus, even though Communist control of government produced very high education spending, Keralan autarky produced a massive brain drain both domestically and internationally. As Zacahariah, Mathew, and Rajan (1999) note, as "the gap between the supply of educated persons and the opportunities available for their placement in [Kerala] worsened ... it became necessary and attractive for the educated Keralan youth to seek employment in the fast developing metropolitan areas in the other states." Thus, Kerala provides a cautionary tale for how economic closure can undermine the best-laid educational plans. As both India and Kerala have opened to the global economy since 1990, these patterns of educated unemployment and emigration have slowed and reversed.

We now turn to Malaysia, a country that much earlier combined a global orientation with educational success.

Malaysia

The Malaysian experience provides a dramatic contrast to India. Since the 1960s, Malaysia has spent over 5 percent of its national income on public education and at various points, including the early and late 1990s, over 7 percent of GDP, which would place it firmly within the top decile of global spenders, despite having fairly slow population growth and a middle-income status. However, for most of this period, Malaysia has been run in a moderately autocratic manner, with a powerful executive that is largely uncontrolled by the legislative and judiciary. Thus Malaysia is a mixed case in terms of our theoretical determinants of democracy: It has a full voting franchise; the legislature is fairly representative but not highly competitive, partly because the long-time ruling National Front coalition controls the press; and the executive is fairly unconstrained by the other branches of government. Thus, on a political level, Malaysia does not appear a prima facie likely candidate to spend large amounts on public education. We shall see that for two key reasons – Malaysia's peculiar ethnic politics and its early entry into the global economy – these unpromising initial conditions have nonetheless supported major investments in education.

Malaysia's experience with British colonialism was a mixed one. On the one hand, Malaysia's abundance of natural resources, particularly rubber, led to its becoming one of the wealthier colonies in the empire. On the other hand, colonial government was beneficial largely for the British and for the Chinese and Indians who migrated during the nineteenth century. The indigenous Malays, who had been largely agricultural, fared significantly less well and soon became a numeric and economic minority. As in most colonies, there was little direct interest in providing public services for the indigenous population; as Snodgrass (1998) notes, "colonial governments in Malaya provided little education.... [M]ost of what happened occurred through private rather than public initiative." Education, then, was mostly limited to the British and Chinese elite until the end of the nineteenth century. Even after some limited public provision to Malays began in 1870, it was very much restricted in its range, and the colonial authorities actively discouraged Malays from progressing beyond elementary education. Ethnically defined economic differences in Malaysia, in Snodgrass's (1998) terms, "in large part reflected differences in education opportunity." This dual economic and education dominance of the British and Chinese over the Malays was to be directly challenged following independence in 1957.

The run-up to independence was accompanied by a new set of demands for education by the Malays. The most important moment was the release of the Razak Report in 1956, which recommended that primary education be publicly offered to all children using a national curriculum. This goal was achieved with astonishing pace, particularly in comparison to other developing countries with similarly ambitious aims during the same period (for example, the Indian Second Five Year Plan). By 1960, 90 percent of Malaysian children were enrolled in primary schools. Between 1955 and 1967, education spending as a percentage of GDP increased from 1.8 percent to 5.5 percent, actually beating the target of 5 percent set in the First Malaysia Plan – in rather sharp contrast to India (Loong-Hoe, 1982).

It is worth noting that this expansion was contemporaneous with two important phenomena: firstly, increasing Malay control of the government, which led to a targeting of education at the previously undereducated Malay population; and secondly Malaysia's program of industrialization, which began as early as the late 1950s and led to increasing exports in manufactured goods and required a more educated workforce. Moreover, before 1969 Malaysia scored strongly in terms of the Polity index. These early steps in education spending came at a time of relative democracy for Malaysia, although the Chinese community was already discriminated against, since public support was only available for secondary schools that taught in Malay or English. More generally, Malaysia maintained an uneasy interethnic compromise, with the United Malay Nationalist Coalition governing together with representatives of the Malaysian Chinese Association and Malaysian Indian Association in a National Alliance that was nonetheless governed largely in the interests of the former group (Neher and Marlay, 1995). The political economy of Malaysia was commonly characterized as "politics for the Malays" and "economics for the Chinese" (Teik, 2006). Despite the advances in education investment following the Razak Report, by 1967 there were still proportionally nearly twice as many Malays without any formal education as Chinese and half as many with secondary education (Taylor, 2007).

The mismatch between economic and political power was uneasy and did not hold. The 1969 "May 13" race riots by the Malay population against the wealthier Chinese led to a political tightening, resulting in the current semi-autocratic regime and the development of Malaysia's well-known form of affirmative action aimed at the Malay population. Education spending, however, did not suffer in the turn to autocracy: Openness proved to be a substitute for democracy in terms of promoting public education spending in Malaysia. Moreover, this combined with a form of ethnic targeting of education that had expansionary effects on overall education spending due to the peculiarities of Malaysian ethnic politics. The policy of promoting the economic and educational status of the Malays was essentially a method of targeting toward a favored minority, which as we saw in Chapter 2 appears to be more common under autocracies. Indeed, this ethnic targeting was combined with targeting of resources to higher education, specifically for Malays, since passing exams in the Malay language in order to enter upper secondary education became compulsory in 1970. However, unlike the case in Chapter 2, where targeting tended to be toward higher education that favored a wealthy elite, the Malaysians were targeting higher education toward a poor but politically dominant minority. This outcome is in line with the general predictions of the formal model that a reduced selectorate will target education toward its own members, although the empirical relationship to income differs substantially from the statistical analysis in Chapter 2.

The peculiar ethnic logic of Malaysian autocracy combined with a shift toward developmental export-oriented industrialization to lead to further education investment. Like India, Malaysian industrialization was conducted through multi-year development plans; however, unlike India, in Malaysia's case, "human development through formal education has always been an important component" (Taylor, 2007). The two-decade New Economic Program (NEP), from 1970 to 1990 in Malaysia, had as one key aim "the development of a strong human resource orientation in order to be internationally competitive during the process of industrialization" (Mukherjee and Singh, 1995). The NEP mixed affirmative action in the realms of education and corporate ownership with the active promotion of export-oriented assembly industries as a way of galvanizing economic growth among the Malay community (Teik, 2006). For Mahathir

Mohammed, later to become Malaysia's premier, the two issues were directly connected; he explicitly argued that Malays did not yet have the skills necessary for the transition to export-driven industrialization (Mahathir, 1970).

Hence openness, affirmative action, and education would go hand in hand. In particular, the Malaysian government concentrated on apparel and the new electronics industry, both of which demanded at least basic educational skills and often command of English. Education provision was expanded to meet these demands, albeit in its somewhat distorted pro-Malay manner. Secondary enrollment by the end of the NEP was nearly 60 percent and higher education had enrollment rates of 7 percent (around half a typical European enrollment of the time). Higher education received substantial funding during the last years of the NEP as the state founded several new public universities and all-Malay residential schools (Teik, 2006). Potential enrollments could have been even higher, since these kinds of ethnic quotas in the tertiary system limited the access of Chinese and Indian students, who often studied abroad. Indeed, the percentage of tertiary students of Malay origin rose from 12 percent in 1970 to 70 percent in 1995 (Mahadevan, 2007).

The massive increase in Malaysian spending was not purely from increased enrollments but also from its targeting to the poorer Malays. By 1989, the poorest quintile of Malaysians received 36 percent of primary education funds and 32 percent of secondary education funds, far higher shares than their counterparts in similarly developed states (Basu and King, 2002). The push from globalization was, if anything, even stronger than the ethnic developmental aims of the government, since by the late 1970s skills gaps were concentrated in the exporting industries, pushing up skilled wages despite the increases in enrollment. This contrasts strongly with the wage decreases and educated unemployment that accompanied increased enrollment in autarkic India.

Once Mahathir Mohammed became premier in 1981, export-driven industrialization intensified further, with a push into heavy industry, particularly the auto industry (Teik, 2006) and the microelectronics industry, which constituted 53 percent of all manufactured exports to the OECD by 1990 (O'Connor, 1993). This required high levels of technology transfer, which in turn amplified the demand for skills in Malaysia. Much of this technology was imported directly from Japan, following Mahathir's "Look East" strategy. Mahathir was particularly inspired by the combination of export-oriented industrialization and human capital investment displayed in Taiwan and South Korea (Neher and Marlay, 1995). Over the period between 1985 and 1995, consequently, the share of manufactures in Malaysian exports increased from 26 percent to 71 percent (Ravenhill, 2008). As O'Connor (1993) notes, the growth in high-tech industries meant that "while semi-skilled labor was becoming less important an input, skilled engineering and technician labor was becoming more important."

The New Development Program, established in 1991, deemphasized affirmative action in order to respond to these export-led demands for skills. The key aim during the 1990s was to supply high-end skills that would facilitate the transition to production higher up the value chain. Taylor (2007) notes

that by this point, "high priority was given to expansion of the higher education sector in response to increasing demand for higher quality labor" arising
from the growing modern export sector. Skills shortages were now considered
a key threat to further development as international demand continued to
push up demands for skills. Even as enrollments expanded, Malaysia's very
high level of global integration meant that returns to skill remained constant
or even increased: Whereas the return to primary education in 1967 was 12.9
percent, by 2000 it was 35.4 percent, and returns for secondary and university
education also grew, albeit more moderately during this time (Taylor, 2007).
During the 1990s, emphasis was placed on more costly forms of education,
including a specialization in science and engineering as well as more vocational education, all of which were costlier than the standard education mix
of the pre-1990 years. As Malaysia crossed the threshold of developed country status, its skills profile and comparative advantage shifted toward tertiary
education.

Thus the export-driven development of Malaysian education followed
a "sequential" logic, moving from universal primary education in the 1950s
and 1960s, to mass secondary enrollments in the 1970s, to a focus on higher
education by the 1990s. Whereas in 1975 fewer than 5 percent of Malaysians
had attained a higher education, and fewer than 30 percent attained secondary education, over 80 percent of citizens had at least a primary education.
By 1995, with the push up the education ladder by the government, over 60
percent had secondary education and 10 percent higher education, and by 2004
three-quarters had completed secondary education, and nearly 20 percent had
higher education (Mahadevan, 2007). Taylor (2007) argues this development
pattern was directly related to export-led industrialization: The NEP tied a
move away from ISI to export orientation to "an increase in the supply of the
semi-skilled and skilled labor force"; from 1981 to 1990, the NEP combined
a shift to high-tech production with science education at the secondary level;
and the Sixth through Eighth Plans of 1991 to 2005 emphasized research and
development and rapidly expanding tertiary education in order to maintain
"productivity-driven growth" (Malaysia, 2001). This sequential pattern of
development, mimicking the skills profile of exports, was typical of the export-
oriented development adopted by East Asian states, as we will explore further
in the next section.

Yet, even with this massive increase in high-end skills, Malaysia still has
major skill shortages: A World Bank survey suggests that 70 percent of
Malaysian managers complain about an insufficient supply of graduates (World
Bank, 2005). As opposed to, for example, the case of India before the mid-
1990s, Malaysia actually lacks the demanded number of graduates. The government has responded fairly strongly to this demand, with the education
budget increasing to over 7 percent of GDP during the early 1990s, although
the Asian crisis knocked down spending temporarily. Whether the Malaysians,
having essentially achieved the government's aim of equalizing Malay and
Chinese economic power, will continue to rely on public investment is an open

question. In 1996, the Malaysians allowed private universities to form for the first time, partly in response to export-led demands for more skilled workers. Nonetheless, this is likely to remain a small percentage of overall spending, given that the government has expanded funding significantly for expensive technical education at the secondary level. The replacement of Mahathir with his UMNO colleague Abdullah Ahmad Badawi has seen the continued rise of education investment. Aggregate spending has further increased to 8.6 percent of GDP in 2004 (Mahadevan, 2007). Abdullah has also introduced substantial tuition schemes to aid poor pupils – now of all races – in transitioning from studying science and mathematics in Malay to doing so in English (Teik, 2006). This latter policy move is revealing. Malaysia remains quasi-autocratic and under the control of the UMNO – yet, the importance of the export sector is such that even the strong pro-Malay slant of education provision is making way for a direct, cross-ethnic focus, on English-based training for competing in world markets.[10]

Summing Up

At the start of the second millennium, both India and Malaysia were desperately trying to meet the skill demands of their nascent high-technology sectors, with varying degrees of success. But for the fifty years beforehand, these two states with similar levels of wealth and democracy in the 1950s had very dissimilar experiences in terms of education funding. Despite its ostensible democracy, India's elite-driven, autarkic economic system meant that the economic elite was threatened by expanded education provision and that domestic technological demands were not strong enough to force increased education spending. Despite its turn to authoritarianism in the 1960s, Malaysia became a regional leader in education spending, partly because its autocracy favored the relatively poorer Malays (and hence targeting education spending was more costly than is typical since an ethnic majority rather than an economic minority was being targeted), and partly in response to a highly export-oriented economy that had voracious skills needs.

Why did regime type not overwhelm the effect of openness? One possible answer is that both India and Malaysia have mixed regime types. The stultifying impact of one-party rule and the caste system on education could explain India's failure to meet rhetoric with education policy (Weiner, 1990). Similarly Malaysia's Malay political elite preferred to target education toward the poorer Malay population and away from the Chinese economic elite, thus weakening the impact of authoritarianism. Still, these structural explanations varied weakly across time and thus fail to explain the *changes* in education spending in these states, particularly India, which retains the caste system but has opened

---

[10] Which is not to say that pro-Malay spending or quotas in hiring have disappeared. Abdullah's first Five Year Plan, released in 2006, emphasized redistribution from the Chinese to the Malays, though also for the first time to the Indian minority (Pepinsky, 2008).

its borders. These cases, then, which appear to lie off the typical path of open democracies and autarkic autocracies, help us to see how the mechanisms laid out in the previous chapter were still manifest in these very unusual cases.

3.4 EAST ASIA AND LATIN AMERICA: RETHINKING THE DEVELOPMENT STORY

The Indian and Malaysian cases are revealing for what they say more broadly about developmental strategies adopted by states in the second half of the twentieth century. A vast literature exists on the political economy of development, typically contrasting the stories of stagnant growth in Latin America since the 1950s with the stunning rise of a set of East Asian countries from the poorest in the world in 1950 to first-tier economic status by the 1990s (for a review, see Haggard, 1990). A set of competing arguments explaining this striking divergence is commonly drawn upon in the literature; in particular, while some scholars emphasize the difference between the outward-looking trade policies of East Asia and the import substitution policies of Latin America, others emphasize the activist role of the "developmental" state in the former region.[11] In this section, I revisit the accepted wisdom on the differences between Latin American and East Asian development, arguing that education policy ties these standard stories together. To support this story, I compare the educational experiences of two paradigmatic states: the import-substituting, "weak state" of Brazil and the export-oriented, "activist" South Korea.

Before moving to the country cases, I begin by briefly recapping the developmental debate among political economists. The standard story told by neoclassical economists focuses on the opposed trade policies of East Asia and Latin America (Belassa, 1988; Harberger, 1988; Krueger, 1985). Although both regions began the postwar era with fairly similar trade policies – typically referred to as "early import substitution industrialization" strategies – by the mid-1960s, the East Asian states had moved to a mixed model combining tariffs and quotas with export processing zones and export subsidies (Haggard, 1990). The gap between the regions' policies widened through the 1970s and 1980s, with Latin American states attempting to move up the production ladder through "late period ISI" strategies, wherein high-technology companies in computing and aerospace were sheltered from foreign competition, whereas the East Asian states focused on selling medium-technology goods to the American and Japanese markets. During this period, though the countries of East Asia and Latin America adopted sharply differing trade policies, their political regimes actually converged, in both cases on a form of technocratic authoritarianism, typically under military control. Thus, this period is one where the sharpest difference between the regions lies in their economic, not political, openness. Culminating with the World Bank's seminal report in 1993, *The East Asian*

---

[11] This does not, of course, exhaust the set of arguments purporting to explain the different growth paths of the regions: others include land inequality (Kay, 2002) and institutional structure (Rodrik, 2000).

Miracle (World Bank, 1993), the mainstream development community settled on this distinction in trade policy as the key explanation for divergent growth. East Asian industries, exposed to international markets, were competitive and growing. Latin American firms, sheltered from competition, were outdated and stagnating.

The early 1990s saw the emergence of an alternative argument, which took on further momentum as the East Asian Crisis of 1997 undermined the view that an export-led policy alone would secure stable development. A number of authors, among them Evans (1995), Wade (1990), and Amsden (1989), dissented from the view that East Asian success could be explained as the result of a non-interfering state that let the market rule. Instead, they argued first that the East Asian states were more protectionist and the Latin American states more accommodating than met the eye; and second, that export orientation was in any case a goal set and actively supported by the state. Activist states managed development by establishing export zones, privileging certain forms of production and financing, and, most critically for our purposes, focusing on the composition of the labor force. Latin American states, conversely, were unable to channel capital effectively, were often subject to capture by major Western multinationals, and without the bureaucratic capacity to build a modern workforce. This approach rejected the simple distinction between trade policies, arguing that export orientation was an outcome of different developmental strategies and growth trends rather than their cause.

I do not attempt to adjudicate between these competing explanations. Rather, I argue that education provides a common, but understudied, thread woven through both developmental stories. Education provision, both in its aggregate level and the composition of that spending, was necessarily determined by the developmental strategies of policy makers, and in the case of East Asia the hand of the state was as heavy with education as it was with other strands of state activism such as access to finance and subsidies. Yet, these developmental strategies were predicated on access to international markets that forced up demand for education and permitted supply to expand without undermining skilled wages. The "sequential" pattern of East Asian education provision, for example, was a decision made by a rather activist state but was viable precisely because of the trade strategies that it accompanied.

Before turning to the cases, it is useful to see the aggregate picture of how the regions diverged in terms of their education spending from 1960 on. Figure 3.5 demonstrates the development of education spending in East Asian and Latin American countries from 1960 to 2000. The vertical axis displays the percentage of national income devoted to public spending on education divided by the percentage of the population under the age of fifteen. This variable measures the *intensity* of educational investment, netting out the "automatic" element produced by demographic change. Although the data are somewhat incomplete, I am able to track the education investment of three East Asian states – South Korea, Malaysia, and Singapore – and six Latin American states – Argentina, Brazil, Colombia, Paraguay, Peru, and

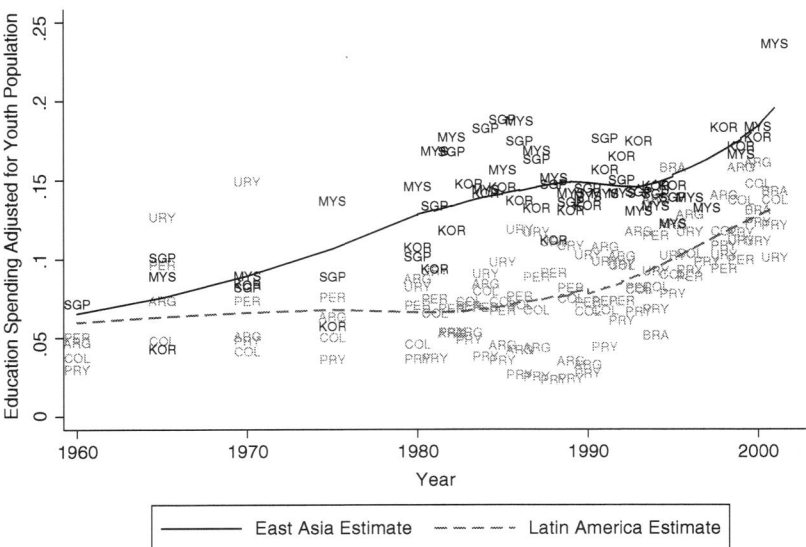

FIGURE 3.5. Comparing East Asian to Latin American Education Spending

Argentina. The two lines on the graph are lowess smoothing curves that fit a moving average for each region.

In 1960, most of these states had fairly similar levels of economic development; indeed, a number of the Latin American countries – for example Argentina, Colombia, and Uruguay – were substantially richer than the East Asian states. Furthermore, through the 1960s, when both Latin American and East Asian states had fairly similar development strategies focusing on import substitution, their levels of educational investment were quite comparable. However, during the 1970s and 1980s, the patterns diverge dramatically. As Latin American countries deepened their ISI strategy, their East Asian counterparts shifted toward an activist export-oriented strategy that (a) galvanized demand for a mass moderate-skill workforce and (b) prevented a collapse in the skill premium accompanying educational expansion. It is noticeable that between 1970 and 1990, Latin American investment in education, adjusted for demographics, was essentially flat, whereas East Asian states averaged a near-doubling of intensity. Of further interest is the surge in Latin American educational investment starting in the early 1990s, which was, not coincidentally, the period of democratization *and* liberalization of their economies. Since 1990, the gap between Latin American and East Asian investment has thus narrowed substantially, though it remains sizable. Moving away from this simple aggregate analysis and to develop this story more closely, I now turn to analyze the experience of Brazil and contrast it with that of South Korea.

Brazil

The titles of major studies of the Brazilian education system reflect a sense of despair: Birdsall and Sabot's edited volume *Opportunity Foregone* (1996); Brock and Schwartzman's *The Challenges of Education in Brazil* (2004); even David Plank's more optimistically titled *The Means of Our Salvation* (1996) opens with the chapter title, "Why Does Brazil Lag behind in Educational Development?" Answers to that question are legion in the existing literature: clientilism, the power of the Catholic Church, ethnic heterogeneity, and poverty. These are certainly all retarding forces on Brazilian education. However, Brazil's postwar authoritarianism and strategy of import substituting industrialization together provide the most compelling explanation for its substandard and misdirected investment in public education.

As Plank (1996) notes, Brazil has declared a constitutional right to free primary education since its independence in 1822. However, perhaps unsurprisingly, the authoritarian Empire of Brazil did not keep to such promises. It was not until the Revolution of 1930 that the central government began active involvement with education policy and even today the state lags behind most of its low-performing Latin American peers in literacy, spending, and enrollment. This poor performance has endured despite the efforts of educational modernizers, the *escolanovistas*, whose 1932 "Manifesto dos Pioneiros da Educacao Nacional" was the founding document of educational reform in Brazil (Plank, 1996). The manifesto argued that the national government was obliged to establish universal compulsory secular schooling at both the primary and secondary levels, and their demands appeared to be heeded by the post-revolutionary government, which reaffirmed the right to education in 1934 and, importantly, committed federal and subnational governments to spending a designated percentage of their revenues on education. Thus Brazil's democratic interlude produced a surge of state involvement in education, as in the case of the Philippines. However, in 1937 Getulio Vargas organized a coup and declared the *Estado Novo*, an authoritarian regime that rewrote the constitution to deemphasize public investment on education, particularly at the secondary level. Instead, as Plank (1996) notes, Vargas "deemed public action to be supplementary to the efforts of families and private agencies including the Catholic Church." Vargas's policies even led to reducing primary schooling in rural areas from four to three years in length (Lawlor, 1985).

The conclusion of the Second World War led to the deposal of Vargas, who soon, however, morphed into a populist democrat and returned to power through election rather than coup in 1950. Democracy meant the reimposition of the constitutional requirement for set levels of education funding (Lawlor, 1985). However, the ability of the state to translate such aims into action was delayed by debate over the Basic Education Law between the staunchly pro-clerical and anti–mass education supporters of the *Estado Novo* and their secular democratic rivals. By the time the law was passed, it was only three years until, in 1964, the military overthrew the democratic government, beginning two decades of military rule during which the Brazilian economy was most profoundly influenced by the economic strategy of import substituting industrialization. During this period, the Brazilian polity in many ways resembled those of the authoritarian East Asian states, with political and civil liberties repressed though not eliminated. Yet, the education stories of Brazil and, for example, South Korea began to diverge dramatically during the 1960s and 1970s.

Import substitution as an economic strategy required mimicking the industrial structure of already developed countries, in order to wean Brazil off its imports. Haggard (1990) identifies three historical phases of import substitution. The first phase (ISI 1) was shared by countries in both Latin America and East Asia. This set of policies involved the production of consumer goods, sheltered from the international market by an array of tariffs and subsidies. Haggard identifies this period as lasting from 1935 to 1955 in Brazil, with the East Asian states adopting it marginally later (between 1945 and the early 1960s). From 1955 onward, whereas the East Asian countries would selectively liberalize trade and promote exports, the Brazilian government of Juscelino Kubitschek deepened the state's support of the import substituting sector (ISI 2), with the establishment of the National Development Council promoting vertical integration of companies key to this process. As in India, the deepening of ISI was not accompanied by increased education spending: As Lawlor (1985) notes, "by 1961 and the end of the Kubitschek presidency... Brazil had a massive deficit and had still not embarked on any noticeable programme of social or educational development." By 1965, following the military coup, Brazil had entered the third stage of import substituting development (ISI 3), according to Haggard (1990). This focused on a "continued deepening" of investment: a focus on heavy industry, financed by foreign borrowing, with gradual attempts made to export in these industries. Industry remained sheltered from foreign competition and increasingly dependent on expensive energy imports, for which the Brazilian economy had little foreign currency to exchange.

This development strategy brought about a debt crisis from the mid-1980s that proved terminal for the military government, and indeed for the Brazilian economy as a whole, until the mid-1990s. And this crisis had harsh consequences for public spending of all varieties. Yet, education was not a casualty of the debt crisis per se but of two decades of misguided policy from the mid-1960s. Education did not suffer from complete neglect; rather, the attention of the military government was focused inopportunely. The government introduced reforms of higher education in 1968 and of primary and secondary education in 1971 (Plank, 1996). These reforms promised significantly more than was delivered – not for the first time in the history of Brazilian education policy. While compulsory primary schooling was extended from four to eight years, no attempts were made to increase funding to basic education, producing a striking surge in dropout rates: Whereas over 50 percent of students completed the four-year primary sequence in 1970, by 1980 only 19 percent were completing the eight-year sequence – in other words, the de jure extension of primary education was not matched by de facto action (Birdsall et al., 1996). This paltry graduation rate remained low even following the transition to democracy, amounting to only 38 percent in 1996. The reforms that the military government made to the secondary education sector – eliminating the distinction between technical and academic streams – which on paper appeared progressive, actually mattered little since the proportion of students actually entering secondary education remained stubbornly low. The fiction of removing the "dual track" system of technical and academic streams was abandoned by 1982 (Plank, 1996).

Funding priorities remained misguided at the aggregate level. The military government "significantly reduced the share of the federal budget that went to education, while simultaneously reducing the shares of state and municipal governments in total tax revenues" (Plank, 1996), thereby leading to a state of endemic underfunding. Haar (1977) estimates a decline in education's share of the federal budget from 10.7 percent in 1969 to 6.6 percent in 1973. The composition of spending was slanted toward higher education and away from basic education; by 1980, the share of expenditures devoted to basic education by the federal Ministry of Education had declined to 7 percent. Contemporaneously, the share of overall funding (federal, state, and municipal combined) going to tertiary education was rising, from 18 percent in 1975 to 26 percent in 1989. Enrollments jumped from 278,000 in 1968 to 800,000 in 1974 (Lawlor, 1985). Combined with the pattern of upper-middle-class children attending private primary and secondary schools but taking the lion's share of publicly funded university places, the Brazilian education system became ever more regressive in regard to socioeconomic background. This pattern of favoring the tertiary sector over universal primary education is, I have argued, emblematic of both autocracies and autarchic states. Ames (1987) argues that the funding of higher education was an explicitly political strategy aimed at securing support for the military regime from the upper-middle classes: Regressive redistribution was firmly in the elite's political interest.

The role of import substitution industrialization in retarding education expansion in Brazil has been noted by observers of Brazilian education policy. Birdsall (1996), mirroring some of the arguments made in Chapter 2 on the demand effects of globalization, argues that "because Brazil adopted an inward-looking development strategy, the demands for educated labor (hence the returns to investment in education and the household demand for education) were not as high as they might have been had Brazil's economy been more open and more oriented toward exports." In particular, Brazilian labor demand was bimodal: a large demand for unskilled agricultural or mining labor and a small demand for highly educated labor in the sheltered industrial sector. Missing was demand for a mass moderately educated workforce such as that which developed in East Asia. Furthermore, import substitution created its own political obstacle to change, since workers in the sheltered industrial sector accrued sizable scarcity rents that they were desirous to protect either from trade liberalization or the widespread expansion of education.

While the authoritarian nature of the Brazilian government certainly supported the favoritism shown to the university sector, even after democratic transition in 1986 the pattern continued. In fact, between 1986 and 1990, the first four years of democratic government, the percentage of federal education funding devoted to higher education actually rose from 50 percent to

65 percent, while funding of basic education declined by 39 percent (Plank, 1996). Clearly democracy was not an immediate salve to the imbalance in funding, accompanied as it was by a continued lack of trade liberalization. It was not until 1990, under the Fernando Collor de Mello administration, that Brazil began a fundamental liberalization of trade, with tariffs reduced from an average of 41 percent to 17.7 percent in three years (Baer, 2008). Exports as a proportion of national income rose from 8.20 percent in 1990 to 18 percent by 2004.

The liberalization of the Brazilian economy provoked increased demand for education, to which the government has responded. Between 1991 and 2002, the gross enrollment rate in secondary education expanded from 40 percent to 75 percent (Guimares de Castro and Tiezzi, 2004). Despite the expansion of education, trade liberalization increased demand for skilled labor substantially, meaning that the skill premium remained steady (Arbache, Dickersson, and Green, 2004). Fernando Enrique Cardoso, president between 1995 and 2002, emphasized that education was his number one social priority (Brown and Hunter, 2004). Under Paulo Renato de Souza, his minister of education, funding targets and – perhaps more importantly – funding floors have been established, reducing the gap between expressed aims and achieved outcomes in education spending (Schwartzman, 2004). Souza explicitly pushed for a reversal in Brazil's traditional funding priorities that privileged tertiary over primary education (Power and Roberts, 2000).

This strategy met with some success. For example, while universal primary enrollment had been achieved by the early 1990s, graduation rates from primary school lagged substantially, at around 60 percent. However, from 1995 to 2000, primary graduation rates finally started moving toward universality, growing at 12 percent per annum (Castro, 2000). Most important was the FUNDEF program, which subsidizes education in poorer schools, providing federal matching to municipalities that cannot meet the federal minimum of 315 reals per student. This program has led to an 89 percent increase in funding in the impoverished North-East region and a 47 percent increase in the North. So successful has the program been that the Luiz Inacio Lula de Silva's government has proposed a constitutional amendment to extend it further (Melo, 2008) Overall, Brazilian education funding has finally shifted to a more fiscally progressive balance.

Summing up the Brazilian experience more generally, the key pattern emerging over both autocratic and democratic regimes since the 1930s has been an overall underfunding of education combined with a misallocation of educational resources. In particular, basic education has been largely neglected whereas higher education has received the lion's share of funding. Arguably, import substitution industrialization created an "ends against the middle" pattern, with the small, sheltered educated class opposing education spending that might reduce their rents and a large group of poor citizens who could be bought off with populist redistributive policies. Lacking has been a sustained expansion of primary and, in particular, secondary education to the bulk of the population. While democracy in Brazil has finally produced a shift in this direction, it is striking that such a change did not manifest itself until trade policy as well as regime type had liberalized. Under the transitional government of Collor, the balance between higher and primary education actually shifted in the former's direction. Thus Brazil, along with many of its Southern Cone neighbors, faces a substantial challenge in catching up with other developing states, whose educational policies were more clearly focused on broad-based skills. In particular, Brazil still greatly lags behind South Korea, a country much poorer than the Latin American norm in 1950 but which has essentially converged with the developed world, both economically and educationally.

South Korea

While analyses of Brazilian education accentuate the negative, the literature on South Korean education has a remarkably different tone. South Koreans are commonly considered to be idiosyncratically education-obsessed, with some estimates of the proportion of South Korean resources spent on public and private education – including tutoring – topping 15 percent (Seth, 2002). Yet, while South Korea's apparently pro-education Confucian culture has been a constant since the early twentieth century, its achievements in education provision have shown dramatic growth, suggesting that, culture aside, other forces have been at work in terms of promoting educational investment. In this case history, I argue that South Korea's educational experience since 1945 has been tied closely to its changing trade policies, as well as the experience of land reform in 1950. In particular, South Korea education followed what Seth (2002) terms a "sequential" strategy: South Korea expanded primary education dramatically during the 1960s, middle-school enrollment in the 1970s, high school enrollment in the 1980s, and university enrollment in the 1990s. This sequential wave closely tracked South Korea's move from first-stage ISI (1955 to 1965) to early export orientation (1965 to 1975), heavy industry export orientation (1975 to 1990), and finally to high-tech export orientation (1990 onward). Each stage of trade-induced industrial development matched the particular level of education provided by the government: As South Korea's comparative advantage shifted toward more human capital–intensive production, the focus of funding shifted up the educational ladder. Figure 3.6 demonstrates the pattern of sequential development of each educational sector, tracking how many thousand students were enrolled at particular points in time since 1960. It is noteworthy that most of this development occurred under autocratic rule, since a freely elected democratic government was not elected until 1993. Hence economic openness, rather than political openness, appears to have been the driving force behind South Korea's pattern of educational development.

The story of sequential development begins under the administration of Korea's first major postwar government, that of Syngman Rhee from 1948 to 1960. Rhee headed the First Korean Republic formed upon the ending of the postwar U.S. occupation in August 1948 and inherited the Korean constitution promulgated by the newly elected National Assembly a month earlier. As was

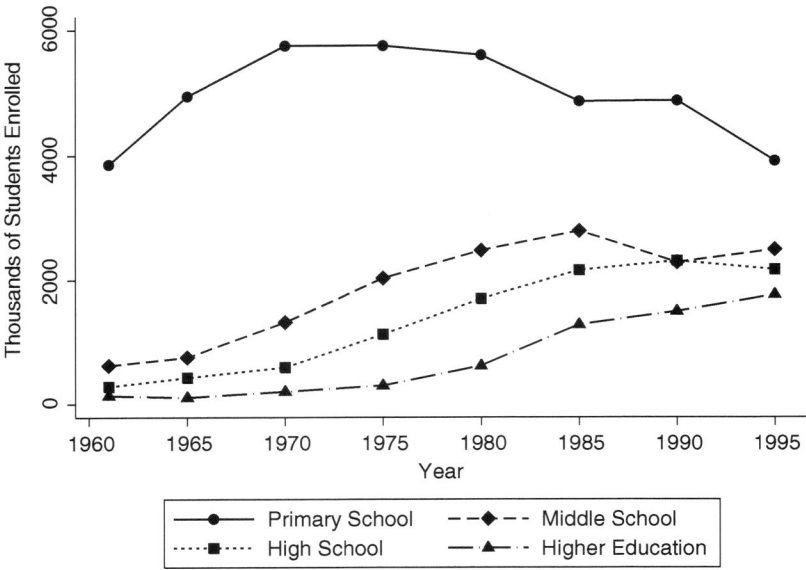

FIGURE 3.6. Sequential Enrollment in Education in Korea
Source: Seth (2002).

the case with many constitutions of newly independent states in the postwar era, the Korean Constitution aimed to address educational issues and declared that elementary education be both universal and compulsory in Korea (Article XVI), with the further stipulation that private elementary education be forbidden. Thus, as had been the case with the Philippines, the political liberalization produced by the end of Japanese colonization (Korea had been under official Japanese control since 1910), followed by American occupation, produced a fairly progressive statutory environment for education. Whereas less than 40 percent of Koreans attended primary education under Japanese rule in 1942 (and fewer than 5 percent went on to middle school [Sorenson, 1994]), following the war, the Rhee government quickly drew up developmental plans for expanding primary education – the 1949 six-year plan intended on achieving 95 percent enrollment in primary education by 1956. Such plans were laudable, and indicative of a political loosening following the stifling Japanese administration, even though Korea remained a somewhat authoritarian republic under Rhee. But achieving these goals was scuppered by a variety of factors: a massive shortage of teachers, endemic poverty, limited government funds, and few classrooms (Adams and Gottlieb, 1993).

And these preexisting problems were clearly worsened by the advent of the Korean War just months after Rhee took office. The war caused massive dislocations and around 80 percent of all educational facilities were damaged or destroyed (Seth, 2002). Surprisingly, while progress toward the initial six-year plan's goal of 95 percent elementary enrollment was delayed, a new six-year plan with the same aim begun in 1954 was successful. Korea moved from having just over 2 million children enrolled in 1953 to 3.6 million by 1960 (Republic of Korea, Ministry of Education, 1963). How did Korea manage to achieve that goal, particularly given the destruction of war? Some potential candidate explanations fail to pass muster – while the Americans gave over $2 billion of aid to the Koreans for domestic development, very little of this was targeted toward education – less than $100 million (Seth, 2002). Furthermore, cultural explanations are not especially helpful in understanding the timing of this massive increase. Instead, the reason for Korea's success in primary education enrollment during the 1950s appears to be related to the aims of the Rhee government to secure popular support. While the First Korean Republic was hardly a paradigmatic democracy, its limited accountability did at least force recognition of popular demands for education. Seth (2002) notes the emphasis on primary education was partly for "economic reasons: primary education was less expensive to implement." However, the "state policy prioritizing primary education was also justified with the slogan 'uniformity of education'." Thus the Rhee government was keen to underline the universal and uniform nature of primary education as a way of promoting its democratic bona fides. Other levels of education slowly expanded too throughout the 1950s but with less pace and, in particular, with little state funding, in sharp contrast to the Latin American countries and India, where developmental emphasis was placed on acquiring higher skills.

In fact, the Rhee government actively discouraged investment in higher education. The government established regulations governing universities in 1955, which set standards for admission, faculty qualifications, and university governance. The university sector faced further restrictions later that year, when Rhee issued a Presidential Decree on the Establishment of College and University Standards, which set actual quotas on admission to try to prevent further expansion of the higher education sector. In 1957, this applied to thirty-two of fifty-two colleges, and by 1958 the law applied to every university or college in South Korea, reducing overall enrollment by just over 1 percent. Part of the concern was that, in the absence of a fully developed external market, graduates from these institutions would be unable to find jobs. Indeed only 40 percent of graduates in the late 1950s could find jobs requiring a college education.

This provides an interesting contrast to India. Like India in the postwar era, South Korea lacked the ability (and in the 1950s the intention) to sell the product of these high-skilled workers abroad; consequently, expansion of higher education led directly to educated unemployment or job mismatch. However, unlike the Indians, the South Koreans resolved this problem by literally cutting back enrollment and focusing their resources on primary (and later secondary) education. Why did they make this restrictive but ultimately beneficial decision? Part of the answer lies in the gradual tightening of the political environment. Rhee's rule during the 1950s was increasingly authoritarian and his overthrow in 1960 did not lead to democracy but rather further political repression under the military government of General Park Chung Hee, which began in 1961. Since South Korea was under authoritarian control, the state could essentially make higher education policy by fiat, permitting them to install quotas. However, there remains a further puzzle. Most authoritarian states, as we saw in Chapter 2, tend to increase elite-targeted higher education and disfavor primary and secondary education for the masses. Yet Rhee and Park's governments both did the reverse. What explains this surprising turn of events?

The answer lies in the close connection between education and trade policy under the Park regime: the paradigmatic "developmental state." Park's strategy for economic growth, an aim he held not purely for altruistic reasons but also as a means of retaining popular support for the military government, involved transitioning to industrialized status through promoting a massive growth in exports. Unlike many authoritarian leaders, Park actively promoted education and moreover did so by focusing on basic education rather than on the dictator's usual preference, higher education. Such concern did not always meet its match in government funding – like most authoritarian governments, Park's regime kept taxation rates low. But the government was able to expand primary and secondary enrollment by fiat and similarly to limit enrollment at higher levels of education. The overall strategy was, in Seth's (2002) terms, to create a "clearly defined pyramid," by increasing the number of children receiving basic education and reducing numbers at higher levels. In the latter case, this was attempted through a 1961 plan to cut the number of students in higher education in half, from 125,000 to 64,000 in three years. This plan did not prove simple to implement, and from 1963 until 1968 the government found itself setting strict quotas that it would rescind annually, consequently pushing overall enrollment in higher education up to 164,000 by 1966. However, by the late 1960s, the government was having more success in limiting enrollments, actively punishing universities for over-enrollment, and managed to check any increases throughout the 1970s. Such control was facilitated by Park's Yushin Constitution of 1971, which granted him near-dictatorial powers and enabled him to literally police the degree to which universities were abiding by the quotas.

Instead, the Park regime envisaged expansion coming in the middle tier of the educational pyramid. In the First Five Year Developmental Plan of the new military government (from 1962 to 1966), a target of 100 percent enrollment in primary education was envisaged. By 1970, this ambition had been achieved. Consequently, with primary enrollment universal and quotas established in higher education, the Park government entered the 1970s with its ambitions firmly focused on achieving universal secondary education. In particular, in tandem with the government's post-Yushin developmental strategy of developing South Korean heavy industry, Park was desirous to alter the structure of South Korean education to concentrate more heavily on vocational training, in contrast to the classic liberal education favored traditionally. There was an explicit "movement to scientificize the whole people" (Sorenson, 1994). In 1974, in connection with the push to heavy industry, the government actually mandated that all major industrial concerns provide systematic training programs. Contemporaneously, the government produced an Industrial Education Promotion Law, which singled out technical high schools and vocational schools for extra funding to support training aimed at specific industries. In fact, vocational education doubled as a proportion of the state's education budget between 1970 and 1979. Thus, in the realm of vocational education, we can most clearly see education and trade policy hand in glove. However, despite the Park regime's intent, vocational education, while expanding significantly, remained, as in most advanced industrial countries, viewed as a second-best option and enrollment in academic high schools increased at roughly the same rate as in vocational schools.

Putting together the expansion of vocational and academic secondary education, we see that, although the composition of secondary education never quite met the government's ambitions, its overall size of enrollment certainly did, helping to underpin South Korea's transition from low-skill manufacturing to heavy industry to high-technological exports between the 1970s and 1990s. The overall growth in secondary education began early in the Park era, with the announcement in 1961 that middle-school entrance exams would be abolished in 1963 and compulsory education extended to nine years (Sorenson, 1994). The government failed to meet that target but did abolish the entrance exams in 1968 (the same year it not coincidentally began really cracking down on higher education enrollment) and by 1978 middle-school enrollment was essentially universal. By that point, and indeed from the early 1970s, the state was focusing its efforts on increasing high school enrollments (with particular focus on vocational training). By the 1980s, given the surge in high school enrollment in the late 1970s (which was itself propelled by the expansion of middle schooling from 1968), the government had even backed off restricting higher education enrollments. In 1981, the government moved from admissions quotas to graduation quotas, allowing a 30 percent increase in admissions (Park, 2007). And starting in the early 1990s, the government promoted diversification in the higher education sector, explicitly in response to changing export strategies. Thus, although South Korea's government was as authoritarian in the 1960s and 1970s as that of Brazil, at this time it focused on universal education aimed at the lower levels of the educational pyramid, in stark contrast to the Brazilian obsession with high-end skills. As South Korea's trade and industrial policies changed, gradually climbing the value-added ladder, by the 1990s the South Korean government was focusing on expansion at higher levels of the educational pyramid.

Did economic openness dominate political closure in South Korea? Certainly when one looks at enrollment, it would appear so. However, in terms of funding, the South Korean government appeared less distant from the autocratic norm. Although primary education was fully public in the sense that private schools were banned at this level, the levels of actual state funding rarely kept up with the statutes on enrollment – essentially the government created an unfunded mandate. To make up the difference, schools relied heavily on supplementary fees that were paid either by families or more collectively by parent teacher associations. In the 1950s, these latter organizations often covered nearly 50 percent of overall funds, even at the primary level (Sorenson, 1994).

The government tried to ban them in 1961, but given the state's incapacity and unwillingness to fund education fully to meet its enrollment targets, they were reintroduced in 1970. Along with the PTAs came extra-school education in the form of private tuition during the 1970s. While the administration of Chun Doo Hwan tried to ban private tuition in 1980, driven underground it remained a large proportion of overall educational expenses. Indeed, by the transition to democracy in 1993, total spending on education from all sources was 12 percent of GDP, only one-third from the central government. Of the total spending of $47.5 billion, $21 billion came from private fees and $6.5 billion from private tuition. South Korea was in one sense a world leader in overall education spending, yet in terms of money from the public purse it remained on the low end of industrial nations, spending only just over 4 percent of GDP (Lee, 2001). Thus open autocracy had two effects. On the one hand, openness drove demand for skills and permitted high levels of enrollment without growth in educated unemployment or a collapsing skill premium (particularly in secondary education). However, on the other hand, the authoritarian government was loath to administer a redistributionist education policy that would heavily tax the elite to pay for the education of the poor. Hence, while overall enrollment was high, spending was only moderate, albeit channeled toward South Korea's comparative advantage (sequentially from primary to secondary education).

The transition to democracy did see a corresponding change in the level of fiscal redistribution undertaken through the education system. Kim Young Sam, in power from 1993 to 1998, pledged to increase the public share of education funding and in 1995 the National Assembly approved a 25 percent increase in the education budget and a push toward overall public spending of 5 percent of national income.[12] Kim Dae Jung, perhaps South Korea's first truly "democratic" leader, pledged a further increase to 6 percent of GDP on assuming office in 1998. However, the Asian Financial Crisis of that year delayed achieving that goal. By 2003, Korea had achieved around 5 percent of GDP in public funding for education, placing it just below the OECD average. Kim Dae Jung also recommended a total ban on all forms of private tuition, but the Constitutional Court ruled in 2000 that such a ban would be unconstitutional. Whereas the military regime had arguably attempted to ban private tuition as a way of shoring up state control of the content of education, for the Kim Dae Jung administration the private tuition sector was an affront to redistributive goals. Either way, the large private sector in South Korea remains thriving, to the point that overall education spending may have far passed the point of efficiency, or even redistributive "social justice," leading to a generic cost creep somewhat reminiscent of that of American health care. Despite the cost inefficiencies of South Korean education, it has nonetheless underpinned South Korea's transition to a high-technology export orientation. Given that

---

[12] Note that this magnitude of spending increase is similar to the estimated effect of transitioning to democracy from the statistical regressions in Chapter 2.

it faced the same political barriers to the expansion of education as its Latin American counterparts, the guiding force behind the South Korean education boom appears to have been its open economic strategy and its sequential development of schooling.

3.5 DUAL SHOCKS: SOUTHERN EUROPE JOINS THE EUROPEAN UNION

Typically, changes in regime type and orientation toward the international economy accompany one another. Trade policy changes are often a large component of the panoply of reforms that take place following democratization. We saw, for example, in the Philippines that political and economic liberalization both had positive impacts on education spending in the post-Marcos era. Given this collinearity, it is often hard within individual cases to pull apart the differential effects of democracy and openness on education spending: There is every risk that we will misattribute causal importance to one factor over another. This section attempts to remedy this problem by examining a set of cases where shocks to regime type and to economic openness happened in identifiably different periods: the Southern European states, Portugal, Spain, and Greece, who all experienced episodes of democratization in the 1970s and joined the European community in the 1980s. In all three cases, though particularly in the Iberian states, we see two separate jumps in education spending, one following each shock.

The 1970s saw a wave of political liberalization across Southern Europe, with first Portugal, then Spain and Greece, exiting from authoritarian military rule. Huntington (1991) termed this the "third wave of democratization," which culminated in the wave of democratizations in Eastern Europe at the end of the Cold War. All three countries had extremely low levels of education spending by European standards, less than 2 percent of national income, partly as a consequence of autocracy and partly because of the long-standing traditions of church involvement in education, which mitigated against public provision and emphasized education as an instrument of cultural socialization rather than economic development. Following democratization in the mid-1970s, all three states saw increases in education spending (though the Greek increase was fairly minimal) before they joined the European Union in the 1980s – in the Greek case in 1981, and for Spain and Portugal in 1986. This second event also appears to have set off a series of increases in education funding, with all three states sharply improving funding and converging towards the European mean.

Portugal

In the 1960s, Portugal had arguably the most backward educational system in Western Europe. Indeed, it was not until the mid-1960s that the country made public education available to all children between the ages of six and twelve. Even then, under the Salazar regime implementation of education policies

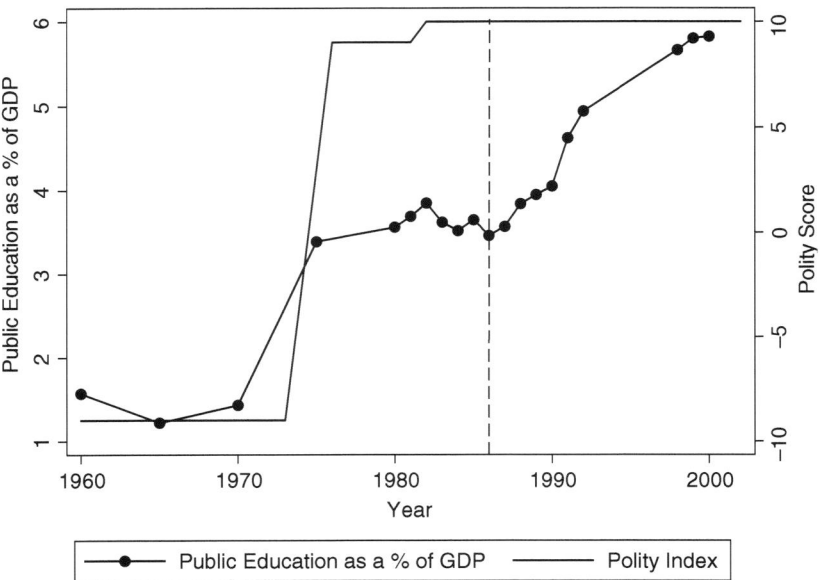

FIGURE 3.7. Democracy and Education Spending in Portugal

sorely lagged any legislative expansion of education, leading to endemic illiteracy. However, the death of Salazar in 1970 and the bloodless coup of 1974 that removed his successor Marcello Caetano led to the imposition of free elections and full democracy by 1980 in Portugal. In the decade before Salazar's death, public expenditure on education had averaged around 1.5 percent of GDP. Following the coup, educational expenditure hovered between 3.5 percent and 4 percent from the mid-1970s through to around 1986 – the year of entry to the European Community – after which it began its climb to just over 5.5 percent in 2000, the OECD norm at the time. This second jump was partly due to the extension of compulsory education from six to nine years in the mid-1980s, which led to an increase in the average years of education within the labor force of one full year between 1982 and 1992 (from five to six years; Hartog, Periera and Vieira, 2001). Figure 3.7 demonstrates the close relationship between democracy and education spending in Portugal and the second climb following access to the European Community in 1986 (the dotted line).

Examining the transition to democracy and its relation to economic policy in more detail, an intriguing tale emerges. While Salazar had largely conceived of education as "teaching one's place in life," Caetano's education minister Jose Veiga Simao (a Cambridge-educated physicist) proposed the "democratization" of Portuguese education in 1972 (Stoer and Dale, 1987). Veiga Simao deliberately modeled his proposed reforms on the standard OECD pattern, conceiving of education as human capital development rather than Salazarian indoctrination. Veiga Simao's reforms included an extension of compulsory education and the reform of higher education. Ironically, according to Stoer and Dale (1987), these very reforms helped to sew the seeds of the regime's demise: Intended to slow the drive to democracy and preserve the old regime by creating "organization without mobilization," the reforms instead "further stretched the credibility of the largely discredited principle of corporatism." While the Caetano regime did not survive 1974, Veiga Simao's unimplemented reforms were adopted by the new socialist left following the coup. The newly elected socialist party did not stop with the Veiga Simao reforms: Further steps were made to develop nursery education, unify the secondary school system, ban child labor, and provide study grants. The reforms of the 1980s (expanding the age of compulsory education to fourteen and increasing funding during the 1990s) were thus legacies not only of the transition to democracy itself but also of the rise of the Portuguese socialists.

Portugal's entry into the European Community in 1986 was also a key determinant of the rise in education spending in the late 1980s and early 1990s. As Figure 3.7 demonstrates, education spending had stabilized at around 3.5 percent of national income in the post-democratization era. However, from 1986 to 1992 education spending rose around 50 percent to 5 percent of national income before beginning a climb in the late 1990s to nearly 6 percent of national income by 2000. Underlying this increase was a massive increase in the demand for skilled labor, precipitated by entry into the common market. Portugal, despite its reputation as a trading state, had remarkably low levels of openness during the early twentieth century, with imports averaging only 5 percent of national income before the interwar era. As Nunes (2003) notes, "this fact... probably proved to be very detrimental to productivity growth, by reducing international diffusion mechanisms, particularly in the case of technical progress."

Portugal consequently lagged Europe in technological terms for the remainder of the twentieth century until the jolt of accession in 1986. Hartog, Periera, and Vieira (2001) argue that this date marks the point at which the returns to education began to rise most significantly in modern Portuguese history. Despite the fact that education was expanding in supply at unprecedented rates during the 1980s, the return to a year of education grew from 4.8 percent in 1982 to 6.1 percent in 1992. The theory that globalization permits states to expand education without reducing the returns to education finds ample support in the Portuguese case. Furthermore, there was also a demand-side effect: According to the same authors, "the liberalization of trade with more developed countries producing capital goods encouraged the importation of technology requiring skilled labor." Combining the supply- and demand-side impetus to education, the political balance of support for education swung sharply toward its proponents, since the previously opposed Portuguese elite retained their skill premium. Thus, in the post-democratization era, openness, along with partisanship, has been the chief driver of Portuguese education expansion.

Spain

Like Portugal, Spain began its transition to democracy in the mid-1970s, with the death of Francisco Franco in 1975. Spain's expenditure on education prior

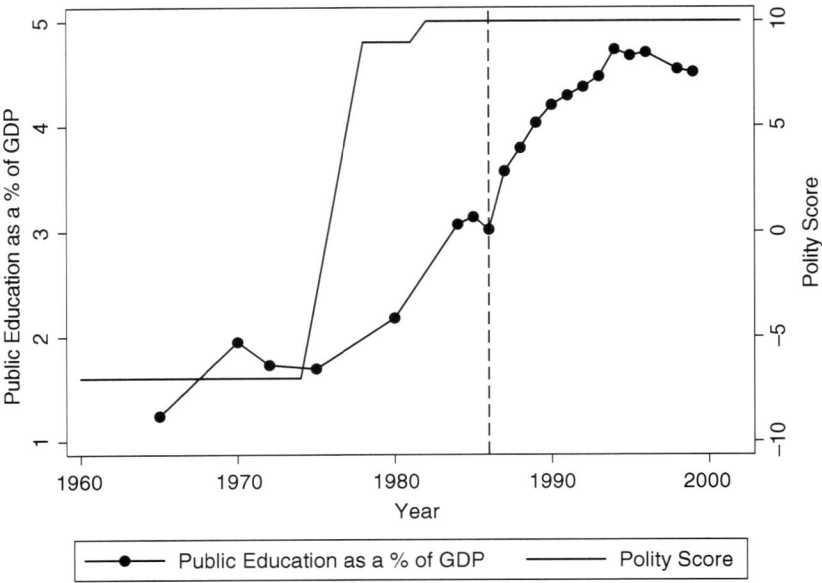

FIGURE 3.8. Democracy and Education Spending in Spain

to Franco's autocracy had hardly been higher than that of poorer Portugal, somewhat under 2 percent of GDP. As Diebolt (1999) shows, Spanish education spending was considerably below its long-run 1850-to-1970 path during the period of Franco's rule: at least a quarter below trend. However, as in the Portuguese case, following democratization, education spending rose to over 3 percent of national income by the mid-1980s and to over 4.5 percent by the mid-1990s – in total, a near-trebling of expenditure. Again, similarly to the pattern in Portugal, Spanish education growth briefly slowed in the mid-1980s before rising steeply following accession to the European Community, although the period of stagnation was much shorter than that occurring in Portugal. The close connection between education and democracy, along with the spurt following accession to the common market (represented by the dotted line), can be viewed in Figure 3.8.

Similarly to Caetano's doomed attempts to bolster autocracy through reform, the floundering Franco regime attempted to reform education in the early 1970s but was unable to implement reforms successfully or to override the chief enemy of widespread public education: the Church. Education in Spain until 1970 had largely been the preserve of the Catholic Church, which ran fee-paying schools with a very limited membership (McNair, 1984). Spanish education was extraordinarily stratified; in 1965, only 3 percent of working-age Spaniards attended secondary schools, mostly the children of the upper-middle class. The 1970 Education Act committed the state to public financing of education for all students, but this largely meant subsidization of the Catholic private school system as a result of the necessary political bargain between the government and the Church, and little expansion was actually achieved (O'Malley, 1995).

The state school system developed slowly along a separate track, but funding was halting until the 1978 post-Franco Constitution, which enshrined the right to secondary education, and then the two Socialist education bills, the Ley Orgánica del Derecho a la Educación (LODE) in 1985 and the Ley Orgánica de Ordinación General del Sistema Educativo (LOGSE) in 1990, the latter of which extended compulsory education to age sixteen (Boyd-Barrett and O'Malley, 1995). The quantitative effects of the passage of these laws were enormous in magnitude: There was a doubling of real expenditure per student contemporaneous with a major increase in enrollment (from 50 to 70 percent of fourteen- to eighteen-year-olds attending school; Boix, 1998). Again, as in the Portuguese case, while the authoritarian regime of the early 1970s gave a nod to human capital development (largely for technocratic economic reasons), it was not until the democratic regime emerged – and in particular the arrival of the Socialist Party – that the state began funding public education at a level even approximating the Western European norm.

The mid-1980s saw a brief stagnation in education spending in Spain, with education spending jumping again following entry into the European Community in 1986. From 1987 to 1995, education spending increased by over 50 percent, from 3 percent of national income to 4.7 percent. While these increases in spending were partly a function of Socialist rule, the impact of European integration was critical in pushing Spain toward the OECD average of education spending. In fact, the preamble to LOGSE specifically references the importance of the common market in justifying massive increases in education spending:

When incorporating the citizens of the next century into the schools of today, the countries with which we are attempting to construct the European project ... place great confidence in the relevance of education and training .... The progressive integration of our society within the framework of the European Community positions us, in an educational context, for a future of competition... (Ley Orgánica de Ordinación General del Sistema Educativo, 1990).

Spanish education spending since accession has converged rapidly with the European norm. As Diebolt (1999) notes, "with the emergence and consolidation of the European Union and more broadly with the increasing globalization of the economy, possible [educational] lags established during the course of history will gradually dwindle or disappear." Moreover, while integration with the regional (and indeed global) economy has pushed up the demand for skill because of technology transfer, supply-side effects have prevented the wage premium to education from reducing, despite the very large increases in enrollment during the 1980s. In fact, Minondo (1999) finds that the Spanish non-manual/manual wage premium (an analog of the skilled/unskilled premium) actually increased during the 1980s from 1.45 to 1.60, with the bulk of the jump happening in the three years following accession. Overall, education spending since democratization appears to have been closely related to the positive trade shock of entering the European Union, with the Spanish labor market converging in structure rapidly to that typical of advanced industrialized nations.

Greece

Unlike Spain and Portugal, Greece had an extended period of postwar democratic government before the autocratic interlude of military rule – "the Regime of the Colonels" – from 1967 to 1974. Between 1952 and 1963, Greece had been governed by a series of conservative governments and then from 1963 to 1967 by centrist and liberal coalitions. Pre-1967 Greece was a constitutional monarchy with an overbearing monarchical influence, particularly between 1963 and 1967, when King Constantine II continually attempted to undermine the centrist governments of the time. In particular, the king's ire was raised by the reformist Center Union government of George Papandreou between 1964 and 1965. Papandreou – the father of the first leader of the post-democratization Greek socialist party PASOK, Andreas Papandreou – was considered by the king to be dangerously radical, and the Center Union government was undermined in 1965 by the king's machinations.

Before George Papandreou left office, he introduced Greece's first modern education bill in 1964. The bill massively increased the role of the government in education and attempted to replace the artificial state language Katharevousa (a form of ancient Greek) with spoken or "demotic" Greek as the language of instruction in primary education. This shift to spoken Greek vastly increased the relevance and accessibility of education to the poor and lower-middle classes. Furthermore, enrollment was substantially increased by the extension of free compulsory education to nine years (Kazamias, 1978). In combination with the use of spoken Greek, the change to compulsory education proved a spur to public spending on education, which rose by 50 percent, from 1.4 percent of national income in 1960 to 2.1 percent by 1965. The reaction of the king to Papandreou's liberal government was merely a precursor of the reaction of the Greek establishment to the emergence of democratic socialism in Greece. In 1967, just before the scheduled elections for that year, Colonel George Papadopoulos seized control of government and established a military junta, which imprisoned opponents, including George Papandreou, and dissolved political parties. The ultraconservative reaction was also felt in the area of education. The generals revoked the 1964 Education Act, with compulsory education reverting back to six years from nine (Gouvias, 1998). Consequently, education spending fell back to 1.7 percent of national income by the mid-1970s. The overthrow of the generals in 1974 marked a return to both democratic politics and an expansionist public education policy. The center-right party New Democracy, headed by Constantine Karamanlis, swiftly moved to reinstate portions of the 1964 Act removed by the generals. Education policy was moved to the top of the agenda; as Kazamias (1978) notes, "the new government, in the tradition of previous reformist regimes, gave educational reconstruction top priority." Compulsory education reverted to nine years, and spoken Greek was to be used exclusively in a reformed secondary system. Education spending had returned to its pre-junta level by entry into the European Community in 1981.

The year 1981 was a momentous one for Greece. Entry into the free market in January was followed in October by the election of Greece's first

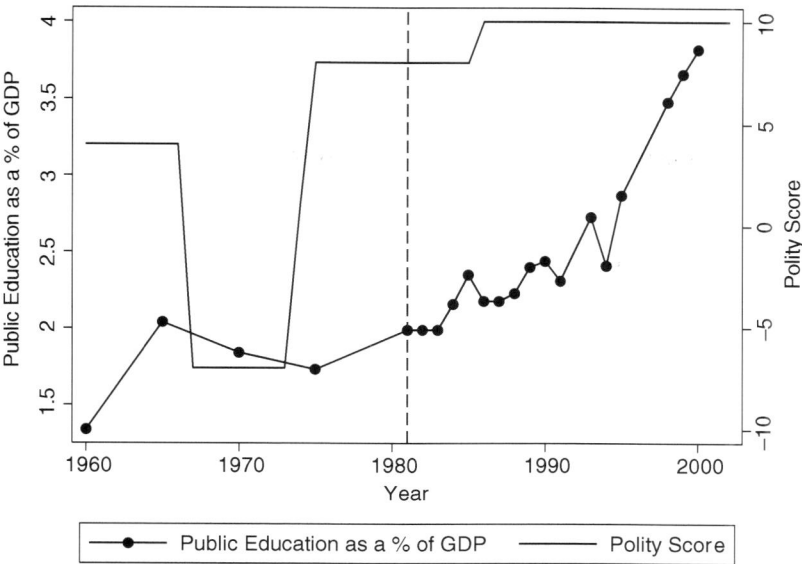

FIGURE 3.9. Democracy and Education Spending in Greece

socialist government. Both events underlay a surge in Greek education spending in the 1980s and 1990s that would push Greece to near the OECD average level of spending. Competition from European firms has driven Greek demand for education significantly. As Giamouridis and Bagley (2006) note, "Greek governments are very interested in participating in the global high-tech 'New Economy' and ... a restructured educational system is now seen as a necessary precondition for increased productivity, competitiveness, and the ability to adapt to the innovative content of the new technologies." Since Greek companies had been heavily sheltered from competition before 1981 and because Greece's industrial structure had been slanted toward labor- and land-intensive production, the arrival of skill-biased European technology has forced a sea change in education policy. The increased demand for skill caused by European integration was accompanied by a series of "democratizing" education reforms introduced by PASOK between 1981 and 1985 (Grollios and Kaskaris, 2003). These involved the establishment of teacher training colleges for the first time and the establishment of parent unions for civic participation in education planning.

As Figure 3.9 shows, the socialists began a gradual increase in funding from 2 percent to 2.5 percent of national income by 1990. In their second period in office, from 1993 to 2004, they introduced a major reform to the structure of secondary education in 1997 and oversaw a rise in education spending from 2.5 percent to 3.8 percent of national income. Yet, despite the massive increases in enrollments, the returns to skill in Greece did not collapse after European integration: A year of schooling increased log hourly earnings by 7.3 percent in 1974 but by 8.3 percent in 1999 (Tsakloglou and Cholezas, 2005). Thus open markets have apparently *increased* the returns to education in modern Greece, even though education is far more abundant than in the 1970s.

3.6 CONCLUSIONS

From the Pacific to the Indian to the Atlantic Ocean, the cases in this chapter have demonstrated the powerful and consistent effects of democracy and globalization on education spending. We have seen that both democratic revolutions and autocratic coups lead to systematic effects on education policy. The robust empirical relationship found between democracy and education spending in Chapter 2 is no mere artifact of a benign upward trend in both variables. Instead, many autocratic leaders such as Marcos, Estrada, Caetano, and Papadopoulos have cut back education funding upon seizing power. Moreover, trade policies have also had enormous impact on education policy. Indian, Brazilian, and Philippine import substitution industrialization stemmed the technological demand for education and protected the children of the elite from competition. It also led to a focus in all three cases on funding for higher education and a neglect of primary education, as these states attempted to jump-start heavy industrialization through import substitution. Conversely, South Korean and Malaysian export-led industrialization and the spurt of trade following entry to the European Community for Portugal, Spain, and Greece have facilitated the transition to a high-skill, high-wage economy in these states. In South Korea and Malayisa, moreover, the export-driven strategy led to a sequential focus on primary and secondary education before the turn to high skills. Even though education provision has expanded massively in these states, the wage premium to education does not appear to have suffered, indicating that the supply effects of globalization on education spending are powerful indeed.

4

The Partisan Politics of Education

4.1 INTRODUCTION

In advanced industrial countries, the politics of education may be more formalized than the struggles between autocratic elites and uneducated masses we saw in the previous chapters, but they are no less consequential. While few politicians actively espouse cuts to education, the harsh realities of budgetary trade-offs mean that the underlying spectrum of partisan preferences over education typically manifests itself in policy outcomes. In fact, even among the world's richest countries, education spending can be extremely volatile, and that volatility hinges on the partisan identity of government. In this chapter, I show that swings in partisanship may have an impact on education spending as large as the effects of democratization that we saw in Chapter 2. Partisanship matters for education and it matters to the tune of billions of dollars.

The idea that partisanship affects policy outcomes is hardly new in political science. Indeed, it would be hard to believe that people would vote as they do if parties entirely failed to represent and execute the policy preferences of their constituencies. Work on this topic in political science has a storied history: from the analyses of Shonfield (1965) and other postwar analysts of comparative economic policy in the "Golden Age," through the "power resources" analysis of writers such as Korpi (1983) and Esping-Andersen (1985), to the more recent heirs to that literature (Bradley et al., 2003; Garrett, 1998; Rueschemeyer, Stephens, and Stephens, 1992). Furthermore, there has also been work, albeit more limited in scale, showing that socialist parties in advanced industrial countries tend to increase public spending on education (Busemeyer, 2007; Boix, 1998).

In all, the field of study devoted to the effects of parties on policy has been tilled to near erosion. It is not, then, the sole aim of this chapter to show that left-wing governments spend more on public education than right-wing governments do, although we will address these results in passing. Instead, my intention is to tell a more nuanced causal story, moving from voter preferences over education, to parties' statements in manifestos, the degree to which those statements correspond to policy outcomes, and finally to the role of electoral institutions in constraining parties and framing trade-offs between policy goals.

I note also, with reference to vocational education, that the pattern of left-wing promotion of education does not hold as cleanly once we examine more targeted education spending – an issue I follow up in Chapter 5. Throughout this chapter, I explore an underlying tension. Do voter preferences or party preferences drive partisan policy making in education? Is education policy a bottom-up process of aggregating voter intent? Or is it a top-down story, where party preferences and institutional constraints determine a country's educational profile? Answering these questions addresses an underlying tension in much modern work on political economy: whether politicians are opportunistic seekers of the median voter's approval, or driven by partisan preferences that mean commitments to the electorate are meaningless (Persson and Tabellini, 2002).

I begin in Section 4.2 by developing a theory of the partisan electoral politics of education. Working within the framework of established democracies, I turn my focus to a more precise elaboration of parties' electoral promises and the constraining role of electoral institutions. I show that left-wing parties are expected to spend more on education, both absolutely and relatively, than right-wing parties but that this pattern appears reversed for vocational education, at least in streamed education systems. I then develop a series of hypotheses about the effect of electoral systems, showing that they both moderate partisan effects and alter the trade-offs that parties make between education and pure redistribution.

The remainder of the chapter tests empirically both the assumptions and the propositions of the theory developed in Section 4.2. Sections 4.3 and 4.4 focus on the preferences of, respectively, voters and political parties over education spending. In Section 4.3, I examine individual level data drawn from the International Social Science Survey Program surveys conducted in 1996 and 1999 across twenty industrialized states. This analysis permits me to test the theoretical assumption that income and individual-level partisanship are strong predictors of preferences over education spending. Section 4.4 analyzes partisan preferences, examining the degree to which party manifestos express a desire to expand education spending. I find a strong left-right pattern, with social democratic and liberal parties consistently promising to expand education more than conservative parties. I also examine whether the pre-election rhetoric of parties actually has an impact on spending over and above the cabinet ideology of the governing party, once these parties actually gain control over the policy process after the election.

The last two sections of the chapter focus on policy outcomes. Section 4.5 looks directly at the effect of cabinet ideology on both absolute and relative education spending. I find substantively strong and statistically robust evidence that as the ideological composition of the cabinet moves rightward, both absolute and relative education spending are reduced. I then provide a more intuitive interpretation of these results by examining the predicted dollar change resulting from typical shifts in party control across several OECD states. I conclude Section 4.5 by showing that the provision of vocational education has rather distinct partisan effects that in some cases actually reverse those for more general education spending. Section 4.6 examines the role of electoral institutions in constraining policy. I find that the general partisan pattern displayed in Section 4.5 is complicated once one distinguishes between proportional and majoritarian electoral systems, with the former displaying much weaker effects of partisanship. I then show how the moderating effect of proportionality is mirrored in the pattern of individual voter preferences over both education and general redistribution. Section 4.7 draws general conclusions about partisanship and education in the advanced industrial world.

4.2 A PARTISAN MODEL OF EDUCATION SPENDING

The formal model in Chapter 2 focused on expanding education throughout the population, from richest to poorest. However, once we turn our gaze to the advanced industrial world, education at the primary and secondary levels is compulsory and universal. Thus, education looks more like a standard redistributive good in such countries, producing a clearer partisan pattern of preferences. Even still, the translation of such preferences into policy outcomes is not obvious. For one thing, voters cannot easily hold political parties to promises made in elections – this is the classic "time inconsistency" problem (Iversen, 2005). Furthermore, the structure of electoral institutions determines the number of political parties, the way in which voters of different preferences are split across them, the necessity of coalition building by politicians, and the degree to which multiple political issues are compacted along fewer dimensions. Thus, the political economy of universal education in advanced industrial countries removes some complications only to add others.

The Basic Model

I begin by revisiting the model developed in Chapter 2 and, as before, I assume that there are three groups (H, M, P) with different levels of non-wage income: y_H, y_M, and y_P. However, whereas before we analyzed the expansion of education provision S from zero to one, we now set S equal to one and examine the uniform level of per-student spending on education, h. Since education is universal, I abstract from scarcity effects (revisiting these in Chapter 5, which focuses on higher education) and thus ignore the difference between "skilled" and "unskilled" workers. I alter the model further by introducing an explicit "lottery" effect of education, which proxies for the meritocratic effects of education spending, discussed in the introductory chapter. Put simply, increased per-student spending on education increases the chances that today's poor will be tomorrow's rich and vice versa. In the absence of scarcity effects, this helps distinguish education from general redistribution. The family utility function can be framed as:

$$U_i = (1 - \tau)\, y_{i0} + m_0 + \delta\Big[\big(1 - p(h_1)\big)\, y_{i0} + p(h_1)\, \overline{y}_0 + g(h_1)\Big]$$

As in Chapter 2, utility is composed of parental income net of taxes and the discounted expectation of children's income plus future externalities produced by education. The distinct elements of this particular formulation are that there is lump-sum redistribution available in period zero, m, and that children's expected income is determined by a lottery effect. The budget constraint is simply $m_0 + h_1 = \tau \bar{y}_0$.

Thus taxes can be spent two ways: on immediate redistribution (m) or on education (h), the benefits of which are realized only by children. The effect of education here is twofold. First, there is a lottery effect – increasing education spending increases the probability $p(h)$ that children's income will be randomly allocated with a one-third chance each of y_H, y_M, y_P, meaning an expected income equal to mean income.[1] With probability $1-p(h)$, children will have the same income as their parents. Thus the effect of h on $p(h)$ determines the degree of meritocracy produced by education spending, assuming that ability is distributed uniformly across income groups. The second effect is a uniform benefit from education spending $g(h)$ received by all individuals – this could either be private gains or a social gain from externalities. Since education provision is uniform, there is no distinction and we can consider this to be each citizen's share of the growth in economic output produced by education. I assume that $g(h)$ is increasing and concave. I now examine the effects of increasing absolute education spending (that is, holding m constant) and increasing relative education spending (that is, holding the tax rate constant):

Absolute spending $\qquad \left. \dfrac{\partial U_i}{\partial h_1} \right|_{m=m^*} = -\dfrac{y_{i0}}{\bar{y}_0} + \delta \left[p_h \left(\bar{y}_0 - y_{i0} \right) + g_h \right]$

Relative spending $\qquad \left. \dfrac{\partial U_i}{\partial h_1} \right|_{\tau=\tau^*} = -1 + \delta \left[p_h \left(\bar{y}_0 - y_{i0} \right) + g_h \right]$

A brief overview of these equations suggests that poorer individuals are more likely to benefit from increased absolute spending than are richer individuals, since taxes increase with family income, but the expected benefit of meritocracy decreases. Relative spending shows a similar pattern of preferences, but purely through the meritocracy effect, since taxes are fixed. I now parameterize $p(h)$ as $h / \bar{y}_0$, which means that the probability of children's income being determined meritocratically is one if the maximum possible tax take of $\bar{y}_0$ is adopted and equals zero if h is set to zero. I rewrite the preceding equations and rearrange to find the optimal level of g_h (the first derivative of output $g(h)$) and consequently the optimal h, since $g(h)$ is increasing and concave:

---

[1] I assume that $p(h)$ is strictly increasing and bounded between zero and one for all possible values of h between zero and $\bar{y}_0$.

Absolute spending $\qquad g_b^* = \dfrac{1+\delta}{\delta} \dfrac{y_{i0}}{\overline{y}_0} - 1$

Relative spending $\qquad g_b^* = \dfrac{1-\delta}{\delta} + \dfrac{y_{i0}}{\overline{y}_0}$

As individual income, relative to mean income, gets larger, in both cases we see the left-hand side also gets larger. Because output $g(b)$ is concave, this means that b^*, the optimal level of education provision, is getting smaller. Put simply, richer individuals demand less education, both absolutely and relatively, than poorer individuals.

> *Hypothesis One (a): Poorer individuals prefer higher absolute and relative education spending than do richer individuals.*

In terms of comparing absolute and relative spending, the optimal choice of education for all individuals with less than mean income will be higher when the tax level is permitted to vary (absolute spending) than when it is fixed (relative spending). In the latter case, such poorer individuals are forced to choose between redistribution now and education later: Education spending forces a trade-off. For richer individuals, the preferences are reversed: Below a certain threshold of education spending, high externalities mean education spending is preferable to further redistribution. This implies that the gap between rich and poor is smaller in terms of relative education spending than absolute education spending.

> *Hypothesis One (b): Partisan patterns should be less pronounced with respect to relative spending.*

Streaming and Vocational Education

A further factor affecting preferences over education spending is whether education spending actually produces a meritocratic income distribution. In highly *streamed* education systems, the future earnings possibilities for students are often fixed at a young age. Such systems typically involve a splitting of secondary education into academic and vocational tracks. From a redistributive perspective, streaming has both positive and negative effects: On the one hand, streaming may permit the development of more productive vocational skills; on the other hand, it may reduce the ability of poorer citizens to enter highly paid professions that require academic qualifications. I alter the family utility function to incorporate streaming ($\alpha = 0$ is a fully streamed system, and $\alpha = 1$ is non-streamed) and vocational training, which increases earnings for the poor and middle class by a parameter $\omega_J(h)$, increasing in h, with $\omega_R = 0$.[2]

---

[2] I assume the rich cannot increase their earnings through vocational education and that vocational education does not change the cost of providing education, just its market returns.

$$U_j = (1-\tau)y_j + m + \delta\left[(1-\alpha p(h))\left[y_j + (1+\varepsilon-\alpha)\omega_j(h)\right] + \alpha p(h)\overline{y} + g(h)\right]$$

Under complete streaming, there is no lottery effect; however, vocational education is more valuable, with an effect of $(1+\varepsilon)\omega_j$. When there is no streaming, the lottery effect works as in the basic model, but vocational training is worth less: just $\varepsilon\omega_j$. I examine the effect of increased education spending for the different groups.

$$\frac{\partial U_P}{\partial h} = -\frac{y_P}{\overline{y}} + \delta\left[\alpha p_h\left(\overline{y} - y_P + (1+\varepsilon-\alpha)\omega_P(h)\right) + \left((1-\alpha p(h))(1+\varepsilon-\alpha)\frac{\partial\omega_P}{\partial h}\right) + g_h\right]$$

$$\frac{\partial U_M}{\partial h} = -\frac{y_M}{\overline{y}} + \delta\left[\alpha p_h\left(\overline{y} - y_M + (1+\varepsilon-\alpha)\omega_M(h)\right) + \left((1-\alpha p(h))(1+\varepsilon-\alpha)\frac{\partial\omega_M}{\partial h}\right) + g_h\right]$$

$$\frac{\partial U_R}{\partial h} = -\frac{y_R}{\overline{y}} + \delta\left[\alpha p_h\left(\overline{y} - y_R\right) + g_h\right]$$

The rich do not receive vocational education and are affected only by streaming. When streaming is complete, $\alpha = 0$, the negative meritocratic effects of education spending drop out and the rich might be happy to increase spending on vocational education. The poor and middle class face more of a trade-off. When streaming is complete, vocational education is worth more, but they are unable to access the benefit of meritocracy – the possibility of becoming as wealthy as the rich. The trade-off is one between the vocational sure thing and the possibility of income mobility. Thus, the surprising result is that while streamed vocational education may be a good or bad thing for the poor and middle class, depending on the trade-off between higher certain wages and lower income mobility, for the rich it is almost always desirable, even though their own children do not receive it. Streaming protects the rich from meritocracy.[3] When, conversely, there is no streaming, the rich turn against education spending, as in the basic model. However, since the poor and middle class receive at least some extra benefit, $\varepsilon\omega_j$, from vocational training, as well as maintaining the possibility of income mobility, they should prefer higher spending on vocational education when there is no streaming. These results produce Hypothesis Two:

> *Hypothesis Two: When education is streamed, richer individuals should prefer higher spending on vocational education. When education is not streamed, poorer individuals should prefer higher spending on vocational education.*

Partisan Politics

I begin my analysis of partisan politics with a simple median voter model with two parties (center-left and center-right) and partisan politicians (that is,

---

[3] In Chapter 5, I argue that vocational streaming protects the scarcity rents that the rich receive through their exclusive access to higher education. If higher education is necessary to achieve income parity with the rich, then the model in this chapter essentially replicates that claim.

politicians represent different income groups and would prefer the optimum education policy of that group) who are unable to make binding commitments to pre-election policy declarations (Iversen and Soskice, 2006). Since the baseline model assumed three groups in the economy (*H*, *M*, and *P*), there are too few parties for each group to be perfectly represented; thus the two parties, *L* and *R*, fully represent *P* and *H* respectively, but the middle group is split across both parties in terms of representation. Each party is thus made up of representatives of either *P* or *H* and an unknown proportion of *M*. For any given election, the leader of the party who will make policy following election may be a member of *M*, with probability θ_K, where $K = (L, R)$, or of one of the fully represented groups, with probability $(1-\theta_K)$. Note that because I limit the number of parties to two, despite greater heterogeneity in the population, this electoral system resembles majoritarianism.

Once in power, the leader of the elected party will make policy according only to their own partisan preferences; that is, they cannot commit to any other group's policy, despite the possible vote gains that such a commitment might encourage. This restriction precludes parties from making commitments in their pre-election manifestos that go against the grain of their partisan identity. Under this probabilistic model, if party *L* is elected, the preferred education policy of group *M*, h^*_M, will be imposed with probability θ_L, and the preferred policy of *P*, h^*_P, with probability $(1-\theta_L)$. A symmetric pattern occurs with party *R*. The key prediction of such a model is that over repeated elections, where $\theta_L = \theta_R = \theta$, the parties will impose the following expected policies:

$$E\left(h^*_L\right) = \theta h^*_M + (1-\theta)\, h^*_P$$

$$E\left(h^*_R\right) = \theta h^*_M + (1-\theta)\, h^*_H$$

This implies that, over repeated elections, the optimal policy for the left party is higher than for the right party since we know from the preceding results that the average of the middle income and poor groups' preferred levels of education spending is higher than the average of the rich and middle income groups. Following Hypotheses One (a) and (b), left-wing government should be associated with greater absolute and relative education spending than right-wing government. This pattern should, however, be more accentuated in the case of absolute spending as opposed to relative spending.

Electoral Systems and Moderation

The simple majoritarian model of partisan politics, then, implies a standard left-right dimension of partisan politics with respect to education, with similar implications for both absolute and relative education spending. Things become somewhat more complicated, however, if we turn to the analysis of proportional electoral systems. The political economy literature provides a vast array of conflicting hypotheses on the impact of electoral systems on public spending, suggesting proportionality leads to increased spending, decreased spending, or an indirect effect on spending through the party system (Iversen and Soskice, 2006; Lizzeri and Persico, 2002; Austen-Smith, 2000; Persson and Tabellini, 2002). Clearly, the distinction between electoral systems is theoretically complex. In this section, I highlight two distinctions between majoritarian and proportional electoral systems that seem particularly germane for our understanding of education spending: firstly, the moderating effect of proportionality on policy volatility; and secondly, the possibility of multidimensional politics.

I begin with a discussion of the moderating effect of proportional electoral institutions, building off Iversen and Soskice (2006), who argue that proportional electoral systems make coalitions between centrist and left-wing parties more likely than coalitions between centrist and right-wing parties. I adapt their model to show that it also implies that the *volatility* (or range across governments) of public spending (including education) should be lower under proportional representation as compared to majoritarianism. Using the three groups – P, M, and H – I assume, following Iversen and Soskice, that because of fiscal progressivity, the maximum tax takes from each group are 0, T_M, and T_H, and that all taxes provide education funding.[4]

Under majoritarianism, as discussed in the preceding section, there are two parties, L and R, with the former being led by a member of P with probability 2/3 and by a member of M with probability 1/3, and the latter being led by a member of H with a probability of 2/3 and by a member of M with probability 1/3. Each party will attempt to maximize the optimal policy of its members, which amounts to, for P, M, and H, respectively: (T_H+T_M), T_H, and 0. Thus the expected tax revenue ρ of the L and R parties and the potential range of policy are:

$$E(\rho_L) = \frac{2}{3}[T_H + T_M] + \frac{1}{3}T_H$$

$$E(\rho_R) = \frac{1}{3}T_H$$

$$E(Range_{MAJ}) = E(\rho_L) - E(\rho_R) = \frac{2}{3}[T_H + T_M]$$

Under proportional representation, there are three parties, L, C, and R, representing P, M, and H. If each group votes for its representative party, policy will be developed through coalitional bargaining in the post-election period. I assume, following Iversen and Soskice, that each party has an equivalent chance of being made fondateur. I assume that once a coalition is formed, Rubenstein bargaining takes place and the final tax revenue therefore lies halfway between the optimal points of each party. I abstract away from the possibility of reneging

---

[4] The assumption of tax progressivity with regard to education seems appropriate when considering universal education. Chapter 5 notes that this story is more complex when analyzing targeted education such as spending on universities.

on bargains.[5] In terms of establishing the range of tax revenue, the key instances we want to look at are when L or R are made fondateur. If L is chosen, they choose between C and R as partner:

$$L \text{ Chooses } C \Rightarrow E(\rho_{LC}) = \frac{1}{2}[T_H + T_M] + \frac{1}{2}T_H$$

$$L \text{ Chooses } R \Rightarrow E(\rho_{LH}) = \frac{1}{2}[T_H + T_M]$$

Unsurprisingly, L will therefore choose to bargain with C, who can offer them a higher tax take. If R is chosen as fondateur, they will likewise choose to bargain with C, and this coalition produces the simple total tax revenue of ½ T_H. Thus, to calculate the potential range of tax revenue, we examine the difference between the tax revenue of the LC coalition and that of the CR coalition:

$$E(Range_{PR}) = E(\rho_{LC}) - E(\rho_{CR}) = \frac{1}{2}[T_H + T_M] + \frac{1}{2}T_H - \frac{1}{2}T_H = \frac{1}{2}[T_H + T_M]$$

The range of partisanship under proportional representation is significantly smaller than that under majoritarianism. This result obtains due to the increased post-election bargaining power of the middle group, with its commensurately more moderate policy preferences, under the PR system, where it counts for half of the post-election governing coalition. Under majoritarianism, the two-party system squeezes the middle class into only a third of either of the two parties. This result produces Hypothesis Three.

Hypothesis Three: Proportional electoral systems should show a more moderate effect of partisanship on education spending than majoritarian systems.

Electoral Systems and Multidimensionality

My analysis of the moderating effect of proportionality showed that electoral institutions matter for policy outcomes even when policy is unidimensional. I now turn to examine the implications of proportionality when parties have multidimensional policy preferences. As in the case of the moderation effect, multidimensionality is possible because proportionality leads to a greater number of political parties.[6] A proliferation of parties means that voters whose preferences over education and redistribution differ from the unidimensional model can more easily find political representation that reflects these preferences. Returning to the basic model, we can see that variation in discount rates, income, and the externalities produced by education could alter an individual's

---

[5] This possibility is dealt with by Iversen and Soskice 2006, who show their results still obtain, provided no group can make credible commitments to underexploit their bargaining power.

[6] In proportional systems, the centripetal force of Duverger's Law does not apply (Cox, 1997). Consequently, these systems tend to have many more viable political parties than do majoritarian ones. The average effective number of political parties in proportional systems in the OECD between 1960 and 2000 was 3.9 compared to just over 2 in majoritarian systems.

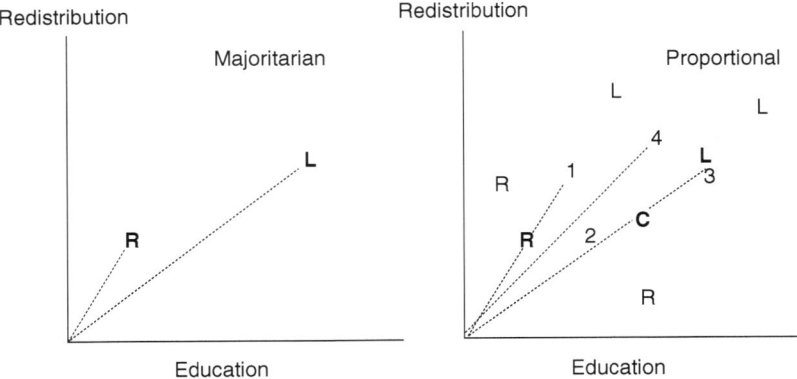

FIGURE 4.1. Party Positions in Multidimensional Space

trade-off between redistribution and education spending. Whereas majoritarianism tends to compact these preferences to one dimension, largely determined by voting over the tax rate, proportional systems allow for considerable variation across both dimensions, permitting the viable coexistence of low-education/high-redistribution and high-education/low-redistribution parties.[7]

Formally modeling multiple parties in a multidimensional policy setting is highly demanding, and typically most theorists argue that equilibrium policies are indeterminate (McKelvey and Schofield, 1986). Thus, rather than attempting to find a determinate outcome, it is more useful to compare the potential configurations of parties across majoritarian and proportional electoral systems in regard to redistribution and education.

I demonstrate possible party placements in multidimensional space in Figure 4.1 (the slopes of the dotted lines reflect relative education spending preferences). Beginning with the majoritarian system, it should be clear that with only two parties in two dimensions, policy must compact to one dimension. Provided that discount rates are not unusually low, redistribution and education preferences will line up on a high/high low/low axis, with the slope of the axis determining the difference in preferences between absolute and relative education spending. Note that in this standard case the left-wing party prefers higher relative education spending than the right wing party and that it lies to the right-wing party's north-east. Thus, when we see education spending increase, we should also expect redistribution to increase, though the ratio of increases will depend on the slope of the relative spending line.

The proportional system looks different in multidimensional space. Here there is room for small parties that might want increased spending on redistribution but less on education and vice versa. Depending on the size of these groups relative to parties sitting on the standard high/high low/low axis, it may be possible to strike coalitions that raise spending on one dimension and lower

---

[7] Electoral systems that incorporate multidimensionality might also allow variation on non-economic preferences such as religion to enter the coalition-building framework.

it on another. In Figure 4.1, the large L and R parties are now no longer capable of forming a majority on their own and must form coalitions with the smaller left-wing, right-wing, and centrist parties. Depending on the size of each party, there are many viable coalitions. Coalition 1, between the large right party and one small right, center, and left party, appears more left wing than Coalition 2 between the large right party, two small right parties, and the center party. Yet Coalition 1 would also have lower education spending, trading this off against the small-left wing party's preference for high redistribution. Coalition 2 would have almost the same ratio of education to redistribution as Coalition 3, but it is a right-wing coalition with much lower absolute spending on both. Coalition 3, between the large left-wing party and one small left, center, and right party would have the same level of redistribution as Coalition 1 but much higher education spending. Finally, Coalition 4 between the three left parties and the center party is significantly more left-wing than Coalition 3, which includes a right-wing party, yet it has lower education spending.

One could clearly provide a multitude of further examples by adding new parties and/or coalitions, but two implications are clear. Firstly, proportional systems show less correlation between preferences over education spending and redistribution than majoritarian ones. Multidimensionality permits the emergence of "ends against the middle" political coalitions against education spending but which are pro-redistribution. Secondly, under proportional systems, the average partisanship of coalitions is not a clear guide to their education preferences. Instead, we need to examine the preferences of parties on each distinct policy item – for example, as expressed in their manifestos – if we are to establish a coalition's likely education and redistribution policies. These implications produce Hypotheses Four and Five.

> *Hypothesis Four: The pattern of individual and party preferences over redistribution and education will be more correlated in majoritarian than proportional electoral systems.*
>
> *Hypothesis Five: Baseline partisanship will be a better predictor of relative education spending in majoritarian systems than proportional ones. Pre-electoral statements will be better predictors than average coalition partisanship in proportional systems.*

4.3 VOTER PREFERENCES OVER EDUCATION

The models of preferences over education spending that I developed in the previous section, and also in Chapter 2, rely quite strongly on the assumption that education has a redistributive component and that consequently, wealthy individuals should be less inclined to support such spending than poorer individuals. This assumption is common in formal models of education (for example, Boix, 1998; Fernandez and Rogerson, 1995; Perotti, 1993), but is it actually empirically valid? Wealthy individuals rarely vocalize anti-education preferences, perhaps because of education's normative "halo." Nonetheless, in this section, I show that there is a robust negative relationship between income and support for public education spending at the individual level. Furthermore, the reverse relationship holds with preferences over private education – here the wealthy are more supportive, the poor less supportive. These patterns hold up across the analysis of twenty-one industrialized states, including both the standard "old OECD" club as well as newer industrializers such as the Eastern European states and Israel. This section also provides assurance that parties largely reflect the educational preferences of their voting blocks – both right-wing voters and right-wing parties appear to share similar preferences for reduced or stagnant education spending.

The data in the following analyses come from various waves of the International Social Survey Program (ISSP). This survey is now a common workhorse for political economy analyses of redistribution, yet to this point there has been no systematic analysis of the determinants of preferences over education spending as opposed to more general redistribution. I begin with the 1996 "The Role of Government" survey, which includes a question on preferences over government spending on education. Specifically, the question asks, "Listed below are various areas of government spending. Please show whether you would like to see *more* or *less* government spending in each area. Remember that if you say 'much more', it might require a tax increase to pay for it." Then respondents are provided with the following choices next to the area of education: "Spend much more," "Spend more," "Spend the same," "Spend less," and "Spend much less," as well as a "Can't choose" option. Removing the final option leaves us with a five-point scale of education preferences, increasing in the respondent's *disapproval* of education spending. One of the strengths of this survey question is that it directly addresses the issue of fiscal trade-offs. This is, however, a very broad measure of education: The survey provides no distinction among types nor levels of education; consequently, it best resembles the concept of *absolute education spending* preferences.[8]

My chief interest is in two particular characteristics of respondents: their income level and their partisan preferences. Given that the formal model distinguishes individuals along their pretax income and suggests that poorer individuals, all else equal, will prefer higher education spending, it is important to support this major assumption empirically. Secondly, since I have assumed that political parties aggregate individual interests along the dimension of income, I want to check whether parties' expected preferences represent those of their voting base. Accompanying these two key variables of interest is a battery of control variables. Rather than use respondents' preferences over policies of interest as controls, I focus solely on their demographic characteristics, which are indisputably exogenous to their education policy preferences. I include controls for gender (male coded as zero, female as one), age, previous education (a seven-point scale: none, incomplete primary, primary, incomplete secondary, secondary, incomplete tertiary, tertiary), religious attendance (a six-point scale from once a week to never), a dummy for being Catholic and one for being

---

[8]   A separate question on higher education support is examined in Chapter 5.

Protestant. The education variable is of particular interest, since education is positively correlated with income but may generate separate pro-education views. Religion is also a potential confound, especially when religious schools are in the private sector – consequently, I try to pick up this effect using both religious identification and intensity.

To measure the effects of income and partisanship, I use a variety of indicators. The ISSP does not provide an income variable that has an exact translation across countries. Family income is measured in units of the country's particular currency, and because I am not interested per se in the difference in overall national per capita income, since countries can only tax *within themselves*, I create a set of four income variables that standardize the income distributions of each country. Firstly, for each country, I use the range of incomes among respondents to divide them into income quartiles for that particular country. Secondly, I take the mean income of respondents in a particular country and divide the income of each of that country's respondents by this mean.[9] Thirdly, I take the logarithm of the previous variable, which reduces its rightward skew substantially. Fourthly, I use a measure of the respondent's subjective social class: a six-point scale from lower class to upper class. Finally, I also use two measures of individual partisanship. The ISSP uses a simple five-point partisanship scale, placing individuals along a line from far-left, to center-left, to center, to center-right, to far-right. I develop a variable "partisanship" that treats this scaling as a simple linear measure and I also turn the categories into dummy variables (using far-left as the baseline category).

I run a series of ordered logit regressions, given that the dependent variable is a five-point scale with unknown distance between categories. In each model, I incorporate country dummies, in order to control for country-specific levels of educational support. I also use the sampling weights provided by the ISSP to adjust the sample appropriately for population demographics. In Table 4.1, Models A through D use, in turn, the four varied measures of income and Models E and F retain the log relative income variable and add measures of partisan identification. The first four models display a robust positive relationship between the income measures and the dependent variable. Recall that increases on the dependent variable correspond to *disfavoring* government spending. Thus, the consistent picture drawn is that higher-income individuals are less favorable to education spending than lower-income individuals, holding their other demographic characteristics constant.

Table 4.2 shows that moving across substantive categories on the income variable has a moderate effect on education preferences, making individuals between 1 and 5 percent less likely to support increased spending strongly, and 1 and 5 percent more likely to prefer spending remain constant. This is a robust but not enormous effect. Note that there is only a tiny probability of actually being more likely to want to reduce spending as income increases, thus we

---

[9] I use the mean given the standard assumption in models of redistribution that individuals with higher than mean income will disfavor redistribution and those with lower than mean income will favor it.

TABLE 4.1. *The Determinants of Voter Preferences on Education Spending*

	Model A	Model B	Model C	Model D	Model E	Model F
Gender	-0.205	-0.198	-0.203	-0.201	-0.179	-0.189
	(0.048)***	(0.049)***	(0.048)***	(0.043)***	(0.064)***	(0.064)***
Age	0.007	0.007	0.007	0.006	0.009	0.008
	(0.002)***	(0.002)***	(0.002)***	(0.002)***	(0.002)***	(0.002)***
Education	-0.103	-0.090	-0.105	-0.114	-0.096	-0.098
	(0.024)***	(0.023)***	(0.023)***	(0.024)***	(0.029)***	(0.029)***
Religious Attendance	-0.055	-0.034	-0.055	-0.046	-0.028	-0.027
	(0.015)***	(0.012)***	(0.015)***	(0.016)***	(0.009)***	(0.010)**
Catholic	0.247	0.059	0.248	0.394	0.053	0.061
	(0.100)*	(0.074)	(0.101)**	(0.130)***	(0.080)	(0.086)
Protestant	0.119	0.070	0.120	0.201	0.087	0.098
	(0.036)***	(0.048)	(0.036)***	(0.083)***	(0.054)	(0.059)
Income Quartile	0.044					
	(0.021)**					
Relative Income		0.040				
		(0.018)**				
Log Relative Income			0.077		0.065	0.063
			(0.036)***		(0.026)**	(0.025)**
Subjective Social Class				0.053		
				(0.024)**		
Partisanship					0.252	
					(0.050)***	
Center-Left						-0.188
						(0.073)**
Center						0.226
						(0.103)**
Center-Right						0.441
						(0.094)***
Far-Right						0.115
						(0.155)
Countries	21	21	21	23	19	19
N	22,285	22,285	22,285	25,594	13,579	13,579

Note: Robust standard errors are in parantheses: ***$p < 0.01$, **$p < 0.05$, *$p < 0.1$. All models contain country dummies.

TABLE 4.2. *Effects of Income/Partisanship Variables on Education Spending Categories*

Spend	Model A Income Quartile	Model B Relative Income	Model C Log Relative Income	Model D Subjective Social Class	Model E Partisanship	Model F Far-Left to Center-Left	Model G Far-Left to Center-Right
Much More	−0.023	−0.012	−0.022	−0.048	−0.172	0.024	−0.073
More	0.003	−0.002	−0.003	−0.005	−0.032	0.001	−0.019
Same	0.023	0.012	0.022	0.045	0.175	−0.022	0.079
Less	0.003	0.001	0.003	0.006	0.024	−0.003	0.011
Much Less	0.001	0.000	0.001	0.001	0.004	−0.001	0.003
Change of IV	1st to 4th quartile	10th to 90th percentile	10th to 90th percentile	Move from 1 to 6	Far-Left to Far-Right	Far-Left to Center-Left	Far-Left to Center-Right

are distinguishing between *relative* support. The effects of partisanship actually appear somewhat stronger than those related to income, which may imply some causal effect of party platforms on voter preferences (that is, voter preferences could be endogenous to elite manipulation) or simply a strong effect of ideology.

Even controlling for income, partisan identification has a robust independent effect on preferences, with voters on the right consistently less favorable to increased spending compared to those on the left. Interestingly, far-left voters appear less favorable to education spending than those on the center-left – a pattern we shall also see reflected in party manifestos in the next section.[10] Nonetheless, center and center-right parties are consistently less favorable to spending than those on the center-left or far-left and voters on the far-right less favorable than the center-left. The substantive effect of partisanship on preferences is large compared to income. Moving along the full length of the partisanship scale implies that an individual is 17 percent less likely to support increased spending strongly, 17 percent more likely to support the same level of spending, and even 2.4 percent more likely to support reduced spending. Similar, albeit smaller effects are found when moving between parties closer in partisan hue.

The control variables largely have the expected effects. Women are more supportive of education spending than men. Older individuals are less supportive than younger ones. Individuals with higher education are indeed more supportive of education than less educated individuals. Overall, this analysis supports the assumptions underlying the formal model: that income is negatively related to support for education spending and that parties appear to be aggregating preferences in a manner that supports a low-income/high-income, left/right divide. The results for education do not show a scarcity effect; in fact, they indicate that educated individuals are more supportive of increased education spending. Note, though, that education provision is universal in all the surveyed countries and thus the debate here is about per-student spending, not the extension of education. We shall see in Chapter 5 that when we examine targeted spending, there is more evidence of a potential scarcity effect.

I now move to the opposite end of the education funding spectrum by examining preferences over private education. The 1999 ISSP, which focuses on social inequality rather than spending preferences, has a question addressing views on the "justness" of private education. The question is, "Is it just or unjust – right or wrong – that people with higher incomes can buy better education for their children than people with lower incomes?" The potential answers are, "Very just, somewhat just, neither just not unjust, somewhat unjust, and very unjust." Notice that this question is framed differently from the previous question. Firstly, there is no reference directly to taxes or public policy. Secondly, the question is cast normatively, about "just" ways in which society

---

[10] This is potentially a reflection of pro-redistribution, anti-education political parties in proportional representation systems, as hypothesized in section 4.2.

TABLE 4.3. *Determinants of Preferences over Private Education*

	Model A	Model B	Model C	Model D	Model E	Model F
Sex	0.115 (0.021)***	0.139 (0.019)***	0.137 (0.026)***	0.132 (0.025)***	0.119 (0.020)***	0.122 (0.020)***
Age	−0.002 (0.001)**	−0.001 (0.001)	−0.002 (0.001)**	−0.002 (0.001)**	−0.001 (0.001)	−0.001 (0.001)*
Education	−0.009 (0.012)	0.004 (0.010)	−0.020 (0.014)	0.018 (0.011)	−0.028 (0.013)**	0.011 (0.010)
Rel. Attendance	0.014 (0.011)	0.013 (0.011)	0.003 (0.011)	0.009 (0.012)	0.006 (0.011)	0.009 (0.012)
Catholic	−0.041 (0.033)	−0.034 (0.032)	−0.030 (0.037)	−0.027 (0.041)	−0.022 (0.030)	−0.034 (0.036)
Protestant	−0.045 (0.034)	−0.043 (0.037)	−0.018 (0.043)	0.015 (0.049)	−0.038 (0.033)	−0.026 (0.039)
Family Income	−0.029 (0.008)***			−0.014 (0.007)**		−0.018 (0.006)***
Social Class		−0.100 (0.020)***		−0.075 (0.016)***		−0.075 (0.016)***
Partisanship			−0.151 (0.025)***	−0.138 (0.024)***		
Center-Left					0.077 (0.029)***	0.079 (0.030)***
Center					−0.060 (0.027)**	−0.051 (0.028)*
Center-Right					−0.224 (0.046)***	−0.196 (0.043)***
Far-Right					−0.247 (0.095)***	−0.234 (0.073)***
Observations	20,750	22,064	14,168	11,892	23,408	19,580

Source: International Social Survey Program (1999).
Note: Robust standard errors are in parentheses.
* Significant at 10 percent; ** significant at 5 percent; *** significant at 1 percent.

could be structured. Thus we should be very careful in comparing answers to this question to those to the questions on public spending analyzed previously. Nonetheless, we would expect income and partisanship to have the reverse relationship to the preceding analysis. The formal model in Chapter 2 suggested that richer individuals prefer private to public education. Aggregated into party preferences, this suggests right-wing support for private education.

In Table 4.3, I conduct a similar set of estimates to the earlier analysis, using an ordered logit model to examine the determinants of views over the justness of private education. For income, I am able to categorize individuals by the country-specific decile into which their family income falls and I also use the subjective social class indicator. For partisanship, I use the same five category indicators. Models A and B examine income and class, and Models C through F use the partisanship indicators, with and without income and class. Throughout all the models, we see the expected patterns. Higher-income individuals are less inclined to think of private education as unjust, as are individuals of higher subjective social class and individuals who identify further to the right on the partisanship scale. As before, center-left identifiers are the most antipathetic to private education, and in this case we do see far-right individuals as the most supportive of private education, with center-right individuals behaving similarly. Overall, across twenty-two countries, the results are remarkably robust, even though in the case of private education, age, education, and religious identification/intensity are not robust predictors of preferences. Thus the analysis of private education produces the expected reversal of voter preferences to that of public education. More broadly, both analyses provide strong support for the assumptions that income and partisanship drive education preferences. We now turn to examine precisely how parties aggregate such preferences.

4.4 PARTY PREFERENCES OVER EDUCATION

Promising to support education is an archetypal political crowd-pleaser. Most parties from left to right make campaign speeches promising that education is a political priority. Yet, when one examines actual party manifestos, different partisan preferences over increased public investment in education appear somewhat more distinct. In one sense, campaign manifestos are cheap talk: Since parties are rarely held accountable to all promises in their campaign literature, mentioning a policy for increased education in the pre-election period does not provide a credible commitment for post-election behavior unless reputation costs are very high. Nonetheless, since manifestos have to be filled with some preferred policy proposals, there is also ample cause to believe that parties are not mentioning education for purely ornamental reasons. Furthermore, as noted in Section 4.2, where politics is multidimensional – proportional electoral systems – there is reason to believe that manifesto statements might provide a guide to how parties view education vis-à-vis their more general redistributive preferences.

As we shall see, there are strong partisan patterns in the degree to which parties emphasize increased investment in education in their manifestos. However, when we examine whether these pre-election promises have any effect on post-election policy outcomes, controlling for the partisanship of government, we find a much more mixed story. In fact, *absolute* education spending does not appear to be independently affected by such promises. However, there does appear to be a direct effect of rhetoric on *relative* education spending, even when partisanship is held constant, implying a rather pessimistic message: Political parties that promise to give out more education spending with one hand may take away funding from other government programs with the other. Rhetoric, in that sense, is merely about priorities under fixed budget constraints.

How can we measure parties' expressed preferences? In this section, I draw on Woldendorp, Kemon, and Budge's (2000) Comparative Manifestos Project (CMP), as adapted by Cusack and Engelhardt (2002), which scores each political party's manifesto along a variety of dimensions, including the percentage of the manifesto devoted to calls for increased education spending. This variable (*EDPOS*) ranges from 0 to 30 percent, with a mean of 3.67 percent and a standard deviation of 3.4 percent. In terms of measuring party type, I employ three techniques. The first technique uses Woldendorp and his colleagues' (2000) party coding, which splits parties into eleven families: ecology (green), communist, social democratic, liberal, Christian democratic, conservative, national, agrarian, ethnic and regional, and special interest. I use party dummies and also combine parties into similar-party groups: the far-left, the center-left, the center-right, and the paleo-conservatives.[11] The second technique I use orders parties along a scale and treats that ordering as a single linear variable (*PARTY*). The third technique abstracts away from party identification and uses the stated positions of parties on issues other than education. I use two ideological variables taken from the CMP in the Cusack-Engelhardt dataset: the CMP policy position variable (*CMPIDEO*), which is compiled from a range of manifesto positions across several policy areas, and a simple measure of general party attitudes toward the markets and the welfare state (*MARKWELF*).

Table 4.4 presents the analysis. Ten party types are entered into the regression in Model A, with the "special interest" party grouping omitted. Three points are immediately noticeable. Firstly, and perhaps most surprisingly, are the very large and significant negative coefficients on the green and communist parties (especially the former). Secondly, there are strong positive and significant coefficients for the social democrats and liberal parties, with the former having the largest positive coefficient of all the parties. Thirdly, all the parties to the right of the liberals – the Christian democrats, conservatives, nationalists, agrarians, and regionalists – have negative coefficients, with particularly large coefficients for the paleo-conservative parties, especially the nationalists.

How ought we to interpret the coefficients in Model A? Figure 4.2 shows 95 percent confidence intervals for each party, with the dashed line representing the estimate for the average *EDPOS* value for special interest parties. The most striking pattern is an inverse-U, with far-left parties barely mentioning education; social democrats and liberals the strongest advocates for increased education spending; and right-wing parties at varying lower levels of advocacy, particularly nationalist parties, who most resemble the green parties. If we exclude the greens and communists from analysis, we see a clear left-right negative pattern. The result for greens and communists is somewhat surprising and may reflect the kinds of variation we saw in section 4.2 among left- and right-wing minor parties under proportional representation, where they cater for individuals whose education and redistribution preferences do not line up along the standard dimension. Figure 4.2 thus provides some empirical evidence for the *possibility* of an "ends against the middle" coalition, though the political feasibility of such coalitions remains less clear.

[11] The communists and greens are in the far-left grouping; the social democrats and liberals in the center-left grouping; the Christian democrats and conservatives in the center-right grouping; and the nationalists, agrarians, regionalists and special interest parties are in the paleo-conservative group. This last group is so named since these parties represent conservative identity politics (e.g., national, rural, regional, special interest) rather than programmatic mass conservatism.

TABLE 4.4. *The Effects of Party Type on the Proportion of Manifestos Devoted to Calls for Increased Education Spending*

	Model A	Model B	Model C	Model D	Model E	Model F
	OLS	OLS	OLS			
Greens	−1.656 (0.297)***	−0.456 (0.166)***				
Communists	−0.869 (0.256)***					
Social Dem.	0.623 (0.239)***	1.109 (0.140)***	0.752 (0.101)***			
Liberals	0.477 (0.237)**					
Christian Dem.	−0.312 (0.253)	0.354 (0.145)**				
Conservative	−0.060 (0.240)					
Nationalist	−1.478 (0.396)***					
Agrarian	−0.555 (0.310)*					
Ethnic / Reg.	−0.526 (0.334)					
Party				−0.047 (0.021)**		
CMPIDEO					−0.045 (0.002)***	
MARKWELF						−0.003 (0.001)***
Constant	3.535 (0.218)***	3.000 (0.120)***	3.390 (0.071)***	3.721 (0.106)***	3.410 (0.041)***	3.471 (0.047)***
N	4,076	4,076	2877	4,076	4076	4,068
R²	0.41	0.40	0.48	0.38	0.41	0.38
Elections	345	345	340	345	345	345

Note: Robust standard errors are in parentheses. ***$p < 0.01$, **$p < 0.05$, *$p < 0.1$.
Observations are party election years. All regressions include election fixed effects.

I simplify matters in Model B by combining the parties into four major groups: far-left, center-left, center-right, and paleo-conservative, with the latter omitted. We see very strong results here, with far-left parties mentioning education even less than the paleo-conservatives, and with the two centrist groups devoting considerably more space in their manifestos to calls for increased education funding. Model C, which includes only center-left and center-right parties in the sample, finds a robust difference of three-quarters of a percentage point between the two groupings. Thus, there appears to be considerable evidence backing the assertion that left-wing parties (at least those likely to actually gain power) express greater pre-election interest in increasing education funding than do right-wing parties, confirming Hypothesis One.

Model D uses the simple linear party measure. Figure 4.2 displayed considerable non-linearity, which suggests that a linear assumption may not be

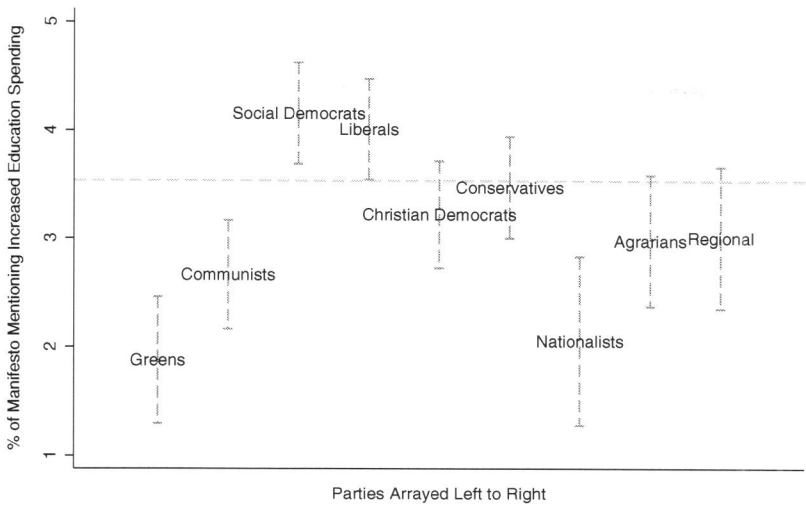

FIGURE 4.2. Comparing Parties' Education Rhetoric

appropriate.[12] A linear fit does, however, appear to be statistically significant at the 5 percent level, although with a much lower magnitude than the preceding regressions suggest because of the inclusion of the far-left parties. Model E uses the CMP ideology index, which ranges between –90.8 and 85, with higher numbers reflecting right-wing ideology. The coefficient on this variable is –0.045, implying that a two-standard deviation ideological shift to the right should be associated with a sizable decrease of over 2 percent points in *EDPOS*. This implies that other ideological factors that are associated with being on the left or the right – for example, attitudes on employment and regulation – are very closely associated with attitudes toward increased education spending. Model F confirms this finding employing a simpler proxy for ideology, using codings of attitudes to the welfare state and market economy, and also finding a robust, albeit somewhat smaller, partisan effect. Overall, there is strong evidence that left-wing parties, however defined, are much stronger pre-electoral advocates of increased education spending than are right-wing parties.

I now shift gear to examine a slightly different question about parties' preferences over education spending. For parties that win a majority, the connection between education rhetoric and education policy should be simple: They can choose to enact their promises or choose to renege on them. For parties that fail to join the government, the strategic environment is also simple: They simply have no control over policy outcomes. However, there is a large subset of cases where parties do not win a majority but do have some hand in government through coalition. They thus have some opportunity to

---

[12] I also conducted these regressions using a quadratic function of party type, finding a statistically significant inverse *U* that peaked between social democrat and liberal parties.

TABLE 4.5. *The Effects of Education Rhetoric on Gaining Education Portfolio*

	Model A	Model B
	Full Sample	**Did Not Have a Prime Minister**
EDPOS	0.043	0.062
	(0.021)**	(0.031)**
Greens	−14.703	−15.698
	(742.158)	(985.049)
Communists	−1.448	−0.584
	(0.555)***	(0.557)
Social Dem.	−0.225	0.013
	(0.490)	(0.525)
Liberals	0.917	0.742
	(0.489)*	(0.511)
Christian Dem.	0.508	1.145
	(0.502)	(0.529)**
Conservative	−0.019	0.156
	(0.495)	(0.540)
Nationalist	−15.180	−16.202
	(897.032)	(1,693.827)
Agrarian	0.277	0.032
	(0.523)	(0.607)
Ethnic / Reg.	−0.823	−1.288
	(0.722)	(0.738)*
Vote Share	11.873	5.330
	(0.594)***	(0.908)***
Observations	3,443	1,494
Elections	297	101

Note: Robust standard errors are in parentheses.
***$p < 0.01$, **$p < 0.05$, *$p < 0.1$.

realize their expressed policy preferences over education spending, but this is likely to depend on whether they are given the education seat in the cabinet. Table 4.5 examines whether non-winning parties that express a strong preference for increased education spending in their pre-election manifestos are more likely to be granted the education portfolio in coalition cabinets in the post-election period. This question pertains to Hypothesis Five, which suggested that the education policies of coalition governments should be examined by addressing the policy platforms of individual members rather than just the average partisanship of the coalition. Here I show that major coalition members often give minor parties with strong education preferences the education portfolio. Figure 4.1 showed a set of potential coalitions in proportional systems, containing parties of quite different sizes. Table 4.5 suggests that education policy is likely to reflect more than just the preferences of the major party in the coalition and hence supports the assertion that proportional electoral systems support multidimensional policy outcomes.

Table 4.5 contains two models. Model A contains the full sample of parties, including those who won the election, whereas Model B includes only those parties that did not win the election. These parties may, however, gain some cabinet portfolios if they form a coalition with the winning party. Both models use logit estimations and include election fixed effects. The regressions have as their dependent variable a simple zero/one coding of whether a party gained the education portfolio in that particular electoral period. I control for all party types, as well as the vote share that party received. The independent variable of interest is *EDPOS*, the percentage of the party's manifesto devoted to calls for increased education spending.

Examining the coefficients shows that advocating education spending in one's manifesto significantly increases the chances of receiving the education ministry. Since Model A includes those parties who win the election, it is not surprising that we see a strong positive result here – presumably those parties who advocate education spending *and* form a coalition government will want to keep the education portfolio to themselves. However, when we exclude election winners from the analysis, we see an even stronger effect of education advocacy on the chances of being granted the education portfolio, even controlling for party type *and* vote share. To get an idea of the predicted effect, a party that increased its proportion of its manifesto devoted to calls for increased public education spending by 10 percent would see its chances of acquiring the education ministry increase by around 15 percent points, a rather sizable effect.

I conclude the analysis of party preferences by asking whether manifesto promises to expand education are merely cheap talk, once general partisanship is controlled for. Thus, I am turning from expressed preferences in manifestos to revealed preferences in policy. I use a dataset, ranging from 1960 to 2002 across twenty-four OECD countries, that incorporates only those parties serving in government during a particular year. To measure partisanship, I now use Cusack and Engelhardt's (2002) *cabinet center of gravity* measure, which compiles the CMP ideology variable for all parties, converting it into a country-year dataset, where the center of gravity is a weighted average of the parties comprising the governing cabinet. If a cabinet contains members of only one party (as in many majoritarian systems), this cabinet center of gravity index will correspond closely to the CMP ideology variable for that party in that electoral period. Coalition government, however, requires weighting each party's ideology index by its share of seats. Similarly, the *EDPOS* index is now a weighted average of the *EDPOS* scores for each party in cabinet, reflecting the average emphasis that parties put on education before the election, weighted by their post-election cabinet seats.

Table 4.6 presents a set of models, all with country fixed effects, examining the impact of cabinet partisanship versus pre-electoral manifesto positions on education spending. Models A and B both have *absolute public spending on education* as their dependent variable. This measure is identical to that used in Chapter 2, although the dataset is now limited to the OECD. The same set of control variables as in earlier chapters is employed. Model A includes the weighted education rhetoric variable – *EDPOS* – whereas Model B includes both this *and* the cabinet partisanship variable. Examining Model A first, we see no direct effect of the weighted education rhetoric measure on actual education outcomes. Once we include the cabinet partisanship variable, the coefficient

TABLE 4.6. *The Effects of Rhetoric on Education Spending*

	Model A PUBED	Model B PUBED	Model C PUBED/GOVEX	Model D PUBED/GOVEX
Lagged DV	0.703	0.702	0.632	0.650
	(0.034)***	(0.035)***	(0.037)***	(0.035)***
EDPOS	0.014	0.002	0.195	0.129
	(0.012)	(0.001)	(0.061)***	(0.056)**
Cab. Party		−0.006		−0.021
		(0.002)***		(0.009)**
Log Openness	−0.881	−0.834	−2.150	−1.958
	(0.241)***	(0.245)***	(1.249)*	(1.154)*
Population < 15	0.030	0.045	−0.066	0.132
	(0.023)	(0.024)*	(0.119)	(0.110)
Log (GDP)	2.472	2.048	12.653	10.009
	(1.437)*	(1.398)	(7.310)*	(6.433)
Log (GDP) Sq	−0.054	−0.057	−0.298	−0.336
	(0.028)*	(0.027)**	(0.141)**	(0.126)***
Log (POP)	0.540	0.382	6.435	4.381
	(0.914)	(0.890)	(4.769)	(4.200)
GOVEX/GDP	−0.039	−0.028		
	(0.020)*	(0.020)		
Year	0.013	0.033	−0.021	0.171
	(0.010)	(0.012)***	(0.050)	(0.056)***
Constant	−56.441	−81.902	−169.950	−427.606
	(25.244)**	(27.178)***	(124.408)	(123.213)***
R^2	0.583	0.617	0.499	0.590
Observations	407	389	406	388
Countries	24	23	24	23

Note: Standard errors are in parentheses.
***$p < 0.01$, **$p < 0.05$, *$p < 0.1$. All regressions include country fixed effects.

on rhetoric essentially vanishes, although cabinet partisanship appears a strong predictor of actual education spending (which we shall explore in much greater depth in the following section). Thus far, then, it appears that despite the clear relationship between partisanship and "expressed preferences" over education spending, these preferences are poor predictors of actual outcomes and, once partisanship is controlled for, rhetoric alone has essentially no effect on absolute education spending.

This rather negative result is, however, counterbalanced by Models C and D, which use *relative education spending* as their dependent variable. Model C just includes the rhetoric measure and finds a strong and robust relationship between rhetoric and relative education spending: A percent point increase in the amount of the "weighted" manifesto dealing with calls for increased public education corresponds to an increase of around 0.2 percent of the amount of overall government spending devoted to education. Is it, however, the case that education rhetoric is merely serving here as a proxy for cabinet partisanship? That appears not to be the case. In fact, Model D, which includes both the weighted education rhetoric variable and the cabinet partisanship variable, estimates that both measures have robust effects on relative education spending. The impact of rhetoric is reduced by around a third, but it remains robust at the 5 percent level.

What then, are the implications of this finding? It appears to be the case that "expressed preferences" over education spending, once general partisanship is controlled for, only correspond to "revealed preferences" in terms of education's relative importance vis-à-vis other government programs. On the one hand, this is perhaps intuitive. If we think about what the rhetoric variable is really measuring, we could construe it as the relative importance of education to other pre-election promises in a given manifesto (or, in this case, weighted manifestos). Since these other promises would presumably also be for other forms of government action and spending, then one could argue that we are simply seeing the zero-sum game of policy emphasis in the manifesto spill over into a zero-sum relationship between objects of actual government spending. On the other hand, there does appear to be an element of subterfuge in government promises to increase public spending on education that actually turn out to be, at best, a fixing of education spending combined with a reduction of other government services. Notice that this relationship is separate from the effects of partisanship. Thus, it implies that right-wing governments with election manifestos that are "unexpectedly" pro-education will not actually expand education once in office but that they will, at least, maintain funding while cutting other programs. Left-wing governments who barely mention education, conversely, may be deciding to tilt the budget toward other preferred public goods. Rhetoric, then, acts as a signal over a government's preferences over education in regard to other policy areas, but it appears to have precious little impact on the aggregate emphasis that is placed on education.[13]

4.5 DERIVING POLICY OUTCOMES

If politicians are not responding to particular commitments made to the electorate in terms of absolute education spending, then what is driving their behavior? In this section, I argue that a party's overall ideological position – that is, its "essential" partisan preference – is a much better predictor of education spending than are pre-electoral statements. Voters would do well to beware the "gift horse" of promises of changes in education spending, whether upward or downward, from politicians whose party's ideological preferences appear to contradict such statements. In fact, cabinet partisanship is a robust and substantively powerful predictor of both absolute and relative education spending, leading to changes of around 1 percent of GDP in a period as short as one electoral term following a shift in government. As we shall see, dramatic changes in government could lead to equally momentous changes in education funding, potentially holding the funding for thousands of schools and millions of teachers in the balance. The empirical analysis in this section examines the cross-sectional

---

[13] In Section 4.6, I revisit this analysis, examining the differential impact of manifesto statements in majoritarian versus proportional electoral systems.

TABLE 4.7. *The Effects of Partisanship on Absolute and Relative Education Spending*

	Model A PUBED/GDP	Model B PUBED/GDP	Model C PUBED/GOV	Model D PUBED/GOV
	PCSE	Fixed Effects	PCSE	Fixed Effects
Lagged D.V.	0.798	0.702	.787	0.658
	(0.0381)***	(0.034)***	(0.038)***	(0.035)***
Partisanship	−0.006	−0.006	−0.023	−0.026
	(0.002)***	(0.002)***	(0.008)***	(0.008)***
Log Openness	−0.285	−0.836	−0.990	−1.830
	(0.107)***	(0.244)***	(0.433)**	(1.161)
Population < 15	0.043	0.046	0.167	0.150
	(0.018)**	(0.023)*	(0.076)**	(0.111)
Log (GDP)	2.483	2.042	4.013	8.988
	(0.730)***	(1.396)	(3.319)	(6.457)
Log (GDP) Sq	−0.038	−0.057	−0.060	−0.330
	(0.012)***	(0.027)**	(0.057)	(0.127)***
Log (Pop)	−0.513	0.399	−0.899	5.283
	(0.141)***	(0.885)	(0.595)	(4.208)
GOVEX/GDP	0.017	−0.030		
	(0.013)	(0.020)		
Year	−0.018	0.033	−0.031	0.192
	(0.006)***	(0.012)***	(0.030)	(0.055)***
Constant	7.048	−82.751	18.583	−462.012
	(17.142)	(26.809)***	(83.631)	(123.087)***
Observations	389	389	388	388
Countries	23	23	23	23
R^2	0.963	.617	0.961	.584
Short-Run Effect	−0.278	−0.319	−1.143	−1.309
Four-Year Effect	−0.818	−0.811	−3.308	−3.110

Note: Standard errors are in parentheses ***$p < 0.01$, **$p < 0.05$, *$p < 0.1$.

and time-series effects of changes in partisanship on changes in education spending for twenty-three countries from 1960 to 2000. As in Chapter 2, our dependent variables of interest are absolute education spending and relative (to other government consumption) education spending.

Models A and B of Table 4.7 examine PCSE and fixed effects regressions of absolute public spending on education. The models used both demonstrate a statistically significant estimated effect of partisanship, with a similar magnitude. To ascertain what kind of substantive effect is implied by these coefficients, I estimate short- and long-run effects of the mean range – fifty points – of partisanship across all twenty-three countries. Short-run (one-year) effects simply amount to the coefficient on cabinet partisanship multiplied by fifty. They imply that a switch from the average left-wing party to the average right-wing party in the dataset is associated with a reduction in spending of between a quarter and a third of a percent point of national income. This implies a 5 to 7 percent decrease in average education spending across the dataset.

The four-year effect – a standard electoral cycle – of this change in partisanship is estimated to be a reduction in spending of around three-quarters of a percentage point of national income, around 15 percent of the average expenditure on education across the dataset. Clearly, a party that won multiple terms would see an even greater change in education expenditure in the long run, albeit with a falling marginal change for each extra year. This implies that consistent partisan control of government will indeed lead to divergence in education policy, but even in the long run it is unlikely to lead to changes of much greater than 1 percent of GDP in education spending. Since the within-country standard deviation of education spending since 1990 is 0.46, this likely range of partisan change seems quite plausible.

Models C and D of Table 4.7 examine the effect of partisanship on relative public spending on education. In both of the models, cabinet partisanship is again a significant predictor of the composition of government spending. Thus Hypothesis One (a) is confirmed: Right-wing governments lead to lower absolute and relative education spending. The short-term predicted change in relative education spending is just over 1 percent of overall government consumption and the predicted four-year effect of changing from the average left-wing to the average right-wing party in the dataset is a reduction of just over 3 points in the percentage of government spending devoted to education. Given that the average percentage of government spending devoted to education across the dataset is 28.7 percent, this would amount to around an 11 percent decline in the proportion of government spending taken by education. Since this predicted effect is around two-thirds the size of that obtained for absolute education spending, it provides confirmation of Hypothesis One (b), which argued that the partisan effect should be slightly weaker with regard to relative education spending.

Table 4.8 provides some intuition of the dollar-value magnitude of these changes, showing the typical partisan range for each state and the associated four-year change in education spending in dollar terms using Model B. This model has the advantage that it measures only changes within states and hence is the most appropriate measure in terms of estimating the effects of partisan change within countries. To use the United Kingdom as an example, a change from Conservative to Labour control of the government is associated with a four-year change in spending of $12.3bn (£7bn at 2006 exchange rates), or $206 (£118) per capita. This a vast figure, with obvious implications for the kinds of educational purchases that could be made. For example, this sum could purchase the services of half a million teachers at the average UK salary for junior teachers. Alternatively, per-student spending in the public primary and secondary sector could rise by $2,750/£1,580 (in fact, from 1997 to 2006, Labour's spending per student rose £2,500, even higher than this estimate). Elsewhere the predicted change in per capita spending from a full shift in partisanship ranges from $57.82 in Spain (which has a low partisan range and low absolute per capita spending) to over $400 in Denmark and Iceland (with high partisan range and high per capita spending).

So far we have seen a striking partisan pattern in education – left-wing parties are much more strongly supportive of education spending at the aggregate level. However, Hypothesis Two, regarding streaming and vocational education, suggested that under some conditions it might actually be right-wing

TABLE 4.8. *Four-Year Predicted Financial Effects of Partisanship on Education*

Country	Range of Partisanship	1999 Education Spending $bn	Change in Total Spending $bn	Change as % of Budget	1990s Mean per Capita Spending	Change in per Capita Spending
Australia	31.8	19.9	2.4	12.0	$1,021	$122.87
Austria	82.4	16.3	3.6	22.3	$1,688	$375.72
Belgium	39.9	17.9	2.1	11.6	$1,284	$148.89
Canada	32.1	37.2	3.7	9.9	$1,271	$126.04
Denmark	71.9	15.9	2.4	15.3	$2,748	$420.39
Finland	67.7	9.6	1.8	18.8	$1,727	$325.06
France	53.0	100.8	15.4	15.3	$1,566	$239.36
Germany	39.8	121.1	17.7	14.6	$1,412	$205.90
Greece	60.9	4.9	1.4	28.1	$350	$98.35
Iceland	81.5	0.4	0.1	28.8	$1,540	$443.80
Ireland	53.6	4.2	0.9	20.8	$905	$187.90
Italy	33.1	53.2	6.6	12.4	$817	$101.11
Japan	32.2	196.5	30.4	15.5	$1,516	$234.39
Luxembourg	34.0	0.8	0.1	16.5	$1,497	$247.68
Netherlands	36.9	23.2	3.0	13.0	$1,387	$180.01
New Zealand	40.6	4.6	0.5	10.1	$1,083	$109.04
Norway	44.8	12.3	1.3	10.3	$2,505	$259.03
Portugal	41.2	7.3	0.9	12.0	$595	$71.36
Spain	22.8	30.5	2.6	8.6	$673	$57.82
Sweden	81.1	20.8	3.7	17.8	$2,095	$372.16
Switzerland	25.0	17.9	1.4	7.7	$2,457	$190.18
UK	56.8	56.8	12.3	21.6	$954	$205.97
USA	53.7	437.5	78.8	18.0	$1,443	$259.85

parties that favor increased spending, even when it is not targeted at their own children. I now turn to examining the empirics of vocational education policy. In doing so, however, I am forced to rely on much less satisfactory data than in the case of aggregate education spending data. There is no reliable, cross-national time-series data available on relative government spending on vocational training.[14] This means direct comparisons to the previous results are not feasible. However, UNESCO does have data on the relative enrollments in academic versus vocational tracks for seventeen countries going back to 1970. While this does not provide a perfect analog to Hypothesis Two, we nonetheless see the expected patterns for spending apparent in the study of enrollment. The variable I analyze is the proportion of total secondary students enrolled in vocational programs and it covers seventeen countries from 1970 to 1997. Since changes in enrollments are very gradual, this measure provides a tough case for a redistributive partisan theory of vocational education, yet even here we see a robust effect of partisanship.

In Table 4.9 I examine a broad variety of models explaining the change in relative enrollments in vocational education. I use both Prais-Winston regressions, which include between-country effects, and fixed effects analyses, which include solely within-country effects. For each type of statistical model, I examine, firstly, all countries; secondly, countries with streamed schooling systems; and thirdly, countries without streaming. I define streaming as whether students are streamed into academic and vocational schools before age sixteen. Thirteen countries qualify as streamed in this analysis, but because of missing data for Australia, Canada, and the United States, only four qualify as non-streamed. Hence, we should view analyses of the latter group with some caution. That caveat aside, across the models we see a very consistent pattern of partisanship.

Models A through C use a basic set of controls and the Prais-Winston technique. In the full sample, partisanship appears to have no effect, but when we break countries into two groups by the presence of streaming, we see that in streamed countries right-wing parties are associated with increased enrollments in vocational education whereas in non-streamed countries that effect is associated with left-wing parties. Models D through F, which add general government spending and public spending on education, produce a near-identical picture. The fixed effects regressions show a similar pattern. Models G through I, using the basic controls, show a very robust right-wing increase in vocational enrollment in streamed states, though the left-wing effect in non-streamed states is not significant. Finally, Models J through L, which add the lagged dependent variable and spending controls, show a right-wing effect in streamed states and a left-wing effect in non-streamed states. Overall, there is a fairly pronounced differential partisan effect across streamed and non-streamed states that conforms to the expectations of Hypothesis Two. The effect, while significant statistically, is not substantively enormous – a fifty-point shift to the right is

---

[14] Even cross-sectional data on spending is limited in scope; for example, Eurostat's data on spending in 2005 only cover six Western European states plus several Eastern European ones.

TABLE 4.9. *Vocational Enrollments as a Proportion of Total Enrollments*

	Model A	Model B	Model C	Model D	Model E	Model F
	PRAIS	PRAIS	PRAIS	PRAIS	PRAIS	PRAIS
	All	Streamed	Not Streamed	All	Streamed	Not Streamed
Partisan	-0.002	0.010	-0.095	-0.004	0.008	-0.088
	(0.012)	(0.004)**	(0.044)**	(0.012)	(0.004)**	(0.048)*
Log GDP	155.457	131.568	417.967	158.928	148.843	519.538
	(37.460)***	(33.238)***	(99.136)***	(35.807)***	(28.996)***	(62.504)***
Log GDP Sq	-2.741	-2.391	-7.591	-2.904	-2.804	-9.703
	(0.695)***	(0.629)***	(1.892)***	(0.668)***	(0.543)***	(1.199)***
Log Pop	-10.023	-3.068	-20.629	-4.581	1.858	-13.159
	(3.255)***	(2.592)	(6.904)***	(2.942)	(2.713)	(5.911)**
GOVEX				0.063	0.213	-0.508
				(0.154)	(0.128)*	(0.373)
PUBED				-0.172	0.191	-0.861
				(0.254)	(0.249)	(0.488)*
Year				0.198	0.205	0.373
				(0.092)**	(0.089)**	(0.150)**
Constant	-2,000.361	-1,725.774	-5,376.872	-2,459.912	-2,385.937	-7,433.897
	(498.913)***	(442.082)***	(1,288.912)***	(517.661)***	(400.742)***	(966.097)***
N	227	173	54	209	159	50
Countries	17	13	4	16	12	4
R²	0.39	0.49	0.54	0.41	0.53	0.73

	Model G	Model H	Model I	Model J	Model K	Model L
	Fixed FX	Fixed FX	Fixed FX	Fixed FX	Fixed FX	Fixed FX
	All	Streamed	Not Streamed	All	Streamed	Not Streamed
Partisan	0.019	0.027	-0.031	-0.001	0.010	-0.093
	(0.011)*	(0.010)***	(0.039)	(0.010)	(0.006)*	(0.041)**
Log GDP	95.301	82.695	176.438	-5.210	6.865	-351.569
	(23.887)***	(21.255)***	(147.093)	(12.999)	(12.912)	(118.022)***
Log GDP Sq	-1.578	-1.260	-3.068	0.128	-0.089	6.984
	(0.462)***	(0.404)***	(2.739)	(0.255)	(0.260)	(2.263)***
Log Pop	-13.858	-53.257	26.221	19.147	-28.561	199.849
	(18.449)	(12.999)***	(27.557)	(12.727)	(7.847)***	(56.216)***
Lagged DV				0.964	0.800	1.074
				(0.062)***	(0.069)***	(0.179)***
GOVEX				-0.092	0.222	0.102
				(0.095)	(0.080)***	(0.298)
PUBED				0.063	-0.018	-0.818
				(0.202)	(0.228)	(0.508)
Year				-0.152	0.060	-1.533
				(0.090)*	(0.068)	(0.455)***
Constant	-1,161.961	-410.399	-2,923.322	43.993	225.024	4,210.558
	(429.598)***	(311.813)	(1,808.612)	(248.362)	(212.151)	(1,431.179)***
N	227	173	54	177	136	41
Countries	17	13	4	16	12	4
R²	0.33	0.44	0.46	0.79	0.87	0.87

Note: Robust standard errors are in parentheses.

***$p < 0.01$, **$p < 0.05$, *$p < 0.1$.

associated with an increase of one-third of a standard deviation in the proportion of students attending vocational education in streamed countries, and a decrease of a full standard deviation in non-streamed countries. Demographic effects and year-to-year autocorrelation appear somewhat stronger.

Nonetheless, from the perspective of the standard political science literature on vocational education, which emphasizes the general complementarity between left-wing government and vocational training systems (Iversen and Stephens, 2008; Iversen 2005), the fact that partisan effects are *conditional* on school streaming is surprising. On closer inspection, though, it appears rather intuitive. Vocational training is a double-edged sword for the poor – it boosts wages at the lower end of the income distribution, but it may also preclude advances up the career ladder, when such training, as in streamed systems, limits access to university and the professions. I pick up this trade-off again in Chapter 5. However, I now turn to another important conditioning effect for education: the role of electoral institutions.

4.6 ELECTORAL INSTITUTIONS AND EDUCATION POLICY

To this point, I have examined the impact of partisanship, whether individual or governmental, on education spending in an institution-free environment. However, in Section 4.2 I asserted that the electoral system facing voters and parties has powerful effects on the kinds of policies that can be made. Specifically, I argued that electoral institutions affect education policy in two manners. Firstly, proportional electoral systems should have a *moderating* effect on the range of partisan policy making, reducing partisan swings in education policy. Secondly, I argued that proportional systems, because they permit the development of multiple political parties, create the possibility of a broad variety of coalitions across *multidimensional* policy domains. Put simply, proportional systems can break the strong relationship between party preferences over education spending and general redistribution found in majoritarian systems.

The Moderating Effect of Electoral Institutions

Hypothesis Three asserted that proportional representation systems should see a smaller range of partisan policy because the coalitional dynamics generated in these systems force parties to bargain over policy and give greater bargaining power to centrist groups. Table 4.10 empirically explores this proposition using three variables: a variable for whether an electoral system has multimember districts; the effective number of parties in the legislature; and an index of proportionality. In each case, the variable is interacted with cabinet partisanship.[15] I measure electoral systems using three variables, each time interacting them with the partisanship variable. The first variable is a three-point indicator

---

[15] There are two reasons for doing this: Firstly, electoral systems are largely constant within states across time, hence in a fixed effects model they essentially drop out; secondly, I am interested in the effect of partisanship *conditional* on the prevailing electoral system.

TABLE 4.10. *The Partisan Effect under Different Electoral Institutions*

	Model A PUBED/GDP	Model B PUBED/GDP	Model C PUBED/GDP	Model D PUBED/GOV	Model E PUBED/GOV	Model F PUBED/GOV
Lagged D.V.	0.654 (0.039)***	0.648 (0.040)***	0.649 (0.040)***	0.587 (0.036)***	0.598 (0.041)***	0.597 (0.041)***
Cabinet COG	-0.014 (0.004)***	-0.020 (0.006)***	-0.014 (0.004)***	-0.054 (0.018)***	-0.081 (0.028)***	-0.042 (0.018)**
Cab * MMD	0.011 (0.005)**			0.042 (0.025)*		
Cab * Parties		0.005 (0.002)***			0.018 (0.008)**	
Cab * PROPORT			0.014 (0.006)**			0.035 (0.026)
LOGOPEN	-0.910 (0.289)***	-0.756 (0.247)***	-0.843 (0.248)***	-02.381 (1.368)*	-1.496 (1.145)	-1.727 (1.157)
Population < 15	0.113 (0.030)***	0.127 (0.027)***	0.126 (0.027)***	0.432 (0.143)***	0.468 (0.130)***	0.471 (0.130)***
Log GDP	0.189 (1.950)	2.991 (2.074)	3.256 (2.072)	5.731 (9.082)	23.824 (9.291)**	25.148 (9.326)***
Log GDP Sq	-0.024 (0.037)	-0.069 (0.038)*	-0.074 (0.038)*	-0.262 (0.173)	-0.593 (0.172)***	-0.618 (0.172)***
Log Population	2.081 (1.077)*	0.908 (0.924)	1.235 (0.926)	13.565 (5.111)***	9.458 (4.272)**	10.506 (4.303)**
GOVEX/GDP	-0.016 (0.023)	-0.008 (0.020)	-0.009 (0.021)			
Year	0.041 (0.014)***	0.040 (0.013)***	0.037 (0.013)***	0.186 (0.065)***	0.219 (0.059)***	0.209 (0.059)***
Constant	-99.868 (34.972)***	-122.877 (35.275)***	-124.802 (35.268)***	-546.871 (161.453)***	-798.410 (155.046)***	-813.570 (155.744)***
Observations	299	293	293	298	292	292
Number of States	19	17	17	19	17	17
R²	0.61	0.65	0.65	0.58	0.65	0.65

Note: Standard errors are in parentheses.
***p < 0.01, **p < 0.05, *p < 0.1.

of whether a state has multimember districts (coded 0 for no MMD, 0.5 for partial MMD, and 1 for full MMD) from Huber, Ragin, and Stephens (1997). The second variable is the "effective number of legislative parties," taken from Laakso and Taagepera (1979). The third variable is a measure of proportionality ranging between 0 and 1, developed by Iversen and Soskice (2006), which combines Lijphart's (1994) measure of the effective threshold of representation with Gallagher's (1991) measure of the disproportionality between votes and seats. Together these three measures pick up slightly different aspects of electoral variation: both the process governing voting and the outcomes of institutions in terms of party number or disproportionality.

Models A through C of Table 4.10 use absolute education spending as the dependent variable. In all three models, the interactive measures of proportionality combined with partisanship are both positive and statistically significant, albeit more so in the measure of party number and the proportionality index. In all cases, the impact of proportionality is to dampen down the negative "pure" effect of cabinet partisanship.[16] Model A implies that the effect of cabinet partisanship is roughly three and a half times stronger in non-MMD systems than in MMD systems (comparing coefficients of –0.014 and –0.004). Model B implies that each additional "effective" party in an electoral system reduces the impact of the partisanship coefficient by around one quarter. Finally, the results for the proportionality index in Model C indicate that the effect of partisanship is basically canceled out as the index asymptotes toward 1.

Substantively, what are the effects? Examining multimember districts, a rightward move of fifty points on the partisan index is associated with a drop in education spending of 0.3 percent of GDP in MMD systems versus around 0.8 percent in non-MMD systems. Comparing the average effective number of parties in proportional systems (3.9) to those in majoritarian systems (2.5), the fifty-point partisanship increase is respectively associated with a drop of 0.2 percent of GDP versus 0.5 percent. Finally, the effect on education spending of a fifty-point partisanship increase for a state scoring one on the proportional index is less than 0.1 percent of GDP, whereas a state scoring zero on the proportional index sees an effect of 0.7 percent of GDP. In general, whereas right-wing partisanship always has a negative effect on education spending in all kinds of electoral systems, it is only substantively large and statistically significant in majoritarian states. Consequently, there is clearly a very significant moderating of partisan policies in proportional electoral systems, however measured. It appears that the increased bargaining power of centrist groups, as outlined in Hypothesis Three, dampens any pull to the extremes.

For completeness, Models D through F of Table 4.10 repeat the empirical exercise using relative education spending as the dependent variable, producing similar results. However, here we see that the impact of proportionality is slightly weaker, though in the same direction as before. These weaker results

---

[16] The effect of proportionality can be interpreted by adding the coefficient of the interactive variable to that of the partisanship variable.

suggest that proportionality may have more complex effects on the trade-off between types of spending than on pure education funding alone. Indeed, the most statistically significant result comes from that examining the effect of the effective number of legislative parties. Thus, rather than proportionality per se, it may be that the proliferation of parties is what splits education from redistribution in proportional systems. It is to precisely this question that we now turn.

Multidimensionality

I now move to the second main effect of proportional electoral systems: their creation of an effective multidimensional policy space thanks to multiple viable political parties. In Hypothesis Five, I argued that because of this multidimensionality, in proportional systems, examining each coalition member's positions on particular policy items would be a better guide to education outcomes than just looking at the average partisanship of the cabinet as a whole. This is because proportional systems allow parties of apparently similar partisanship to have rather distinct preferences on education versus other redistribution. In majoritarian systems, the reverse should apply, since these systems compact policy along one partisan dimension – thus, in these countries, partisan identification alone is a better predictor than manifesto statements. I test this proposition in Table 4.11 by reintroducing the manifesto statement variable *EDPOS*. Models A through C examine the effects of cabinet partisanship and manifesto statements on absolute education spending, and Models D through F examine these effects on relative education spending. Models A and D include all countries; Models B and E include just proportional systems; and Models C and F include just majoritarian systems.

The results match closely the expectations of Hypothesis Five. As in Table 4.10, cabinet partisanship does not matter in proportional systems, either in terms of predicting absolute or relative education spending. In majoritarian systems, conversely, partisanship is always a strong predictor of both variables.[17] However, when one looks at the role of manifesto statements, we find the reverse pattern, at least in the case of relative education spending. While majoritarian systems never show a significant effect of manifesto statements, controlling for cabinet partisanship, in proportional systems these statements have a positive and statistically robust effect on relative education spending, even though partisanship does not. This suggests that the greater proliferation of parties in proportional systems allows the creation of coalitions that may appear on the surface to be similar in partisan terms but have starkly different education policies. In the next section, I follow up on this suggestion, showing how parties with very similar redistributive preference profiles can have starkly distinct education preferences, but only in countries with proportional electoral systems.

---

[17] Whereas Table 4.10 used an interactive variable, here I split the sample. The moderating effects of proportionality hold in both cases.

TABLE 4.11. *Partisanship versus Campaign Promises across Electoral Systems*

	Model A	Model B	Model C	Model D	Model E	Model F
	Absolute	Absolute	Absolute	Relative	Relative	Relative
	ALL	PR	MAJ	ALL	PR	MAJ
Lagged DV	0.702	0.680	0.641	0.650	0.572	0.662
	(0.034)***	(0.053)***	(0.051)***	(0.035)***	(0.056)***	(0.049)***
Cab. Partisan	−0.006	−0.002	−0.010	−0.021	−0.006	−0.032
	(0.002)***	(0.003)	(0.002)***	(0.009)**	(0.014)	(0.011)***
Manifesto	−0.000	0.018	−0.012	0.129	0.182	0.063
	(0.012)	(0.019)	(0.015)	(0.056)**	(0.085)**	(0.076)
Log Openness	−0.839	-.961	−0.536	-1.958	−2.379	−1.209
	(0.245)***	(.468)**	(0.287)*	(1.154)*	(2.103)	(1.458)
Population < 15	0.045	0.087	0.049	0.132	0.289	0.271
	(0.024)*	(0.046)**	(0.034)	(0.111)	(0.192)	(0.163)*
Log (GDP)	2.048	-1.513	7.265	10.009	−15.808	23.382
	(1.398)	(4.162)	(1.955)***	(6.432)	(18.958)	(9.100)***
Log (GDP) Sq	−0.057	0.017	−0.143	-0.336	0.232	-0.577
	(0.028)**	(0.087)	(0.035)***	(0.126)***	(0.395)	(0.162)***
Log (Pop)	0.382	0.974	−1.553	4.381	4.649	−1.156
	(0.889)	(2.415)	(1.115)	(4.200)	(10.983)	(5.521)
GOVEX/GDP	−0.028	-0.006	−0.057			
	(0.020)	(0.030)	(0.030)*			
Year	0.033	0.026	0.042	0.171	0.087	0.266
	(0.012)***	(0.021)	(0.018)**	(0.056)***	(0.093)	(0.090)***
Constant	−81.902	−35.773	−146.293	−427.606	22.600	−713.059
	(27.178)***	(64.510)	(37.861)***	(123.231)***	(287.079)	(185.207)***
Observations	389	187	202	388	187	201
Countries	23	13	22	23	13	22
R²	0.62	0.59	0.64	0.59	0.50	0.67

Note: All regressions use fixed effects. Standard errors are in parentheses.
***$p < 0.01$, **$p < 0.05$, *$p < 0.1$.

Multidimensional Voter Preferences

Having analyzed how electoral institutions impact partisan policy making, I turn now to examine whether electoral institutions impact voter preferences more generally. In this section, I return to the individual level analysis of Section 4.3 to demonstrate how electoral institutions can shape the multidimensional pattern of individual preferences over (a) education spending, and (b) general redistribution, as suggested by Hypothesis Four. Whereas majoritarian systems appear to compact preferences over both dimensions onto one plane, in proportional systems there is no such effect, and redistributive and educational preferences by party supporters do not covary that strongly.

In the following pages, I present a series of figures. In each figure, I compare the mean scores on the educational and redistributive dimensions for individuals who identify with particular parties. The educational dimension is the same five-point scale (1 to 5) as used in the analyses in Section 4.3. The redistributive dimension taps more general preferences over whether the government should

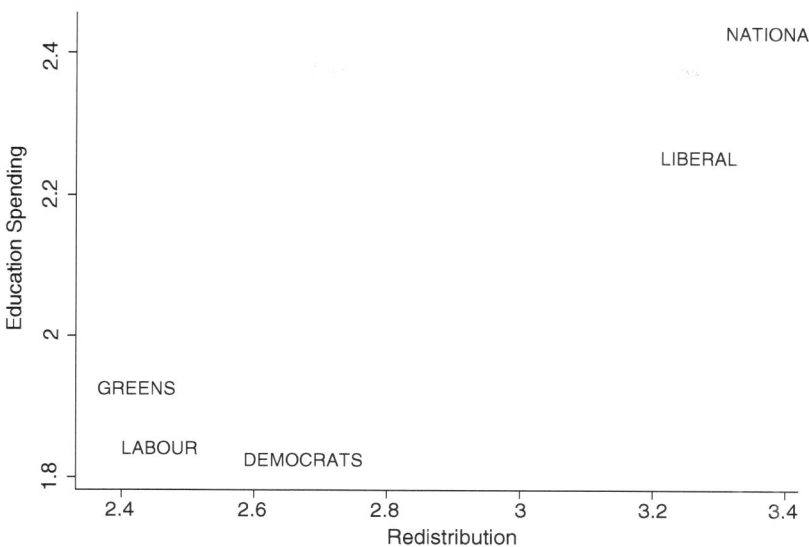

FIGURE 4.3(a). Majoritarian Systems and Voter Preferences – Australia

redistribute resources from the rich to the poor. It comes from the following question in the 1996 ISSP: "What is your opinion of the following statement: It is the responsibility of the government to reduce the differences in income between people with high incomes and those with low incomes." The potential answers are, "Agree strongly, agree, neither agree nor disagree, disagree, disagree strongly."[18] I split the analysis by type of electoral system: majoritarian, proportional, and those two countries that shifted systems in the mid-1990s (Italy and New Zealand). Each figure demonstrates the degree to which voter preferences over education and general redistribution covary across the partisan spectrum.

I begin with five majoritarian countries: Australia, Canada, France, the United Kingdom, and the United States, displayed in Figures 4.3 (a) through (e). In each case, there is a striking pattern: Voter preferences by political party line up along one dimension cutting from the bottom-left to the top-right of each figure (note that higher numbers mean *less* support for education and redistribution). Equivalently, educational and redistributive preferences of voters, as represented by party identification, covary extremely strongly.

In Australia, voters for the Labour Party and the two left-wing minor parties of the Green Party and the Democrats cluster at the bottom-left of the figure with the right-wing National and Liberal Party clustering at the top-right. In Canada, there is more of a spectrum, but the pattern remains diagonal: voters for the social democratic NDP at the bottom-left, those for the Bloc Quebecois and Liberals next, then those for the center-right Progressive Conservatives, and finally those for the right-wing Reform Party at the top-right. The only

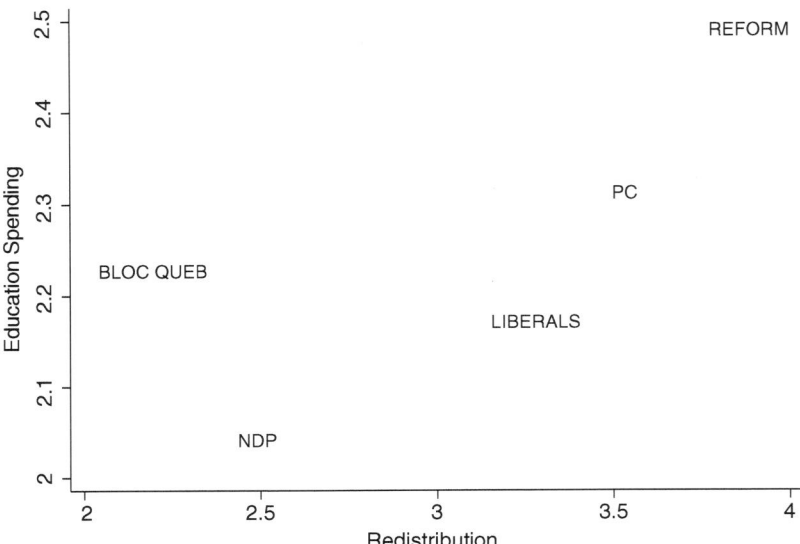

FIGURE 4.3(b). Majoritarian Systems and Voter Preferences – Canada

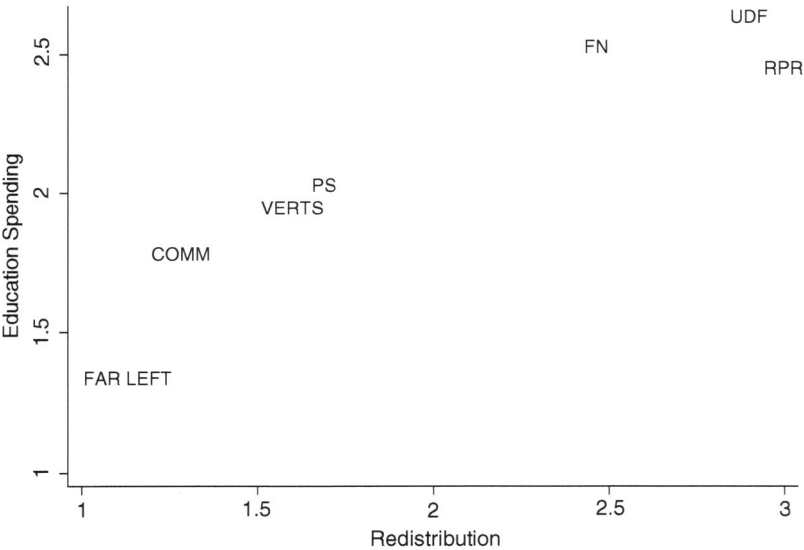

FIGURE 4.3(c). Majoritarian Systems and Voter Preferences – France

group to deviate slightly from the diagonal is voters for the Bloc Quebecois, whose support of education does not match their support of redistribution. France's electoral system trends majoritarian, although the existence of two-round voting dilutes its system from pure plurality. Consequently, France has more viable parties than other majoritarian systems, though in terms of governance, it rarely produces coalitional government. Despite the existence

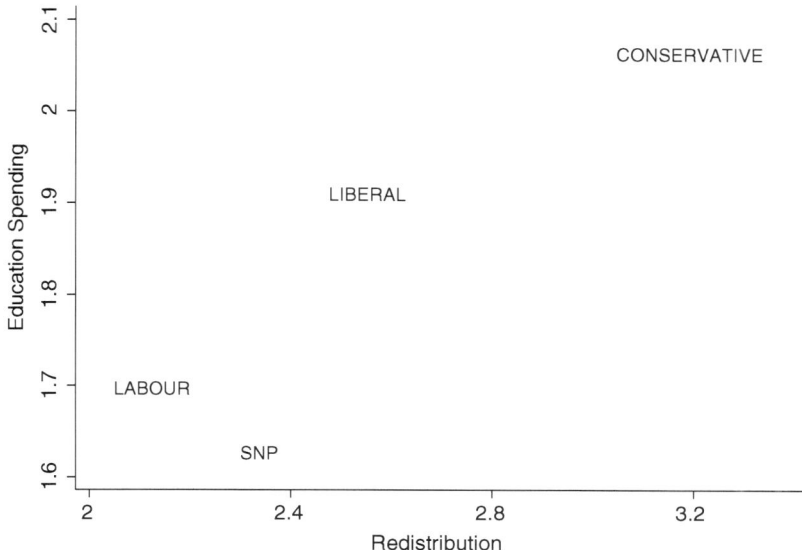

FIGURE 4.3(d). Majoritarian Systems and Voter Preferences – United Kingdom

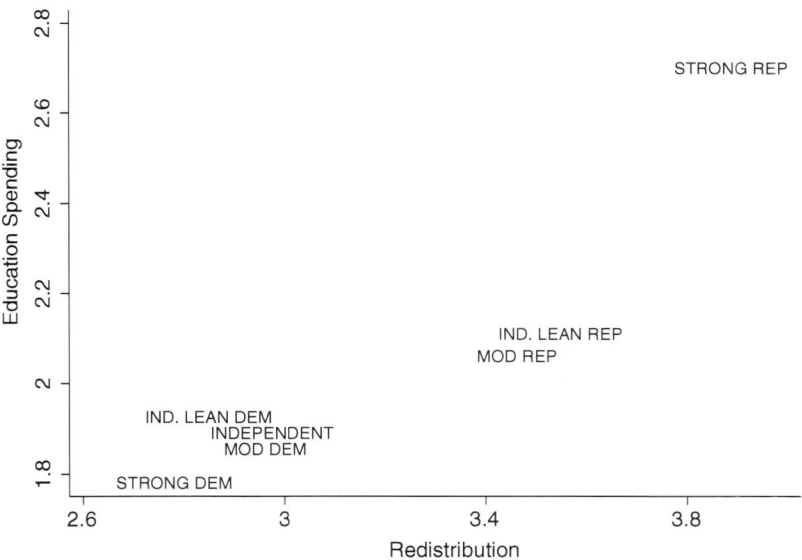

FIGURE 4.3(e). Majoritarian Systems and Voter Preferences – United States

of several viable parties, the diagonal pattern remains, with the Far Left and Communists at the bottom-left, then the Greens and Socialists, with the Front National, the Union for French Democracy (UDF), and Rally for the Republic (RPR) clustering at the top-right.

I now turn to the classic majoritarian systems, the United Kingdom and the United States. Again we see a very clear diagonal pattern. In the United

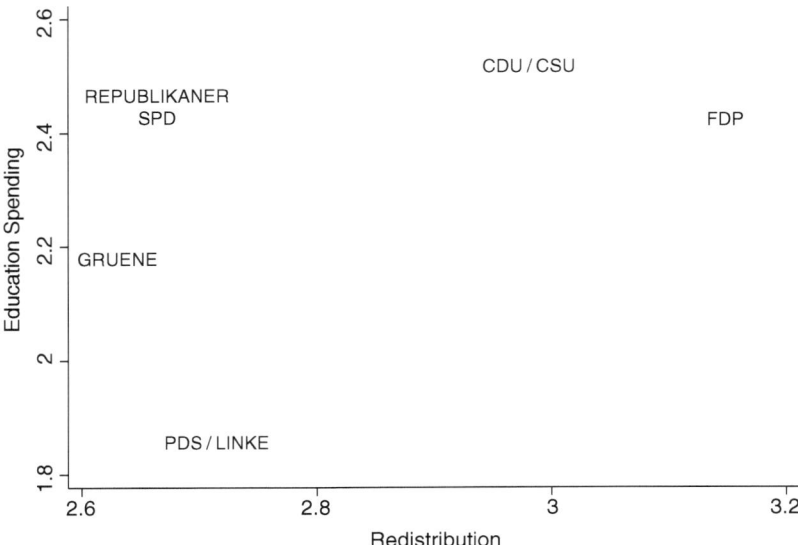

FIGURE 4.4(a). Proportional Systems and Voter Preferences – Germany

Kingdom, this shows the voters for the Labour Party at the bottom-left, for the Liberals in the center, and for the Conservatives at the top-right. Scottish National Party voters are slightly more favorable to education than their redistributive preferences would predict, which may be a function of the fact that Scotland has a different system of educational governance than England. In the United States, there are only two viable political parties, but the ISSP breaks out support of these parties into the strength of partisan identity and also includes independents. Intriguingly, even within political parties we can see the same diagonal pattern we expect in majoritarian systems: Strong Democrats are at the bottom-left, then soft Democrats, independents who lean Democrat, then independents, then independents who lean Republican and soft Republicans around the center, and finally strong Republicans at the far top-right. It is noteworthy just how distant this latter group is from the others – perhaps a result of the right-wing "Gingrich revolution" that produced the Republican takeover of the House of Representatives in 1994. Overall, the five majoritarian systems provide strong evidence that education and redistribution are closely tied in these states and that partisan preferences are quite extreme.

Figures 4.4 (a) through (e) examine countries with proportional electoral systems: Germany, Ireland, Norway, Sweden, and Switzerland. Here we find a starkly different pattern: In most cases, the clean diagonal of the majoritarian countries is gone and furthermore the educational preferences of supporters of major parties are typically much closer than in the majoritarian cases. Beginning with Germany, we see almost no pattern at all across parties. While four parties are centered on the left side of the figure (high redistribution), they have quite distinct educational preferences, with voters for the ex-communist

FIGURE 4.4(b). Proportional Systems and Voter Preferences – Ireland

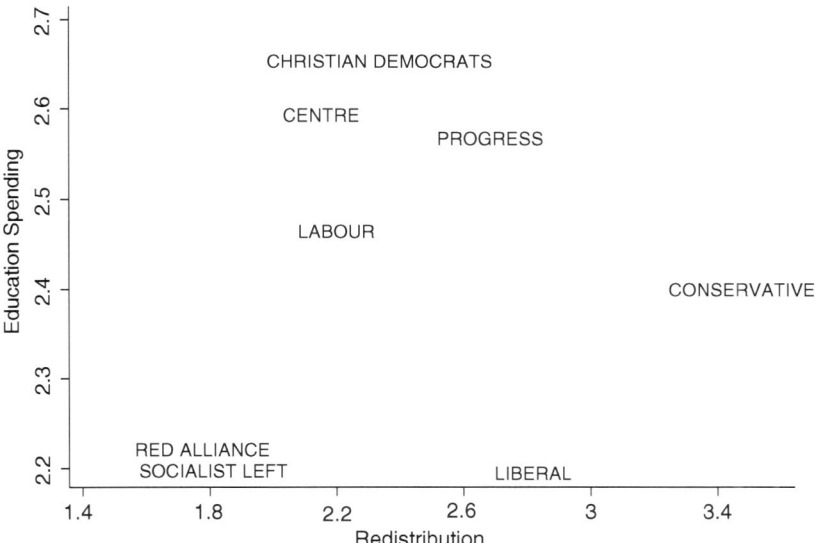

FIGURE 4.4(c). Proportional Systems and Voter Preferences – Norway

Party of Democratic Socialism (PDS) favoring high levels of educational spending, the Greens more moderate, and the Social Democrats even less favorable. While voters for the center-right Christian Democratic Union (CDU) and Free Democratic Party (FDP) favor less redistribution than the other parties, their views on education are indistinguishable from those who vote for the Social Democrats. Thus the three main parties show barely any distinct educational

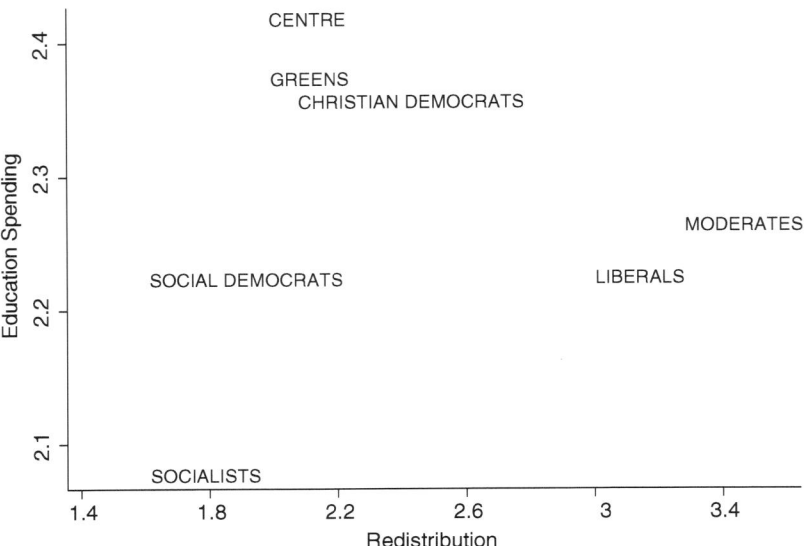

FIGURE 4.4(d). Proportional Systems and Voter Preferences – Sweden

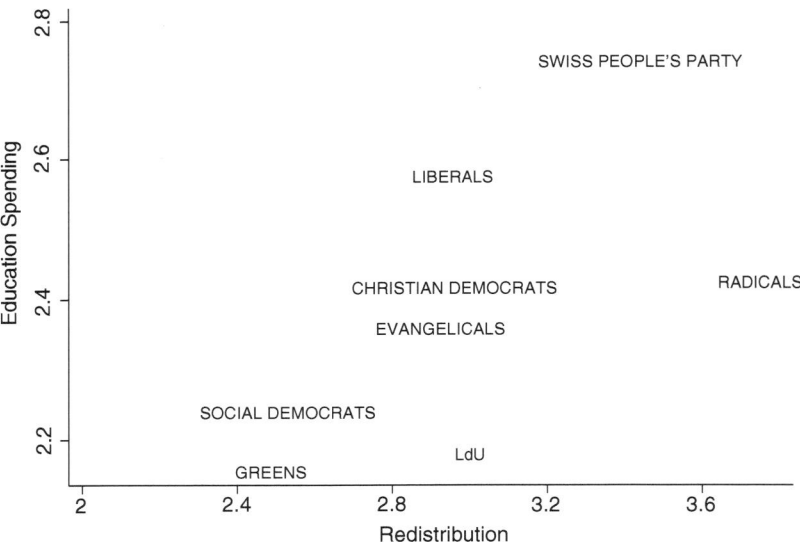

FIGURE 4.4(e). Proportional Systems and Voter Preferences – Switzerland

preferences. Turning to Ireland, even though superficially there appears to be a diagonal effect, in fact, voters for the two main parties, Fianna Fail and Fine Gael, cluster right in the center with almost no distinction in their preferences over education and redistribution.

The two Scandinavian countries, Norway and Sweden, like Germany, show almost no pattern at all in the relationship between preferences over education and redistribution. In Norway, voters from the two largest parties, the Labour Party and the Progress Party, have fairly similar preferences, along with the smaller center/center-right Center and Christian Democrat parties. All these voters have moderate views on redistribution, but are relatively opposed to increased education spending. Voters from the third largest party, the right-wing Conservatives, are strongly antiredistribution but are actually more positive toward education spending than those of other major parties, whereas voters for the centrist Liberal Party are moderate on redistribution but very supportive of increased education spending. Finally, we do see one majoritarian style cluster of the Red Alliance and the Socialists at the bottom-left. However, collectively this group amounted to less than 9 percent of the electorate in 1996. It is intuitive examining the graph to see that (a) shifts between the two largest parties as "formateurs" of the coalition government are unlikely to lead to large shifts in education policy, and that (b) many crosscutting coalitions offering different packages of education and redistributive policy could be formed across the several parties. A similar pattern appears when considering Sweden. Here voters for the three major parties – the Social Democrats, the Moderates, and the Liberals – differ quite sharply in their preferences over redistribution yet barely at all over education. Furthermore, what differences there are in educational preferences occur among parties with very similar redistributive preferences – for example, voters for the Socialists and Centre Party differ substantially on the education dimension but have similar redistributive preferences.

Finally, we turn to Switzerland, where a slight diagonal pattern appears but with the considerable fuzziness we would expect in a proportional system. While voters from the left-wing Social Democrats and the right-wing Swiss People's Party are at opposite ends on both redistribution and education, those for the Radical Party are very antiredistribution while being quite moderate on education. Furthermore, voters for a host of smaller parties share similar redistributive preferences while differing substantially over education: the Liberals, Christian Democrats, Evangelicals, and the Ring of Independents (LdU). One noteworthy element of Swiss politics is that education spending is relatively low in Switzerland and is very reliant on private training – in sharp contrast to the high levels of spending in Sweden and Norway. The pattern of voter preferences thus might reflect this lack of political consensus over the state's role in education in Switzerland. I return to the Swiss case in Chapter 5.

Figures 4.5 (a) and (b) examine two countries that altered their electoral systems, in opposite ways, during the mid-1990s. In 1993, Italy changed from a proportional system, blamed for a multiplicity of unstable coalitions since 1945, to a majoritarian system. In 1996, conversely, New Zealand changed from a majoritarian system to a multimember proportional system. Since the ISSP was conducted in 1996, it is interesting to examine whether in New Zealand individual partisan preferences still reflected majoritarian characteristics and whether Italian preferences still appeared proportional. Beginning with Italy, we do see the kind of diagonal pattern one might expect in a majoritarian system. Voters for the Communists are at the bottom-left and those for the

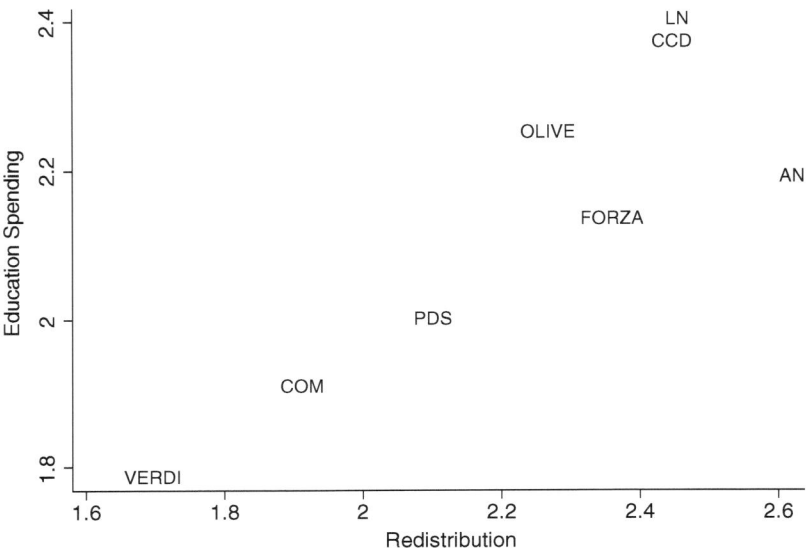

FIGURE 4.5(a). Changing Electoral Systems and Voter Preferences – Italy

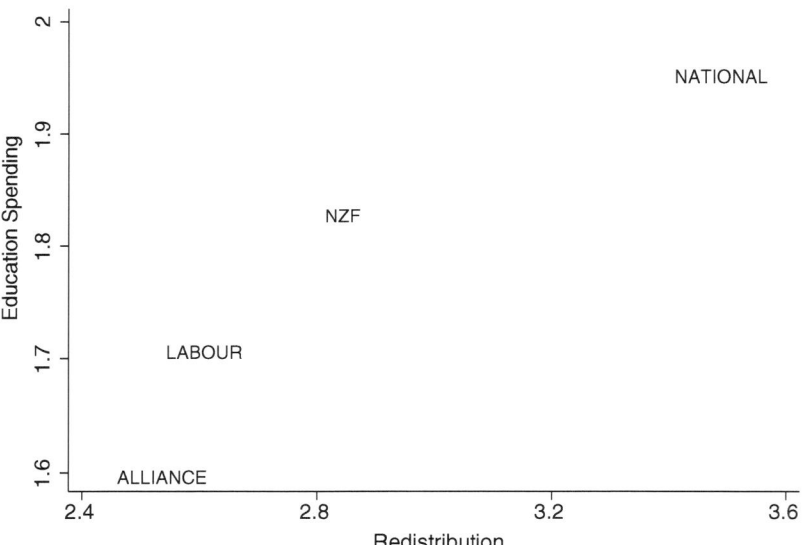

FIGURE 4.5(b). Changing Electoral Systems and Voter Preferences – New Zealand

Northern League, National Alliance, and Christian Democrats are toward the top-right. However, voters for the two main parties around which coalitions would form in the post-transition period – Silvio Berlusconi's Forza Italia and Romano Prodi's Olive Tree coalition (minus the Democratic Party of the Left [PDS]) – have fairly similar preferences over redistribution and (slightly less so) over education. Thus, more generally, we see the formation but not fruition of the kind of majoritarian diagonal pattern we saw in, for example, France. In New Zealand, conversely, we see that the decision to transition to proportionality in 1996 had not had a strong impact on preferences by the time of the ISSP survey. Here voters for the center-right National Party are firmly at the top-right and those for the center-left Labour Party toward the bottom-left, with the left-wing Alliance firmly at the bottom-left.

4.7 CONCLUSION

Education policy in the OECD might best be characterized as constrained volatility. I characterize it as volatile because we have seen very large swings in education spending in response to typical changes in the partisan control of government, in many cases with magnitudes similar to the predicted effects of democratization from Chapter 2. I characterize this volatility as constrained because the size of this volatility depends on the institutional context in which politics operates. Specifically, proportional electoral systems appear both to moderate the partisan effect on education spending and to detach it from broader partisan preferences over redistribution. I found these effects at the level of both voters and parties, suggesting that political parties do aggregate voter preferences fairly effectively but that both groups are constrained by the electoral environment. Clearly, educational politics in advanced industrial countries are complex and at the behest of a variety of actors and institutions. Still, the overall message is clear: Partisan politics have a profound impact on education spending in the OECD. Education, even of the vocational kind, is far from a political ceasefire – in fact, it appears to be the source of a particularly fierce redistributive battle. And this is not just an effect of polarized political parties. Voters themselves disagree profoundly on the parameters of desired education policy, even in a world of universal education. As we turn to education provision that is rather less than universal – higher education – we shall see even sharper contrasts.

5

High Politics in Higher Education

5.1 INTRODUCTION

This chapter explores the politics of higher education spending in the OECD. In 1950, almost all OECD states had a publicly subsidized higher education system limited to a small fraction of the population. Since then, however, many states have witnessed a transformation of that elite model into a mass higher education system, with enrollment levels often exceeding 50 percent. This transition to a mass system has provoked differing funding reforms. Several states, including Australia and England, have radically altered their funding structure of higher education, moving toward the use of tuition fees. Other states, such as Sweden and Finland, have seen a huge surge in public investment in higher education accompanying mass enrollment. Finally, many states, such as Germany and Austria, retain the same elite public higher education structure with which they began the postwar era. Why did some states expand higher education while others remained in stasis? Why did some states choose to introduce tuition fees, whereas others continued to restrict investment to the public sector? Do these patterns hold at the subnational level in contexts such as the American states? In this chapter, I argue that redistributive politics plays a key role in higher education policy, but its effect is strongly conditioned by existing institutions, both political and educational – for example, the existence of a vocational education sector and the size of the existing higher education system. Higher education may sit at the apex of the educational establishment, but it is hardly insulated from partisan politics.

It is somewhat ironic that scholars have not adequately addressed where higher education falls into the skills and production profiles of OECD states, given the proliferation of typologies generated by scholars since the foundational work of Esping-Andersen (1990). In particular, the Varieties of Capitalism literature (Hall and Soskice, 2001) that famously splits countries into two groups, partly determined by their relative investment in general versus specific skills, barely touches on the role of higher education. This omission is rather surprising considering the theoretical importance in the research program of firm strategies and international competitiveness, two concepts likely to be heavily influenced by different patterns of higher education provision and funding. Nor have scholars addressed in detail the partisan politics of higher education. Iversen and Stephens (2008) have suggested that higher education might be incorporated into the Varieties of Capitalism *and* the "power resources" typologies of OECD countries by outlining what they refer to as "three worlds of human capital formation." Thus, higher education finally appears to be surfacing on the agenda of scholars of comparative political economy of advanced industrial nations. However, this synthesis remains somewhat unsatisfying since its predictions of the impact of partisanship on higher education are unidirectional – left-wing control of government always and everywhere leads to higher public spending.[1]

This chapter develops the argument that higher education policy in the OECD is driven by a set of partisan choices within a "trilemma" among the level of enrollment, the degree of subsidization, and the overall public cost of higher education. I argue that governments can achieve at most two out of the following objectives: mass enrollment, full subsidization, and a relatively low total public cost. Consequently, some governments will choose mass, partially private, inexpensive higher education systems: the Partially Private model. Others will have mass, fully public, but expensive higher education systems: the Mass Public model. Finally, some governments will retain the status quo of inexpensive, publicly funded, but elite higher education systems: the Elite model.

What explains movement within this trilemma? As in Chapter 4, I argue that political partisanship determines policy choices over higher education. However, because the provision of higher education is typically regressive – since access is biased toward the wealthy – the pattern of partisanship and public spending is quite different from that of universal education. When existing enrollment is low, I expect right-wing parties to favor greater public spending on higher education and expansion of enrollment, since they can target resources to their own constituents. Conversely, left-wing parties should be more reluctant to expand public funding and enrollment until enrollment has already reached mass levels. Accordingly, I expect initial moves toward the Mass Public model to be made by right-wing governments and moves toward the Partially Private system to be made by left-wing governments. However, once a mass enrollment system has been attained, these partisan preferences will reverse, with left-wing parties keen on expanding enrollment universally and right-wing parties seeking to limit further expansion. Unlike the Iversen-Stephens conjecture, I argue that the impact of partisanship is thus conditional on the structure of the existing higher education system. Moreover, partisan choices are not made in a frictionless environment. Subnational veto players can block reforms, and vocational education and school streaming can channel students away from higher education.

I begin the chapter by developing a formal model of the trilemma, starting by establishing the aggregate trade-off among subsidization, enrollment, and

---

[1] Iversen and Stephens justify this expectation by arguing that the structure of taxation in OECD countries renders higher education financing less regressive. I show in section 5.3 that the extent to which this claim is true depends rather heavily on the progressivity of tax systems, which varies dramatically.

public cost before moving to individual preferences among the three possible configurations within the trilemma and concluding by examining how individual preferences are aggregated into party preferences and political decisions. The model is intended to provide a comprehensive micromechanism to understand institutional change in higher education, linking individual preferences to policy outcomes. I then turn to an empirical analysis of whether these trade-offs exist cross-sectionally at the national level, demonstrating the apparent clustering of OECD states along these dimensions. I then turn to the individual level, using survey data on preferences over government support for low-income students accessing higher education, noting the contextual effect of the preexisting level of enrollment on these preferences. I then examine higher education policy itself, using data drawn from twenty OECD countries to explore the effects of partisanship on spending and enrollment levels. I find a strong conditional effect of partisanship, with right-wing parties favoring increased spending at low levels of enrollment but left-wing parties favoring spending at mass levels of enrollment. I also show a powerful limiting role of vocational education and school streaming. I then move to a series of country cases that draw out the historical development of the trilemma. I focus first on England, a Partially Private system; then move on to Sweden, a Mass Public system; and conclude with Germany, an Elite system. I also discuss whether the "dual system" of vocational training in Germanic states is responsible for their limited higher education systems. I conclude with an analysis of patterns of higher education appropriations and tuition fees across the U.S. states, demonstrating that the conditional effect of partisanship also appears to hold at the subnational level.

5.2 MODELING THE TRILEMMA IN HIGHER EDUCATION

In this section, I develop a simple model of political preferences over higher education systems. I characterize the move from an Elite model of higher education to a mass system as involving choices within a trilemma.[2] In most public services, the government must decide both the extent of coverage and the degree to which the service will be publicly subsidized. For a fixed budget constraint, any increase in one of these measures will force a decrease in the other. Thus, a trilemma is the trade-off between any two of the budget constraint, the extent of coverage, and the degree of subsidization, when the other variable is held constant. How does this pattern play out in the case of higher education? I measure coverage with the gross enrollment rate of a given cohort in higher education.[3] Within the OECD, this ranges from one-third of the population in Belgium and Germany to over 80 percent in New Zealand and Sweden. Given the substantial range along this measure, we can identify elite higher education systems (those with gross enrollment rates less than a third)

---

[2] The concept of a "trilemma" was popularized by Iversen and Wren (1998).

[3] Gross enrollment rates include multiple entries into higher education by the same individual and thus are a more appropriate index of overall budgetary strain on the government than net rates.

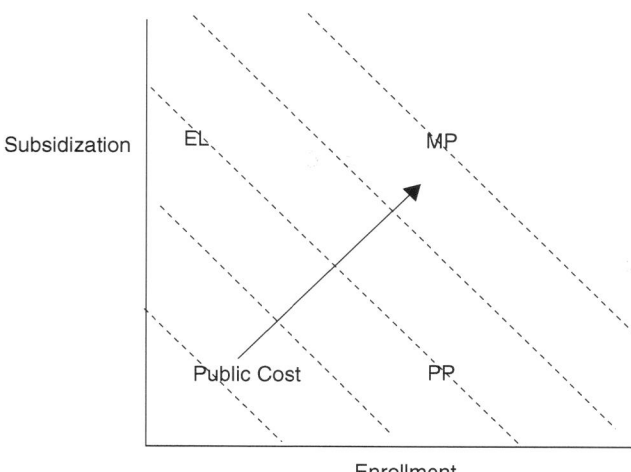

FIGURE 5.1. The Trilemma in Abstract

and mass higher education systems (those with gross enrollment over a half). The degree of subsidization also varies widely in higher education. Some systems are almost totally publicly funded – for example, Denmark, Norway, and Finland – whereas others have over 50 percent of funding from private sources– for example, the United States, Japan, and Australia. Finally, some higher education systems take relatively little from the public purse – less than 1 percent of GDP in Britain, Italy, and Japan, whereas others cost over 1.5 percent of GDP, including Denmark, Finland, and Sweden.

Trade-offs within the trilemma can be characterized using the "ideal types" of Elite, Partially Private, or Mass Public higher education systems. Some states will have high levels of enrollment at a lower level of subsidization (Partially Private systems), whereas others, spending the same amount of public money, will have higher degrees of subsidization but lower coverage (Elite systems). Conversely, for a fixed level of enrollment, states can trade off budgetary restraint versus subsidization. Some states will have mass systems with low levels of subsidization and low overall public cost (Partially Private systems), whereas others will have mass systems with high levels of subsidization and high overall costs (Mass Public systems). Finally, for a given level of subsidization, states can trade off enrollment with overall cost. Some states will have low levels of private funding, low overall costs, but also low enrollment (Elite systems); others will have similarly low levels of private funding but with high costs and high enrollment (Mass Public systems).[4] Figure 5.1 demonstrates these trade-offs.

---

[4] One further configuration is possible: an inexpensive, elite, and partially private higher education system. Such a system does not exist in any fully industrialized state, but is fairly common in the developing world. However, most middle-income countries – for example, Mexico, Brazil, and Turkey – have highly subsidized higher education along the lines of the Elite model, as did high-income states in 1950.

I now move to a theoretical analysis of the effects of subsidization, enrollment, and taxation on individuals to determine the micro-preferences underlying higher education policy.[5] To focus on the redistributive impact of higher education, I make some simplifying assumptions about the economy – in particular, I assume that economic activity requires two key inputs: skilled labor (which in this instance refers to higher education) and unskilled labor (which for the purposes of this chapter includes both lower levels of education and "pure" labor).[6] The returns to skill, as in Chapter 2, depend negatively on the relative supply of higher education and positively on the productivity or "quality" of higher education provided. I assume that unskilled wages are fixed with respect to both skill supply and higher education quality. Consequently, skilled wages are $w_s = As^{\alpha-1}$, where A is the "quality" of higher education, s is the proportion of individuals with higher education, and $(\alpha-1) \in [-1,0]$ is the elasticity of skilled wages with respect to skill supply. Unskilled wages are fixed as w_u. I also assume that people vary in their level of non-market income so that even among skilled workers, some are "richer" than others.

So far, I have set up an economy where some people, with higher education, receive skilled wages, whereas others do not receive higher education and consequently receive unskilled wages. But how is higher education distributed? Here I start by making an assumption similar to that made in Chapter 2: that higher education expands from the richest person in society to the poorest. As s increases, enrollment into higher education includes poorer and poorer citizens until at $s = 1$ all citizens receive higher education. While the assumption that access to higher education is income dependent is clearly a simplification, it conforms closely to the empirical record (Halsey, 1993; Barr, 2004). In fact, there is a large sociological literature on the "Maximally Maintained Inequality" hypothesis, in which expansion only reduces inequality in higher education once nearly all (80 percent) citizens above a certain income level have already been enrolled (Raftery and Hout, 1983; Shavit, Arum, Gamoran, 2007). Hence the empirical pattern is that expansion favors those "next in line" along the income distribution, which I refer to as income dependence.

Along with the level of enrollment, we need to examine the degree of subsidization of higher education, which I model as $p \in [0,1]$, where $p = 1$ is a fully public system of higher education and $p = 0$ is a totally private system. To keep the analysis simple, I assume that higher education is a uniform good, determined only by its relative quality A. This means that I am not distinguishing among different mixes in the types of skills provided by universities (business versus medicine versus classics) nor among different kinds of university (research universities, liberal arts colleges, and technical colleges). Finally, there are no externalities to higher education. While there may be social benefits to higher education, most labor economists find that higher education has lower social returns than primary or secondary education (Psacharopoulos and Patrinos, 2002).

[5] In the appendix to this chapter, I derive these micro-preferences formally.
[6] To simplify the analysis to one dimension, I hold constant the level of state investment in other education and focus only on taxes paying for higher education.

In the appendix, I develop the model fully, noting the budget constraint facing the government, and how families attempt to maximize their utility across two generations in their preferences over subsidization and enrollment. Here, more informally, I establish the broad preferences of families over higher education policy by distinguishing them based on their level of (parental) income, which comes from their skilled/unskilled wages and their non-market income. Since the distribution of higher education is perfectly determined by non-market income in this setup, we can distinguish between skilled individuals who have higher non-market income and unskilled individuals who have lower levels. When we examine expanding enrollment, we will also examine the preferences of a third group: those previously unskilled families who newly acquire higher education and have middling levels of non-market income.

I begin by considering changes in the rate of subsidization: that is, what are the effects on different income groups if the government increases the share of funding that comes from public sources? For families who never receive higher education but must pay taxes that fund it, any increase in subsidization just means the loss of more tax dollars. Since I am assuming that access to higher education is dependent on income, this implies ceteris paribus that poorer families will be less supportive of increased subsidization and quality improvements than are richer families. However, there is a little nuance to this claim. As families get richer, the absolute amount they pay in taxes increases while the benefits accrued from access to higher education remain constant. Consequently, the richest members of society may prefer to fund their own higher education privately rather than pay in taxes to subsidize the "poorer skilled."

Figure 5.2 compares the impact of subsidization on individuals with varying degrees of income The horizontal axis represents parental income and the vertical axis displays the impact of increasing subsidization on the family's utility. Thus for families with incomes below the threshold to receive higher education, y_s, the impact of increased subsidization on their utility is negative. These poorer families are having to pay to subsidize the education of richer families' children. A similarly negative impact is felt by the very richest families, who pay absolutely more in taxes than they receive in benefits from subsidization. Thus, both rich and poor might find common alliance against increased subsidization: an "ends against the middle" coalition. However, for those people who do receive higher education and whose income is not so high that the cost of taxation outweighs the benefits of subsidization, any increase in subsidization leads to a positive impact. All else equal, this middle group would advocate increased subsidization whereas the poorer and richer groups would oppose any such policy.

I now turn to examine the impact of expanding enrollment. I assume that if parents have higher education, then their children will also receive it, provided that enrollment is steady or increasing.[7] Consequently, individuals fall into three

[7] While the case of decreasing enrollment is theoretically possible, it has been historically rare. Instead, quotas and stagnation are more likely than an outright decline in enrollment, as in the case of South Korea in Chapter 3.

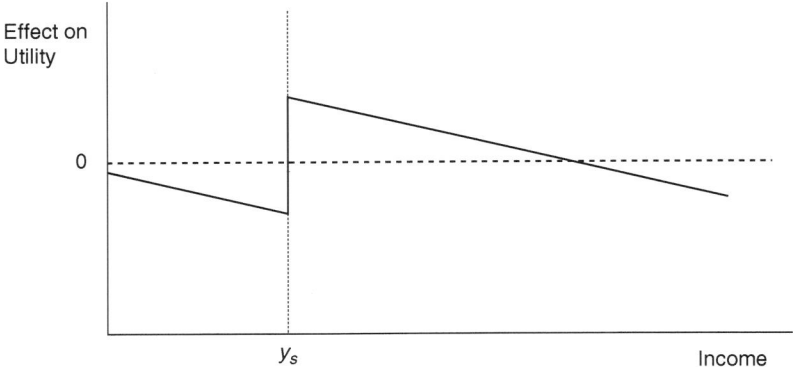

FIGURE 5.2. Increasing the Rate of Subsidization (Partially Private versus Mass Public)

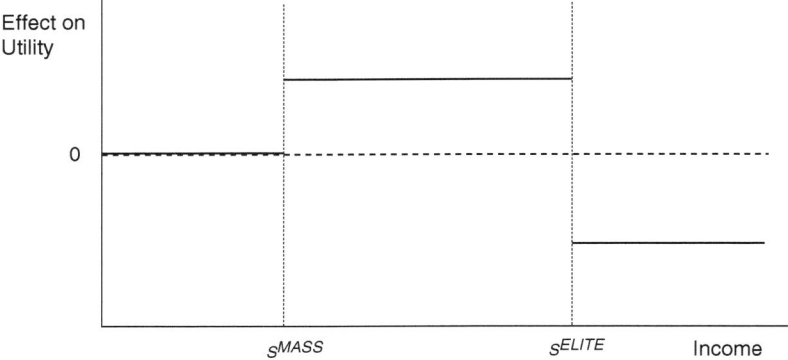

FIGURE 5.3. Increasing Enrollment (Elite to Partially Private)

types: (a) those for whom neither parents nor children receive higher education in a given expansion of enrollment, (b) those whose parents did not receive
higher education but whose children are beneficiaries of expanded enrollment,
and (c) those for whom both parents and children receive higher education at
the pre-expansion level of enrollment. However, here we must turn back to the
trilemma, since I have argued that expansion comes in two flavors. If expansion
is accompanied by decreased subsidization, then we have a transition from an
Elite to Partially Private model. If, conversely, expansion is financed from public
money, we have a transition from an Elite to a Mass Public model.

I begin by examining expansion from an Elite to a Partially Private model,
which bears some resemblance to the case of subsidization just discussed, albeit
in inverse since we are *reducing* subsidization. Figure 5.3 demonstrates the
effects of increasing enrollment from an Elite to a Partially Private level on
families of different income. Because the increase in enrollment is countered
by a decrease in subsidization, the net tax burden of moving from an Elite to a
Partially Private system is zero. Consequently, the lines for each group are flat
with respect to income, since their tax costs are unchanged. Thus, for those

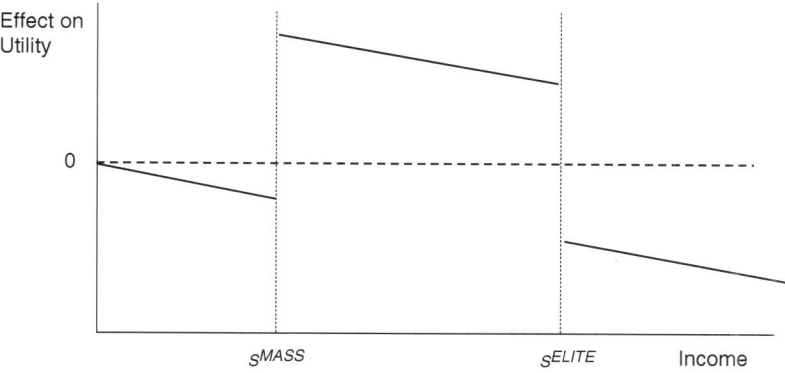

FIGURE 5.4. Increasing Enrollment (Elite to Mass Public)

families who never receive higher education, there is no impact on their utility of moving between these systems. For the other two groups, there is an impact that comes not from taxes but from the direct effects of increased enrollment on wages. For members of the middle group, who receive higher education only under a Partially Private system, there is a jump up in their income since they now receive skilled rather than unskilled wages. However, for the richer members of society, who were already recipients of higher education, expansion is harmful. This negative impact occurs because the increased abundance of skilled labor reduces the skill premium, thereby lowering their children's wages. This is a similar kind of scarcity effect to that we saw in Chapter 2.

I now turn to analyze expansion from an Elite to a Mass Public model. For poorer families, this is similar to the pattern we saw in Figure 5.2, examining subsidization. Since expanded enrollment is at least partly funded from public sources, these families must pay taxes for an enrollment expansion that does not directly benefit them – hence they oppose expansion. The middle group is the real winner of expansion. Whereas previously they had paid in taxes for the richest members of society to attend university, now they are also recipients of higher education, without the need to pay fees. Finally, the richest group is the enemies of expansion. Not only must they pay for more citizens to attend university, thereby increasing their taxes, but also they must confront a decline in the skill premium as a university degree becomes less exclusive. Hence, when considering increasing enrollment through a Mass Public system, an "ends against the middle" pattern emerges, with the rich and poor preferring to limit expansion and the middle advocating it.

Figure 5.4 shows that the middle group is the only one that directly benefits from increased enrollment, whereas the poor and wealthy would prefer to limit expansion of enrollment. Furthermore, expansion of higher education has a stronger negative effect on the very rich than does subsidization. Subsidization affects everyone who receives higher education, though tax costs may outweigh this benefit. Expansion, conversely, only directly benefits those who receive higher education for the first time.

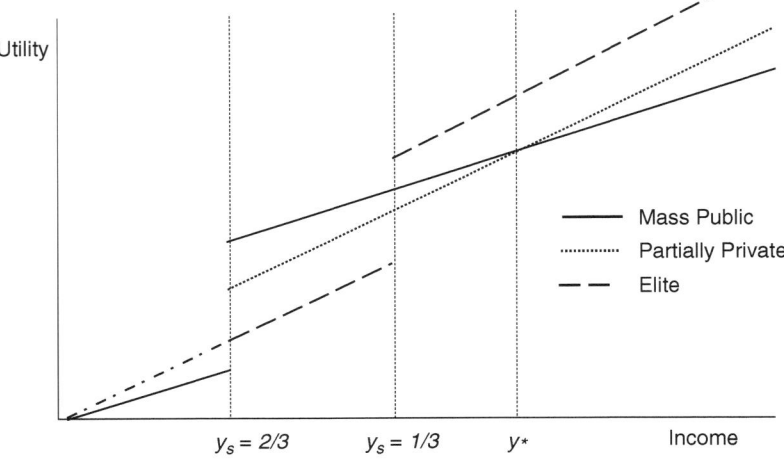

FIGURE 5.5. The Trilemma and Individual Utility

We can assert several conclusions about the preferences of different income groups over higher education systems. Firstly, if access to higher education is income dependent, the poor prefer lower rates of subsidization and enrollment. Turning to the trilemma, this implies the poor prefer both the Elite system with limited enrollment and the Partially Private system with limited subsidization to the Mass Public system since the former systems impose a lower tax burden than the latter. This follows from the basic logic of regressive redistribution that emerges when public goods are available only to the wealthy.[8] Those who receive higher education for the first time under an expansion of enrollment – loosely middle-class families – benefit from both increased enrollment (since it now includes them) and increased subsidization. They consequently prefer a Mass Public to a Partially Private system, and both to an Elite system that excludes them.

Finally, the richest families in society, who already receive higher education, suffer from both increased subsidization and enrollment. They would consequently prefer to maintain an Elite system. If forced to choose between mass systems, their preferences would depend on their precise level of income, with those individuals with incomes above a certain threshold y^* preferring to pay themselves for some of the cost of higher education in a Partially Private system, and those with a lower income preferring a Mass Public system. Figure 5.5 summarizes this ranking of preferences over higher education systems for individuals of different incomes.[9]

---

[8] This reverses the Meltzer-Richard model, wherein the poor demand high levels of public spending since they receive public goods but pay lower taxes than the rich (Meltzer and Richard, 1981).

[9] The Partially Private model has $s = 2/3, p = 1/2$; the Mass Public system has $s = 2/3, p = 1$, and the Elite model has $s = 1/3, p = 1$. The precise values of the parameters are chosen because of their resemblance to the empirical patterns in Section 5.3.

The preference orderings over the three systems have four permutations. The first section, for those individuals with income less than the 33rd percentile, has a preference ordering as follows: the Partially Private and Elite models first with the Mass Public model last. Thus the poorest third of society are most disadvantaged by a mass *and* fully public higher education system. This pattern may seem counterintuitive since we are used to thinking of mass public services as benefiting the poor; however, the ability to target goods alters the typical outcome of fiscal progressivity. This preference ordering is reversed for individuals with incomes between the 33rd and the 67th percentile. In this group, the preference ordering is as follows: Mass Public, then Partially Private, then Elite. The reason for this reversal is that these individuals receive higher education in the Mass Public and Partially Private systems. However, in an Elite system, they would be paying for the rich group to attend higher education without receiving it themselves. The members of this group, one-third of the total population, can be considered the middle class and they are clearly the key beneficiaries of the transition from an elite to a mass higher education system.

The final two subsections occur for those individuals with incomes higher than the 67th percentile. For this group, the Elite system is always preferred to the Partially Private and Mass Public systems. This comes as little surprise. The rich receive fully subsidized higher education in the Elite system, without having to pay for anyone else to receive higher education – a classic case of targeted expenditure. However, the Mass Public and Partially Private systems shift in preference ordering around the individual with income y^*. Below this point, the Mass Public system is preferred, whereas above this point the Partially Private system is favored. Since taxation is a proportion of income but higher education is a fixed benefit, some particularly rich individuals would prefer to pay the cost of higher education privately rather than subsidize the "poorer rich."

In terms of the politics of choice within the trilemma, we see the following patterns. The Elite model displays a clear "ends against the middle" dynamic, with both the poor and the wealthy content with that system over the others and the middle group unhappy at exclusion from higher education. The Mass Public model is the preferred outcome for the middle group and may be preferential to the Partially Private model for a subsection of the wealthy. Thus, the Mass Public model represents a coalition of the middle and upper-middle classes. The Partially Private model is preferred to the Mass Public model by the poor and the very wealthy but is less preferable for the middle and upper-middle classes. However, for the middle class, it is preferable to the Elite system, which would shut that group out of higher education. Thus, while the Partially Private model looks like an "ends against the middle" coalition in comparison to the Mass Public model, it appears to be a middle- and lower-class coalition if compared to the Elite model.

The "Quality" of Higher Education

So far, I have argued that the key distinctions across higher education systems are the level of enrollment and the degree of subsidization, which together determine the public cost of the system. However, implicitly I have been assuming that the per-student cost of higher education is uniform both across time and countries. This per-student cost could be assumed to reflect the "quality" of higher education (though obviously it might also reflect imperfect competition and rent seeking in the university market). What happens if we relax this assumption of fixed quality? At first glance, it might seem to create a potential way out of the trilemma. Governments wishing to reduce public spending while maintaining both enrollment and subsidization can in fact do so by reducing the quality of higher education. In this manner, overall costs would decrease because per-student funding has decreased. The long-term viability of this strategy is certainly questionable and where quality deterioration has occurred there has been pressure from students, universities, and voters to restore per student funding.[10] Nonetheless, governments do sometimes temporarily reduce (or increase) quality. For example, in Section 5.4, we shall see that the English Conservative Party permitted expansion to the lower-middle classes during the late 1980s while maintaining full public subsidization, by reducing per-student spending. Conversely, parties might be interested in increasing quality in order to satisfy their constituents' demands.

What happens when parties alter the quality of higher education? In fact, the results are surprisingly similar to those obtained when one examines subsidization. From a fiscal perspective, the two are rather similar. Holding subsidization and enrollment constant, increasing quality will mean a transfer of resources through the tax system from those who do not receive higher education to those who do. Thus, increasing quality is likely to be fiscally regressive, assuming that access to higher education is strongly correlated with income. This implies that the partisan pattern of preferences over quality should resemble that with subsidization, with the main losers the poorest group in society, the chief winners the middle-income recipients of higher education, and potential losers among the richest citizens who pay the most in taxes.

Progressive Taxation and Higher Education

I now turn to alter a second assumption underlying the argument made previously: that taxation is linear. This is the standard assumption made in models of political economy inspired by the well-known Meltzer-Richard (1981) model, in which individuals pay a set proportion of their income but receive a fixed good. In such models, the richer the individual, the more he or she pays absolutely in taxes, and since everyone receives the same good, at least some individuals will be paying for more than they receive; these are voters with incomes higher than the mean. However, I have already noted that where *not everyone* receives a public good, the redistributive impacts are more complex. And in particular, where the access to the good is positively correlated with income, this Meltzer-Richard model almost flips on its head (it is still true, though, that the richer

---

[10] A relevant parallel emerges in Iversen and Wren (1998), where service productivity cannot be increased to resolve their trilemma because doing so reduces service quality.

members of the group that receive the good pay more for it than do the poorer members).

Furthermore, few countries have a perfectly linear tax system. In fact, tax systems vary widely in their degree of progressivity (Cusack and Beramendi, 2007). It is not unreasonable to think that the change in tax burden under different systems will have a substantial effect on how citizens view public spending on higher education.[11] Formally modeling progressive taxation is not simple, as demonstrated in the appendix, but the standard way of doing so involves assuming that individuals pay a level of tax that is a quadratic function of income – that is, a continually increasing proportion of income. In such a setup, the poorest citizens pay almost no tax and the richest citizens pay a very large proportion of their income in taxes.

What is the impact of progressive taxation on preferences over higher education spending? The distinction, unsurprisingly, emerges only on the tax side of the fiscal equation – that is, the benefits of receiving higher education remain constant but the relative costs paid by individuals change. We can in fact define the threshold individual who pays more under progressive taxation than linear taxation as having mean income plus a term reflecting the level of inequality.[12] This implies that individuals who have less than the mean income *always* prefer higher education to be funded from progressive taxation. Since in all OECD countries mean income is higher than the median income (Kenworthy and Pontusson, 2005), at least half of the population will be more favorably disposed to higher education spending when taxation is progressive. All else equal, then, I expect greater spending on higher education when taxation is progressive. Furthermore, as income inequality increases, more and more people feel similarly because the threshold individual becomes richer. Thus, there is an interactive effect between tax progressivity and income inequality. Under conditions of high income inequality and tax progressivity there will be even greater support for higher education spending *even if* most people do not receive it, because where income inequality is high, progressive taxation harms a smaller, richer group. Conversely, the bulk of the population pays a lower rate under progressive taxation. Thus, popular support for higher education hangs on the assumptions one makes about how citizens are taxed. Just as targeting education to specific groups changes the politics of education, so does targeting taxation.

Equal and Unequal Access to Higher Education

The last assumption I alter is a critical one: that access to higher education is dependent on income. What if, instead, all citizens had an equal chance to attend university? I term this scenario income-independent access. Income independence is more likely when secondary schooling is not streamed into vocational and academic schools. Typically, where streaming exists, students can easily

---

[11] This point is also made in Iversen and Stephens (2008), though they claim that progressive taxation always cancels out the regressive effects of income-dependent access to higher education.

[12] I solve for this threshold formally in the appendix to this chapter.

access university only if they took the academic track: Vocational students are either prohibited or must take further courses to advance. Income independence is also higher when race or income-based affirmative action programs exist. Finally, income independence may be higher when income inequality is low and hence differences in aptitude are relatively more important than differences in income in determining access (Halsey, 1993; Usher and Cervenan, 2005; Shavit, Arum and Gamoran, 2007). Since under complete income independence every family has the same likelihood of receiving higher education, the differential impact of taxation on persons with different levels of income will fully determine their preferences regarding subsidization and enrollment. In other words, when every citizen is equally likely to receive higher education (when 50 percent enrollment implies a 50/50 chance for each family), higher education looks much like a standard public good, and a simple rich-poor redistributive cleavage emerges as in the analysis in Chapter 4.

It is instructive to compare the case of income independence with cases in which access to higher education is income dependent (as assumed in the preceding). In terms of subsidization (and quality), there is a striking flattening of the impact of income on preferences. Poor citizens can now actually receive higher education when access is income dependent. Thus, they may actually support increased subsidization, which they opposed under income dependence. Rich citizens are no longer "guaranteed" higher education, thus they are likely to be less supportive of subsidization and indeed may increasingly prefer a privatized system of higher education that would continue to advantage them.

In terms of preferences over enrollment, there is a muddier picture. For the poor, expanding enrollment under an income-independent access system is preferable to doing so under an income-dependent system, since the latter almost always excludes them. However, the middle class will prefer access to be income dependent as opposed to the lottery of income-independent access, since they are "next in line." Consequently, they will be less supportive of increasing enrollment when access is income independent than when it is income dependent. Finally, a surprising result emerges when examining the wealthiest group of families. These families would actually prefer expanding enrollment when access is income independent rather than income dependent, since in the former case they are not "assured" of receiving higher education. More simply, under income independence, any expansion of enrollment increases the chances of higher education for *their* children, whereas under income dependence, such expansion solely helps *other people's* children. Thus, since both rich and poor prefer expanded enrollment under income independence, provided they collectively politically outweigh the middle class, we should expect higher levels of enrollment when access to higher education is independent of income.

From Preferences to Parties to Policies

I now turn to partisan preferences over higher education policies. The propositions developed in the preceding sections tie individual income to preferences over higher education. But to understand the determinants of actual policy, we need to explore how political parties might aggregate these preferences and how partisan policies are affected by the existing level of enrollment. This section develops a set of propositions about partisan preferences over subsidization and enrollment and maps these onto choices between the Elite, Partially Private, and Mass Public systems.

In this section, I assume that political parties have preferences over higher education based on those of their constituencies. Hence parties do not choose higher education policies to attract votes – specifically, there is no convergence to the median voter's preferred set of higher education policies for electoral reasons. Given that higher education is very rarely the focal point of pre-election debate, this seems a sensible assumption. Furthermore, Chapter 4 showed a powerful effect of cabinet partisanship alone on education policy. Making this assumption permits us to separate out left-wing and right-wing party preferences over higher education policy as determined by their base of support. I assume a two-party system, where the left party can always rely on the support of the poorest third of society and the right party on that of the richest third.[13] Both parties compete for the support of the middle third, with the left earning α and the right earning $(1-\alpha)$ of that group's support, where $\alpha \in [0,1]$ is given probabilistically and exogenously (that is, it is not determined by higher education policy promises). Each group has a population of one-third with total population equaling one. Elections take place between period zero and period one, and period zero's policies are taken as exogenous. The aggregated preferences of the constituencies of left and right will depend on the size of the governing coalition (determined by α) and the current level of enrollment (modeled as s_0). I start by assuming that access to higher education is income dependent.

If s_0 is less than one-third, skilled individuals belong only to the voting bloc of the right. In this Elite scenario, the left-wing party shares the preferences of those unskilled in period zero for lower subsidization and per student spending. The left-wing party will support increased enrollment only if $s_1^* > (2-\alpha)/3$ (that is, if left-wing constituents are benefited) or if increased enrollment is accompanied by a decrease in subsidization to offset tax increases. Conversely, the right-wing party will prefer higher levels of subsidization and per-student spending provided enrollment stays below the threshold where left-wing constituents benefit. The right-wing party's preferences regarding increasing enrollment depend on the weighting it attaches to the poorer members of its voting bloc (that is, whether the tax increase on richer members is outweighed by the advantage of enrolling poorer right-wing voters) and will be strictly negative for any expansion of enrollment past $s_1^* = (2-\alpha)/3$. Where enrollment is already mass – that is, $s_0^* > (2-\alpha)/3$ – these preferences reverse. Left-wing parties will advocate higher subsidization and per-student spending once enrollment passes this point, since the chief burden of increased taxation falls on the rich. Left-wing parties will also favor expanding enrollment further under these conditions,

---

[13] This setup approximates that used in Chapter 4, based on Iversen and Soskice (2006).

since the new recipients will be left-wing constituents. Conversely, right-wing parties will increasingly disfavor subsidization and per-student spending once enrollment passes half of the population and will also wish to halt further expansion of enrollment.

Turning to the broader question of institutional change, how do these preferences translate into the three "ideal types" of higher education system: Elite, Mass Public, and Partially Private? We must first assume that parties *actually have* the freedom to alter higher education policy without institutional constraints. If veto players can totally block reform, the Elite system will remain in place. Although I do not explicitly model such institutional obstacles in the model, since creating a coalition supporting expansion is difficult – due to opposition from both the rich and poor – it is likely only to be feasible under conditions of high party autonomy.

Where parties are unconstrained, their preferences will depend on the size of their electoral support and the current level of enrollment, as noted previously. Parties with little support from the middle of the income distribution are likely to retain an Elite model, since this is favored by both the rich and poor. This is thus similar to the outcome one might expect when veto players are strong – but in this case, it is party preferences rather than institutional constraints that underpin stasis. If parties do have a middle-class constituency that stands to gain from expansion, whether they choose a Partially Private or Mass Public model depends on partisanship. Right-wing parties will push for increased subsidization and per-student spending, and potentially support expansion up to, but no further than, $s_1^* = (2-\alpha)/3$. Thus expansion from an Elite model is likely to produce a Mass Public system under the leadership of the right, albeit with the somewhat knife-edge result that once enrollment has reached s_1^*, it should be capped. From this point onward, in fact, we might expect right-wing parties to increasingly favor fees as access to the higher education system becomes universal.

Conversely, starting from an Elite system, we should expect left-wing parties to tolerate increased enrollment only if the tax burden on left-wing constituents, who fail to receive higher education, is restricted to a relatively low level. Hence left-wing parties should support expansion into a Partially Private model, which keeps the tax burden constant by lower subsidization while increasing enrollment. However, when a mass system is attained, left-wing parties become increasingly interested in public subsidization and per-student spending as it is *their* constituents who increasingly benefit. This suggests a potential three-stage move from an Elite model to a Partially Private model and finally to a Mass Public model. As we shall see in the case studies, the politics of the original expansion of higher education thus contrast with the politics of higher education *once a mass expansion has occurred.*

One further policy option remains unexplored: the role of income dependence. Previously, I argued that the rich-poor split over subsidization (and quality) is lessened when access is income independent. Intuitively, as higher education looks more like a universally accessible public good, partisan preferences conform more to the standard model, where left-wing parties favor increased spending. Though no higher education system is de facto income independent, when a system is *less* income dependent, I expect the standard partisan pattern of preferences over spending (a) to be less pronounced and (b) to have a lower threshold after which left-wing parties are the chief proponents of increased spending.[14]

Furthermore, income dependence may itself be endogenous. Left-wing parties typically seek to reduce income dependence and will subsidize entry by poor groups, either through class-based affirmative action or through targeted grants and loans. Another strategy is altering the structure of schooling to promote access by poorer students, perhaps by removing streaming. The Labour Party in the UK, for example, largely replaced the tripartite streaming of British secondary education with a single comprehensive scheme. Right-wing parties, conversely, have tended to maintain streaming, since they prefer to maintain income dependence. Another important policy is tuition fees. Empirical work shows that tuition fees can actually reduce the inequality in access to higher education itself – that is, they can increase the income independence of the system (Shavit, Arum, and Gamoran, 2007). Though fees might present a direct financial obstacle to poorer students, the effect they have on financing increased overall enrollment may outweigh this effect. The surprising conclusion emerges that substantial fees often increase income independence more than small fees, since the latter provide an obstacle to access without enabling expanded enrollment (the latter are also typically unsubsidized for the poor). Thus, left-wing parties will introduce tuition fees to increase income independence, provided (a) the fees are large enough to sustain expanded enrollment and (b) grants and loans for poorer students are established. If fees are introduced, absent these conditions, then they may reduce income independence and will be favored by right-wing parties.

In Summary

To summarize the theoretical expectations, I expect low institutional constraints and large majorities to be associated with shifts from the Elite model to one of the mass models. I expect right parties to favor moving to Mass Public systems (especially in states with low inequality) and for left parties to favor Partially Private systems. As higher education expands past half of the population, these partisan preferences will weaken, as higher education more closely resembles a uniform public good. If institutional and electoral constraints are too strong for the left to move from an Elite to a Partially Private system, increasing the system's level of income independence may constitute the left's preferred higher education strategy in an Elite system. Finally, progressive taxation and high inequality will interact to produce greater higher education spending.

---

[14] There is no clear partisan pattern; however, both rich and poor groups prefer increasing enrollment more under income independence, cutting across standard partisan cleavages.

Hypothesis One: At elite levels of enrollment, right-wing parties prefer higher subsidization, enrollment, and quality than left-wing parties.

Hypothesis Two: As enrollment expands, this partisan pattern is diluted and, past a certain threshold, left-wing parties prefer higher subsidization, enrollment, and quality.

Hypothesis Three: More veto players will produce reduced spending and enrollment.

Hypothesis Four: More progressive taxation will produce increased levels of higher education spending, with this effect amplified by the level of inequality.

Hypothesis Five: When income independence increases, left-wing parties will sooner favor increased subsidization and quality, and all parties will favor higher enrollment. Left-wing parties will try to increase, and right-wing parties to reduce, income independence.

5.3 EMPIRICAL ANALYSIS OF THE TRILEMMA

I now turn to analyzing empirically the propositions developed in the formal model. In particular, I examine three questions. First, is the trilemma apparent at a cross-sectional level within the OECD? That is, do countries appear to cluster in the three ideal types I set out in the preceding sections and do the trade-offs among subsidization, enrollment, and cost play out in actual policy outcomes? Second, do individuals approach university funding in the manner suggested by the formal model? While survey data on higher education preferences are scarce, I am able to use data from the 1996 ISSP (also used in Chapter 4) to examine the determinants of preferences over aiding low-income students in accessing university. Third, do political parties aggregate these preferences in the manner suggested by the formal model? I use panel data on national higher education funding and enrollment levels from twenty-two OECD states from 1980 to 1997 to test the conditional partisan hypotheses developed in the preceding section. I leave the analysis of subnational higher education policy until Section 5.5, which focuses on the U.S. states. As in the analyses in the previous chapter, the intent is to demonstrate the empirical validity of the assumptions I have made, and hypotheses I have drawn, at both the individual and national levels.

The Trilemma at the Macro Level

I begin with examining whether the theoretical pattern of a trilemma plays out at the macro level across the OECD. To examine this question, I use cross-sectional data on enrollment, subsidization, and public cost for nineteen OECD states. The gross enrollment rate in higher education in 2002 ranged from one-third of the university-age cohort in Belgium and Germany to over 80 percent in New Zealand and Sweden.[15] The degree of subsidization also varies widely. Some systems, such as Denmark's and Finland's, are almost totally publicly

[15] Gross enrollment rates include multiple entries into higher education by the same individual and thus are a more appropriate index of overall budgetary strain on the government than net rates.

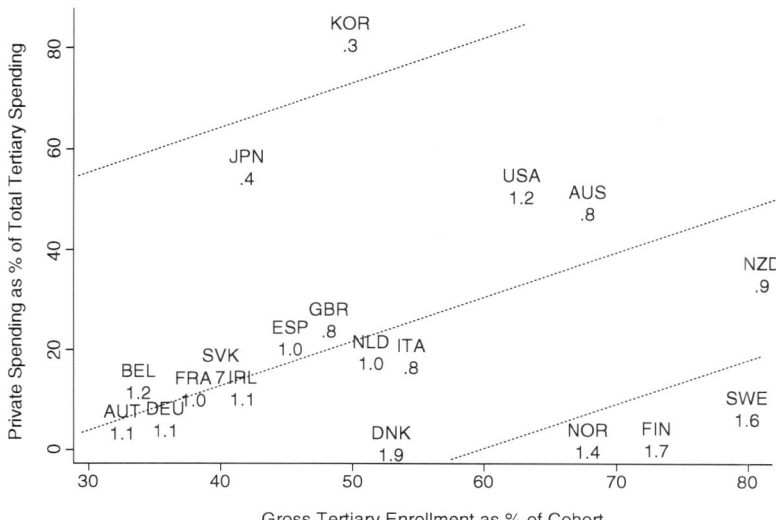

FIGURE 5.6. Enrollment, Private Spending, and Public Cost in 2002

funded, whereas others, such as the United States' and Australia's, are over 50 percent privately funded. Finally, some higher education systems take relatively little from the public purse – less than 1 percent of GDP in England and Italy – whereas others, such as Finland's and Sweden's, cost over 1.5 percent of GDP. The empirical relationship between all three variables is displayed in Figure 5.6, which plots gross tertiary enrollment against the share of tertiary spending from private sources (that is, inverse subsidization) for nineteen OECD states in 2002.[16] For each state, I label its country code and its level of overall public spending on higher education.

In bivariate terms, there does not appear to be a strong relationship between the variables. However, once we examine the public spending variable, we see an interesting pattern. There are three distinct southwest-northeast isocost lines in the figure. In the northwest corner are the two East Asian states with low levels of public funding. Along the main diagonal axis are a dozen states spending between 0.8 percent and 1.2 percent of GDP on public-funded higher education. In the southwest corner are the Elite states such as Austria, Belgium, and Germany with low enrollment and low private financing. At the northeast end are Australia, New Zealand, and the United States with high enrollment and higher private spending but levels of public spending similar to that of the Elite states. Finally, we have a line of states in the southeast corner: the Nordic Mass Public states, which spend at least 1.4 percent of GDP on tertiary education, with high enrollment and high subsidization.

Cross-sectional statistical tests on this data in Table 5.1 confirm this pattern. Since the trilemma implies that enrollment, subsidization, and total cost determine one another, it is not clear that any of the variables can be considered

---

[16] These data are taken from OECD (2005).

TABLE 5.1. *The Trilemma in OECD States in 2002*

	Model A	Model B	Model C	Model D	Model E	Model F
	% Private	% Private	Enrollment	Enrollment	Public Cost	Public Cost
Enrollment	0.194	0.571			0.007	0.010
	(0.281)	(0.177)***			(0.005)	(0.003)***
Public Cost		−51.708	14.021	35.390		
		(10.756)***	(9.149)	(15.501)**		
% Private				0.489		−0.012
				(0.235)**		(0.004)***
GDP Cap	−0.789	0.328	−0.106	−0.237	0.0216	0.012
	(0.791)	(0.535)	(0.421)	(0.475)	(0.009)**	(0.008)
Constant	33.887	41.398	40.606	9.041	0.145	0.553
	(24.869)	(17.073)**	(10.966)***	(15.275)	(0.305)	(0.251)**
N	19	19	19	19	19	19
R^2	0.11	0.66	0.12	0.36	0.36	0.76

Note: Small-sample robust standard errors are in parentheses. ***$p < 0.01$, **$p < 0.05$.

exogenous. Accordingly, I alternate each trilemma variable as the dependent variable, under the caveat that potential endogeneity means that it is difficult to make robust causal claims using cross-sectional data.[17] The estimations use ordinary least squares (OLS) regression with standard errors adjusted for small-sample heteroskedasticity and control for per capita income as well as the trilemma variables.[18] A striking pattern emerges from the data analysis: Each variable is a substantive and significant predictor of another variable only after the third variable is controlled for – hence a trilemma is apparent.

Models A and B use the percentage of tertiary spending from private sources as the dependent variable. Model A incorporates only enrollment and per capita income, both producing statistically insignificant results. However, the addition of the public cost variable in Model B leads to robust results for both enrollment and public cost and a jump in magnitude for the coefficient on enrollment. Substantively, this implies that a 10 percent increase in enrollment is associated with a 5 percent increase in the share of spending from private sources, provided public cost is held constant. An increase in public spending of 1 percent of GDP, conversely, is associated with a reduction of 50 percent points in private spending, given constant enrollment.

Models C and D use enrollment as the dependent variable. Model C finds no effect of public cost alone on enrollment. However, the inclusion of private spending in Model D leads to larger and more robust results for both public cost and private spending. An increase of 0.1 percent point of GDP in public spending on higher education is now associated with an increase of 3.5 points in

[17] As a robustness check, I conducted two-stage least-squares (2SLS) regression of private spending on public cost and enrollment, using other government spending and tertiary attainment in the adult population as instruments. While these instruments are not ideal, 2SLS regression produces stronger and more robust results than OLS, assuaging concerns about endogeneity.

[18] I use the HC3 technique developed in Long and Ervin (2000).

enrollment, and an increase of 10 percent points in the proportion of funding from private sources is associated with an increase of 5 percent in enrollment. Finally, Models E and F use public cost as the dependent variable. Enrollment alone has no significant impact on total public spending, but once I control for private spending in Model F, I again find robust and substantial effects for both variables. An increase of 10 percent points in enrollment is associated with a 0.1 percent point of GDP increase in public spending. Conversely, there is a substitution effect between private and public spending, similar to that seen in Chapter 2: An increase in the proportion of funds coming from private sources of 10 percent points is associated with a decline in public spending of 0.1 percent of GDP. In all cases, the addition of the excluded trilemma variable improves the model fit by over 100 percent. Models A through F imply that we can best understand the cross-national interplay between enrollment, subsidization, and public cost of higher education in the OECD by examining all three variables simultaneously.

Individual Preferences over Higher Education Support

Sharp trade-offs in higher education appear to exist at the national level, but do citizens really view these trade-offs through a political lens? To address this question, I now turn from cross-sectional aggregate outcomes to the micro-foundations of individual preferences regarding higher education. In doing so, I am able to test some of the assumptions I made about individual behavior in the formal model in Section 5.2. I use data from the 1996 International Social Survey Program, which asks participants if they believe that the government should financially support students from low-income families in accessing higher education. This question is slightly tangential to the preceding focus on the preferred levels of enrollment, subsidization, and public funding for higher education. Thus, this question most closely resembles the issue of income-independent access addressed previously. It also pertains to expanding enrollment, since if no quotas are in place, presumably aiding the access of low-income students will cause expansion in overall enrollment. Consequently, following Hypotheses One, Two, and Five, I expect (a) that all else equal, higher income individuals will be less supportive of this kind of policy, and (b) that as the higher education system expands, thereby permitting more low-income individuals to become enrolled, higher-income individuals should become even less supportive of such policies. In this section, I test in turn these two hypotheses, beginning by looking at individual preferences, ignoring the national higher educational context (that is, the size of the higher education system), before turning to examine how the size of higher education in any given country impacts these preferences.

Table 5.2 begins the analysis of individual preferences. As in Chapter 4, I develop a variety of measures of income, since the ISSP does not directly provide a cross-country comparable score. I also examine individual partisanship, looking at both a simple continuum of partisanship and then at more discrete

TABLE 5.2. *Individual Preferences over Support for Low-Income Students in Higher Education*

	Model A	Model B	Model C	Model D	Model E	Model F
Gender	−0.194	−0.207	−0.193	−0.217	−0.193	-0.182
	(0.031)***	(0.031)***	(0.031)***	(0.028)***	(0.039)***	(0.031)***
Age	0.003	0.002	0.003	0.001	0.004	0.002
	(0.001)***	(0.001)**	(0.001)***	(0.001)	(0.001)***	(0.001)**
Education	0.019	0.034	0.020	0.031	−0.007	0.014
	(0.013)	(0.013)**	(0.013)	(0.012)**	(0.017)	(0.013)
Religiosity	0.003	0.005	0.004	0.003	0.017	0.019
	(0.010)	(0.010)	(0.010)	(0.009)	(0.013)	(0.010)*
Catholic	0.015	0.034	0.022	0.003	−0.095	-0.010
	(0.050)	(0.050)	(0.050)	(0.044)	(0.069)	(0.050)
Protestant	0.085	0.093	0.087	0.068	0.000	0.055
	(0.049)*	(0.049)*	(0.049)*	(0.045)	(0.062)	(0.049)
Income Quartile	0.189					
	(0.016)***					
Relative Income		0.161				
		(0.027)***				
Log Relative Income			0.283		0.301	0.266
			(0.027)***		(0.034)***	(0.027)***
Subjective Class				0.096		
				(0.014)***		
Partisanship					0.285	
					(0.021)***	
Center-Left						−0.258
						(0.050)***
Center						0.210
						(0.056)***
Center-Right						0.465
						(0.051)***
Far-Right						0.256
						(0.178)
Observations	22,155	22,155	22,155	25,421	13,451	22,155

Note: Standard errors are in parentheses. ***$p < 0.01$, **$p < 0.05$, *$p < 0.1$.

identification with parties of the far-left, center-left, and so on. Finally, I also include the same array of controls as those used in Chapter 4: gender, age, religiosity, dummies for being Protestant or Catholic, and a categorical variable measuring educational attainment. The dependent variable is an ordered categorical variable measuring preferences for funding low-income students in higher education. The precise question asked by the ISSP 1996 survey is (in English), "On the whole, do you think it should be or should not be the government's responsibility to give financial help to students from low income families?" The answers to this question are coded such that *higher numbers reflect less support for the policy.* Consequently, "definitely should be" is coded as one, "probably should be" is coded as two, "probably should not be" is coded as three, and "definitely should not be" is coded as four. Thus the dependent variable is a four-category ordered measure and, consequently, as in Chapter 4,

I use an ordered logit model with country dummies and clustered standard errors.

In Table 5.2, I run six models, alternating different measures of income and/or partisanship. Across all the models there is an extremely robust positive effect of income. Recall that this means that higher-income individuals are *less* predisposed to government support for low-income individuals than are lower-income individuals. Model A (using income quartiles), Model B (using income relative to the mean), Model C (using the log of relative income), and Model D (using subjective social class) all show this very similar and robust pattern. Furthermore, partisanship is also an extremely strong predictor of support for government aid to students from low-income families. Importantly, Models E and F suggest that the estimated effect of income remains significant (and similar in magnitude) even controlling for partisan preferences. Thus, as in Chapter 4, income remains an important determinant of education preferences, even when we limit our analysis to higher education.

Model F suggests that the partisan pattern of support for higher education aid is approximately linear around the center of the partisan distribution (that is, from center-left to center-right), but as we saw on several occasions in Chapter 4, preferences are more unexpected around the extremes, with far-left voters less supportive of student support than center-left voters, and far-right voters more supportive than center-right supporters. Given the smaller sample of voters at the partisan extreme, this could reflect sample composition quirks or conversely it might adhere to the kind of *U*-shaped expectation of education spending developed in Chapter 4. As for the remaining control variables, women appear more favorable to student support than men, and older individuals are less supportive of student aid. The effect of education varies in robustness, although a potential "supply-side" effect is implied where college-educated individuals are less supportive of minting new low-income graduates than individuals with less education. The religion variables are rarely statistically significant, although they lean in an antisupport direction.

The estimated effects of different levels of income and partisanship vary substantially. Moving from the first to the fourth income quartile is estimated to decrease the chance of definitely supporting student aid by 14.2 percent points, increase the chances of probably supporting it by 9.2 percent points, probably opposing it by 3.9 percent points, and definitely opposing it by 1.1 percent points. Note that most of the effect is to transfer people from definitely to probably supporting such aid. Very few people in the dataset *claim* that they outright oppose such aid (that is, they are unwilling to tell the interviewer they oppose such support, as we saw in the case of the general pro-education bias in surveys in Chapter 4). But there is still substantial variation in the degree of support for such measures and this does correlate very strongly with income. Very similar patterns hold in the other income/class models: Models B, C, and D. In Model E, a shift in partisanship from center-left to center-right (that is, ignoring the most extreme categories) is associated with a 14.1 percent point decrease in category one, and increases in the other categories of respectively 8.5, 4.4, and 1.3

TABLE 5.3. *Preferences over Higher Education Support Interacted with Enrollment*

	Model A	Model B
Gender	−0.187	−0.191
	(0.036)***	(0.051)***
Age	0.003	0.003
	(0.002)*	(0.002)
Education	0.165	0.144
	(0.052)***	(0.059)**
Religiosity	0.007	0.023
	(0.011)	(0.010)**
Catholic	0.045	0.015
	(0.082)	(0.088)
Protestant	0.146	0.106
	(0.043)***	(0.057)*
Log Relative Income	0.187	0.272
	(0.066)***	(0.077)***
Income*Enrollment	0.003	0.001
	(0.001)***	(0.001)
Education*Enrollment	−0.003	−0.003
	(0.002)**	(0.001)**
Partisanship		0.063
		(0.155)
Partisanship*Enrollment		0.006
		(0.003)**
Observations	16,738	10,943

Note: Robust standard errors in parentheses. ***$p < 0.01$, **$p < 0.05$, *$p < 0.1$.

percent points. The similarity across these measures suggests that income, class, and partisanship matter in determining preferences over providing support to students from low-income families. This provides robust microfoundations for the claim that right-wing parties will disfavor income independence.

Table 5.3 provides a more contextual exploration of higher education policies by examining whether individual preferences are partially shaped by the preexisting level of enrollment in higher education in the particular country that they live in. In this set of models, I run the same estimations as in Models C and E of the previous table but include interactions between the national level of gross tertiary enrollment in 1995 (the year before the survey was taken) and the individual-level variables of income, education, and partisanship. Put simply, I want to see whether income, education, and partisanship effects are dependent on the type of higher education system (here distinguishing between elite and mass systems) in which an individual lives. Model A adds the interactions with education and income. Most of the estimated coefficients on the control variables, as well as education and income, remain in the same direction as in Model C of Table 5.2. Most pertinently, the interaction of individual income with national enrollment levels is positive and robust, implying that high-income individuals are more opposed to student aid in mass enrollment systems than in elite systems. The effect of education, however, is in the reverse direction, implying that college-educated individuals are less concerned about student aid in mass systems. Model B introduces the individual partisanship variable and a variable that interacts this with the national level of enrollment. Here the estimate for partisanship itself, while still positive, is not statistically significant, but its interaction with the enrollment level is, implying that right-wing voters are more opposed to student aid in systems with high levels of existing enrollment.

What are the implications of this contextual analysis? Since there are a lot of moving parts, due to the interaction terms, the estimated effects of changing an individual's income, for example, are quite distinct from those in Table 5.2. Using Model A, I examine the effect of moving from the 5th to 95th percentile on log relative income, first in a country with an elite level of enrollment of 30 percent, and second in a country with a mass level of enrollment of 60 percent. In the elite case, this change in income is associated with a decrease in the first category of 12.5 percent points and increases in the latter categories of 8.7, 2.9, and 0.9 percent points. In the case of mass enrollment, we see a decrease of 14.3 percent points in the first category, and increases of 5.0, 6.9, and 2.3 percent points in the latter categories. Note, then, that in the mass systems, richer individuals become much more likely to prefer that the government *not* support low-income students (that is, there are sharp jumps in the likelihood of answering positively in the latter two categories).

Turning to Model B, the effect of moving from the center-left to the center-right in elite systems is to decrease the first category by 12.0 percent points and increase the latter categories by 8.7, 2.6, and 0.7 percent points (all highly robust estimates). In a mass system, conversely, this change in partisanship decreases the first category by 16.8 percent points and increases the latter ones by 6.6, 7.9, and 2.3 percent points (again, all robust). Note that this mirrors the results for income (the interactive variable that is now not robust in Model B), suggesting that the conditional effects of partisanship and income are very similar in scope. Right-wing voters in mass systems are much more antipathetic to student support than their equivalents in elite systems.

Overall, Table 5.3 provides firm evidence that institutional context matters quite strongly in determining whether individuals favor government support in the realm of higher education. But, of course, it is not individual voters themselves who pull the policy levers that increase enrollment or student support – that task is delegated to governments. Thus, I now turn to the governments themselves. What do partisan actors do to higher education once in office? Do they follow the apparent demands of voters that we saw in this section?

Partisan Policies in the World of Higher Education

In this section, I turn from the preferences of the voting public to the parties that may, or may not, enact those preferences. I examine two particular issues pertaining to the trilemma: the funding of higher education and the level of enrollment. The data on university financing and enrollment are drawn from

UNESCO's "Education and Literacy" and "World Education Indicators" data-sets and the World Bank's EdStats databases.[19] Annual data are available for these indicators from 1980 through 1997, a period of analysis that is also coter-minous with the expansion of university systems in many states. To examine the determinants of spending, I use public spending on tertiary education rela-tive to spending on other forms of education, which has a mean of 20.7 percent and a within-country standard deviation of 3.5 percent. By controlling for the lagged level of tertiary enrollment and overall education spending, this mea-sure picks up changes in either subsidization *or* per-student spending ("qual-ity"). Unfortunately, I cannot distinguish between subsidization and quality because data on private spending (which would allow us to determine the level of subsidization) are extremely limited in time-series availability.[20] However, our theoretical expectations about the effect of partisanship on both subsidiza-tion and quality are very similar since both involve increasing the level of public support per student. For testing the determinants of enrollment, I use the gross tertiary enrollment ratio, with a mean of 38.8 percent, median of 34.3 percent, and within-country standard deviation of 9.7 percent.

The formal model suggested that the partisanship of government should affect spending and enrollment outcomes. To measure the effects of partisan-ship, I use the lagged cabinet center of gravity index used in Chapter 4. The formal model implied that right-wing parties seek higher levels of subsidization and per-student spending than left-wing parties when enrollment is low but that this pattern is reversed for high levels of enrollment. Accordingly, I also create an interactive variable that is the product of lagged partisanship and enrollment. The extensions to the theoretical model examined the effects of differential access to higher education and different tax systems. I develop three measures that address whether access to higher education is income dependent. First, I employ a simple dummy operationalization of whether pupils are streamed into general and vocational schools by age sixteen. Since entering university from vocational schools is unusual and difficult, and poorer students tend to choose vocational training, access in education systems with streaming will be more income dependent than in those without streaming.[21] Second, I use the average proportion of secondary students enrolled in vocational streams, taken from the UNESCO dataset used in Chapter 4. Finally, I employ the Gini coefficient of household pretax income taken from the Luxembourg Income Study. I expect that states with higher levels of inequality will have more income-dependent higher education systems. In these states, the impact of inequalities in income,

---

[19] Gross enrollment data are from EdStats (2004). Tertiary spending in absolute amounts of national currency is from UNESCO (2007), which also provides information on absolute spend-ing on other levels of education, permitting the development of a relative spending indicator.

[20] In the next two sections, I examine the politics of reducing subsidization through the introduc-tion of tuition fees in the country cases and statistical analysis of U.S. states.

[21] Data on streaming come from the International Association of Universities database on Higher Education Systems at http://www.unesco.org/iau/onlinedatabases/index.html (accessed July 12, 2007).

as opposed to aptitude, on access will be greater, either because of greater differences in public secondary school quality or the ability of parents to "purchase" access through tutoring or private schooling.

To measure tax regressivity, I use data taken from Carey and Tchilinguirian's (2000) estimates of average effective tax rates. Specifically, I measure tax regressivity by calculating the ratio of the average effective tax rate on labor income to that on net capital.[22] I argue that the effect of the progressivity of taxation depends on the level of income inequality, thus I interact this variable with the Gini coefficient. The discussion of aggregating political preferences into policy briefly highlighted the potential institutional blockage caused by veto players. Accordingly, I use Huber et al.'s sixteen-point measure of the number of veto players (Huber et al., 1997). Finally, I also employ a set of control variables that potentially affect both enrollment and spending. I use a measure of GDP per capita to control for income effects on higher education policy, the proportion of population younger than fifteen to control for changing demographics, and overall public spending on education to control for the possibility that higher education financing and enrollment are increasing as part of a broader trend toward education spending.

Tables 5.4 (a) and (b) examine the determinants of public spending on tertiary education relative to other education spending.[23] Model A of Table 5.4 (a) provides a "naïve" benchmark, including just the basic partisanship variable and the control variables. In this model, the effects of cabinet partisanship on relative tertiary spending are essentially nil. The key determinants of tertiary spending appear to be demographics and the expansion of public education spending. However, the preceding theoretical section argued that the impact of partisanship on subsidization and per-student spending is *dependent* on the existing level of enrollment. Thus Model B, which includes measures of enrollment and the interaction of cabinet partisanship and enrollment, provides our "sophisticated" benchmark model, testing Hypotheses One and Two. Here we see that partisanship, enrollment, and the interactive variable are all significant at the 5 percent level and that the effect of the former two variables is estimated to be positive, with the latter variable negative. This implies that while at low levels of enrollment right-wing parties increase relative tertiary spending, as enrollment increases above a certain threshold, the partisan effect switches, with left-wing parties increasing relative tertiary spending. In Model B, this threshold occurs when gross enrollment reaches 32 percent.

Model C adds the veto players measure, testing Hypothesis Three, which produces the expected negative effect on tertiary spending with a move from

---

[22] I employ their estimates for labor and net capital taxation for 1980–5, 1986–90, and 1991–7. Results are similar using consumption taxation instead of (or combined with) labor taxation or replacing net capital taxation with gross capital taxation. Tax regressivity is simply the inverse of tax progressivity.

[23] I employ a pooled OLS regression with a lagged dependent variable, a linear time trend, panel autocorrelated error terms, and panel-corrected standard errors to adjust for serial contemporaneous correlation between states.

TABLE 5.4(a). *Partisan Effects on the Composition of Education Spending*

	Model A	Model B	Model C	Model D	Model E	Model F	Model G
Lagged DV	0.910	0.869	0.862	0.860	0.814	0.805	0.728
	(0.037)***	(0.054)***	(0.053)***	(0.055)***	(0.058)***	(0.058)***	(0.069)***
Partisanship	-0.011	0.052	0.061	0.056	0.094	0.106	0.083
	(0.009)	(0.024)**	(0.025)**	(0.024)**	(0.031)***	(0.031)***	(0.315)***
Enrollment		0.047	0.049	0.046	0.042	0.046	-0.016
		(0.020)**	(0.020)**	(0.020)**	(0.021)**	(0.021)**	(0.028)
Partisan X Enroll		-0.002	-0.002	-0.002	-0.002	-0.003	-0.002
		(0.001)***	(0.001)***	(0.001)***	(0.001)***	(0.001)***	(0.001)**
GDP per Cap	-0.037	-0.041	-0.028	-0.033	-0.011	0.004	0.024
	(0.021)*	(0.026)	(0.029)	(0.027)	(0.047)	(0.052)	(0.060)
Population < 15	0.053	0.094	0.115	0.094	0.034	0.074	0.049
	(0.080)	(0.086)	(0.100)	(0.088)	(0.149)	(0.192)	(0.169)
Public Ed Spend	0.364	0.212	0.201	0.164	0.618	0.581	1.330
	(0.087)***	(0.128)*	(0.140)	(0.157)	(0.227)***	(0.282)**	(0.413)***
Veto Points			-0.164			-0.156	-0.135
			(0.074)**			(0.075)**	(0.075)*
Streaming				-0.435		-0.135	-4.844
				(0.433)		(0.647)	(1.618)***
Vocational Share					-0.054	-0.047	-0.221
					(0.023)**	(0.029)*	(0.074)***
Stream*VOC							0.217
							(0.072)***
Year	0.048	-0.005	-0.005	-0.002	-0.001	-0.006	0.118
	(0.039)	(0.047)	(0.047)	(0.049)	(0.054)	(0.056)	(0.062)*
Constant	-95.988	8.010	8.076	2.385	1.247	12.010	-231.962
	(77.421)	(94.444)	(95.380)	(97.635)	(109.245)	(112.404)	(122.487)*
Threshold		32.07	34.90	31.75	38.76	40.64	43.45
N	271	266	266	266	228	228	228
Countries	22	22	22	22	18	18	18
R²	0.958	0.963	.961	0.963	0.963	0.961	0.963

Note: Robust standard errors are in parentheses. ***$p < 0.01$, **$p < 0.05$, *$p < 0.1$.

TABLE 5.4(b). *The Effects of Inequality on the Composition of Education Spending*

	Model A	Model B	Model C Low Gini	Model D High Gini
Lagged DV	0.850	0.755	0.845	0.454
	(0.059)***	(0.064)***	(0.046)***	(0.071)***
Partisanship	0.066	0.122	0.051	0.116
	(0.028)**	(0.040)***	(0.034)	(0.059)**
Enrollment	0.045	0.031	0.026	−0.004
	(0.021)**	(0.025)	(0.023)	(0.004)
Partisan X Enroll	−0.002	−0.003	−0.0015	−0.002
	(0.001)***	(0.001)***	(0.0007)**	(0.001)**
GDP per Capita	−0.040	−0.104	−0.215	0.040
	(0.028)	(0.072)	(0.101)**	(0.071)
Population < 15	0.108	0.308	0.246	−0.322
	(0.113)	(0.234)	(0.260)	(0.138)**
Public Ed Spend	0.314	1.782	0.213	5.868
	(0.145)**	(0.459)***	(0.190)	(0.633)***
Veto Points		−0.175	−0.172	−0.133
		(0.121)	(0.170)	(0.143)
School Stream		0.905	0.554	−5.343
		(0.849)	(0.623)	(1.826)***
Regressivity	−1.152	24.433	1.087	−3.585
	(0.678)*	(11.023)**	(1.063)	(3.270)
Gini		95.306		
		(34.491)***		
Gini*Regress		−89.396		
		(41.428)*		
Year	0.022	.072	0.229	0.094
	(0.054)	(.088)	(0.109)**	(0.114)
Constant	−44.197	-179.453	−454.360	-194.920
	(107.683)	(176.851)	(218.117)**	(226.360)
Threshold	35.28	42.451	34.78	49.32
N	251	177	109	93
Countries	21	18	9	9
R²	0.962	0.966	0.970	0.988

Note: Robust standard errors are in parentheses. ***$p < 0.01$, **$p < 0.05$, *$p < 0.1$.

the 10th to 90th percentile of veto players associated with a decrease in relative spending of 0.7 percent points. I next examine the effect of school streaming in Model D. Here I find that streamed systems are estimated to have lower spending, as suggested in Hypothesis Five, but the estimate is insignificant at conventional levels. Model E examines the effect of the average level of vocational education in each country, and here we do see a statistically significant negative effect of the structure of secondary schooling on relative spending. A one standard deviation increase in vocational enrollments is associated with a decrease of 0.8 percent points in relative spending – an effect similar to that of veto players. Model F incorporates these three measures concurrently, showing that veto players and vocational education remain fairly robust predictors. Model G turns to the interactive effect of vocational education and school streaming that we explored in Chapter 4. Here we see a very robust pattern that is rather intriguing. In states without streaming, only the vocational education effect applies, and this remains negative. In states with streaming, there is a robust negative effect of streaming itself and then a positive interaction term, which largely cancels out the effect of changes in the share of vocational enrollment. Thus, in streamed systems, the effect of streaming itself dominates vocational enrollments, whereas in non-streamed systems, vocational enrollments matter. This suggests that streaming itself – as in, for example, Germany and Austria – provides an obstacle to increased higher education funding, regardless of enrollments. In non-streaming states such as Sweden and the United States, what matters instead is the choice of students to enter vocational paths *within* their school. In the streaming states, the choice of accessing university is made for their student by their choice of school; in the non-streaming states, the choice appears more voluntary – the choice of a program within a school.

Table 5.4(b) focuses on the interactive effects of the tax system and inequality. I now move away from analyzing vocational education, retaining solely the school-tier dummy. Model A adds the tax regressivity variable, which has a strong negative effect (and hence progressivity has a positive effect) on tertiary spending. Model B presents a full estimation including both inequality and its interaction with regressivity. The model shows that the interaction of inequality and regressivity is statistically significant and negative, implying that more progressive tax systems have higher tertiary spending when inequality is also high, confirming Hypothesis Four.[24] The conditional partisan effect predicted by Hypotheses One and Two also holds, with an estimated threshold of just over 40 percent.

Figure 5.7 provides predicted values and 95 percent confidence intervals for the short-term marginal effect of a fifty-point shift rightward in partisanship on relative tertiary spending at different levels of existing enrollment.[25] There is a robust finding that when enrollment is below around 30 percent, right-wing parties prefer higher relative tertiary spending, but beyond around 50 percent enrollment, left-wing parties prefer higher spending, with partisan preferences switching between these points. At 25 percent enrollment, a fifty-point shift to the right produces a standard deviation increase in relative tertiary spending, but at 60 percent enrollment it produces a standard deviation *decrease*.

Finally, Models C and D split the sample into two groups, using the median level of national inequality in 1990 as the cutpoint. Here I test whether partisanship on subsidization and quality is moderated in systems with lower income dependence, as suggested by Hypothesis Five. As expected, the partisan switching pattern is more robust in Model D, the high inequality subsample, than in Model C. In particular, the threshold point of enrollment for switching is

---

[24] The vocational education variable produces extremely similar effects. Both are highly collinear with inequality, which dominates the regression.

[25] This is produced using code provided by Brambor, Clark, and Golder (2006).

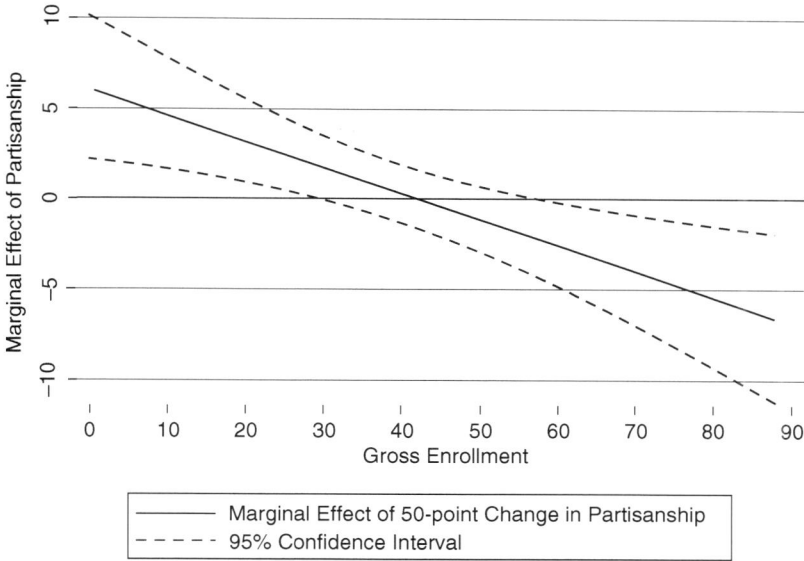

FIGURE 5.7. Marginal Effect of a Fifty-Point Change in Partisanship on Relative Tertiary Spending at Different Levels of Enrollment

substantially higher in Model D, occurring when enrollment reaches almost 50 percent. Conversely, in Model C the threshold occurs at around 35 percent. This implies that right-wing parties continue to favor public investment in higher education significantly longer in high-inequality states, presumably because inequality of income is related to inequality in access. The negative effect of streaming is also more pronounced, and statistically robust, in the high-inequality states. In the low-inequality states, Model C robustly estimates that left-wing parties favor increased investment once enrollment has passed 50 percent, but the estimate that right-wing parties prefer investment at lower levels of enrollment is not robust at conventional levels. Moreover, the partisan switching effect is weaker and happens at lower levels of enrollment when inequality is low, suggesting that left-wing parties will sooner support transition to a Mass Public model in such countries. Figure 5.8 demonstrates the estimated short-term effect of a fifty-point rightward shift in partisanship on relative tertiary spending at different levels of enrollment for high- and low-inequality states.

Table 5.5 turns to the determinants of gross tertiary enrollment. I use as independent variables cabinet partisanship, per capita income, population under age fifteen, public education spending, veto players, and the school streaming dummy variable.[26] I also add the relative tertiary spending measure that was the dependent variable in Table 5.4 (a). Model A presents the estimates from this

---

[26] As before, I use a pooled OLS with a lagged dependent variable, panel-specific autocorrelation, and panel corrected standard errors and I omit the inequality and regressivity variables, which pertain to the tax structure, since I focus on enrollment, not spending.

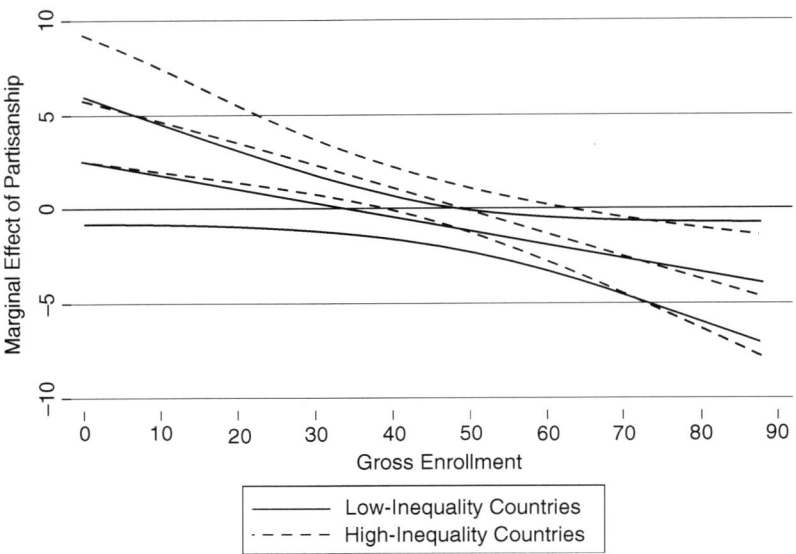

FIGURE 5.8. Marginal Effects in High- and Low-Inequality States

baseline equation. There are two significant findings here. First, lagged cabinet partisanship is robustly and negatively related to enrollment, such that a shift of fifty points to the left is estimated to increase gross tertiary enrollment by 1.35 percent points. This implies that left-wing parties are associated with increased enrollment across the dataset. Secondly, school streaming is associated with systematically lower tertiary enrollment, as suggested by Hypothesis Five, with streaming systems having enrollment rates 2 percent points lower than non-streaming systems.

To examine whether the partisan switching threshold effects suggested by Hypotheses One and Two are also present for enrollment, I divide the sample into two groups, using as a threshold the figure of 35 percent, which is the median threshold estimate from Table 5.4. Model B re-estimates the baseline equation on states whose lagged level of tertiary enrollment was less than 35 percent. Here I find the negative effect of cabinet partisanship vanishes – left-wing parties are not keen to expand enrollment when the next citizens "in line" are right-wing constituents. Right-wing parties appear more ambivalent – they trade off increased political support with higher taxes – and it seems that these effects net out. Furthermore, in these elite systems, school streaming appears not to effect enrollment levels. Model C, which examines states with a lagged enrollment above 35 percent, shows that the partisan pattern switches in mass systems – here the coefficient is larger than in Model A – a fifty-point switch to the left increasing tertiary enrollment by over 2 percent points – albeit at slightly lower levels of statistical significance. Thus, left-wing parties expand enrollment only after substantial levels of enrollment have occurred and their own constituents will be the beneficiaries. Streaming also has a larger negative

TABLE 5.5. *Determinants of Gross Enrollment*

	Model A	Model B	Model C	Model D	Model E	Model F
	All	Lag < 35	Lag > 35	ECM All	ECM Lag < 35	ECM Lag > 35
Lagged DV	0.957	0.993	0.896	-0.010	0.092	-0.068
	(0.034)***	(0.035)***	(0.054)***	(0.026)	(0.033)***	(0.040)*
Partisanship	-0.027	0.002	-0.042	-0.023	0.015	-0.055
	(0.011)***	(0.012)	(0.023)*	(0.010)**	(0.012)	(0.025)**
				0.006	-0.006	0.018
				(0.012)	(0.014)	(0.022)
Tertiary/Ed	-0.030	-0.004	-0.043	0.021	-0.015	-0.032
	(0.038)	(0.026)	(0.046)	(0.046)	(0.032)	(0.057)
				0.030	0.011	0.019
				(0.068)	(0.058)	(0.115)
GDP per Capita	-0.020	-0.039	0.151	-0.035	-0.020	-0.079
	(0.029)	(0.025)	(0.061)**	(0.025)	(0.022)	(0.057)
				-0.096	-0.640	0.138
				(0.354)	(0.319)**	(0.608)
Population < 15	-0.098	-0.052	-0.296	-0.156	0.100	-0.031
	(0.091)	(0.063)	(0.184)	(0.087)*	(0.081)	(0.089)
				2.143	-0.621	6.192
				(0.825)***	(0.701)	(2.720)**
Public Ed Spend	0.186	-0.046	0.028	0.006	-0.325	-0.159
	(0.193)	(0.237)	(0.463)	(0.159)	(0.171)*	(0.348)
				0.269	0.319	-0.077
				(0.513)	(0.484)	(0.890)
Veto Points	-0.007	0.041	0.093	0.027	-0.031	-0.153
	(0.080)	(0.070)	(0.151)	(0.073)	(0.069)	(0.148)
School Tier	-1.956	-0.008	-6.112	-0.878	0.157	-2.921
		(0.261)	(2.418)***	(0.637)	(0.266)	(1.147)**
Year	0.246	0.239	0.087			
	(0.960)**	(0.051)***	(0.169)			
Constant	-483.243	-470.733	-158.019	6.801	3.396	11.731
	(172.208)***	(101.669)	(336.070)	(1.960)***	(2.263)	(2.792)***
N	271	158	113	262	154	108
Countries	22	19	21	22	19	21
R^2	0.961	0.986	0.980	0.124	.224	0.260

Note: Robust standard errors are in parentheses. ***$p < 0.01$, **$p < 0.05$, *$p < 0.1$.

impact on enrollment – mass higher education systems become constrained in size in the presence of streaming.

Finally, Models D through F use an error correction model, appropriate in cases like enrollment where there is very strong year-to-year autocorrelation. This model includes lagged transformations of each variable and the difference in each variable between the current and lagged period. The dependent variable is now the difference in enrollment between the current and lagged period. Models D through F replicate the previous three models using this different structure. I find results similar to those found previously, with left-wing parties the advocates of increased enrollment in states with lagged enrollment above 35 percent but not below that threshold. This effect comes only from the "permanent" lagged level of partisanship rather than the "temporary" difference between current and previous partisanship, suggesting that partisan changes to enrollment are affected over the medium term. School tiering also remains significant in systems above the threshold, but not in the full sample. Overall, the error correction model confirms that the basic findings of Models A through C are robust to removing the strong effect of a lagged dependent variable.

In summary, the empirical results strongly support the expectations of the formal model. As expected, partisan preferences over higher education spending are *conditional* on the level of current enrollment and on the level of income dependence of access, proxied for by inequality. When higher education systems have elite enrollment, we expect right-wing parties to be the chief advocates of increasing subsidization (or quality). However, once a mass system has been reached, the partisan effect switches such that left-wing parties are most interested in increasing spending. Thus, as noted in the model, the partisan story behind the journey to a mass system (and consequently the transition from Elite to Mass Public or Partially Private) is quite distinct from partisan preferences once a truly mass system has been obtained. Importantly, in low-inequality countries, this partisan story is more muted and left-wing parties become favorable to increased spending somewhat earlier. The positive effect of progressive taxation, interacting with inequality, is also confirmed as is, with somewhat less robustness, the negative effect of veto players on spending. The story of enrollment expansion also conformed to expectations. When systems have elite levels of enrollment (under 35 percent), there is little partisan effect on expansion (and, if anything, there is a right-wing bias). However, once enrollment has expanded beyond this point, future increases in enrollment are strongly associated with left-wing parties.

5.4 HISTORICAL ANALYSIS OF THE TRILEMMA

In this section, I examine three states that are emblematic of the three ideal types of the trilemma: England, Sweden, and Germany. In doing so, I am able to more closely trace the pattern of partisan preferences over higher education and the transition between higher education systems. All three states had very similar higher education systems in 1945. However, whereas the Germans have retained an essentially elitist higher education system, both the Swedes and the English have moved rapidly toward a mass system. The financing of this expansion differed substantially between England and Sweden, with the Tony Blair government enacting a series of reforms introducing tuition fees, while the Swedes have opted for a prolonged expansion of public funding at the tertiary level. I examine in turn the Partially Private English system, the Mass Public Swedish system, and the Elite German system, also comparing the latter to the similarly elite systems of Austria and Switzerland.

Higher Education in England

In 1950, English higher education was more of a rite of passage for the children of the elite than a necessary educational step for would-be professionals. In the immediate postwar era, fewer than 3 percent of children went on to university (Chitty, 2004), and most individuals who ended up in professions that we would today think of as classic "college-level" careers – for example, engineers, journalists, and stockbrokers – never entered the university system. Generally, most students who attended university were either beneficiaries of the elite British "public school" system (meaning, in actuality, fee-paying schools of considerable antiquity) or increasingly those middle- and working-class children who had attended the publicly funded grammar school system.[27] However, the relative affluence of the 1950s led to increases in applications to university. The existing structure of English higher education, constructed around the "ancients" (Oxford, Cambridge, Durham, and the Scottish schools) and the nineteenth century urban "redbricks" (London, Manchester, Birmingham, and Bristol), could not easily absorb such demand. While 80 percent of students applying to university in 1956 obtained places, this proportion had dropped to 60 percent by 1964 (Layard, King, and Moser, 1969).

The strains on the system presented a quandary for the ruling Conservative Party, by 1961 reaching a decade of unbroken government. On the one hand, most Tory ministers were themselves products of both the elite university system (typically Oxbridge) and the elite public schools (typically Eton) and were thus direct beneficiaries of the rationing of higher education. However, on the other hand, the Tory electoral base would be the chief beneficiaries of any limited expansion of higher education, given that they were starting from such a low point of coverage (by 1961, around 5 percent of the population). Furthermore, the subsidization of higher education was beyond debate at this time, and certainly a fully public system of funding was in the Conservative interest given its regressive fiscal structure. Consequently, as Gordon and his colleagues note, "as the 1950s closed…the Conservative government had committed itself to growth in higher education" (Gordon, Aldrich, and Dean, 1991). The chosen

---

[27] The grammar school system was the top stream of English public secondary education, access to which was determined by the "Eleven Plus," an exam taken at the end of primary schooling.

resolution to the enrollment issue was the creation of a committee on potential expansion, led by Lord Robbins, reporting in 1963.

The Robbins report was an unprecedented call to expand higher education. Robbins recommended that all universities and technical colleges be governed under a unitary system, the construction of six more universities, and that "courses of higher education should be available for all those who are qualified by ability and attainment to pursue them and wish to do so" (British Ministry of Education, 1963). The Conservatives accepted the Robbins recommendations within twenty-four hours of publication. The legislation demonstrates three key implications of the model developed in this chapter. Firstly, the report envisaged expanding enrollment to around 15 percent of the population – a group well within the Conservative Party's base electoral support. Secondly, the subsidization of higher education was not in debate since the current regressive fiscal structure was firmly in the Conservative interest. Thirdly, the streamed structure of English public secondary education – split into grammar schools, secondary moderns, and technical schools – and the high level of English income inequality meant that access to higher education was largely income dependent and hence destined for students from Conservative families.

Labour, elected in 1964, soon departed from Robbins' orthodoxy. Anthony Crosland, the education secretary, rejected the call for a unitary system of higher education, instead establishing a "binary policy," retaining the split between universities and technical colleges (referred to as "polytechnics") with the latter under direct public control.[28] Moreover, Labour rejected Robbins' calls for the construction of six new universities. Why did Labour choose to undermine Robbins? Crosland argued in 1965 that the binary policy was preferable to a "unitary system, hierarchically arranged on the 'ladder' principle"; instead, he advocated "a move away from our snobbish caste-ridden hierarchical obsession with University status" (quoted in Silver, 2003). Expanding the number of universities was undesirable because it overly favored Conservative constituents. Crosland did, however, alter the structure of secondary schooling through the introduction of "comprehensive" schools, which were intended to break down the streamed structure of English education (Bognador, 1977). Thus, access to higher education would over time depend decreasingly on income.

The Labour Party was not the only enemy of expansion. In response to Labour's successful attempts at expanding the use of "comprehensive" secondary schools and also in reaction to the increasing acceptance of "progressive" teaching methods and student participation at the university level, a group of right-wing iconoclasts published a series of antiprogressive education pamphlets known as the "Black Papers" between 1969 and 1970 (Cox and Dyson, 1971). Their complaints against the universities were legion, including a general

---

[28] Universities, conversely, have long had a peculiar relationship to the state in the UK, with nominal autonomy in the area of governance but funded largely from public sources, until Labour's Teaching and Higher Education Act of 1998. In practice, through the Research Assessment Exercise and other funding devices, the government has been able to acquire considerable indirect control over university governance.

aversion toward student protest and participation (Amis, 1971).[29] The most pointed attack on university expansion was the author Kingsley Amis's well-known assertion that "more will mean worse." In particular, the group's claimed concern was not with expansion per se but with the "reduction in appropriate resources" per student. This reflected the elite's concern that the regressive structure of higher education would be "progressivized" to the detriment of their offspring. This view was typical among the "Establishment Tories," whose socioeconomic status was far removed from the majority of the Conservatives' voting base. Despite rhetorical caveats that they were not recommending quotas, their underlying preferences are best summed up by Kingsley Amis and Robert Conquest's remark that, "For our part, we believe in giving everyone all the education which he can take: we only wish it to be education not eyewash" (quoted in Cox and Dyson, 1971). The split among the Tories mirrors that presented in the model between the upper-middle-class proponents of a Mass Public system and the very wealthy who prefer an Elite model.

The Tory schism over higher education flared up again in the mid-1980s, following concerns that England was lagging in international terms, with only 15 percent of young adults attending universities or polytechnics. The 1988 Education Act, passed by Education Minister Kenneth Baker, attempted to kickstart the university sector by ending the binary system. Baker also called for a doubling of enrollment, from 15 to 30 percent over the next twenty-five years, and suggested that private tuition fees might be a suitable mechanism for financing this expansion. These proposed changes in enrollment and subsidization met in-party resistance, and Baker's successor, John MacGregor, abandoned these policy aims on taking office in 1989 (Chitty, 2004). This disagreement is not surprising. Tory support was split between the middle-class advocates of a Mass Public system and the wealthy, who preferred maintaining an Elite system or else a transition to tuition fees. The disagreement led to inaction. Since no quotas existed, enrollment had expanded to 30 percent by 1993. However, financing was not keeping up. Baker later referred to this challenge as a "time bomb" set by his original expansion proposal (Barr and Crawford, 2005).

Split over higher education policy, the Tories chose the path of least resistance: They maintained overall funding levels while permitting increased enrollment, thus reducing per-student spending by around 50 percent (Lawton, 1994). In 1995, with ever-increasing enrollments and plummeting quality, the Conservatives decided to halt the spiral by capping student numbers (Williams, 2004). With most of their core constituency now entitled to higher education and with vocal complaints about declining quality, a limit on enrollment was the only sustainable option for the party. One thing the Conservatives were able to agree on was a reduction in the system of student support that aided working-class children attending college. In 1990, the Conservatives froze the level of

---

[29] Kingsley Amis's famous phrase 'pernicious participation' summed up the Black Paper authors' attitudes towards student democracy (Amis, 1971).

the student maintenance grant available to poorer students and began to phase it out to be replaced by a loan system available to all students. As Callender (2003) notes, this shifted the system of student support from a large subsidy benefiting poorer students to a smaller subsidized loan available to all.

Blair's Labour Party, elected in a landslide in 1997, was consequently faced with a dilemma. Overall enrollment was approaching mass levels. Yet because of high English inequality and the persistence of streaming, the social composition of the universities had changed very little; even by 1997, private schools, with only 7 percent of secondary school pupils, accounted for nearly 40 percent of the students of the "top" thirteen universities (Chitty, 2004). According to some estimates, income inequality among students had actually *increased* during the era of expansion. Blanden and colleagues (2004) estimate that whereas the enrollment gap between children of parents in the top income quintile and those of parents in the bottom quintile was 14 percent points (20 percent versus 6 percent), this had increased to 37 percent points by 1999 (46 percent versus 9 percent). It was clear that university expansion under the Conservatives had largely benefited their own constituents. Consequently, increases in public funding would lead to a Mass Public system, mostly serving the interests of Conservative voters. However, the Elite system was unsustainable because of the demand for enrollment, now coming increasingly from Labour supporters. Instead, Labour shifted to a Partially Private system that would lessen the fiscal burden on the poor.[30]

The Education Act of 1998 removed the enrollment cap and introduced up-front tuition fees of £1,000 per annum – the first time private funding had been sought for university education in England. This was furthered in 2004 by legislation setting £3,000 per annum "top-up fees." This measure was accompanied by student grants for poorer families and income-contingent repayment of loans. The government also announced the establishment of an Office of Fair Access to ensure that working-class children were supported in entering higher education. Finally, the government announced a "soft target" of 50 percent enrollment by 2010. Estelle Morris, the education minister between 2001 and 2002, had justified these latter two moves by noting "our pledge to increase participation is one of this Government's highest priorities…. [U]niversities are not birthrights of the middle classes" (quoted in Blanden and Machin, 2004). Thus higher education would be expanded but in a manner that would benefit Labour's working-class constituents: shifting the burden of payment onto middle-class students and attempting to create a more income-independent system of access.

The Act proved highly controversial and barely scraped through against Conservative, Liberal, and Labour backbench opposition (Stevens, 2004).[31]

---

[30] The transition to tuition fees in other "early expanders" was also undertaken by center-left parties – for example, Australia in 1989 and New Zealand in 1990. In both cases, as enrollment has expanded beyond 50 percent, the Labour parties of both states have moved away from fees and toward increased funding.

[31] The opposition of Labour backbenchers may seem surprising given the progressive nature of tuition fees. Some of the opposition may have been a function of ideological inertia – a deep

However, the contents of the Act were generally beneficial to Labour's core constituency. Tuition fees replaced a large tranche of regressive public spending. As Barr and Crawford (2005) put it, the Labour government was no longer "subsidizing champagne." The slanting of student support to benefit those who either come from poor families (the new grant) or end up in them (the payback threshold for fees) was highly progressive. Finally, Labour's establishment of an access regulator tried to ensure that this increase in enrollment benefited the poorer members of society.

The reactions of all three major parties to the 2004 reforms mirrored those suggested by the formal model. Labour advocated the transition from an Elite system to a Partially Private one, which would benefit the poor and the middle class. The Conservatives argued instead for the retention of the system as it was, campaigning on the basis of revoking all fees and instituting a quota on admissions. This would have amounted to retrenching into an Elite system. Finally, the centrist Liberal Democrats demanded the revoking of fees but campaigned for increased overall funding of higher education on the Mass Public model, a position popular with students and many middle-class voters but unpopular with both the poor and the wealthy (Williams, 2004).

Following the 2005 election, the Conservatives moved toward the political center with the election of David Cameron. This centripetal pattern was mirrored by Cameron's acceptance of fees on principle. Thus, the political battles over higher education in the UK appear to be temporarily over, with the acceptance of the Anglo-American model. As Stevens (2004) notes, "English Higher Education has undergone a remarkable transformation…. In 1960, the visible part of the English university system was small, academic, liberal arts oriented and socially elitist. Today it is an extensive system where the emphasis is on mass higher education with a practical bent." This change was enormous in scale, yet its final shape was politically determined.

We move now to Sweden, which has taken a very different route from the UK and where politicians made very different choices in moving from an elite to a mass higher education system.

Higher Education in Sweden

Swedish higher education looked remarkably similar to English higher education in the pre-expansion era: In 1945, fewer than 5 percent of Swedes attended university. Nugent (2004) notes that "those students who entered the university were few and privileged." The political system was firmly set against expansion, as Jonsson and Erikson (2007) note, "politically influential people… emphasized the need to divert students from the system who did not meet high

---

disabiding for private money in the public sector and a concern that fees would create stratification among universities (Heller and Rogers, 2006). However, there was considerable concern that fees would inhibit enrollment by poorer students. An alternative explanation is that as higher education passed the 50 percent threshold, it would be Labour's core constituency that benefited from public spending on higher education.

standards." As in England, there was little concerted parliamentary interest in higher education until the mid-1960s, at which point enrollments had begun to rise substantially, doubling between 1962 and 1967, albeit from very low levels (Elzinga, 1993). However, unlike in England, the policy response to increased demands on enrollment came from the politically dominant left. The Social Democrats passed a higher education finance bill in 1965, providing study assistance for all full-time students in higher education (set at 25 percent grants and 75 percent loans; Salerno, 2002). This reform achieved the Social Democratic goal of creating greater income independence of access within the limited level of existing enrollment. Then in 1968 they appointed a higher education commission, known as U68.

However, in sharp contrast to the Conservative-appointed Robbins report in England, the Social Democrat–led U68 commission recommended that "a limitation in total resource availability was necessary" in the higher education sector (Swedish Ministry of Education and Science, 1993). Such recommendations conformed to Social Democratic interests: Since higher education had limited enrollment, any expansion would be unlikely to include many Social Democratic constituents and was hence undesirable. The year 1968 also marked a decision by the Social Democrats to amalgamate all streams of upper-secondary schooling into one comprehensive system, similar to that envisaged by Crosland in England (Nugent, 2004). Thus, given the elite enrollment higher education system of the 1960s, the Social Democrats' response was to focus on ensuring higher levels of income independence rather than on moderate expansion of an income-biased system.

The higher education reforms recommended by U68 were passed in 1975 following a "principle proposition" from the Social Democrats, though these reforms would not enter law until 1977, during the period of the center-right "bourgeois coalition" from 1976 to 1982. The final law, H-77, largely represented the demands of the Social Democrats' proposition, with the bourgeois coalition too fragile to make major changes (Bauer et al., 1999). The 1977 Higher Education Act unified the various systems of higher education into one nationwide system: the *hogskola* (OECD, 1993). This system would now be run under the aegis of the Ministry of Education, which would also define enrollment levels. It also devolved higher education governance to some degree by creating regional boards in order to further regional development (OECD, 1993). The most interesting aspect of the reforms was their impact on access. Although a nominal quota was established (known as *numerus clausus*), there was also a major effort made to integrate the adult population into the higher education system (Salerno, 2002). For the first time, people over twenty-five were put on equal footing with school-leavers, leading to a massive increase in adult enrollments (Johansson, 2004). Thus the Social Democrats' intentions to limit the size of the sector but to encourage broader socioeconomic participation within these limits found ample support in H-77.

The return of the Social Democrats to power in 1982 was accompanied by little major reform, given that H-77 fulfilled most of their demands. Enrollment levels remained fairly steady throughout the 1980s because of the *numerus clausus* system, and the most major piece of reform was a further adjustment to student grants and loans coming in 1989 (Reuterberg and Svensson, 1994). This reform increased the size of grants and made loans income contingent, but despite this small act of progressivity, the Social Democrats did not undertake any more major reforms; indeed, they hoped to cut the higher education budget in the late 1980s, despite concern that Sweden's enrollment levels compared poorly internationally (Fritzell, 1998). Jonsson and Erikson (2007) argue that this stasis was driven by the Social Democrats' ambivalence toward higher education: "the problem was not a lack of demand but political unwillingness to expand the system."

As Salerno (2002) notes, "it would eventually take change in government before calls for reform turned to action." When Carl Bildt led the right-wing Moderate Party to victory in the 1991 election, little time was spared in rethinking higher education policy. Already in 1984, the Moderates had committed to "free admission" of students in their party program (Bauer et al., 1999). In 1992, the bourgeois coalition released its *Memorandum on Independence of Universities and University Colleges*, which resulted in the Higher Education Act of 1993. This Act granted universities considerable autonomy in their admission standards, thus marking the end of the *numerus clausus* era. Financing henceforth would be undertaken on a per-student basis, rather than on the basis of national demand forecasts (Marton, 2000).

This reform led to an enormous increase in enrollments, leading to a doubling of new entrants from 1990 to 2000. Unlike the English Conservatives, the Swedish Moderates permitted the overall university budget to rise along with enrollments. Thus, the Swedish Moderates sparked a series of enrollment and funding increases that mark the Mass Public model. This was accompanied by a deemphasis on equal access and support for university control of admissions: The government's recommendations argued that "equality between men and women or between background characteristics should not be written in the higher education law" (Nugent, 2004). This move back toward income dependence combined with low inequality meant that, unlike the English Conservatives, there was little internal split within the Swedish right over expansion to a Mass Public system.

However, the huge expansion of higher education in Sweden during the 1990s has begun to weaken the earlier partisan split. With some of the highest enrollment rates in the world, funding of higher education increasingly resembles a universal public good rather than a targeted one. Consequently, the Social Democrats have supported the transition to a mass system. However, they have emphasized somewhat different reforms than the Moderates, focusing on further reducing income dependence. Their 2001 Open Higher Education Bill aimed at a 50 percent participation rate and established a recruitment commission to help broaden access. Funding for the sector has increased further, with Sweden now spending over 1.5 percent of GDP on higher education, and with over 50 percent enrollment, it is now the Social Democrats who are the chief advocates of increased enrollment and funding (Marton, 2000). Thus, as the conditional partisanship hypothesis suggests, in truly "mass" higher education systems, the politics of the trilemma are reversed.

Since inequality is low in Sweden, tuition fees remain off the table for the right. Henrik von Sydow, a Moderate parliamentarian, stated in 2003 that "it is not on the agenda .... [W]e don't want to have a system where students have to pay for higher education. It's not the Swedish model and it's not the way to go" (*The Guardian*, 2003). Of course, von Sydow is not alone among European right-wingers in his antipathy toward fees – the English Conservatives wanted to revoke them – but unlike New Labour, even the Social Democrats have no interest in tuition fees, since enrollments are so large (in 2002, Swedish gross enrollment was 80 percent, compared to 48 percent in England). Instead, the higher education system has become part of the "Nordic model" over the past decade – on its way to becoming a universal entitlement.

Higher Education in Germany

Germany has a storied tradition of higher education. The system of research universities established in nineteenth century Prussia became a model for many of the world's best universities, especially in America (Fischer-Appelt, 1996). Although the Nazi regime neutered German universities, converting them into Nazi educational institutions, the postwar era of German higher education saw significant expansion under the control of the Länder, who were granted control over university education by Germany's Basic Law, since higher education landed in the realm of "cultural autonomy." Even in 1960, German higher education was as expansive as that in England and Sweden: Around 4 percent of each cohort of school-leavers entered the higher education system, which as in the UK and Sweden was divided into an academic sphere of universities and a vocational sphere of technical colleges, named *Fachhochschulen*, as well as a variety of professional colleges.

However, unlike England and Sweden, Germany faced a set of institutional constraints that would make future expansion and reform of higher education much more difficult. First, Germany had sixteen higher education systems rather than one, since the Basic Law provided the Länder with control over universities, creating a broad set of potential veto players. Coordination between the Länder was slow and piecemeal: Helmut Kohl referred to the council of Länder education ministers as "the most reactionary institution in the Federal Republic" (Hufner, 2003).[32] Second, each year's higher education budget was negotiated in the Länder legislations as a lump sum, rather than through per-student funding as in England and Sweden (Konow, 1996). This meant that expansion of student numbers would not necessarily be met by a commensurate increase in funding. Third, the structure of German law, based on the

---

[32] Such was the control of the Länder over higher education that even undergraduate examinations and admissions policy came under their jurisdiction (Onestini, 2002). Moreover, all university employees were employees of the Länder governments.

Basic Law, meant that reform to the higher education system would have to be achieved through constitutional mechanisms. Fourth, Germany had a streamed schooling structure that limited university access to students in the academic *gymnasia* (despite the occupying forces' postwar attempt to integrate schools; Nugent, 2004).

Finally, German universities themselves were based on the Humboldtian doctrines of "academic freedom" and "the unity of research and teaching." While these may not appear dissimilar to the principles underlying American research, in practice they have led to an ill-structured system of undergraduate and graduate training, where students typically take seven years to finish their first degree, with high drop-out rates of around 30 percent. Thus, the costs of per-student funding to degree significantly exceed those in the United States or the United Kingdom (though perhaps not Sweden, which also tends to have long average duration for first degrees), potentially causing "financial decimation" to the system if enrollments do increase (Heller and Rogers, 2006). Moreover, there has been a general concern that German graduates are neither systematically prepared for the job market nor for further study, weakening incentives for students to enroll and leading to generalized cost creep in the system (Schleicher, 2006).

Although German enrollment had expanded to around 10 percent by 1970, there was concern over the universities' ability to meet this rising demand, with both Länder and universities extremely cautious about increased enrollment (Onestini, 2002).[33] In 1969, the grand coalition government consisting of the Christian Democrats (CDU), the Christian Socialists (CSU), and the Social Democrats (SPD) passed an amendment to the Basic Law (the *Finanzverfassungsreform*), which stipulated a new role for the federal government in higher education, particularly in terms of funding university expansions, for which the federal government would pay 50 percent.[34] The grand coalition permitted legislative expansion of higher education since the middle class – the chief beneficiary of expansion in the formal model – was no longer split across parties. However, partisan preferences became much more distinct following the Social Democrats' (SPD) victory later in 1969. The left-wing SPD government that controlled German government until 1982 introduced a variety of higher education reforms reflecting their particular ideological concerns.

Chief among these SPD reforms was the introduction of the BAFöG (*Bundesausbildungsförderungsgesetz*) system of student financing. This provided student grants aimed at low-income students and was funded two-thirds by the federal government (Onestini, 2002). This was followed in 1974 with the introduction of student loans, with the left more concerned with working-class children being able to access higher education than with increasing per-student

[33] The association of university presidents, the Westdeutsche Rektorkonferenz, was against building even a single new university; see Nugent (2004).

[34] The federal government also gained control over the regulation of faculty salaries and student grants, the latter permitting the development by the SPD of the BAFöG system.

financing or enrollment, which would mostly benefit CDU/CSU constituents. The countervailing position of the CDU/CSU became clear in 1983, one year after entering office, when they changed the BAFöG system into an interest-free loan instead of a grant (Lingens, 1998). Furthermore, the CDU/CSU were content to let inflation reduce the number of eligible recipients from 44.6 percent in 1972 to just 12.6 percent by the time the Social Democrats returned to power in 1998 (Hufner, 2003). Gerhard Schröder's government reacted to this starving of the BAFöG system by increasing the generosity of grants and eligibility significantly in 2002. Thus, in terms of increasing the progressivity of access to university, partisan patterns played out in Germany in a similar manner to England and Sweden, with the left pushing grants and access by the working class and the right limiting such support. In terms of overall expanded access, however, neither was willing to encourage the transition to a mass system, partly because of the institutional constraint of overriding the Länder, and partly because of the SPD's disinterest in encouraging middle-class access (Ostermann, 2002). The institution of a *numerus clauses* national quota system for enrollment occurred under SPD government in 1972 and was followed by a lottery system in 1976, which increased the probability of working-class children receiving one of the limited number of places (Nugent, 2004). Thus, like the Swedish Social Democrats, the SPD kept overall enrollment low, thereby avoiding benefiting the middle-class constituents of the conservative opposition while promoting working-class access.

However, unlike in England and Sweden, the size of the overall system continued to stagnate once the conservative coalition consisting of the CDU, the CSU, and the Free Democrats (FDP) came to power in 1982. Gross enrollment increased from 18 percent to only 25 percent from 1985 to 1995. Part of the problem lay in the antipathy of the universities toward expansion. Mayer, Muller, and Pollak (2007) note that "many university professors are still vehemently opposed to the opening of the universities to what they perceive as the nonacademic masses." Consequently, the Education Council (*Wissenschaftsrat*) recommended in 1993 that new students be channeled away from the universities to the technical *Fachhochschulen*. One of the Kohl government's final acts of legislation furthered this stagnation: the 1998 Amendment to the Higher Education Framework Act. This amendment established quotas on the number of students entering medicine, dentistry, architecture, business management, or psychology. These restrictions allowed the CDU/CSU to limit entry into a number of the professions best represented in their constituency, and this strategy resembles that of the English Conservative Party in 2005.

The return of the SPD to power further retarded expansion: By 2000, the rate of attendance had risen only to 27 percent, by this point almost 20 points lower than in England and Sweden (Hufner, 2003). Whereas England and Sweden saw sudden surges of enrollment in the late 1990s, Mayer, Muller, and Pollak (2007) note that in Germany, the late 1990s "was followed by a period of stagnation and a slight reduction in the number of students." Why has German enrollment remained low? Three potential explanations emerge. First, the streamed nature of German secondary education remains in place, unlike in England and Sweden, where it has been mostly attenuated, thus limiting the number of students taking the necessary qualification for university. Baker and Lenhardt (2008) argue that "at the core of the resistance to the expansion of higher education is the extreme selectivity of German secondary education." Second, the Länder have had control over the admissions process and appear to have been unwilling to increase funding or enrollment, thereby acting as veto players. Thirdly, the SPD have been unwilling to countenance expansion of a system where few working-class students gain access (in the 1990s, only 12 percent of university students had working-class parents), while the CDU/CSU have for their part enrolled the lion's share of their support (Windholf, 1997).

In 1997, there were widespread national protests over the underfunding of higher education. The SPD was unable to break the endemic *Reformstau* (reform jam) blocking change, and many Germans now believe a crisis point has been reached (Schleicher, 2006). There is little consensus on whether a Partially Private or Mass Public path is the way forward. The SPD split over fees in 1996 (Fuhr, 1997), when its education spokesperson suggested them, and appeared to reject a Partially Private system by passing a bill preventing tuition fees in 2002 (Heller and Rogers, 2006). The CDU and CSU conversely have made recent rhetorical nods toward fees. Nonetheless, they are unlikely to be able to enact these fees, since they would directly hurt their own constituency of the upper-middle class, who are the vast majority of university students. Ironically, a grand coalition, as in the late 1960s, could be the savior of expansion. Or since federal reform is constrained, change may come from the veto players themselves – the Länder, who managed to overturn the SPD ban on fees in the Federal Constitutional Court in 2005 (Ziegele, 2006). Nordrhein Westfalen introduced limited tuition fees in 2006 to much student opposition. However, these fees are extraordinarily low by contemporary standards: around 500 Euros per semester. As I noted earlier, small fees are more likely to provide an obstacle to access by credit-constrained working-class students than to alter fundamentally the funding of higher education so as to lessen the fiscal burden on the working class. Put simply, minimal fees are on net negative for poorer citizens. It is not surprising, consequently, that it has been the Länder, dominated by conservative governments, that have introduced fees, since they are likely to bias access towards upper-middle-income students at fairly minimal cost to that constituency. For the most part, though, the German system remains in stasis: Quotas, streaming, and the Länder have prevented transition to mass higher education.

It is instructive to compare briefly the experience of Germany to that of its neighbors, Switzerland and Austria. These latter two states also have elite enrollment levels and have showed little trend toward expansion. Switzerland, if anything, has doubled down on an uber-elite strategy of increased public funding for higher education (1.4 percent of GDP), while enrollments remain lower than in even Germany – only two universities have been founded since 1900 (Strauf, Scherer, and Bieger, 2007). The three countries share a variety of factors, beyond cultural similarity, that help explain this common trend toward higher education elitism: subnational veto players and well-established, streamed vocational training systems.

The former effect of veto players was strongest in Switzerland, where referenda over expanding higher education in the 1970s were rejected at the cantonal level, where the bills failed to gain a majority of cantons (Heidenheimer, 1997). Funding for students outside of their home canton relies on a set of complicated intercantonal deals that exclude the federal government (Werner and Shah, 2006). In Austria, the Länder were less powerful, with higher education policy set at the federal level; however, like their German counterparts, Austrian academics had significant institutional power to prevent expansion, thus veto players at the local level still had significant impact. As in Germany in 1969, it took a grand coalition at the national level of the Social Democrats (SPÖ) and the Austrian People's Party (ÖVP) in 1966 to pass the first major higher education expansion bill (Pechar, 2005).

The systems of vocational education in these states were, if anything, even stronger obstacles. Streaming at an early age (ten or eleven years in all three states) means that the totality of secondary education is defined as academic or vocational – with the latter streams providing access to specific skills and a decent salary but typically precluding students from entering university. Thus expanding university enrollments in these conditions necessarily means reducing the size of the vocational system. The wage gap between vocational training and academic training has typically been smaller than in most industrial states, reducing demand for university education – in both Austria and Germany, the marginal returns to a year of education are similar across apprenticeship and university (Fersterer and Winter-Ebmer, 2001; Lauer and Steiner, 2001). The Swiss return to university education relative to vocational training is even lower (OECD, 2003). While left-wing political parties have altered the structure of streaming somewhat in order to reduce the income dependence of university access – for example, the Austrian SPÖ abolished the entrance exam to the academic stream in 1971 – altering the aggregate structure of secondary education would be extremely challenging, particularly given the reliance of private employers on apprentices through the "dual system" of training. Thus, vocational training may have had a particularly strong retarding effect on university expansion across these three states. That said, Sweden also has a large proportion of vocationally trained workers but nonetheless also has a mass higher education system. The key distinction is that Swedish students are only streamed *within* schools; they are all free to apply to university. Thus, given the likely institutional continuity of the dual system in the Germanic countries, they may not find transition to mass higher education as simple as their Scandinavian counterparts.

5.5 HIGHER EDUCATION IN THE U.S. STATES

The United States provides a stark contrast to almost all other advanced industrial economies, in that it has had a "mixed" system of private and public universities (the latter themselves Partially Private in that they uniformly require tuition fees) since the establishment of the great land grant state universities in the mid-nineteenth century (Goldin and Katz, 1999). Furthermore, the United States achieved a "mass" higher education status considerably in advance of most other states, partly in response to the G.I. Bill, which granted subsidies to veterans of the Second World War to attend university. A further distinction is that the United States has a mixed system of public governance and funding, with per-student appropriations and tuition fees often set at the state level, but student aid and research funding centralized at the national level through systems such as the Pell Grant and the National Science Foundation (Lowry, 2001). For two reasons, the arguments I developed previously explaining both subsidization and expansion may not be as appropriate in examining the national American experience.

First, the United States began the postwar era as a Partially Private system and has essentially retained that character; thus whatever institutional change there has been in U.S. higher education does not fit neatly into the categories that I developed for OECD states more broadly. Second, the mixed level of centralization of governance and funding means that attributing policy change to political actors is more complex; for example, Democratic control of Congress and the presidency might see increased student aid, but cuts made by state governments to per-student appropriations could in the aggregate counterbalance this federal effort. Given these two caveats, focusing on national politics is less helpful in understanding higher education policy in the United States. Conversely, the quite varied experience of the fifty states in funding higher education over the past two decades is analytically intriguing, albeit with the qualification that these states are not independent of federal policy. Consequently, in this section, I abstract from the historical analysis of central government machinations that I undertook in analyzing England, Sweden, and Germany and move to a statistical analysis of appropriations and tuition fees at the state level. I show that, as with the broader OECD dataset, there appears to be a partisan effect on higher education policy *conditional* on the level of enrollment in states.

I begin with an overview of the cross-sectional pattern of enrollment by states. Figure 5.9 shows the proportion of the state population enrolled full-time in that state's public universities in 2007, with the states arrayed by their logged population on the x-axis. Broadly, we can see that enrollment varies considerably across the states, ranging from just over 2 percent of the population (Connecticut and Massachusetts) to over 5 percent (North Dakota). This range partially reflects the existence of a large private sector in the Northeast states (New Hampshire, New York, New Jersey, Maine, and Rhode Island have among the lowest public enrollment). There also appears to be a slight negative relationship between population and enrollment levels, potentially reflecting economies of scale in university provision. California is an intriguing outlier: Despite having much the largest population of any state, it also has very high levels of enrollment, perhaps because it has three public higher education systems and because of the attractiveness of the University of California

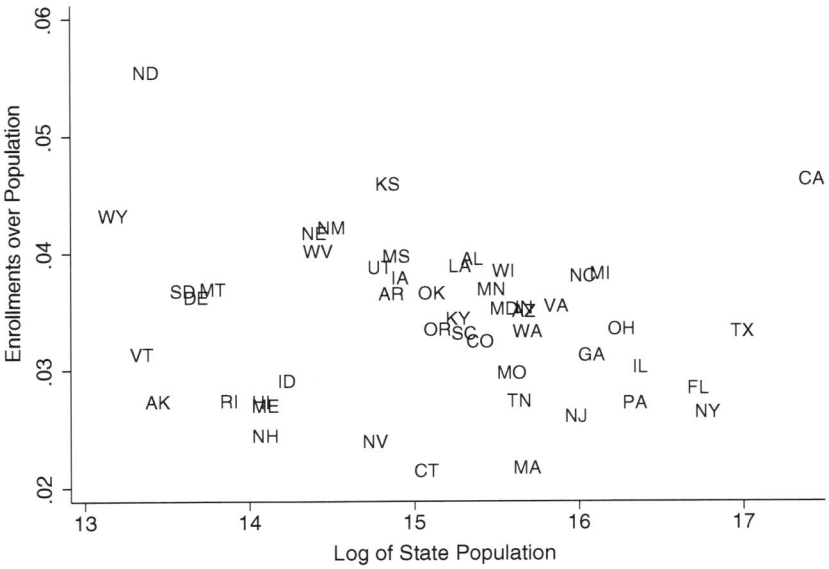

FIGURE 5.9. Enrollment Levels in Public Universities across the U.S. States in 2007

(UC) system for out-of-state students. More generally, this sizable variation in enrollment levels may have important implications for the politics of university financing, as we shall see in the empirical analysis that follows.

In the statistical analysis, I use two dependent variables, both taken from the Illinois State University's Grapevine data collection on state tax appropriations and tuition fees. I normalize each measure by the number of full-time enrolled students in each state and by state GDP per capita to create two variables: (a) state tax appropriations per full-time student as a percentage of GDP per capita in that state, and (b) net tuition fees per full-time student as a percentage of GDP per capita in that state. These measures thus provide us with indices of per-student public and private spending (in public universities) proportional to average state income. Figure 5.10 compares tuition and appropriations across the U.S. states in 2007.

The figure shows quite substantial variation in public and private funding of public universities across the U.S. states. Appropriations range between just over 5 percent of GDP per capita in Vermont to over a quarter in Hawaii and New Mexico. Tuition fees range from nearly 30 percent of GDP per capita in Vermont to under 5 percent in California and New Mexico. As the names of the extreme states on each distribution suggest, there appears to be a negative relationship across the fifty states between tuition fees and educational appropriations.[35] Tuition fees range between 4 percent and 28 percent of GDP per

---

[35] Indeed, it is statistically robust with a *t*-statistic of 3.34. However, once we remove the four states most at the extreme on the two measures (Vermont, New Hampshire, Hawaii, and New Mexico – all small and rather idiosyncratic states) that relationship essentially disappears (producing a *t*-statistic of 1.19).

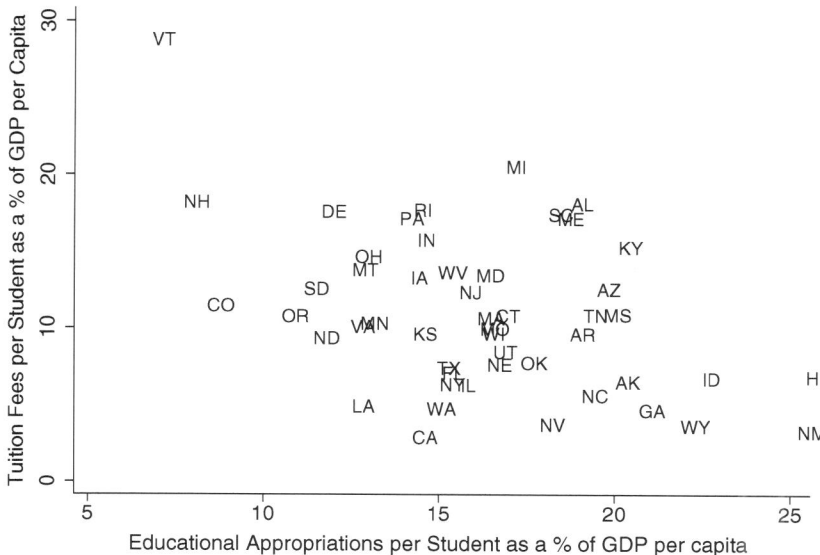

5.10. Per-Student Appropriations and Tuition Fees in the U.S. States in 2007

capita and appropriations between 7 and 26 percent of GDP per capita. While some of this variation is driven by GDP per capita differences across the states – for example, Alabama, Kentucky, and Maine have high scores on both measures partly because of low GDP per capita – much comes from deliberate political choice, such as Colorado's very low level of educational appropriations – likely a function of Colorado's Taxpayer Bill of Rights introduced in 1992. At the opposite extreme, Michigan's use of both high state funding and tuition fees reflects a deal struck between the University of Michigan and the state to maintain the high standards of its flagship campus.

To examine the determinants of appropriations and fees, I run a similar set of estimations to those used in Table 5.4, albeit now considering the U.S. states rather than OECD countries. I use all U.S. states (excluding Delaware for data availability reasons) from 1982 to 2004. Both dependent variables are measured at the state level. The first, examined in Table 5.6, is the per-student level of appropriations for higher education divided by the state's GDP per capita – this measures direct per-student funding. The second, examined in Table 5.7, is the per-student level of net tuition fees normalized again by state GDP per capita. This measure shows the extent to which the financial burden of attending public university is taken on by private citizens.

In terms of independent variables, since I am now examining subnational units, I require a new measure of partisanship and use state-level, rather than nation-level, demographic measures. Following Doyle (2007), I use an updated version of the measure of citizen and governmental partisanship developed by Berry and his colleagues (1998), which comes in two forms: estimates of citizens' ideology and estimates of the state government's ideology.[36] It is not obviously apparent which measure is most appropriate. If we think that governments essentially make policy according to the general preferences of voters within the state, then the former seems more apposite. If we think that the state's legislators are able to operate independently of general voter preferences, then the latter might be more useful. In fact, the way that Berry and his colleagues construct their variables means that the gap between the measures is not as stark as it may appear. Both measures are constructed from Americans for Democratic Action (ADA) and the AFL-CIO's Committee on Public Education (COPE) scores for individual congress members. Berry and his colleagues take these scores for incumbents and derive estimated scores for unsuccessful challengers. They then count the votes for incumbent and challenger to create an average level of citizen ideology for each congressional district and average across congressional districts to create the state's citizen ideology index. To generate the government ideology index, they use the same congressional ideology estimates, apply them to the governor and state houses, and average across these state institutions. Thus, both scores come from *voting for national level representatives*, but the government ideology variable is adjusted to reflect state-level elections.

As in Table 5.3, I want to model the effect of partisanship conditional on existing enrollment; thus, for each measure of partisanship, I also include its interaction with the number of enrollees divided by the state's population. This enrollment variable is also included separately on its own. Finally, I also employ a battery of control variables. Like Doyle (2007), I use a measure of state income inequality taken from Galbraith and Hale (2005). I also include measures of the state's population, to control for potential economies of scale in higher education finance, and of the state's gross domestic product, to control for income effects. I also add a linear time trend to capture the well-known secular decrease in per-student state appropriations and the accompanying increase in tuition fees (Heller and Rogers, 2006). Table 5.6 examines the determinants of educational appropriations across forty-nine states from 1982 to 2004. I run two sets of estimations. In Models A through C, I use a fixed effects OLS regression, and in Models D through F, I employ a pooled OLS model with panel-corrected standard errors. Table 5.6 begins by estimating the determinants of per-student appropriations as a percentage of state GDP per capita. Models A and D include the full specification, whereas Models B and E include only the citizen ideology variables and Models C and F include only the government ideology variables.

Across the models, a number of results jump out. Firstly, other than citizen ideology, enrollment, and their interaction, no other control, except the time trend, is statistically significant across all the models. Notably, government ideology is a significant predictor only when citizen ideology is controlled for and even then only when between-state differences are included (that is, in Model

---

[36] Doyle (2007) conducts a similar analysis to that in Table 5.6, though he focuses on the role of inequality and he does not view partisanship as mattering conditional on the level of enrollment. The updated data extend to 2006 and is available at Fording (2008).

TABLE 5.6. *Educational Appropriations in the U.S. States*

	Model A	Model B	Model C	Model D	Model E	Model F
	Fixed	Fixed	Fixed	PCSE	PCSE	PCSE
Lagged DV	0.666	0.665	0.623	0.921	0.922	0.915
	(0.035)***	(0.034)***	(0.034)***	(0.021)***	(0.021)***	(0.022)***
FTE/Population	-3.776	-3.837	-2.789	-1.248	-1.528	-0.124
	(0.428)***	(0.443)***	(0.328)***	(0.300)***	(0.323)***	(0.168)
Citizen Ideology	-0.126	-0.122		-0.124	-0.090	
	(0.029)***	(0.025)***		(0.021)***	(0.018)***	
Citi. Ideo*FTE/Pop	0.038	0.036		0.037	0.026	
	(0.009)***	(0.008)***		(0.007)***	(0.006)***	
Govt. Ideology	0.007		-0.015	0.050		-0.001
	(0.012)		(0.011)	(0.013)***		(0.009)
Govt Ideo*FTE/Pop	-0.002		0.004	-0.015		-0.001
	(0.004)		(0.004)	(0.004)***		(0.003)
Log State GDP	-0.273	-0.282	-1.068	0.456	0.461	0.356
	(0.983)	(0.981)	(0.979)	(0.363)	(0.367)	(0.393)
Log Population	0.481	0.447	0.682	-0.613	-0.623	-0.513
	(1.132)	(1.130)	(1.136)	(0.413)	(0.414)	(0.445)
State Inequality	-1.563	-2.320	-4.556	6.249	4.941	4.732
	(4.963)	(4.591)	(4.927)	(3.104)**	(3.031)	(3.080)
Year	-0.048	-0.047	-0.037	-0.051	-0.051	-0.060
	(0.021)**	(0.021)**	(0.022)*	(0.022)**	(0.022)**	(0.024)**
Constant	110.921	108.953	93.328	109.422	110.211	123.518
	(39.360)***	(38.507)***	(39.674)**	(44.219)**	(44.259)**	(47.723)***
Observations	1,078	1,078	1,078	1,078	1,078	1078
Number of ID	49	49	49	49	49	49
R^2	0.66	0.66	0.65	0.96	0.96	0.95

Note: Robust standard errors are in parentheses. ***$p < 0.01$, **$p < 0.05$, *$p < 0.1$.

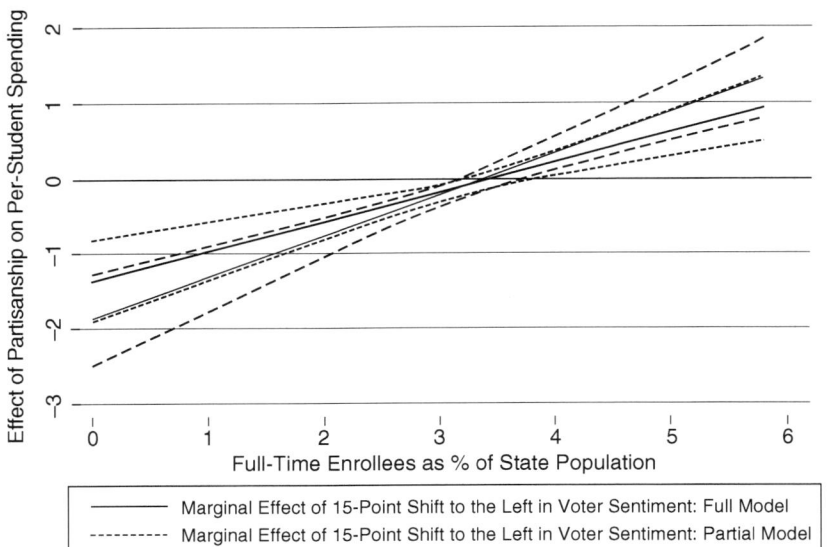

FIGURE 5.11. Citizen Ideology and Per-Student Spending in the U.S. States

D). The effect of citizen ideology on educational appropriations is conditional on a state's level of enrollment (both within and across states). The implied pattern is that at low levels of enrollment, a shift in citizen ideology to the left (or in the pooled model, a state with more left-wing citizen ideology) is associated with declines in per-student educational appropriations. However, at high levels of enrollment, a shift to the left is associated with increases in educational appropriations.

The impact of citizen ideology can be seen more clearly in Figure 5.11, which shows the conditional effect of a fifteen-point (one standard deviation) shift left in citizen ideology in the full pooled Model D and in the model without government ideology, Model E. I present the estimated effect of partisanship for both models as well as the 95 percent confidence intervals around this estimate. The figure shows that below an enrollment level of just over 3 percent of the state's population, a move to the left in citizen sentiment is associated with a reduction in educational appropriations, but when enrollment is higher than just under 4 percent, there is a robust association with increased spending. This is precisely the pattern we saw with OECD countries, thus it is reassuring to see that the same pattern appears to be holding at the subnational level.

As previously noted, the effect of government ideology is much less robust and in fact in the opposite direction to citizen partisanship in Model D. Furthermore, when citizen partisanship is removed, there is no robust effect at all for government ideology. Thus the most we can say about government ideology is that it may have the opposite effect to citizen partisanship cross-sectionally – when the state is already to the left, a left-wing government moderates the predicted effect of citizen ideology. But this is pretty thin gruel. Overall, it

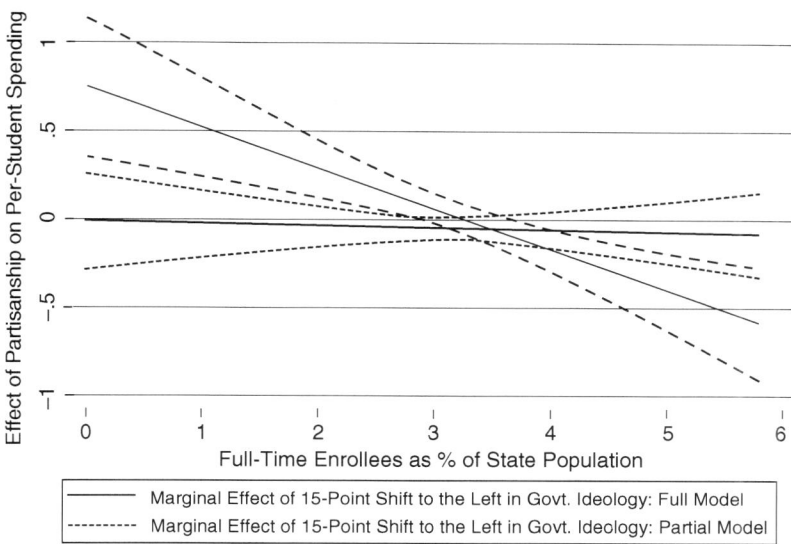

FIGURE 5.12. Government Ideology and Per-Student Spending in the U.S. States

seems that only citizen partisanship has a robust effect. The impact, such as it is, of government ideology can be seen in Figure 5.12, which demonstrates its estimated conditional effect in Models D and F.

What explains why government ideology has a less robust effect than citizen ideology? While it might superficially appear that government ideology is more reflective of the ideology of state policy makers, the measure, like the citizen ideology one, is derived from congressional delegations, not actual estimates of governor and/or state house ideology. As such, the government ideology variable acts like a citizen ideology with greater variance (that is, it tracks the citizen ideology variable but spikes up and down as control of the house and/or governorship changes hands). More generally, these results indicate that overall trends in state ideology appear to be driving university financing rather than sharp changes in control of state institutions. This provides a potential counter to the finding in Chapter 4 that policy makers have some independence from voter preferences – at least in the U.S. states, it appears that overall citizen preferences are key, though, of course, policy making is quite different at the national and subnational levels.

I now turn to examine the determinants of tuition fees. Across the dataset, educational appropriations and tuition fees are negatively related, both cross-sectionally and within states. However, as Table 5.7 shows, there is a remarkably similar estimated effect of partisanship, conditional on enrollment, as in the case of educational appropriations. As citizen ideology moves to the left, at low levels of enrollment tuition fees will be lower, but at high levels of enrollment they will be higher. The effects of government ideology also show some similarity to the previous analysis in that government ideology is significant only once citizen partisanship is controlled for (although unlike in the earlier analysis,

TABLE 5.7. *Tuition Fees and Partisan Preferences in the U.S. States*

	Model A	Model B	Model C	Model D	Model E	Model F
	Fixed	Fixed	Fixed	PCSE	PCSE	PCSE
Lagged DV	0.807	0.808	0.812	0.973	0.971	0.978
	(0.028)***	(0.028)***	(0.029)***	(0.013)***	(0.013)***	(0.012)***
FTE /Population	−1.235	−1.336	−0.335	−0.440	−0.505	−0.012
	(0.185)***	(0.182)***	(0.146)**	(0.148)***	(0.147)***	(0.100)
Citizen Ideology	−0.085	−0.077		−0.031	−0.022	
	(0.010)***	(0.009)***		(0.009)***	(0.008)***	
Citi. Ideo * FTE/Pop	0.029	0.027		0.012	0.010	
	(0.003)***	(0.003)***		(0.003)***	(0.003)***	
Govt. Ideology	0.013		0.001	0.012		0.004
	(0.006)**		(0.006)	(0.006)**		(0.005)
Govt. Ideo * FTE/Pop	−0.004		0.001	−0.004		−0.000
	(0.002)**		(0.002)	(0.002)**		(0.001)
Log State GDP	−1.702	−1.681	−2.015	−0.413	−0.430	−0.397
	(0.362)***	(0.360)***	(0.388)***	(0.160)***	(0.162)***	(0.159)**
Log Population	1.080	0.993	1.215	0.424	0.436	0.418
	(0.418)***	(0.423)**	(0.442)***	(0.171)**	(0.173)**	(0.171)**
State Inequality	0.897	−0.420	−0.585	−1.112	−1.145	−2.065
	(2.306)	(2.073)	(2.330)	(1.054)	(1.091)	(1.046)**
Year	0.057	0.059	0.062	0.009	0.009	0.008
	(0.011)***	(0.010)***	(0.011)***	(0.007)	(0.007)	(0.007)
Constant	−107.179	−107.956	−115.998	−18.111	−17.360	−17.167
	(18.726)***	(18.495)***	(19.743)***	(14.847)	(14.231)	(13.995)
Observations	1,078	1,078	1,078	1,078	1,078	1,078
States	49	49	49	49	49	49
R^2	0.82	0.82	0.80			

Note: Robust standard errors are in parentheses. ***$p < 0.01$, **$p < 0.05$, *$p < 0.1$.

government ideology is significant in Model A, which uses state fixed effects). The control variables, unlike in the previous analysis, are mostly significant (excluding inequality). States with higher income, both cross-sectionally and temporally, have lower tuition fees, whereas size in population has a positive effect on fees. Finally, whereas there was a secular downtrend in state appropriations, the long-run trend is upward for fees.

The effect of citizen ideology on tuition fees appears somewhat surprising, since it appears that left-wing governments want higher tuition fees when enrollment is higher. On the one hand, we could view this as being more supportive of the funding of higher education institutions more generally when enrollment is already high and thus supporting a potential vehicle of upward mobility for poorer students. On the other hand, in fiscal terms, charging fees is most progressive when enrollment is low rather than when it is high. In our earlier analysis of OECD countries, we did not have equivalent information about tuition fees and thus it is difficult to ascertain whether this result is idiosyncratic to the United States or indicative of a broader left-wing support for higher education institutions, regardless of the funding mechanism, when enrollment is high. Since I lack data on student aid in this analysis, I am unable to tell whether the regressive effects of tuition fees at high levels of enrollment are counterbalanced by student aid to poorer students.

Thus, this is somewhat of a puzzle to put alongside our analysis of appropriations. The estimated effect of government ideology is more intuitive, although it is robust only when controlling for citizen ideology. Here it appears that a shift to the left in state government is associated with a rise in tuition fees when enrollment is low but with a drop in fees when enrollment is high. More generally, despite the mixed results in the analysis of tuition fees, this section nonetheless confirms the more general argument made in this chapter that higher education policy should be analyzed with reference to the conditional effect of partisanship. It is particularly revealing that these conditional patterns hold at both the national and subnational levels in terms of policy outcomes and at the individual level in terms of preferences. The empirical lesson is that how one views the redistributive costs and benefits of higher education depends on one's starting position.

5.6 CONCLUSION

Although political economists have recently reexamined education policy as part of the broader literature on the welfare state (Boix, 1998; Hall and Soskice, 2001; Iversen, 2005), there has been almost no work on the political economy of higher education. This chapter has provided a corrective to this oversight, highlighting the stark choices that governments make between different institutional systems of higher education and the partisan determinants of change between these systems. Critically, I have shown that the impact of partisanship on higher education spending is *conditional* on the structure of the existing system, a finding that even holds up at the subnational level in the

U.S. states. The assumption made by Busemeyer (2007), Iversen and Stephens (2008), and others that partisanship has had a constant effect on higher education spending ignores the massive distinction in the scope of higher education in 1970 as compared to today, and indeed contemporaneously, *among* OECD countries.

By examining the conditional effect of partisanship, the analysis in this chapter helps to situate Iversen and Stephens' findings on the positive effect of left-wing government on higher education spending. This effect exists, but only when higher education is already at a mass level. When systems are elite, the incentives for left-wing parties are very much against increased subsidization of higher education for the rich. The conditional theory of partisanship thus also explains institutional change in higher education more generally since expansion under left-wing governments, which preferred to reduce subsidization, produced Partially Private systems, whereas expansion under right-wing governments has tended to produce Mass Public systems. I further argued for the important role of subnational political institutions and the structure of vocational training as potential obstacles to expanding higher education – both suggesting that a mass higher education may not be soon forthcoming in the Germanic states. By teasing out these nuances, this chapter provides a more contextually valid account of the mass expansion – or, in some countries, the lack thereof – of higher education, perhaps the key development in contemporary labor markets.

APPENDIX TO CHAPTER 5: MODELING PREFERENCES
OVER HIGHER EDUCATION

The formal model examines a society split into two generations, where parents in period zero are taxed to pay for the higher education of children in period one. I normalize total population to equal one; thus average revenues equal total revenues. The economy is modeled by a representative firm that produces a good using both unskilled labor u and skilled labor s, which comes from workers with higher education and is augmented by the "quality" of higher education A. I use the following CES production function, where $\alpha \in [0,1]$: $Y_t = \left[A_t s_t^\alpha + u_t^\alpha \right]^{1/\alpha}$. Normalizing output to equal unity and assuming competitive labor and product markets, this implies that unskilled wages are $w_{ut} = u_t^{\alpha-1}$ and that skilled wages are $w_{st} = A_t s_t^{\alpha-1}$, where $\partial w_{st} / \partial s_t < 0$ and $\partial w_{st} / \partial A_t > 0$. All citizens provide one unit of labor u and skilled citizens also provide one unit of skilled labor s. Citizens are also endowed with individual wealth, q_i, which follows a standard lognormal distribution $f(q_i)$.[37] Income for people who do not receive higher education is $y_{ut} = w_{ut} + q_i$ and income for people who receive higher education is $y_{st} = w_{ut} + w_{st} + q_i$.

---

[37] I introduce the wealth parameter to distinguish among skilled (unskilled) workers. This could be considered to be income from non-labor market sources such as capital gains or wealth bequests.

Individuals receive higher education if their income exceeds a threshold y_{it}^*, determined by the level of enrollment $s \in [0,1]$; specifically $s_t = 1 - F(y_{it}^*)$, where $F(y_{it}^*)$ is the cumulative income distribution. To denote whether an individual receives higher education, I use the function $h_{it}(s_t) \in \{0,1\}$, where $h_{it} = 1$ if an individual receives higher education, and $h_{it} = 0$ otherwise. The per-person public cost of higher education is the product of the rate of public subsidization of children's education $p_1 \in [0,1]$ and the "quality" of higher education A_1. The total public cost of provision equals this per-person cost multiplied by the level of enrollment in period one s_1. This total cost is met by taxing parental income at a linear tax rate τ. Total tax revenues equal τ multiplied by average parental income $\bar{y}_0$. This produces the budget constraint $\tau \bar{y}_0 = A_1 s_1 p$. Each family's utility function is defined over two periods, with period one discounted by $\delta \in [0,1]$. This function has two parts: first, parental income net of taxes $(1-\tau)y_{i0}$; second, discounted children's income, determined by whether they receive higher education, $y_{i1}(s_1)$, minus the unsubsidized proportion *(1−p)* of the cost A of education, if the children receive it.

(A1) $$U_i = \left(1 - \frac{A_1 s_1 p_1}{\bar{y}_0}\right) y_{i0} + \delta \left[y_{i1}(s_1) - [1 - p_1] A_1 h_{i1}(s_1) \right]$$

Subsidization

I begin by analyzing the effect of increasing the rate of subsidization p_1 for a fixed enrollment s_1 (i.e., comparing Partially Private and Mass Public systems), comparing the effects of increasing subsidization on (a) families below the threshold income, whose children remain unskilled (U_U); and (b) families above the threshold income, whose children receive higher education (U_S):

(A2a) $$\frac{dU_U}{dp_1} = -\left(\frac{A_1 s_1}{\bar{y}_0}\right)(w_{u0} + q_i) < 0$$

(A2b) $$\frac{dU_S}{dp_1} = -\left(\frac{A_1 s_1}{\bar{y}_0}\right)(w_{s0} + w_{u0} + q_i) + \delta A_1 \gtrless 0$$

The effects of increasing subsidization are always negative for those families who never obtain university education. For families whose children do receive higher education, the effect of subsidization will be positive, provided their saving on the cost of higher education δA_1 is greater than the increase in their round one taxes. However, for individuals with particularly high incomes, the tax loss, which is proportional to income, will outweigh the fixed benefit from higher education; this occurs when $y_{i0} > \bar{y}_0 \delta / s_1$.

Enrollment

Examining increased enrollment, we must distinguish between two scenarios. Firstly, by holding subsidization constant and allowing total public cost to vary, we can contrast Elite and Mass Public systems. Secondly, by holding public cost constant and varying subsidization in response to changes in enrollment, we can distinguish between Elite and Partially Private systems. For a given increase in enrollment from s_0 to s_1, I distinguish between (a) families who never receive higher education (subscripted UU) with incomes $y_{io} < y_{io}^*(s_1)$; (b) families whose children but not the parents receive higher education (subscripted US), with incomes $y_{io}^*(s_1) \leq y_{i0} < y_{io}^*(s_0)$; and (c) families for whom both generations receive higher education (subscripted SS), with incomes $y_{i0} \geq y_{i0}^*(s_0)$.

	Move from Elite to Mass Public	Move from Elite to Partially Private
(A3a) UU	$-\left(\dfrac{A_1 p_1}{\overline{y}_0}\right)(w_{u0} + q_i) < 0$	0
(A3b) US	$-\left(\dfrac{A_1 p_1}{\overline{y}_0}\right)(w_{u0} + q_i) + \delta\left[w_{s1} - A_1(1 - p_1)\right] \begin{smallmatrix} > \\ < \end{smallmatrix} 0$	$\delta\left[w_{s1} - A_1(1 - p_1^*) - \dfrac{A_1 p_1}{s_1}\right] \begin{smallmatrix} > \\ < \end{smallmatrix} 0$
(A3c) SS	$-\left(\dfrac{A_1 p_1}{\overline{y}_0}\right)(w_{s0} + w_{u0} + q_i) - \delta\left[(1 - \alpha)\dfrac{w_{s1}}{s_1}\right] < 0$	$-\delta\left[(1 - \alpha)\dfrac{w_{s1}}{s_1} + \dfrac{A_1 p_1}{s_1}\right] < 0$

We begin with the poorest families (UU) who never receive higher education. If subsidization is fixed (moving from Elite to Mass Public), then enrollment increases must be paid for by increased taxation; hence the poor dislike expansion. If public cost is fixed (moving from Elite to Partially Private), then enrollment increases are countered by decreases in subsidization, leaving the poor indifferent since their tax loss remains constant. The middle group (US) is the only group that can benefit from increased enrollment in either system, since they are the new recipients of higher education. They will prefer expansion to take place in a Mass Public form rather than a Partially Private one provided that $y_{i0} / \overline{y}_0 < \delta/s_1$, which will hold for nearly all permutations of expansion to this group. The wealthy (SS), conversely, are keen to prevent expansion to either system since not only do they not directly benefit but they also see the value of that education diminished as higher education becomes relatively more abundant. Thus, the wealthiest group would prefer to retain an Elite system. Like the middle group, they will prefer a Mass Public expansion to a Partially Private one, when $y_{i0} / \overline{y}_0 < \delta/s_1$. Note that the richest members of the wealthy group will prefer a Partially Private to a Mass Public system, and that this proportion increases along with enrollment.

Extending the Model (1) Quality

I now consider the impact of changing quality of higher education (per-student spending). The effects are similar to subsidization, differing between (a) those who do not receive higher education and (b) those who do:

(A4a) $\quad \dfrac{dU_U}{dA_1} = -\left(\dfrac{p_1 s_1}{\overline{y}_0}\right)(w_{u0} + q_i) < 0$

(A4b) $\quad \dfrac{dU_S}{dA_1} = -\left(\dfrac{p_1 s_1}{\overline{y}_0}\right)(w_{s0} + w_{u0} + q_i) + \delta\left[\dfrac{w_{s1}}{A_1} - (1 - p_1)\right] \gtrless 0$

Thus changes in quality produce a pattern very similar to those from changes in subsidization, with unskilled families preferring lower quality and skilled families more tolerant of increased spending on quality, albeit less so at higher levels of income. The threshold at which wealthier individuals would prefer less spending on quality is defined as $y_{i0}^* > (\delta/\tau)\left[w_{s1} - A_1(1 - p_1)\right]$. This threshold is always lower than that for preferring decreased subsidization. This implies that the potential for an antiquality coalition between poor and rich is larger than an antisubsidization coalition.

Extending the Model (2) Progressive Taxation

I now consider introducing progressive income taxation. Each parent is now taxed in period zero according to the quadratic schedule: $\tau(y_{i0}) = ay_{i0}^2$. Total (and average) tax take is $E(ay_{i0}^2) = aE(y_{i0}^2) = a\left[Var(y_{i0}) + \overline{y}_0^2\right]$. Tax take is consequently increasing in economic inequality and the budget constraint is $A_1 s_1 p_1 = a\left[Var(y_{i0}) + \overline{y}_0^2\right]$. Family utility is now:

(A5) $\quad U_i = \left(1 - \dfrac{A_1 s_1 p_1 y_{i0}}{Var(y_{i0}) + \overline{y}_0^2}\right) y_{i0} + \delta\left[y_{i1} - (1 - p_1) A_1 b_{i1}(s_1)\right]$

The only difference from linear taxation is the impact on net parental income. Consequently, for a given change in subsidization, enrollment, or quality, these tax systems can be compared by contrasting the tax loss in parental income. I compare the effect of changing subsidization on taxes paid in (a) linear versus (b) progressive systems.

(A6a) $\quad \dfrac{A_1 s_1 y_{i0}}{\overline{y}_0}$

(A6b) $\quad \dfrac{A_1 s_1 y_{i0}^2}{Var(y_{i0}) + \overline{y}_0^2}$

The tax take is larger in linear systems, and hence progressive taxation is less costly, if $y_{i0}/\overline{y}_0 < 1 + c^2$, where c^2 is the squared coefficient of variation, a standard indicator of income inequality. Thus, progressive taxation as a means of funding higher education is always preferred to linear taxation for parents with incomes below the mean. This implies that a larger group of people will support increased higher education spending when taxation is progressive. Thus, we would expect greater levels of higher education spending when taxation is progressive. Furthermore, as inequality rises, more and more individuals prefer to use progressive rather than linear taxation to fund higher education and thus this result should intensify as inequality rises.

Extending the Model (3) Income Independent Access

Finally, I alter the earlier assumption about access to higher education by assuming that access to higher education is uniformly distributed with respect to income. In this extreme case, the level of enrollment s equals the probability of receiving higher education for *all* individuals. Under perfect income independence, all families have the following utility function:

$$(A7) \qquad U_i = \left(1 - \frac{A_1 s_1 p_1}{\overline{y}_0}\right) y_{i0} + \delta\left[s_1\left(w_{s1} - (1 - p_1)A_1\right) + w_{u1}\right]$$

The effects of increasing subsidization and enrollment on family utility are as follows:

$$(A8a) \qquad \frac{\partial U_i}{\partial p_1} = -A_1 s_1 \frac{y_{i0}}{\overline{y}_0} + s_1 \delta A_1$$

$$(A8b) \qquad \frac{\partial U_i}{\partial s_1} = -A_1 p_1 \frac{\left(y_{i0}\right)}{\overline{y}_0} + \delta\left[\alpha\, w_{s1} - (1 - p_1)A_1\right]$$

We can compare the preceding equations to the income-dependent cases in Equations A2 and A3. Families too poor to receive higher education in the income-dependent case will be more favorable toward subsidization when access to higher education is income independent. The reverse pattern applies for parents rich enough to receive higher education under income dependence. Examining enrollment, a more complex pattern emerges.[38] The poor will be more supportive of increased enrollment under income independence rather than income dependence, since they are always excluded in the latter scenario. However, the middle group prefers the sure thing of being "next in line" to receive higher education in the income-dependent system over a probabilistic income-independent system. Finally, high-income families, like the poor, will prefer expanding enrollment under the auspices of an income-independent rather than an income-dependent system.

[38] Here I compare Equation A8b to the left column of Equation A3, which refers to moving from Elite to Mass Public systems.

6

Conclusion

I began this book with an intriguing puzzle. If creating a mass education system, and enjoying the fruits of economic growth that accompany it, is the equivalent of a policy "silver bullet," why do countries vary so greatly in their education spending? Surely, the massive positive externalities associated with public education ought to override whatever institutional costs there are in creating and maintaining a mass education system. Yet, education spending differs so massively among states that at the extreme, Denmark spends twenty times more on public education as a proportion of national income than Equatorial Guinea and three times more than its near-neighbor Greece. This latter comparison is particularly intriguing. OECD countries are now engaged with ever-deepening trade with the developing world, meaning that their comparative advantage increasingly lies in high-skilled production. Yet, even among the developed world, aggregate education spending varies dramatically – across neighboring states and even within states across election cycles. Furthermore, while some states have mass higher education systems that educate a majority of the population, others retain elite, restrictive university systems, even while popular commentators and politicians across the OECD emphasize the dependence of the industrialized world's future welfare on "education, education, education" (Blair, 1996; Friedman, 2004). Education may be an engine of growth, but governments in the developing and developed world appear willing to sacrifice these potential gains. Why do states engage in such self-defeating behavior?

Throughout this book, we have seen that redistributive politics, in multiple guises, underlies the observed variation in education spending. Solving collective action problems is difficult in the best of circumstances, when all citizens pay the same tariff and receive the same benefit. But when providing a public good such as education, the politics of redistribution easily overwhelm the political economy of efficiency because people pay different fees and receive different amounts of education. Public education has fiscally redistributive effects under progressive taxation, with the rich paying more but receiving the same education as everyone else. Like most public goods, it is no surprise then that the rich might, all else being equal, prefer to buy the good on private markets.

But expanding education has even more undesirable impacts for the elite. Where only the elite are educated, they reap the benefits of the scarcity of education. As education provision expands, their prized and exclusive education is diluted by the skilling of the masses. Furthermore, not only does education expansion threaten the rents to education, it also undermines the hereditary transmission of income and status. Education has a "lottery effect" in that it substitutes meritocracy for birthright, allowing the clever poor-born to replace the duller elite. All in all, education poses threats to the rich and opportunities to the poor like no other public good.

And this menace to the rich does not go unnoticed. Many options exist for the elite to prevent public education from sapping their income. The simplest tactic would simply be to block education spending and cut its undesirable redistributive effects off at the source. And where the elite can rule by decree, or where they have temporary control of the wheel of political decision making, such an outcome is highly likely. However, the demands of the masses for public education may not be politically feasible to ignore. If the elite cannot directly reduce public education spending, they can instead try to manipulate what spending there is to their best advantage. Many forms of education are limited to a subset of the population, typically the richer members of society, and if spending can be targeted toward these areas and away from universally provided education, the elite may be able to curtail the negative effects of increased education spending. Universities have typically been the domain of the elite, whereas primary education has been accessible to the nation at large. Hence, the rich will try to bias spending in the direction of the former, while the masses advocate the latter. To the extent that any public good can be made excludable through targeting, its redistributive effects can thus be curbed.

Thus the battle between the rich, the middle classes, and the poor over education spending may take many forms. Chapter 2 showed that education is riven with crosscutting paths of redistribution that alter the economic effects of education on different groups and open up different political possibilities for manipulation. The model developed in that chapter suggested a variety of hypotheses relating education to democracy and globalization. I tested these hypotheses on a dataset of over one hundred countries from 1960 to 2000, finding that shifts in democracy and openness had large, substantive effects on the level of investment states made in education, both absolutely and relative to other types of spending. These results were, however, conditional on the prevailing regime type and level of development in a state. It appears, in particular, that the positive effect of openness on education is stronger in autocratic and developing states and, in fact, is reversed in advanced industrial countries. I also showed that private spending and the composition of education spending between primary and tertiary investment are closely related to changes in political and economic openness.

Chapter 3 provided flesh to the bones of the empirical analyses of the previous chapter by examining several case studies of the impacts of democracy and globalization on education spending. I began with the Philippines, noting that its fluctuations in regime type and trade policy over the past century have been closely correlated with outcomes in education policy. Particularly noteworthy is the collapse of education funding under the period of martial law under Ferdinand Marcos and the stipulation that education spending reach 6 percent of GDP in the post-democratization constitution. I then turned to a case comparison of India and Malaysia, two states that lay "off the diagonal" of open democracies and autarkic autocracies. Even in these "extreme" cases, we saw the expected effect of changes in trade policy on education policy, with the replacement of the Indian "permit Raj" by liberalization accompanying a long-awaited increase in education funding and Malaysia's export-led development strategy leading to a massive investment in skills. East Asia and Latin America provided a regional level analysis of this comparison between protectionist and export-oriented states. I further focused on the contrast between two similarly autocratic countries, Brazil and South Korea, that had quite distinct trade policies, which I argue were the proximate causes of their very different paths of educational reform. Finally, I examined three states where democratic transitions and trade liberalization were distinct: Portugal, Spain, and Greece. In each case, democratization in the 1970s was followed by a jump in education spending, which then stagnated until entry into the European Community, following which education spending again spiked upward.

Chapter 4 moved to the analysis of aggregate education spending in the OECD, in terms of both individual and party promises as well as actual policy outcomes. The formal model was extended to the analysis of political parties, noting that they face potential constraints from below, in making commitments to voters, and above, through electoral institutions. Empirically, I found that the latter constraint was much more effective than the former. Party rhetoric over education spending matches closely to party type and more general ideology. Where rhetoric differs from cabinet partisanship, it does not appear to have any substantive effect on the actual level of education spending. At most, it appears that pre-election promises only signal to voters the party's priorities among education spending and other forms of public goods. When I turned to the size of the effect of cabinet partisanship on education spending, I found that a "typical" change in partisanship in the OECD would be associated with a four-year change in education spending of almost 1 percent point of national income, a predicted effect not dissimilar to that produced by democratization. Even vocational education is affected by partisanship, though apparently in the reverse direction from aggregate spending. Clearly, the rise of democracy hardly ends the redistributive politics of education. However, institutional constraints appear to have a stronger effect on parties' ability to enact their preferred levels of education spending than do voters. We saw that the effects of partisanship are radically different in majoritarian electoral systems compared to proportional ones. The latter electoral systems force consensus building and may moderate partisan education policy making, but they also create the possibility of unlikely coalitions among parties with diverse views about education and redistribution.

Chapter 5 moved from the analysis of aggregate education spending to partisan preferences over higher education policy. The logic of education targeting was spelled out in this chapter, with the typical redistributive preferences over education spending seen in earlier chapters flipping when one considers selective education such as universities. Through the lens of a "trilemma," I examined how different configurations of university systems could be constructed, building off a trade-off among enrollment, subsidization, and public cost. I argued that, depending on the existing size of the higher education system, political parties would have quite distinct preferences over these policy instruments. I then demonstrated the robustness of the trilemma and the conditional partisan hypothesis of higher education spending through a series of statistical tests and case studies of England, Sweden, and Germany, along with an analysis of the level of appropriations and fees chosen by U.S. states. Again, I showed that redistributive politics plays a huge role in shaping education, even at the apex of the educational pyramid.

Is education sui generis? Are there lessons of this book for politics at large? While one must be careful in applying findings from one policy arena to another, three lessons stand out most boldly. First, to comprehend education policy fully, it was necessary to understand the crosscutting redistributive forces that drive citizens' and parties' behavior. In particular, the ability of groups to target public goods such as education to themselves complicates the standard unidimensional rich/poor analysis of public spending prevalent in the political economy literature. Goods such as higher education that are targeted to a wealthy elite will be fiscally regressive, whereas universal and uniform goods, such as primary education, tend to be fiscally progressive. As I showed in Chapter 5, the extent of progressivity depends not only on who receives the good but who pays for it. Where taxes are highly progressive, a regressively distributed good such as higher education becomes less of a fiscal burden on the poor. Conversely, where education is funded by indirect taxation on goods and services or imports, even uniformly distributed services might be fiscally regressive.

The logic of targeted redistribution outlined in this book could be fruitfully applied elsewhere. For example, Cusack and Beramendi (2007) show that differences in the tax structure among OECD countries affect preferences about general redistribution. One might extend this further to look at how the tax structure affects goods targeted to the poor, such as food stamps, and those targeted to the wealthy, such as arts spending. Furthermore, as noted in Chapter 5, there are likely to be powerful interactions between the level of income inequality and the tax structure, meaning that the secular increase in inequality across the developed world might impact public spending quite differently depending on the way that citizens are taxed. Examining targeting would also be fruitful on the spending side. For example, do the lessons I drew on the politics of higher education also apply to other targeted spending such as culture, policing, and investment regulation, all of which potentially advantage the rich more than the poor? Are there threshold effects as the middle class accesses publicly funded goods previously only available to the elite, whereby what was once a "right-wing" policy becomes a "left-wing" policy? Are scarcity effects apparent with goods other than education? For example, the construction of public housing might not affect aggregate private house prices until a threshold level of construction is reached. Thus, there are several lessons from this book for the study of public goods that are differentially financed or distributed.

The second lesson is that in order to clarify how political institutions affect public policies, we need to disaggregate broad and blunt concepts such as democracy and partisanship and to specify and test more precise mechanisms. Many studies in political economy merely correlate democracy or government partisanship at a national level with a spending variable of interest (Lake and Baum, 2001; Rudra and Haggard, 2005). The problem with this approach is that multiple potential theoretical mechanisms could connect a political institution as multifaceted as democracy with spending variables. For example, in Chapter 2 I identified several competing theories of democracy: the stability, contestation, and monopolistic theories, as well as my own redistributive theory. To sift among these competing explanations, it was important to break down the aggregate Polity index into its constituent elements, thereby showing that the stability of succession and reduced factionalism were not important factors in explaining education spending. Furthermore, we saw that not all forms of autocracy are identical. Communist regimes were major educators, whereas oil-exporting autocracies were paltry spenders.

Similarly, the analysis of partisanship and electoral institutions would benefit greatly from a more fine-toothed analytical comb. As we saw in Chapter 4, broad aggregates of cabinet ideology are useful predictors of public spending, but they neglect institutional constraints, which can moderate partisanship. Simply analyzing whether socialist parties are in government (Boix, 1998; Bradley et al., 2003; Busemeyer, 2007) as a proxy for all the potential impacts of partisan preferences on social policy is a blunt instrument. Instead, this book has attempted to define the particular preferences over education spending of different types of voters and political parties and has examined whether these stated preferences actually match policy outcomes. Furthermore, this study has developed a set of models precisely defining how electoral institutions impact partisan policy making. Many studies of electoral institutions either simply make broad correlatory statements about the relationship between electoral institutions and public spending without specifying clear causal mechanisms (Persson and Tabellini, 2003) or rely on purely cross-sectional data, which does not permit us to distinguish how electoral institutions affect partisan changes in government *within* any one state (Rogowski and Kayser, 2002). But electoral institutions do not just impact policy by themselves – they matter inasmuch as they channel existing patterns of partisanship in different ways.

Third, the study of education is just one component of a broader analysis of inequality in the twenty-first century. While this book has focused on education as a dependent variable, it is also the cause of increases or decreases – depending on how it is distributed – in income inequality more broadly. Thus, we might usefully conceive of education provision as "inequality of opportunity" that contributes powerfully to the rising "inequality of income" that concerns commentators and scholars across the developed world (Kenworthy and Pontusson, 2005; Hacker, 2006). Indeed, Goldin and Katz (2008) characterize changes in American income inequality as a "race between education and technology." This book has shown that even if mass education is a salve for income inequality, it has many political enemies and there is no inevitability that education will "overtake" the technological shifts driving increased inequality. Furthermore, the very types of education that are growing in the developed world, particularly higher education, are likely to lead not to declining inequality but to a bifurcation in the economy between a well-to-do college-educated segment and the struggling remainder of high school graduates and dropouts whose relative wages will continue to decline. Unless governments can achieve universal college education – and the findings of Chapter 5 suggest that such change is politically extremely difficult – we should not expect the shadow of inequality to shorten.

Thinking more broadly about inequality, we might also consider the implications of differential education provision for other less-studied areas of disparity. For example, there is a long-standing literature linking education to other social outcomes such as health and crime (Usher, 1997; Feinstein and Hammond, 2004; Lochner, 2004). Given that sharp inequalities are apparent in citizens' access to health care and to healthy and safe environments, analyzing whether access to education is a proximate cause of these social disparities is overdue. If education improves earnings potential, as assumed in this book, and income is positively related to better personal health and to reduced likelihood of committing crime, then we might want to trace back the origins of health and welfare inequalities to the very political causes that shape disparities in education provision. One further form of understudied inequality that appears increasingly significant, at least in the advanced industrial world, is inequality in ownership of assets – for example, housing and equities. Since such assets are used by families to transfer wealth between generations, they are likely to affect the ability of citizens to afford private forms of education for their offspring, thereby altering once more the politics of education. Similarly, disproportionate returns to various types of education, combined with clustering of similarly educated citizens, may themselves have strong effects on the value of housing markets, as seen in Silicon Valley or Greater Boston (Shiller, 2005). Consequently, education's political import extends beyond its powerful effects on income inequality and to broader lines of division among citizens, from their personal well-being to the houses and cities in which they live.

Thus, the study of education then provides several lessons for the study of public policy more generally. But whether these other public policies are likely to have a larger impact on economic growth and human welfare than education is open to question. Education is a critical area of study for political economists not merely because of its intriguing analytical nature but because it has enormous potential to improve the lot of the developing world, as testified to by the recent interest in development through education propounded by international agencies such as the World Bank. However, the good intentions of international institutions may be for naught if the underlying reasons for educational elitism are not rectified. Many groups have a direct interest in limiting education for quite individually justifiable reasons. It will require political and economic liberalization for the path to mass education to be cleared. Even then, education is likely to be tossed on the political tides, for it is a public good with deep private impacts.

Bibliography

Acemoglu, D. 1998. "Why Do New Technologies Complement Skills? Directed Technical Change and Wage Inequality." *Quarterly Journal of Economics.* **113**(4):1055–89.

2003. "Patterns of Skill Premia." *Review of Economic Studies* **70**(2):199–230.

Acemoglu, D., S. Johnson, J. A. Robinson, and P. Yared. 2005. *From Education to Democracy?* Cambridge, MA: National Bureau of Economic Research.

Acemoglu, D., and J. A. Robinson. 2006. *Economic Origins of Dictatorship and Democracy.* New York: Cambridge University Press.

Acharya, P. 1987. "Education: Politics and Social Structure." In R. Ghosh and M. Zachariah (eds.), *Education and the Process of Change.* Sage: New Delhi.

Achen, C. H. 2000. "Why Lagged Dependent Variables Can Suppress the Explanatory Power of Other Independent Variables." Annual Meeting of the Political Methodology Section of the American Political Science Association, UCLA, July 20–22.

Adams, D., and E. Gottlieb. 1993. *Education and Social Change in Korea.* New York: Garland.

Alesina, A., Baqir, R., and W. Easterly. 1999. "Public Goods and Ethnic Divisions." *Quarterly Journal of Economics.* **114**(4):1243–84.

Alvarez, M., J. Cheibub, F. Limongi, and A. Przeworski. 2000. *ACLP Political and Economic Database Codebook. Democracy and Development: Political Institutions and Material Well-Being in the World, 1950–1990.* Online database at https://netfiles. uiuc.edu/cheibub/www/datasets.html.

Ames, B. 1987. *Political Survival: Politicians and Public Policy in Latin America.* Berkeley: University of California Press.

Amis, K. 1971. "Pernicious Participation." In Cox and Dyson (1971).

Amsden, A. 1989. *Asia's Next Giant: South Korea and Late Industrialization.* New York: Oxford University Press.

Anderson, B. 1988. "Cacique Democracy in the Philippines." *New Left Review* **169**(May–June):3–31.

1997. "The First Filipino." *London Review of Books* 19:20.

Arbache, J, A. Dickerson, and F. Green. 2004. "Trade Liberalisation and Wages in Developing Countries." *Economic Journal* **114**(February):73–96.

Arora, A., A. Gambardella, and S. Klepper. 2005, "Organizational Capabilities and the Rise of the Software Industry in the Emerging Economies." In A. Arora and A. Gambardella (eds.), *From Underdogs to Tigers.* Oxford: Oxford University Press.

Athreye, S. 2005. "The Indian Software Industry." In A. Arora and A. Gambardella (eds.), *From Underdogs to Tigers*. Oxford: Oxford University Press.

Austen-Smith, D. 2000. Redistributing Income under Proportional Representation. *Journal of Political Economy* **108**(6):1235–69.

Autor, D., F. Levy, and R. Murnane. 2001. *The Skill Content of Recent Technological Change: An Empirical Exploration*. Cambridge, MA: National Bureau of Economic Research.

Baer, W. 2008. *The Brazilian Economy: Growth and Development*. London: Lynne Riener.

Baker, D., and G. Lenhardt. 2008. "The Institutional Crisis of the German Research University." *Higher Education Policy* **21**(1):49–64.

Bardhan, P. 1984. *The Political Economy of Development in India*. New York: Blackwell.

Barr, N. 2004. "Higher Education Funding." *Oxford Review of Economic Policy* **20**(4):264–83.

Barr, N., and I. Crawford. 2005. *Financing Higher Education: Answers from the UK*. New York: Routledge.

Barro, R., and D. Gordon. 1983. "Rules, Discretion, and Reputation in a Model of Monetary Policy." *Journal of Monetary Economics* **12**:101–21.

Barro, R. J., and J. W. Lee. 1994. "Sources of Economic Growth." *Carnegie-Rochester Conference Series on Public Policy* **40**(0):1–46.

Basu, A., 2001. "The Dialectics of Hindu Nationalism." In Atul Kohli (ed.), *The Success of India's Democracy*. Cambridge: Cambridge University Press.

Basu, A., and E. King. 2002. "Does Education Promote Growth and Democracy?" In L. Whitehead (ed.), *Emerging Market Democracies*. Baltimore: Johns Hopkins University Press.

Bates, R. H. 1981. *Markets and States in Tropical Africa*. Berkeley: University of California Press.

Bauer, M., B. Askling, S. Marton, and F. Marton. 1999. *Transforming Universities*. London: Jessica Kingsley.

Beck, N., and J. N. Katz. 1995. "What to Do (and Not to Do) with Time-Series Cross-Section Data." *American Political Science Review* **89**(3):634–47.

Becker, G. S. 1964. *Human Capital*. New York: Columbia University Press.

Belassa, B. 1988. "The Lesson of East Asian Development: An Overview." *Economic Development and Cultural Change* **36**(3):273–90.

Bello, W. 2005. "Introduction." In W. Bello, M. de Guzman, M. Malig, and H. Docena (eds.), *The Anti-development State: The Political Economy of Permanent Crisis in the Philippines*. Manila: Zed Press.

Berry, W. D., E. J. Ringquist, R. C. Fording, and R. L. Hanson. 1998. "Measuring Citizen and Government Ideology in the American States, 1960–93." *American Journal of Political Science* **42**(1):327–48.

Besley, T., and S. Coate. 1991. "Public Provision of Private Goods and the Redistribution of Income." *American Economic Review* **81**(4):979–84.

Birdsall, N. 1996. "Education in Brazil: Playing a Bad Hand Badly." In N. Birdsall and R. Sabot (eds.), *Opportunity Foregone: Education in Brazil. Inter-American Development Bank*. Washington, DC: Johns Hopkins University Press.

Birdsall, N., and R. Sabot (eds.). 1996. *Opportunity Foregone: Education in Brazil. Inter-American Development Bank*. Washington: Johns Hopkins University Press.

Blair, T. 1996. *New Britain: My Vision of a Young Country*. London: Fourth Estate.

Blanden, J., S. Machin, G. Street, and H. Street. 2004. "Educational Inequality and the Expansion of UK Higher Education." *Scottish Journal of Political Economy* **51**(2):230–49.

Bognador, V. 1977. "The Politics of Comprehensive Education." *Oxford Review of Education* 3(2):185–93.

Boix, C. 1997. "Political Parties and the Supply Side of the Economy: The Provision of Physical and Human Capital in Advanced Economies, 1960–90." *American Journal of Political Science* 41(3):814–45.

1998. *Political Parties, Growth and Equality: Conservative and Social Democratic Economic Strategies in the World Economy.* New York: Cambridge University Press.

2003. *Democracy and Redistribution.* New York: Cambridge University Press.

Boli, J., and F. O. Ramirez, and J. W. Meyer. 1985. "Explaining the Origins and Expansion of Mass Education." *Comparative Education Review* 29(2):145–70.

Bose, S., and A. Vaugier-Chatterjee. 2004. "Primary Education in India Today: Is Decentralization the Way Out?" In A. Vaugier-Chatterjee (ed.), *Education and Democracy in India.* New Delhi: Manohar.

Bourdieu, P., and J. C. Passeron. 1977. *Reproduction in Education: Society and Culture.* London: Sage.

Bowles, S., and H. Gintis. 1976. *Schooling in Capitalist America.* New York: Basic Books.

Boyce, J. K. 1993. *The Philippines: The Political Economy of Growth and Impoverishment in the Marcos Era.* Honolulu: University of Hawaii Press.

Boyd-Barrett, O., and P. O'Malley. 1995. *Education Reform in Democratic Spain.* New York: Routledge.

Bradley, D., E. Huber, S. Moller, F. Nielsen, and J. D. Stephens. 2003. "Distribution and Redistribution in Postindustrial Democracies." *World Politics* 55(2):193–228.

Brambor, T., W. Clark, and M. Golder. 2006. "Understanding Interaction Models: Improving Empirical Analyses." *Political Analysis* 14(1):63–82.

Braumoeller, B. F. 2004. "Hypothesis Testing and Multiplicative Interaction Terms." *International Organization* 58(04):807–20.

British Ministry of Education. 1963. Report of the Committee on Higher Education. London: Her Majesty's Stationery Office.

Brock, C., and S. Schwartzman. 2004. *The Challenges of Education in Brazil.* Oxford: Symposium.

Brown, D. S., and W. Hunter. 2004. "Democracy and Human Capital Formation: Education Spending in Latin America, 1980 to 1997." *Comparative Political Studies* 37(7):842–64.

Bueno de Mesquita, B., J. D. Morrow, R. M. Siverson, and A. Smith. 2003. *The Logic of Political Survival.* Cambridge, MA: MIT Press.

Busemeyer, M. 2007. "Determinants of Public Education Spending in 21 OECD Democracies, 1980–2001." *Journal of European Public Policy* 14(2):582–610.

Callanta, R. 1988. *Poverty: The Philippine Scenario.* Manila: Bookmark.

Callender, C. 2003. "Student Financial Support in Higher Education: Access and Exclusion." In M. Tight (ed.), *Access and Exclusion: International Perspectives on Higher Education Research.* London: Elsevier.

Cameron, D. R. 1978. "The Expansion of the Public Economy: A Comparative Analysis." *American Political Science Review* 72(4):1243–61.

Carey, D., and H. Tchilinguirian. 2000. "Average Effective Tax Rates on Capital, Labor, and Consumption." OECD Working Paper 258.

Carneiro, P., and Heckman, J. 2002. "The Evidence on Credit Constraints in Post-Secondary Schooling." *Economic Journal.* 112(482):705–34.

Castro, C. 2000. "Education: Way behind but Trying to Catch Up." *Daedalus* 129(2):1–13.

Chitty, C. 2004. *Education Policy in Britain.* Basingstoke: Palgrave Macmillan.

Congressional Budget Office. 1997. *The Role of Foreign Aid in Development.* Washington: Congressional Budget Office.

Corbridge, S., G.Williams, M.Srivastava, and R.Veron. 2005. *Seeing the State: Governance and Governmentality in India.* New York: Cambridge University Press.

Cox, C. B., and A. E. Dyson. 1971. *The Black Papers on Education.* London: Davis-Poynter Ltd.

Cox, G. 1997. *Making Votes Count.* New York: Cambridge University Press.

Crone, D. 1993. "States, Elites, and Social Welfare in Southeast Asia." *World Development* **21**(1):55–66.

Cusack, T. R., and P. Beramendi. 2007. "Taxing Work." *European Journal of Political Research.* **45**(1):43–73.

Cusack, T. R., and L. Engelhardt. 2002. *The PGL File Collection: File Structures and Procedures.* Berlin: Wissenschaftszentrum Berlin für Sozialforschung.

Dahl, R. A. 1972. *Polyarchy: Participation and Opposition.* New Haven: Yale University Press.

De Dios, E., and P. Hutchcroft. 2003. "Political Economy." In A. Balisacan and H. Hill (eds.), *Political Economy. The Philippine Economy: Development, Policies, and Challenges.* New York: Oxford University Press.

de Donder, P., and J. Hindriks. 2003. "The Politics of Progressive Income Taxation with Incentive Effects." *Journal of Public Economics* **87**(4):2491–2505.

Dewey, J. 1916. *Education and Democracy.* New York: Free Press.

Diebolt, C. 1999. "Government Expenditure and Education and Economic Cycles in the Nineteenth and Twentieth Centuries." *Historical Social Research* **24**(1):3–31.

Downs, A. 1957. *An Economic Theory of Democracy.* New York: Harper & Row.

Doyle, W. 2007. "The Political Economy of Redistribution through Higher Education Subsidies." In J. C. Smart (ed.), *Higher Education: Handbook of Theory and Research*, vol. XXII. New York: Springer.

Edstats. 2004. *World Bank Database of Education Statistics.* Available at http://www.worldbank.org/education/edstats/. Accessed July 12, 2007.

Elzinga, A. 1993. "Universities, Research and the Transformation of the State in Sweden." In S. Rothblatt and B. Wittrock (eds.), *The European and American University since 1800.* London: Cambridge University Press.

Erdman, H. L. 1963. "India's Swatantra Party." *Pacific Affairs* **36**(4):394–410.

Esping-Andersen, G. 1985. *Politics against Markets: The Social Democratic Road to Power.* Princeton, NJ: Princeton University Press.

——— 1990. *The Three Worlds of Welfare Capitalism.* Cambridge: Polity.

Estevez-Abe, M., T. Iversen, and D. Soskice. 2001. "Social Protection and the Formation of Skills: A Reinterpretation of the Welfare State." In P. Hall and D. Soskice (eds.), *Varieties of Capitalism.* New York: Oxford University Press.

Evans, P. 1995. *Embedded Autonomy.* Princeton, NJ: Princeton University Press.

Feinstein, L., and C. Hammond. 2004. "The Contribution of Adult Learning to Health and Social Capital." *Oxford Review of Education.* **30**(2):199–221.

Fernandez, R., and R. Rogerson. 1995. "On the Political Economy of Education Subsidies." *Review of Economic Studies* **62**(2):249–62.

Fersterer, J., and R. Winter-Ebmer. 2001. "Austria." In C. Harmon, I. Walker, and N. Westergaard-Nielsen (eds.), *Education and Earnings in Europe.* Cheltenham: Edward Elgar.

Fischer-Appelt, P. "Europeanization of Universities." In S. Muller (ed.), *Universities in the Twenty-First Century.* Providence, RI: Berghahn.

Fording, R. 2008. Updated dataset for Berry et al. (1998). Available at http://www.uky.edu/~rford/Home_files/page0005.htm. Accessed June 2008.

Franco, J. C. 2000. *Elections and Democratization in the Philippines*. New York: Routledge.

Friedman, T. 2002. *The World Is Flat*. New York: Allen Lane.

Fritzell, A. 1998. *The Current Swedish Model of University Governance: Background and Description*. Stockholm: National Agency for Higher Education.

Führ, C. 1997. *The German Education System since 1945*. Bonn: Inter Nationes.

Galbraith, J., and T. Hale. 2005. "Within-State Income Inequality and the Presidential Vote 1992–2004: A First Look at the Evidence." University of Texas Inequality Project (UTIP) Working Paper No. 29.

Gallagher, M. 1991. "Proportionality, Disproportionality, and Electoral Systems," *Electoral Studies* 10(1):33–51.

Garrett, G. 1998. *Partisan Politics in the Global Economy*. New York: Cambridge University Press.

Gellner, E. 1983. *Nations and Nationalism*. Ithaca, NY: Cornell University Press.

Ghosh, R. 1987. "Introduction." In R. Ghosh and Mathew Zachariah (eds.), *Education and the Process of Change*. New Delhi: Sage.

Ghosh, S. 2000. *The History of Education in Modern India*. New Delhi: Orient Longman.

Giamouridis, A., and C. Bagley. 2006. "Policy, Politics, and Social Inequality in the Educational System of Greece." *Journal of Modern Greek Studies* 24:1.

Goldin, C., and L. F. Katz. 1998. "The Origins of Technology-Skill Complementarity." *Quarterly Journal of Economics* 113(3):693–732.

1999. "The Shaping of Higher Education: The Formative Years in the United States: 1890 to 1940." *Journal of Economic Perspectives* 13(1):37–62.

2008. *The Race between Education and Technology*. Cambridge, MA: Harvard University Press.

Gordon, P., R. Aldrich, and D. Dean. 1991. *Education and Policy in England in the Twentieth Century*. London: Woburn Press.

Gordon, R., and W. Li. 2005. "Tax Structure in Developing Countries: Many Puzzles and a Possible Explanation." National Bureau of Economic Research (NBER) Working Paper 11267.

Gouvias, D. 1998. "The Relationship between Unequal Access to Higher Education and Labour Market Structure: The Case of Greece." *British Journal of Sociology of Education* 19(3):305–33.

Gradstein, M., M. Justman, and V. Meier. 2005. *The Political Economy of Education: Implications for Growth and Inequality*. Cambridge, MA: MIT Press.

Grollios, G., and I. Kaskaris. 2003. "From Socialist-Democratic to 'Third Way' Politics and Rhetoric in Greek Education (1997–2002)." *Journal for Critical Education Policy Studies* 1(1). Available online at http://www.jceps.com/?pageID=article&article ID=4. Accessed July 12, 2009.

Guardian, The. 2003. "Tuition Fees Gain Allure in Cash-Hit European Campuses." October 13.

Guimarães de Castro, M., and S. Tiezzi. 2004. "The Reform of Secondary Education and the Implementation of ENEM in Brazil." In C. Brock and S. Schwartzman (eds.), *The Challenges of Education in Brazil*. Oxford: Symposium.

Haar, J. 1977. *The Politics of Higher Education in Brazil*. New York: Praeger.

Hacker, J. 2006. *The Great Risk Shift*. New York: Oxford University Press.

Haggard, S. 1986. "The Newly Industrializing Countries in the International System." *World Politics* 38(2):343–70.

1990. *Pathways from the Periphery: The Politics of Growth in the Newly Industrializing Countries*. Ithaca, NY: Cornell University Press.

Hall, P., and D. Soskice (eds.). 2001. *Varieties of Capitalism*. New York: Oxford University Press.

Hall, R. E., and C. I. Jones. 1999. "Why Do Some Countries Produce So Much More Output per Worker Than Others?" *Quarterly Journal of Economics* 114(1):83–116.

Halsey, A. H. 1993. "Trends in Access and Equity in Higher Education." *Oxford Review of Education* 19(2).

Hanson, G. H., and M. J. Slaughter. 2002. "Labor-Market Adjustment in Open Economies: Evidence from US States." *Journal of International Economics* 57(1):3–29.

Harberger, A. 1988. "Growth, Industrialization, and Economic Structure: Latin American and East Asia Compared." In H. Hughes (ed.), *Achieving Industrialization in East Asia*. Cambridge: Cambridge University Press.

Hardgrave, R., Jr., and S. Kochanek. 2000. *India: Government and Politics in a Developing Nation*. London: Wadsworth.

Hartog, J., P. Pereira, and J. Vieira. 2001. "Changing Returns to Education in Portugal during the 1980s and Early 1990s: OLS and Quantile Regression Estimators." *Applied Economics* 33(8):1021–37.

Hawes, G. 1987. *The Philippine State and the Marcos Regime: The Politics of Export*. Ithaca, NY: Cornell University Press.

Heidenheimer, A. 1997. *Disparate Ladders: Why School and University Policies Differ in Germany, Japan, and Switzerland*. New York: Transaction.

Heller, D., and K. Rogers. 2006. "Shifting the Burden: Public and Private Financing of Higher Education in the United States and Implications for Europe." *Tertiary Education and Management* 12:91–117.

Herrara, Y., and D. Kapur. 2007. "Improving Data Quality: Actors, Incentives, and Capabilities." *Political Analysis*. 15:365–86.

Hiscox, M. J., and S. L. Kastner. 2005. "A General Measure of Trade Policy Orientations: Gravity-Model-Based Estimates for 82 Nations, 1960 to 2000." University of California, Harvard University. Available at http://weber.ucsd.edu/skastner/HiscoxKastner.pdf.Accessed July 5, 2007.

Huber, E., C. Ragin, and Stephens J. 1997. Comparable Welfare State Dataset. Northwestern University and University of North Carolina. Available at http://www.lisproject.org/publications/welfaredata/welfareaccess.htm. Accessed July 27, 2007.

Hufner, K. 2003. "Governance and Funding of Higher Education in Germany." *Higher Education in Europe* 28(2):145–63.

Huntington, S. P. 1991. *Third Wave: Democratization in the Late Twentieth Century*. Norman: University of Oklahoma Press.

International Social Survey Program. 1996. "Role of Government" module. Köln, Germany: Zentralarchiv fuer Empirische Sozialforschung (producer); Ann Arbor, MI: Interuniversity Consortium for Political and Social Research (distributors).

1999. "Social Inequality" module. Köln, Germany: Zentralarchiv fuer Empirische Sozialforschung (producer); Ann Arbor, MI: Interuniversity Consortium for Political and Social Research (distributors).

Iversen, T. 2005. *Capitalism, Democracy, and Welfare*. New York: Cambridge University Press.

Iversen, T., and D. Soskice. 2001. "An Asset Theory of Social Policy Preferences." *American Political Science Review* 95(4):875–93.

2006. "Electoral Institutions and the Politics of Coalitions: Why Some Democracies Redistribute More Than Others." *American Political Science Review* 100(2):165–81.

Iversen, T., and J. Stephens. 2008. "Partisan Politics, the Welfare State, and Three Worlds of Human Capital Formation." *Comparative Political Studies* **41**(4/5):600–37.

Iversen, T., and A. Wren. 1998. "Equality, Employment, and Budgetary Restraint: The Trilemma of the Service Economy." *World Politics* **50**(4):507–46.

Jayasuriya, S. 1987. "The Politics of Economy Policy in the Philippines during the Marcos Era." In R. Robison et al. (eds.), *Southeast Asia in the 1980s*. Sydney: Allen and Unwin.

Johansson, M. 2004. "The Swedish Model for Capital Expenditure in Higher Education from a Lifelong Learning Perspective." Ph.D. diss., Stockholm University.

Jonsson, J. O., and R. Erikson. 2007. "Sweden: Why Educational Expansion is Not Such a Great Strategy for Equality: Theory and Evidence." In Y. Shavit, R. Arum, and A. Gamoran (eds.), *Stratification in Higher Education: A Comparative Study*. Stanford, CA: Stanford University Press.

Kalyvas, S. N. 1996. *The Rise of Christian Democracy in Europe*. Ithaca, NY: Cornell University Press.

Kang, D. C. 2002. *Crony Capitalism: Corruption and Development in South Korea and the Philippines*. New York: Cambridge University Press.

Katzenstein, P. J. 1985. *Small States in World Markets*. Ithaca, NY: Cornell University Press.

Kaulisch, M., and J. Huisman. 2007. *Higher Education in Germany Country Report*. Center for Higher Education Policy Studies, Universiteit Twente, Holland.

Kay, C. 2002. "Why East Asia Overtook Latin America: Agrarian Reform, Industrialization, and Development." *Third World Quarterly* **23**(6):1073–1102.

Kazamias, A. M. 1978. "The Politics of Educational Reform in Greece: Law 309/1976." *Comparative Education Review* **22**(1):21–45.

Kenworthy, L. and J. Pontusson. 2005. Rising Inequality and the Politics of Redistribution in Affluent Countries. *Perspectives on Politics*. **3**(3):449–71.

King, G., M. Tomz, and J. Wittenberg. 2000. "Making the Most of Statistical Analyses: Improving Interpretation and Presentation." *American Journal of Political Science* **44**(2):347–61.

Kingdon, G., R. Cassen, K. McNay, and L. Visaria. 2004. "Education and Literacy." In T. Dyson, R. Cassen, and L. Visaria (eds.), *Twenty-First Century India: Population, Economy, Human Development and the Environment*. New York: Oxford University Press.

Konow, G. 1996. "Planning, Financing and Accountability of German Universities." In S. Muller (ed.), *Universities in the Twenty-First Century*, vol. 2. New York: Berghahn.

Korpi, W. 1983. *The Democratic Class Struggle*. London: Routledge & Kegan Paul.

Kothari Commission. 1968. *Report of the Indian Education Commission*. New Delhi: Government of India.

Krebs, R. 2006. *Fighting for Rights: Military Service and the Politics of Citizenship*. Ithaca, NY: Cornell University Press.

Krueger, A. B. 1999. "Experimental Estimates of Education Production Functions." *Quarterly Journal of Economics* **114**(2):497–532.

Krueger, A. B., and M. Lindahl. 2001. "Education for Growth: Why and for Whom?" *Journal of Economic Literature* **39**(4):1101–36.

Krueger, A. O. 1974. "The Political Economy of the Rent-Seeking Society." *American Economic Review* **64**(3):291–303.

   1985. "Import Substitution versus Export Promotion." *Finance and Development* **22**(2):20–3.

Kumar, K. 1998. "Agricultural Modernisation and Education: Contours of a Point of Departure." In S. Shukla and R. Kaul (eds.), *Education, Development, and Underdevelopment*. New Delhi: Sage.

Kumar, R. 2006. "Introduction." In R. Kumar (ed.), *The Crisis of Elementary Education in India*. New Delhi: Sage.

Laakso, M., and R. Taagepera. 1979. "Effective Number of Parties: A Measure with Application to West Europe." *Comparative Political Studies* **12**(1):3–27.

Lake, D. A., and M. A. Baum. 2001. "The Invisible Hand of Democracy: Political Control and the Provision of Public Services." *Comparative Political Studies* **34**(6):587–621.

Lambert, R., and N. Butler. 2006. *The Future of European Universities: Renaissance or Decay?* London: Center for European Reform.

Lauer, C., and V. Steiner. 2001. "Germany." In C. Harmon, I. Walker, and N. Westergaard-Nielsen (eds.), *Education and Earnings in Europe*. Cheltenham: Edward Elgar.

Lawlor, H. 1985. "Education and National Development in Brazil." In C. Brock and H. Lawlor (eds.), *Education in Latin America*. London: Croom Helm.

Lawton, D. 1994. *The Tory Mind on Education 1979–94*. London: Routledge.

Layard, R., J. King, and C. Moser. 1969. *The Impact of Robbins*. New York: Penguin.

Lee, J. 2001. "Education Policy in the Republic of Korea. Building Block or Stumbling Block?" International Bank for Reconstruction and Development No. 37164.

Ley Orgánica General del Sistema Educativo. 1990. Madrid: Spanish Ministry of Education.

Lijphart, A. 1994. *Electoral Systems and Party Systems: A Study of Twenty-Seven Democracies, 1945–90*. New York: Oxford University Press.

Lindert, P. H. 2003a. "Voice and Growth: Was Churchill Right?" *Journal of Economic History* **63**(2):315–50.

2003b. "Why the Welfare State Looks Like a Free Lunch." NBER Working Paper 9869.

2004. *Growing Public: Social Spending and Economic Growth since the Eighteenth Century*. New York: Cambridge University Press.

Lingens, H. 1998. *German Higher Education: Issues and Challenges*. Bloomington, IN: Phi Delta Kappa International Studies in Education.

Lipset, S. M. 1959. "Some Social Requisites of Democracy: Economic Development and Political Legitimacy." *American Political Science Review* **53**(1):69–105.

Lizzeri, A., and N. Persico. 2001. "The Provision of Public Goods under Alternative Electoral Incentives." *American Economic Review* **91**(1):225–39.

Lochner, J. 2004. "Education, Work, and Crime: A Human Capital Approach." *International Economic Review* **45**(3):811–43.

Long, J., and L. Ervin. 2000. "Using Heteroskedasticity Consistent Standard Errors in the Linear Regression Model." *American Statistician* **54**(3):217–24.

Loong-Hoe, T. 1982. "The State and Economic Distribution in Malaysia." Discussion Paper 31. Singapore: Institute of Southeast Asian Studies.

Lowry, R. 2001. "Governmental Structure, Trustee Selection, and Public University Prices and Spending: Multiple Means to Similar Ends." *American Journal of Political Science* **45**(3):845–61.

Machin, S. 1998. "Recent Shifts in Wage Inequality and the Wage Returns to Education in Britain." *National Institute Economic Review* **166**(1):87–96.

Mahadevan, R. 2007. *Sustainable Growth and Economic Development: A Case Study of Malaysia*. Cheltenham: Edward Elgar.

Mahathir, M. 1970. *The Malay Dilemma*. Singapore: Times Books International.

Malaysia. 2001. *Eighth Malaysia Plan 2001–2005*. Kuala Lumpur: Government Press.

Marjit, S., S. Kar, and D. Maiti. 2007. "Regional Trade Openness Index and Income Disparity: A New Methodology and the Indian Experiment." Working Paper. Calcutta: Centre for Studies in Social Sciences.

Marton, S. 2000. *The Mind of the State: The Politics of University Autonomy in Sweden, 1968–1998*. Göteborg, Sweden: BAS.

Marshall, M. G., and K. Jaggers. 2002. *Polity IV Project: Political Regime Characteristics and Transitions, 1800–2002*. Dataset Users Manual. College Park: Center for International Development and Conflict Management, University of Maryland.

Mayer, K., W. Muller, and R. Pollak. 2007. "Germany: Institutional Change and Inequalities of Access to Higher Education." In Shavit, Arum, Gamoran (2007).

McKay, S. C. 2006. *Satanic Mills or Silicon Islands? The Politics of High-Tech Production in the Philippines*. Ithaca, NY: ILR Press.

McKelvey, R., and N. Schofield. 1986. "Structural Instability of the Core." *Journal of Mathematical Economics* 15(4):179–98.

McNair, J. M. 1984. *Education for a Changing Spain*. Manchester, UK: University Press of Manchester, UK.

Mehrotra, S. 2006. "What Ails the Educationally Backward States?" In S. Mehrotra (ed.), *The Economics of Elementary Education in India*. New Delhi: Sage.

Melo, M. 2008. "Unexpected Success, Unanticipated Failures: Social Policy from Cardoso to Lula." In P. Kingstone and T. Power (eds.), *Democratic Brazil Revisited*. Pittsburgh: University of Pittsburgh Press.

Meltzer, A. H., and S. F. Richard. 1981. "A Rational Theory of the Size of Government." *Journal of Political Economy* 89(5):914–27.

Miguel, E. 2004. "Tribe or Nation? Nation-Building and Public Goods in Kenya versus Tanzania." *World Politics* 56(3):327–62.

Mill, J. S. 1856. *Considerations on Representative Democracy*. South Bend, IN: Gateway Editions.

Mincer, J. 1974. *Schooling, Experience, and Earnings*. New York: Columbia University Press.

Minondo, A. 1999. "The Labour Market Impact of Trade in Middle-income Countries: A Factor Content Analysis of Spain." *World Economy* 22(8):1095–1117.

Morrisson, K. 2005. "Oil, Non-Tax Revenue, and Regime Stability: The Political Resource Curse." Working Paper. Ithaca, NY: Cornell University.

Moulin S. 2004. "Financing Elementary Education in India." In A. Vaugier-Chatterjee (ed.), *Education and Democracy in India*. New Delhi: Manohar.

Mulligan, C., R. Gil, and X. Sala-i-Martin. 2004. "Do Democracies Have Different Public Policies Than Nondemocracies?" *Journal of Economic Perspectives* 18(1):51–74.

Mundell, R. 1968. *International Economics*. New York: Macmillan.

Mukherjee, H., and J. Singh. 1995. "Malaysia." In P. Morris and T. Sweeting (eds.), *Education and Development in East Asia*. New York: Garland.

Myrdal, G. 1972. *Asian Drama*. New York: Allen Lane.

Naik, J. 1965. *Educational Planning in India*. New Delhi: Allied.

Nambissan, G. 2006. "Terms of Inclusion: Dalits and the Right to Education." In R. Kumar (ed.), *The Crisis of Elementary Education in India*. New Delhi: Sage.

Neher, C., and R. Marlay. 1995. *Democracy and Development in Southeast Asia*. Boulder, CO: Westview Press.

Nooruddin, I., and J. W. Simmons. 2006. "The Politics of Hard Choices: IMF Programs and Government Spending." *International Organization* 60(4):1001–33.

Nugent, M. 2004. *The Transformation of the Student Career: University Study in Germany, the Netherlands, and Sweden*. New York: Routledge.

Nunes, A. B. 2003. "Government Expenditure on Education, Economic Growth and Long Waves: The Case of Portugal." *Paedagogica Historica* 39(5):559–81.

O'Connor, D. 1993. "Electronics and Industrialisation: Approaching the 21st Century." In K. Jomo (ed.), *Industrialising Malaysia: Policy, Performance, Prospects*. London: Routledge.

OECD. 1993. *Economic Survey: Sweden.* Paris: OECD Press.

   1998. *Education at a Glance.* Paris: OECD Press.

   2003. *Tertiary Education in Switzerland.* Paris: OECD Press.

   2005. *Education at a Glance.* Paris: OECD Press.

Olson, M. 1993. "Dictatorship, Democracy, and Development." *American Political Science Review* **87**(3):567–76.

O'Malley, P. 1995. "Turning Point: The 1970 Education Act. Education Reform in Democratic Spain." In Boyd-Barrett and O'Malley (1995).

Onestini, C. 2002. *Federalism and Länder Autonomy: The Higher Education Policy Network in the Federal Republic of Germany, 1948–1998.* New York: Routledge.

Orwell, G. 1945. "Politics and the English Language." In *Shooting an Elephant and Other Essays.* New York: Harcourt Brace Jovanovich.

Ostermann. H. 2002. "The Higher Education Debate in Germany." *German Politics* **11**(1):43–60.

Panagariya, A. 2008. *India: The Emerging Giant.* New York: Oxford University Press.

Park, H. 2007. "South Korea: Educational Expansion and Inequality of Opportunity for Higher Education." In Shavit, Arum, and Gamoran (2007).

Parsons, T. 1957. "The Distribution of Power in American Society." *World Politics* **10**(1):123–43.

Pechar, H. 2005. "Backlash or Modernization? Two Reform Cycles in Austrian Higher Education." In A. Gornitzka et al. (eds.), *Reform and Change in Higher Education.* Dordrecht: Springer.

Pepinsky, T. 2008. "Institutions, Economic Recovery, and Macroeconomic Vulnerability in Indonesia and Malaysia." In A. McIntyre, T. Pempel, and J. Ravenhill (eds.), *Crisis as Catalyst.* Ithaca, NY: Cornell University Press.

Perotti, R. 1993. "Political Equilibrium, Income Distribution, and Growth." *Review of Economic Studies* **60**(4):755–76.

Persson, T., and G. E. Tabellini. 2002. *Political Economics: Explaining Economic Policy.* Cambridge, MA: MIT Press.

   2003. *The Economic Effects of Constitutions: What Do the Data Say?* Cambridge, MA: MIT Press.

Piore, M. J., and C. F. Sabel. 1984. *The Second Industrial Divide.* New York: Basic Books.

Pissarides, C. A. 1997. "Learning by Trading and the Returns to Human Capital in Developing Countries." *World Bank Economic Review* **11**(1):17–32.

Plank, D. 1996. *The Means of our Salvation: Public Education in Brazil 1930–1995.* Boulder, CO: Westview Press.

Poterba, J.M. 1995. "Government Intervention in the Markets for Education and Health Care: How and Why?" NBER Working Paper No. 4916.

Power, T., and J. Roberts. 2000. "A New Brazil?" In P. Kingstone and T. Power (eds.), *Democratic Brazil.* Pittsburgh: University of Pittsburgh Press.

Prakash, B. 1998. "Gulf Migration and Its Economic Impact: The Keralan Experience." *Economic and Political Weekly* **33**(50):3209–13.

Pritchett, L. 1995. *Divergence, Big Time.* Washington: World Bank, Office of the Vice President, Development Economics.

Przeworski, A., M. E. Alvarez, J. A. Cheibub, and F. Limongi. 2000. *Democracy and Development: Political Institutions and Well-Being in the World, 1950–1990.* New York: Cambridge University Press.

Psacharopoulos, G., and H. Patrinos 2002. "Returns to Investment in Education Policy." Research Working Paper 2881. Washington: World Bank.

Quinn, D. and J. Wooley. 2001. "Democracy and National Economic Performance: The Preference for Stability." *American Journal of Political Science* **45**(3):634–57.

Raftery, A., and M. Hout. 1983. "Maximally Maintained Inequality: Expansion, Reform, and Opportunity in Irish Education, 1921–75." *Sociology of Education* **66**(1):41–62.

Ravenhill, J. 2008. "Trading out of Crisis." In A. McIntyre, T. Pempel, and J. Ravenhill (eds.), *Crisis as Catalyst*. Ithaca, NY: Cornell University Press.

Rehm, P., and A. Wren. 2008. "Service Expansion, International Exposure, and Political Preferences." Working Paper. Dublin: Trinity College.

Reuterberg, S., and A. Svensson. 1994. "Financial Aid and Recruitment to Higher Education in Sweden." *Studies in Higher Education* **19**(1):33–45.

Rizal, J. P. 1997. *Noli Me Tangere*. Honolulu: University of Hawaii Press.

Rodrik, D. 2000. "Why Do More Open Economies Have Larger Governments?" *Journal of Political Economy* **106**(5):997–1032.

Roemer, J. 2006. *Democracy, Education, and Equality. Graz Schumpeter Lectures.* New York: Cambridge University Press.

Rogowski, R. 1989. *Commerce and Coalitions*. Princeton, NJ: Princeton University Press.

Rogowski, R., and M. A. Kayser. 2002. "Majoritarian Electoral Systems and Consumer Power: Price-Level Evidence from the OECD Countries." *American Journal of Political Science* **46**(3):526–39.

Ross, M. L. 2001. "Does Oil Hinder Democracy?" *World Politics* **53**(3):325–61.

    2005. "Is Democracy Good for the Poor?" Working Paper. Los Angeles: Department of Political Science, University of California Los Angeles.

Rudolph, S., and L. Rudolph. 1972. *Education and Politics in India*. Cambridge, MA: Harvard University Press.

Rudra, N. 2003. "Globalization and the Decline of the Welfare State in Less-Developed Countries." *International Organization* **56**(2):411–45.

Rudra, N., and S. Haggard. 2005. "Globalization, Democracy, and Effective Welfare Spending in the Developing World." *Comparative Political Studies* **38**(9):1015–49.

Rueschemeyer, D., E. H. Stephens, and J. D. Stephens. 1992. *Capitalist Development and Democracy*. Chicago: University of Chicago Press.

Rybczynski, T. M. 1955. "Factor Endowment and Relative Commodity Prices." *Economica* **22**(88):336–41.

Sadgopal, A. 2006. "Dilution, Distortion and Diversion: A Post-Jomtien Reflection on the Education Policy." In R. Kumar (ed.), *The Crisis of Elementary Education in India*. New Delhi: Sage.

Saint-Paul, G., and T. Verdier. 1993. "Education, Democracy and Growth." *Journal of Development Economics* **42**(2):399–407.

Sala-i-Martin, X. 2002. "The 'Disturbing' Rise of Global Income Inequality." NBER Working Paper 8904.

Salerno, C. 2002. "Higher Education in Sweden." CHEPS Higher Education Monitor Country Report. Center for Higher Education Policy Studies, University of Twente, Enschede.

Samuelson, P. A. 1948. "International Trade and the Equalisation of Factor Prices." *Economic Journal* **58**(230):163–84.

Scheve, K. F., and M. J. Slaughter. 2001. "What Determines Individual Trade-Policy Preferences?" *Journal of International Economics* **54**(2):267–92.

Schleicher, Andreas. 2006. "The Economics of Knowledge: Why Education is Key for Europe's Success." Lisbon Council Policy Brief. Paris: OECD Press.

Schultz, T. W. 1961. "Investment in Human Capital: Reply." *American Economic Review* **51**(5):1035–9.

Schwartzman, S. 2004. "Introduction." In C. Brock and S. Schwartzman (eds.), *The Challenges of Education in Brazil*. Oxford: Symposium.

Sen, A. 2000. *Development as Freedom*. New York: Oxford University Press.

Seth, M. 2002. *Education Fever*. Honolulu: University of Hawaii Press.

Shavit, Y., R. Arum, and A. Gamoran. 2007. *Stratification in Higher Education: A Comparative Study*. Stanford, CA: Stanford University Press.

Shiller, R. 2005. *Irrational Exuberance*. New York: Doubleday.

Shleifer, A., and R. W. Vishny. 1994. "The Politics of Market Socialism." *Journal of Economic Perspectives* **8**(2):165–76.

Shonfield, A. 1965. *Modern Capitalism: The Changing Balance of Public and Private Power*. London: Oxford University Press.

Silver, H. 2003. *Higher Education and Opinion Making in Twentieth Century England*. London: Woburn Press.

Singh, J. S., and H. Mukherjee. 1990. *Education and National Integration in Malaysia: Stocktaking Thirty Years after Independence*. Kuala Lumpur: Institut Pengajian Tinggi, Universiti Malaya.

Sinha, A. 2006. "Operationalising the Constitutional Guarantee of the Right to Education: Issues of Resource Crunch and State Commitment." In R. Kumar (ed.), *The Crisis of Elementary Education in India*. New Delhi: Sage.

Smart, J. C. 2007. *Higher Education: Handbook of Theory and Research*, volume XXII. New York: Springer.

Snodgrass, D. R. 1998. *Education in Korea and Malaysia. Behind East Asian Growth: The Political and Social Foundations of Prosperity*. London: Routledge.

Sorenson, C. 1994. "Success and Education in South Korea." *Comparative Education Review* **38**(1):10–35.

Spence, M. 1973. "Job Market Signaling." *Quarterly Journal of Economics* **87**(3):355–74.

Stasavage, D. 2005. "Democracy and Education Spending in Africa." *American Journal of Political Science* **49**(2):343–58.

Stevens, R. 2004. *University to Uni: The Politics of Higher Education in England since 1944*. London: Politico's.

Stoer, S. R., and R. Dale. 1987. "Education, State, and Society in Portugal, 1926–1981." *Comparative Education Review* **31**(3):400–18.

Stolper, W. F., and P. A. Samuelson. 1941. "Protection and Real Wages." *Review of Economic Studies* **9**(1):58–73.

Strauf, S., R. Scherer, and T. Bieger. 2007. "The Role of Universities for Regional Labour Markets: The Example of Central Switzerland." Working Paper. St. Gallen, Switzerland: University of St. Gallen.

Subramanian, A. 2008. *India's Turn: Understanding the Economic Transformation*. New Delhi: Oxford University Press.

Swedish Ministry of Education and Science. 1993. *Knowledge and Progress: A Summary of the Swedish Government's Bill on Higher Education and Research (White Paper on Research)*. Stockholm: Government Bill 1992/93.

Swinerton, E. N. 1991. *Philippine Higher Education*. New York: Praeger.

Synott, J. P. 2002. *Teacher Unions, Social Movements and the Politics of Education in Asia: South Korea, Taiwan and the Philippines*. Aldershot: Ashgate.

Taylor, R. 2007. *Technical Progress and Economic Growth: An Empirical Case Study of Malaysia*. Cheltenham: Edward Elgar.

Teichler, U. 1993. "Structures of Higher Education Systems in Europe," in C. Gellert (ed.), *Higher Education in Europe*. London: Jessica Kingsley.

Teik, K. 2006. "Malaysia: Balancing Development and Power." In G. Rodan et al. (eds.), *The Political Economy of Southeast Asia*. New York: Oxford University Press.

Thelen, K. 2004. *How Institutions Evolve: The Political Economy of Skills in Germany, Brtain, the United States, and Japan.* New York: Cambridge University Press.

Tilak, J. B. G. 2003. *Public Expenditure on Education in India: A Review of Trends and Emerging Issues.* New Delhi: Ravi.

Toh, S., and Floresca-Cawagas, V. 1993. *From the Mountains to the Seas: Education for a Peaceful Philippines in Disarming: Discourse on Violence and Peace.* Norway: Arena.

Tordesillas, E. 2000. *The Nocturnal President. Millions, Mansions and Mistresses: Investigating Estrada.* Quezon City: Philippine Center for Investigative Journalism.

Trow, M. 1973. *Problems in the Transition from Elite to Mass Higher Education.* Berkeley: Carnegie Commission on Higher Education.

2006. "Reflections on the Transition from Elite to Mass to Universal Access." In J. J. Forest and P. Altbach (eds.), *International Handbook of Higher Education.* Dordrecht: Springer.

Tsakloglou, P., and I. Cholezas. 2005. "Education and Inequality in Greece: A Literature Review." Finnish Economy ETLA, Series B 209.

UNESCO. 2007. *Data Centre of UNESCO Institute for Statistics.* Available at http://stats. uis.unesco.org. Accessed July 12, 2008.

Usher, A., and A. Cervenan, 2005. *Global Higher Education Rankings 2005.* Toronto: Educational Policy Institute.

Usher, D. 1997. "Education as a Deterrent to Crime." *Canadian Journal of Economics* **30**(2):367–84.

Vanaik, A. 1990. *The Painful Transition: Bourgeois Democracy in India.* New York: Verso.

Verdier, T., and F. Bourguignon. 2000. "Oligarchy, Democracy, Inequality and Growth." *Journal of Development Economics* **62**:285–313.

Vieira, J., J. Hartog, and P. Pereira. 1997. "A Look at Changes in the Portuguese Wage Structure and Job Allocation during the 1980s and Early 1990s." Discussion Paper TI 97–008/3, Tinbergen Institute, Amsterdam.

Wade, R. 1990. *Governing the Economy.* Princeton, NJ: Princeton University Press.

Weber, Eugen. 1976. *Peasants into Frenchmen.* Stanford, CA: Stanford University Press.

Weiner, M. 1990. *The Child and the State in India: Child Labor and Education Policy in Comparative Perspective.* Princeton, NJ: Princeton University Press.

2001. "The Struggle for Equality: Caste in Indian Politics." In A. Kohli (ed.), *The Success of India's Democracy.* Cambridge: Cambridge University Press.

Werner, J., and A. Shah. 2006. "Financing of Education: Some Experiences from Ten European Countries." Institute of Local Public Finance Working Paper.

Wibbels, E. 2006. "Dependency Revisited: International Markets, Business Cycles, and Social Spending in the Developing World." *International Organization* **60**(2):433–68.

Williams, G. 2004. "The Higher Education Market in the United Kingdom." In P. Teixeira, B. Jongbloed, D. Dill, and A. Amaral (eds.), *Markets in Higher Education: Rhetoric or Reality?* Norwell, MA: Kluwer.

Windholf, P. 1997. *Expansion and Structural Change: Higher Education in Germany, the United States, and Japan, 1870–1990.* London: Westview.

Woldendorp, J., H. Keman, and I. Budge. 2000. *Party Government in 48 Democracies (1945–1998): Composition, Duration, and Personnel.* Dordrecht, Netherlands: Kluwer Academic.

Wood, A., and M. Calandrino. 2000. "When the Other Giant Awakens: Trade and Human Resources in India." *Economic and Political Weekly* **35**(52):30.

World Bank, 1993. *The East Asian Miracle: Economic Growth and Public Policy.* Washington: World Bank.

2004. *World Development Indicators.* Washington: World Bank.

2005. *Malaysia: Firm Competitiveness, Investment Climate, and Growth.* Washington: World Bank.

Zachariah, K., E. Mathew, and S. Rajan. 1999. "Impact of Migration on Kerala's Economy and Society." Working Paper. Thiruvananthapuram: Center for Development Studies.

Ziegele, F. 2006. "The German Tuition Fee Debate: Goals, Models, and Political Implications of Cost-Sharing." In P. Teixeira et al. (eds.), *Cost-Sharing and Accessibility in Higher Education.* Holland: Springer.

Index

10505925R00157

Printed in Great Britain
by Amazon